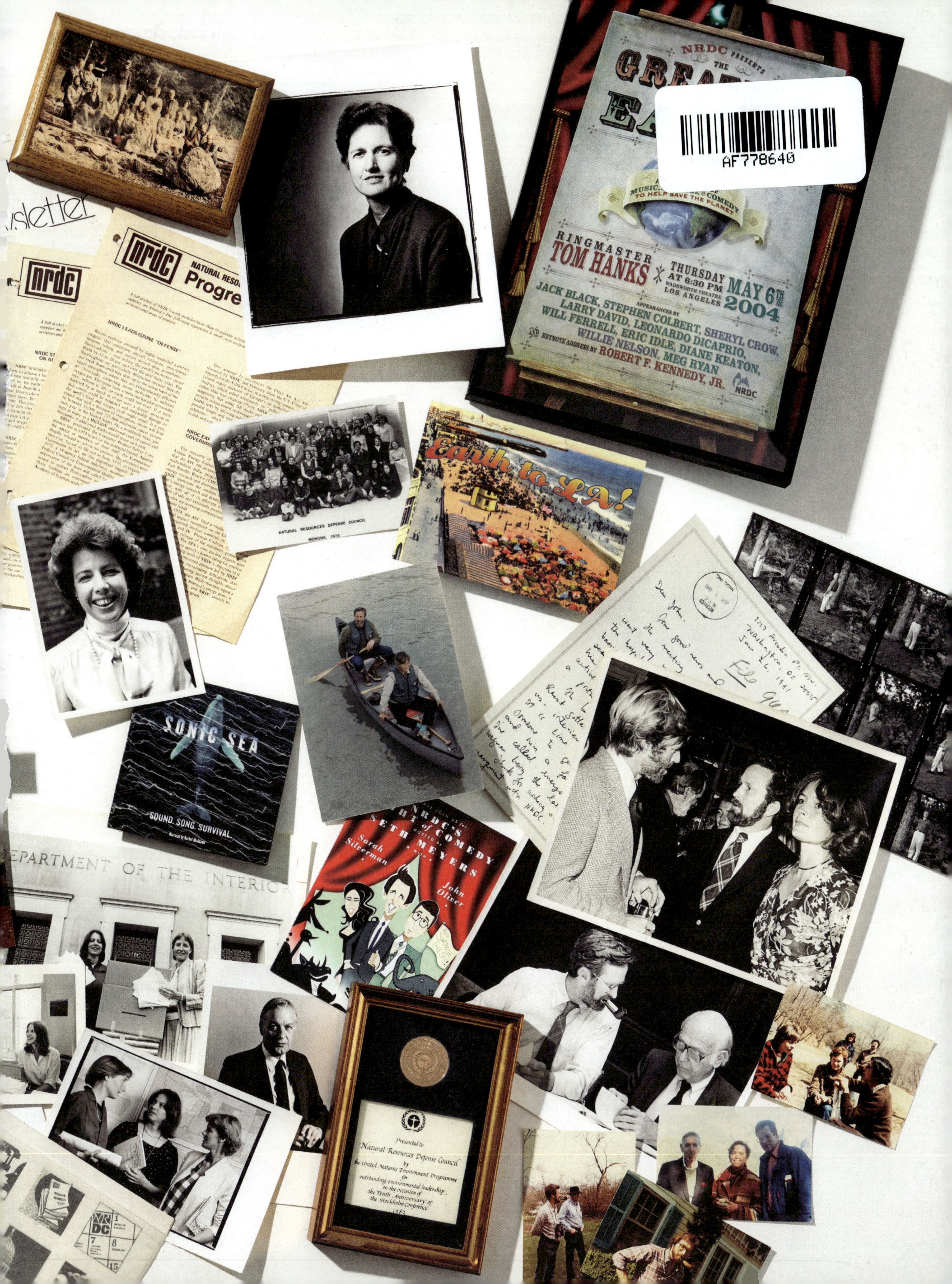

NRDC PRESENTS
RINGMASTER
TOM HANKS
THURSDAY
AT 6:30 PM
WADSWORTH THEATRE
LOS ANGELES
MAY 6TH
2004
APPEARANCES BY
JACK BLACK, STEPHEN COLBERT, SHERYL CROW,
LARRY DAVID, LEONARDO DICAPRIO,
WILL FERRELL, ERIC IDLE, DIANE KEATON,
WILLIE NELSON, MEG RYAN
KEYNOTE ADDRESS BY ROBERT F. KENNEDY, JR.
NRDC
TO HELP SAVE THE PLANET
Earth to LA!
NATURAL RESOURCES DEFENSE COUNCIL
MOHONK 1975
nrdc
NATURAL RESO
Progre
NRDC LEADS OZONE "DEFENSE"
SONIC SEA
SOUND. SONG. SURVIVAL.
DEPARTMENT OF THE INTERIOR
NRDC'S
NIGHT of COMEDY
SETH MEYERS
Sarah Silverman
John Oliver
Presented to
Natural Resources Defense Council
by
the United Nations Environment Programme
for
outstanding environmental leadership
on the occasion of
the Tenth Anniversary of
the Stockholm Conference
1982

NRDC

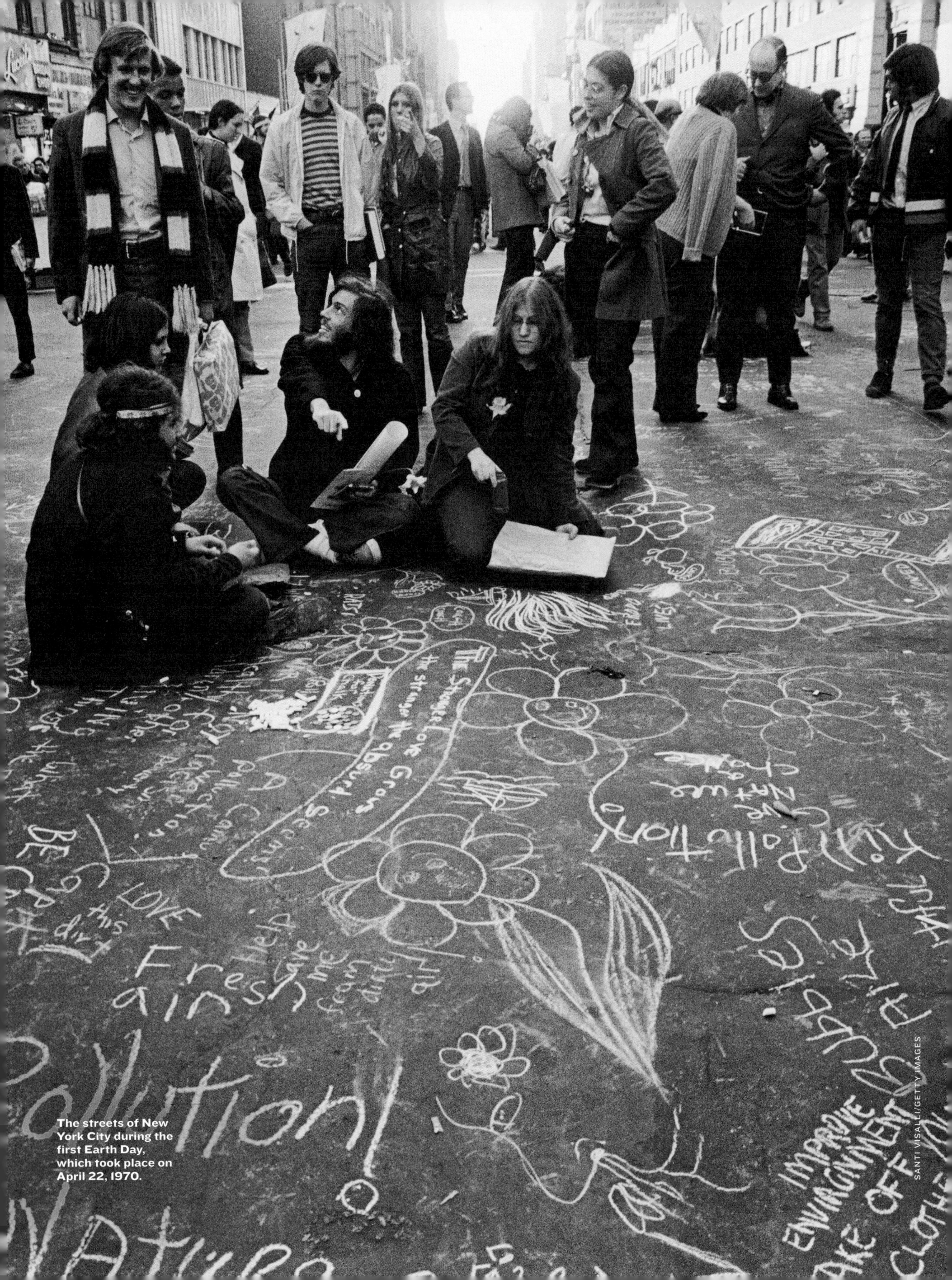

The streets of New York City during the first Earth Day, which took place on April 22, 1970.

SANTI VISALLI/GETTY IMAGES

NRDC

A FORCE *for the* FUTURE

INSIDE NRDC'S FIGHT TO SAVE THE PLANET AND ITS PEOPLE

John H. Adams

ABBEVILLE PRESS PUBLISHERS
NEW YORK—LONDON

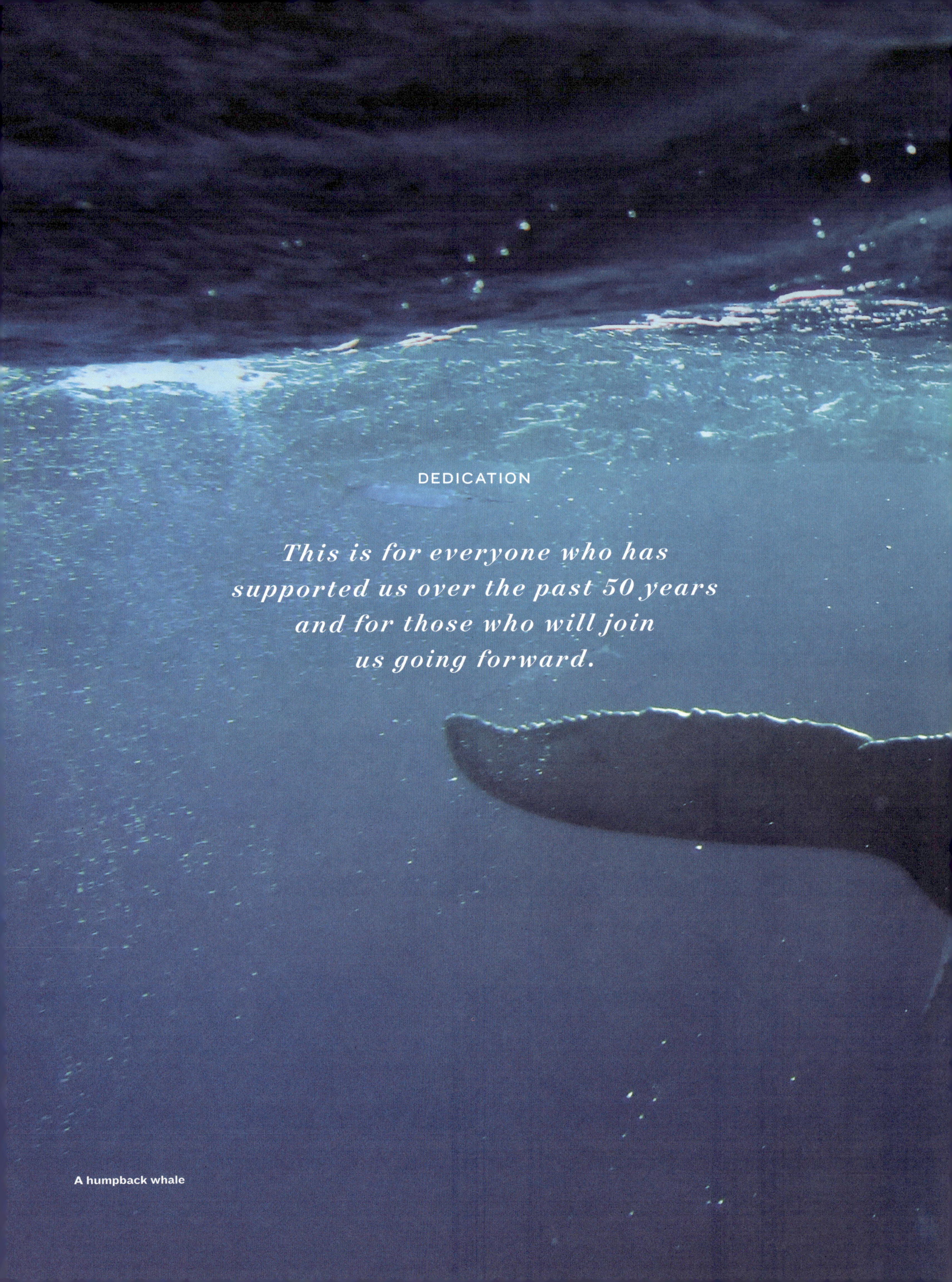

DEDICATION

This is for everyone who has supported us over the past 50 years and for those who will join us going forward.

A humpback whale

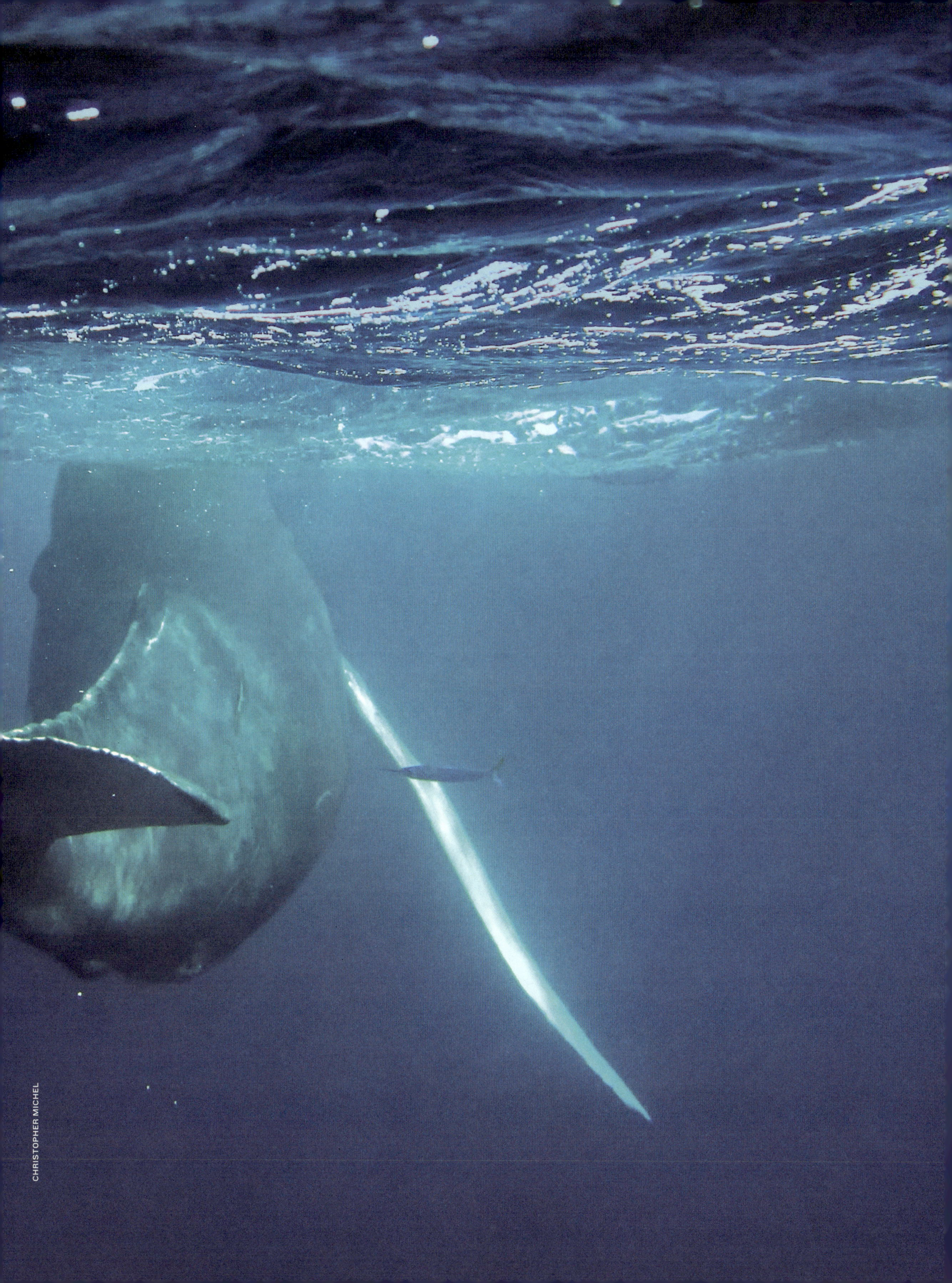

CHRISTOPHER MICHEL

CONTENTS

The Alatna River and Brooks mountain range in the Arctic National Wildlife Refuge.

PATRICK J. ENDRES/GETTY IMAGES

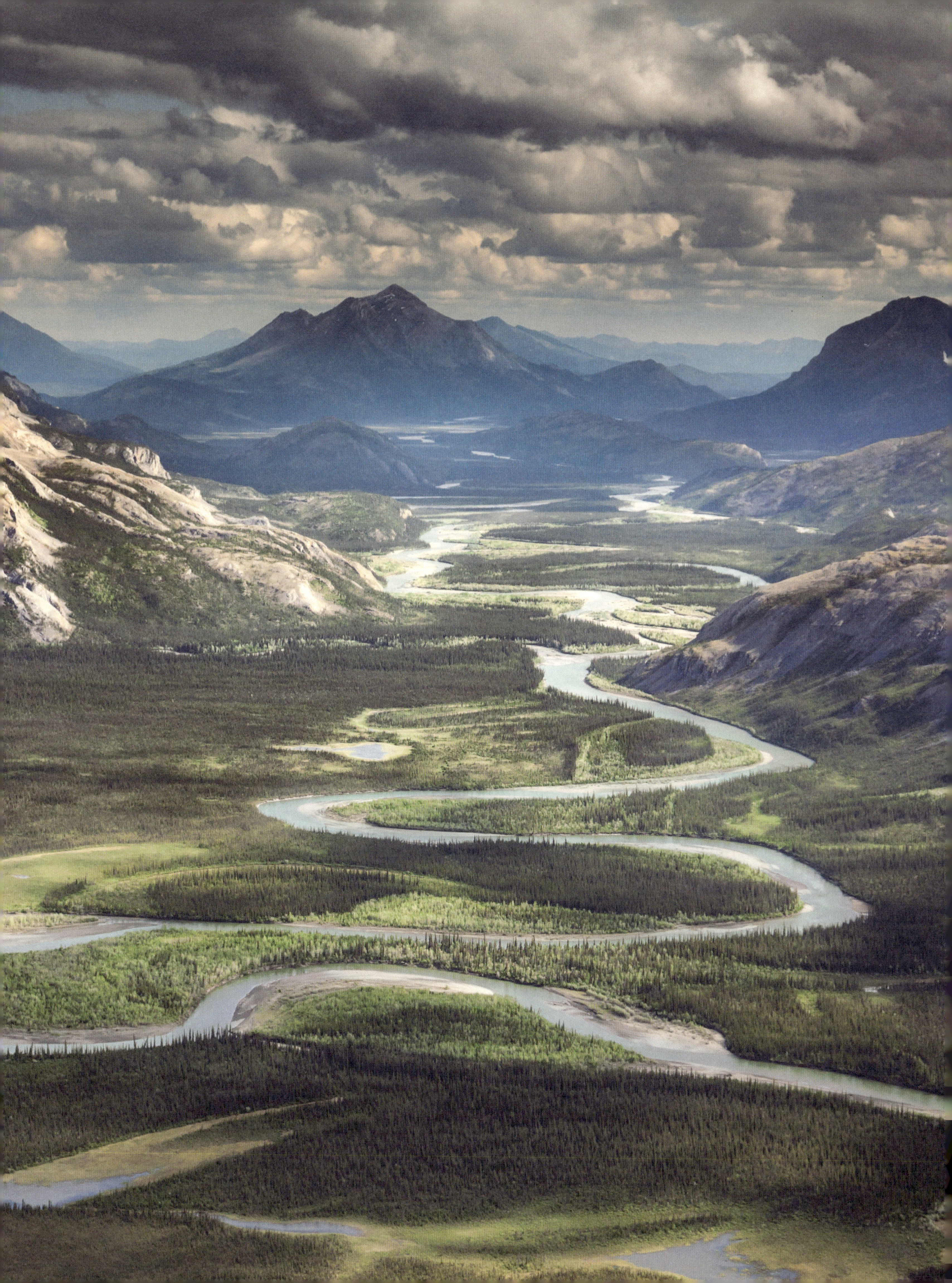

LETTER FROM

Robert Redford

ACTOR, DIRECTOR, CONSERVATIONIST
NRDC TRUSTEE

WHEN I MET JOHN ADAMS FOR LUNCH ONE DAY IN 1973, the concept of legally "representing" the environment in our court system was still a fresh one. Congress had just passed three major laws—the National Environmental Protection Act, the Clean Water Act, and the Clean Air Act—and for the first time, our nation had a regulatory framework for protecting the country's most valuable natural resources. We also had a then-brand-new U.S. Environmental Protection Agency to enforce it. The legal apparatus, in other words, was in place. But for the system to work, we needed people who understood these laws: what they entailed, if they were being followed, and what the consequences should be for violating them. If a factory owner was dumping toxic waste into a local stream or a state was blatantly ignoring air-quality rules, someone had to set the legal process in motion by identifying the perpetrators, bringing a case against them, and winning.

Growing up in California in the 1950s, I'd been immersed in nature: swimming in the ocean, hiking in the mountains, even working for two summers in Yosemite National Park as a teenager. By the early 1970s, it was glaringly evident to me and millions of other Americans that our air, water, and most treasured natural spaces were at grave risk from the actions of corporate polluters and their enablers in government. I had already decided, at that point, to make fighting for the environment a cornerstone of my life. But I knew that fight would require more than signs and slogans. Moral and rhetorical victories weren't enough. I wanted to contribute to legal victories that would result in substantive remedies and lasting protections.

Since joining NRDC's board in 1974, I've gladly wielded my voice and visibility to amplify NRDC's message, expand its reach, and otherwise help it carry out its all-important stated goal of safeguarding the natural systems on which all life depends.

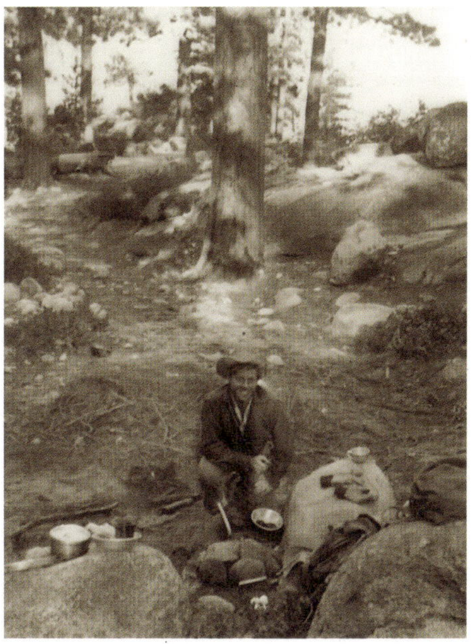

Though NRDC was only three years old when I met John that afternoon, the organization had already made a name for itself by winning important cases relating to offshore oil drilling in Louisiana and environmental impact studies in North Carolina—victories that would end up having a major impact nationally. As I heard him describe NRDC's recent triumphs as well as challenges on the horizon, I knew I wanted to be a part of his team. I joined NRDC's board in 1974, and I've proudly served the organization ever since. Together, NRDC and I have stopped coal-fired power plants from going up next to some of the West's most beloved national parks, saved Bering Sea fisheries from the ravages of offshore oil and gas development, and developed new models for negotiating with industry that move past acrimony and toward real progress. Throughout, I've gladly wielded my voice and visibility to amplify NRDC's message, expand its reach, and otherwise help it carry out its all-important stated goal of safeguarding the natural systems on which all life depends.

Nearly five decades into that relationship, I feel privileged to call John my friend and to stand alongside NRDC as we continue to fight polluters, protect wildlife, pursue environmental justice for disadvantaged communities, champion policies that promote clean energy, and slash the emissions that are warming our planet. Anniversaries are typically opportunities for retrospection, but here at the 50-year mark, John has given us a book that explains where we are—and what's at stake—in this pivotal moment for humanity.

In 2020, we are living through the sixth mass extinction event, while also staring down the climate crisis. Our world is changing—and fast. And even though our nation's air and water have grown demonstrably cleaner since the early 1970s, when NRDC first began taking polluters to court, millions of Americans continue to live in places where these most basic of natural resources, so utterly essential to human life, have been tainted by corporate malfeasance and civic neglect: the twin engines of environmental injustice that reflect the ingrained biases and outright discrimination unfortunately still present in our society.

Still, amid all the horror, there's real cause for hope. In each chapter of *A Force for the Future*, John reveals how NRDC is building upon its experience to craft the solutions we need to protect nature and public health going forward, with the help of the best legal minds, policy experts, scientists, and communicators in the environmental movement. That's why I don't just recommend this book to people as a great read. Instead, I urge people to view it as the blueprint for the planet's—and humanity's—future. We've never needed a book like this one more than we do right now.

Robert Redford as a teenager in Yosemite National Park.

COURTESY OF ROBERT REDFORD

PREFACE

Alan F. Horn

CO-CHAIRMAN AND CHIEF CREATIVE OFFICER, THE WALT DISNEY STUDIOS
NRDC BOARD CHAIR

THERE WERE A LOT MORE QUESTIONS THAN ANSWERS THAT JANuary day in 1970, when a group of young, idealistic attorneys first huddled in a borrowed Manhattan office to form the Natural Resources Defense Council.

How would the country enforce the environmental laws that were beginning to take shape? How would industries respond? Who would make sure the newly created U.S. Environmental Protection Agency would protect people and not polluters? How would communities prepare for the threats of the future? And who would help the American public understand when it's time to demand change?

Unbeknownst to many in the room that afternoon, the answers to those questions would be found within the very organization they were dreaming up and creating from square one. NRDC will hold the government accountable for following its own rules. NRDC will push for the policy solutions the planet needs. NRDC will tell the public the truth about the dangers to our collective health and natural environment. And, finally, NRDC will be there during the moments when Americans need to rise up, stand together, and call for a better world.

We began with a small cadre of people who had the courage to imagine a better future and then started making that future happen—time and again through hard-fought battles in the courts, scientific acumen, and a relentless drive to find a better way for society to progress. For someone like me who deals in the human capacity to dream—in the creation of new worlds and the heroes who fight for them—NRDC's story is worth sharing and celebrating.

For the past half century, we've been calling out industries when they threaten ecosystems and communities or harm people outright. We've been taking state and federal agencies to task—and often to court—when they fail to work for the public interest. We've helped ensure the enforcement

The stories you are about to read will confirm that the human ability to drive change is unstoppable when you have science, laws, and the will of the people in your corner—this is NRDC's playbook.

of our environmental laws in a way that keeps faith with the will of the people, as expressed through the elected officials who put these systems in place for the good of us all. And we've worked with policy makers at the local, state, and federal levels to develop solutions that are effective, just, equitable, and enduring.

Always at the heart of our work is sound science. NRDC's staff scientists investigate the threats to the planet and its people and wildlife, such as water and air pollution, dangerous pesticides, habitat loss and degradation, and the climate crisis. By following the facts, wherever they lead, we are able to form a deep understanding of the challenges before us and clarify what's at stake for our families, communities, and future.

Those young lawyers imagined something beyond what was in front of them—skies clear of smog, a country without its rivers in flames. They turned something impossible into something essential, so much so that many of us today take clean air, clean water, and a healthy environment as givens, not hard-won rights. Their dreams were *that* powerful.

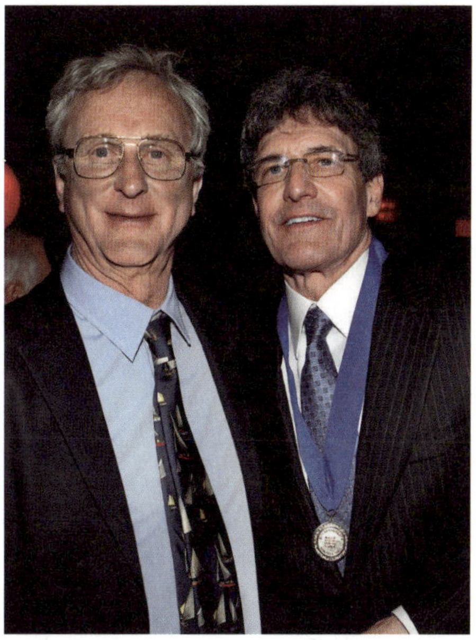

To dream big today, however, is a tremendous task, as we face environmental perils on a scale our founders could scarcely have fathomed five decades ago. The seas are rising. Croplands are turning to desert. The Arctic is melting. The Amazon is burning. The Great Barrier Reef is dying. We're losing species faster than at any other time since the dinosaurs disappeared 65 million years ago.

These and other ravages of climate change are imposing rising costs and mounting dangers on us all. They threaten the future of all humankind.

Our founders may not have foreseen this moment, but they built an organization fit to take on this challenge. NRDC has been pushing for the policies we need to cut the country's carbon footprint in half over the next decade and shrink it to net-zero by midcentury or sooner. While we work to promote American innovation and enterprise to speed up the clean energy revolution, we are also working with states and cities across America to make their infrastructure more climate resilient and their communities healthier.

But NRDC can't do this work alone, and it never has. The power of the people—the collective voice of our partners, members, and activists—gives us our strength and focus. Our charge now is to grow this power, to stand alongside the low-income communities, people of color, and Indigenous groups who have disproportionately borne the hazard and harm of environmental degradation. At the same time, we need to make sure that every worker in America, from West Virginia to Ohio to Alaska, has a shot at success in the clean energy economy of tomorrow.

To say this is hard work is an understatement, but those young visionaries in that borrowed office space 50 years ago redefined what was possible—and we take our cue from them. Today, as an international organization with a staff of more than 700, we are marshalling the power of our three million-plus members and online activists and the grassroots knowledge of our partners to carry out a mission that hasn't changed: to safeguard the earth—its people, its plants and animals, and the natural systems on which all life depends.

There's history in this book, but make no mistake: This isn't a book about all the things NRDC has done. It's about what NRDC is *doing* for our shared future. The stories you are about to read will confirm that the human ability to drive change is unstoppable when you have science, laws, and the will of the people in your corner. This is NRDC's playbook and the story of how we've become an indispensable environmental advocacy organization—one that is shaping a world in which every one of us can thrive and continue to dream.

Alan Horn (right) with John Adams at NRDC's 20th anniversary celebration.

JEFF VESPA/GETTY IMAGES

FOREWORD

Frances Beinecke

NRDC PRESIDENT EMERITA (2006–2015)
HONORARY TRUSTEE

I FIRST ARRIVED AT NRDC IN 1973 AS A SUMMER INTERN, MIDWAY THROUGH my master's program at the Yale School of Forestry & Environmental Studies. Inspired by the civil rights and women's liberation movements in the 1960s, I wanted to find work that advanced the cause of social justice and addressed the environmental degradation we were surrounded by. I had developed a love for nature and the wild through a childhood on the beaches of Cape Cod and in the Adirondack mountains. NRDC was the right place to do that. The first assignment John Adams handed me was to help protect his beloved Catskills, where he grew up loving the region's deep woods and pure waters.

After graduation, I was fortunate to join NRDC's staff. I spent the next decade working with NRDC's heroic ocean champion, Sarah Chasis, to protect our coastal waters and shorelines from the powerful oil industry and from uncontrolled development. The work was daunting but extremely rewarding, leading to some of NRDC's greatest success stories. We beat back the plans of the Carter administration to open up the Atlantic coast to drilling, and then the even more pernicious schemes of the Reagan administration to add Alaska's coastal waters to the list of areas targeted for drilling. And when proposals to open the Eastern Seaboard to offshore drilling resurfaced in 2015 as part of President Obama's "all-of-the-above" energy policy, we stopped them too. (Partisan favor has never been part of our playbook.) Those fights to protect our coastlines and the creatures of the sea continue to this day.

When I succeeded John as NRDC's president in 2006, we were in the second term of the George W. Bush administration. The influence of the fossil fuel lobby was growing in intensity, even as scientists were painting an ever-grimmer picture of the very real and immediate consequences of climate change. NRDC's litigation and advocacy has always rested on a solid foundation of science, but we knew we had to infuse science into every aspect of our work in order to ensure its vital messages would be heard. In 2006, we established NRDC's Science Center to make sure that peer-reviewed science permeated every aspect of our work.

With every decade, NRDC has added the tools that allow us to communicate more broadly and to develop alliances and partnerships in communities across America that have borne the brunt of environmental degradation.

We also knew that we'd be able to fight climate change and protect our environment and the health of our citizens more effectively if we didn't limit ourselves to being a purely bicoastal organization. We needed to put down roots in the Midwest, a bastion of dirty coal-fired power plants but also where renewable energy industries were showing great promise, especially across the Great Plains states. In 2007, we opened NRDC's Midwest office in Chicago, under the inspired leadership of Henry Henderson. The same conviction that we needed to be physically grounded in the places we fought for led to the creation of our Rocky Mountain office in Montana, unleashing our frontline advocacy and growing the strength of activists seeking to protect the charismatic wildlife and great public lands of the West.

As the threats to the atmosphere, our oceans, and biodiversity became increasingly global, we knew NRDC needed to expand internationally as well. We doubled the size of our Beijing staff and opened a permanent office in China in 2006, and in 2009, we launched our India initiative. NRDC's creative engagement and long-term commitment in both countries are focused on energy solutions that will increase efficiency, boost renewables, and reduce dangerous emissions.

In 2010, a series of shocks hit almost simultaneously. The Supreme Court's Citizens United decision let loose a flood of dark money into politics. The fight over climate change became even more intense and more partisan. The American Clean Energy and Security Act, commonly known as the Waxman-Markey bill, which passed the House in 2009, failed to pass the Senate in 2010. And in April 2010, the Deepwater Horizon oil rig exploded in the Gulf of Mexico, killing 11 workers, shutting down three major industries across four states overnight, and causing long-term ecological effects to the rich marine environment of the Gulf that continue to this day. I was honored to be asked by President Obama to sit on the National Commission set up to uncover the root cause of this disaster. That experience gave me an unparalleled look into the inner workings of the oil industry and its determination to go to the ends of the earth to feed our voracious appetite for fossil fuels.

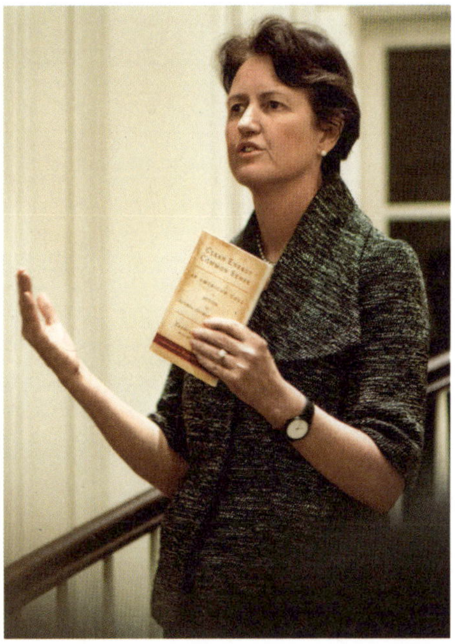

After the seismic events of 2010, we realized the environmental movement needed to be stronger politically to win. So we created the Center for Policy Advocacy to develop new alliances and partnerships and build a presence on the ground in more and more states around the country, along with the NRDC Action Fund, which allows us to do direct political lobbying of a kind we hadn't done before. We also saw a great need for the environmental movement to broaden its constituency. So we launched La Onda Verde, a website reaching out to the country's Latino communities, which have been besieged by pesticides, pollution, and climate change. La Onda Verde, in turn, gave birth to Voces Verdes—*voces* being the key Spanish word for "voices." Politicians needed to hear Latino voices from affected communities coast to coast, loud and clear.

NRDC has evolved significantly over the years. With every decade, we have added the tools that allow us to communicate more broadly and to develop alliances and partnerships in communities across America that have borne the brunt of environmental degradation. A protected environment is not a special interest; it's a common goal shared by all. In a time marked by glaring inequalities of wealth and opportunity, it's increasingly clear that our transition away from fossil fuels and toward a clean energy economy is inseparable from a transition to greater social justice.

When I came to NRDC as a young student, the country had just awakened to the need to take responsibility for actions that cause environmental and human harm. With the climate crisis, we face an epic threat, one that will affect all the natural systems that we depend on for life—the air, the water, the soils that nourish us. As NRDC enters into its sixth decade of holding polluters accountable and advancing the solutions needed to catalyze real progress, I know NRDC has the experience, knowledge, and grit to tackle this challenge from all sides. At every turn, we have grown stronger and more agile, and more diverse. With our new president, Gina McCarthy, at the helm, NRDC is more than ready to take on the climate crisis and to protect the future of humanity.

Frances Beinecke speaking at an event for the publication of her first book, *Clean Energy Common Sense: An American Call to Action on Global Climate Change.*

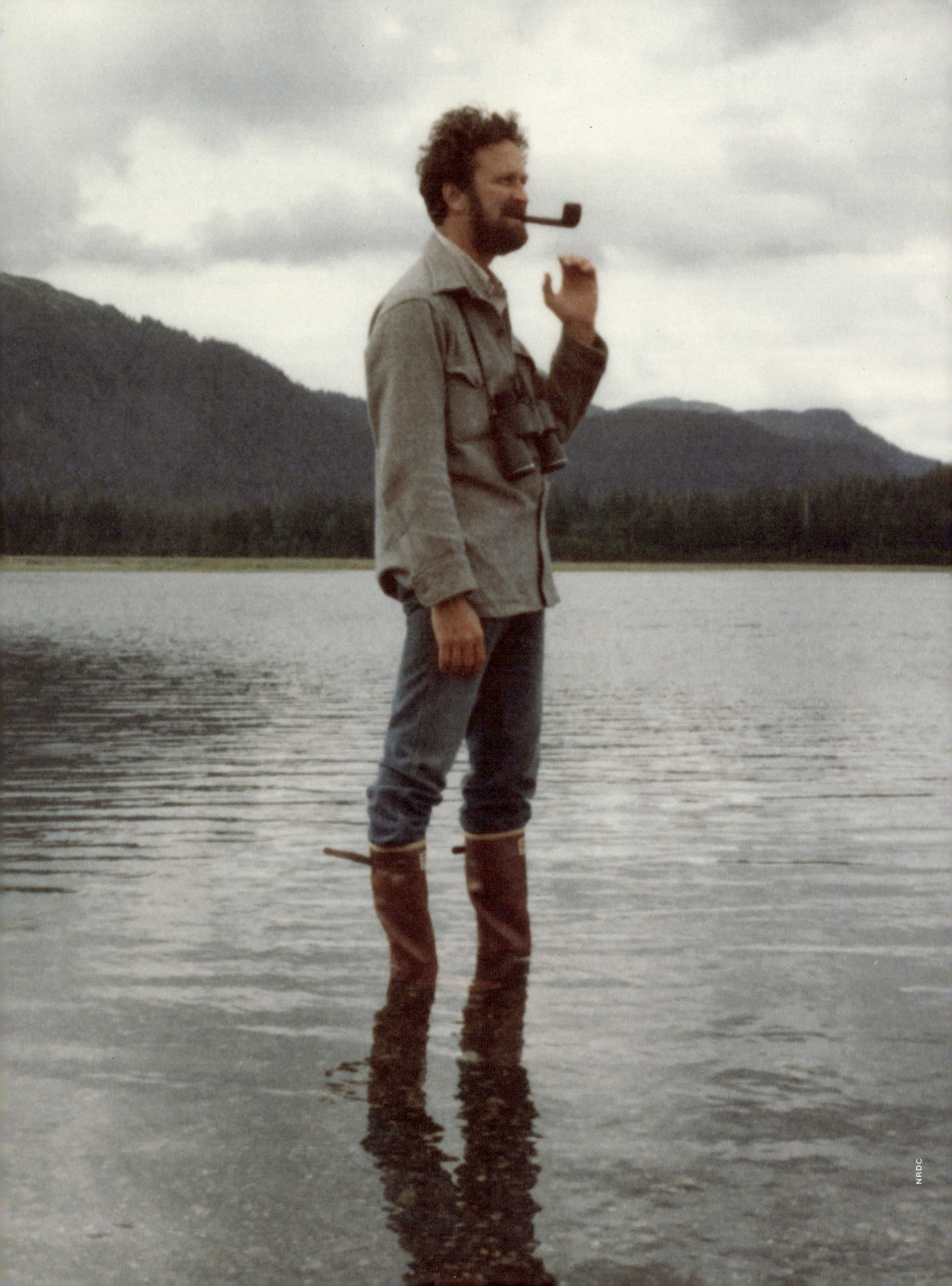

NRDC

INTRODUCTION

John Adams

NRDC FOUNDING DIRECTOR, TRUSTEE,
EXECUTIVE DIRECTOR (1970–1998), PRESIDENT (1998–2005)

IT WAS 1970. WE WERE YOUNG, MAD AS HELL, AND WEREN'T GOING TO take it anymore. The "it" was the destruction of the natural world we loved by greedy and unregulated polluters. The "we" were a group of idealistic lawyers. Most of us were twentysomethings; at 33, I was the old man of the bunch.

We were sickened by TV images of oil spilling into the coastal waters of California and polluted rivers catching fire. My wife, Patricia, and I could walk over to the Hudson River from our apartment in Manhattan's Greenwich Village and watch raw sewage float by. We wanted to change the world, and the tools we would use were the raft of new laws introduced during the Nixon administration. Those laws—the National Environmental Policy Act, the Clean Air Act, and the Clean Water Act—came to us with bipartisan support, something hard to imagine in today's polarized America.

The key to those new laws is that they enshrined the right of ordinary citizens to fight for the environment in court, a principle that had first been established in a landmark case a few years earlier. That case was intimately connected to NRDC's creation story and began with a mortal threat to an iconic mountain on the Hudson River named Storm King.

A giant utility, Con Edison, had proposed to lop off the summit of Storm King to build a pump-storage power plant. Leading the fight to stop this atrocity was Stephen Duggan, a partner at the Wall Street law firm Simpson Thacher & Bartlett, and his wife, Beatrice. In 1970, with the battle in full swing, "Mr. Duggan," as I always called him, became the first chair of NRDC's board, and 50 years later, his law firm continues to provide us with invaluable pro bono support. NRDC is built on a foundation of this kind of enduring loyalty.

The twentysomethings who came together to found NRDC proved to be passionate and visionary leaders. Gus Speth, now an honorary trustee, would later go on to chair President Carter's Council on Environmental Quality and head the United Nations Development Programme. Trustee Dick Ayres is one of the nation's leading experts on the Clean Air Act. John Bryson would serve as President Obama's secretary of commerce. Ed Strohbehn is one of America's leading environmental educators. George Woodwell, one of our earliest board members, was the first scientist to publicly speak out about the transcendent challenge of our time: the warming of the planet.

NRDC stands on the shoulders of giants.

It took 15 years to stop Con Edison's Storm King scheme, from which we drew two vital lessons: first, that even the most powerful special interests aren't invincible; second, that such fights require huge resources—and there's no way to predict how long they'll last. We never let that deter us. From

John Adams wades in Prince William Sound, Alaska, in 1979.

the beginning, NRDC's philosophy was always to dig in for the long haul and somehow find the resources needed. This strategy has been nerve-racking at times, but our dedicated donors, three million members and online activists, and countless other supporters have always come through for us.

The law of evolution states that the species that thrive are those that adapt best to change. NRDC is thriving; it evolves constantly. We don't nibble around the edges of a problem; we play for all the marbles, and as the stakes get higher, we adapt accordingly. When Frances Beinecke took my place as president in 2006, the transition was seamless. She had been with NRDC for more than 30 years, eight of those as executive director, and had established herself not just as a leader of NRDC but of the entire environmental movement.

Since then, NRDC has grown into an organization of more than 700 people. They are some of the best lawyers, scientists, policy advocates, and communicators on the planet, attacking the most urgent environmental problems on all fronts, from the corridors of global diplomacy to the nation's courtrooms to our cities' streets.

The stories in this book are only snapshots of what we've accomplished in the past 50 years. I've chosen them because they emphasize three things that are central to NRDC's work. The first is our obligation to tell the unvarnished truth, based on hard scientific fact, about how the planet and our health are being wounded, so that people understand what is at stake. The second is that it's not enough just to hold powerful corporations and government entities accountable for their actions; we also have to offer practical solutions in order to make progress. The third is the determination to amplify our voice by seeking out new alliances. As Rhea Suh, who became NRDC's president in 2015, so keenly

As Storm King proved, saving the environment is a long-distance race. You never know where the finish line may be, but dropping out early is not an option.

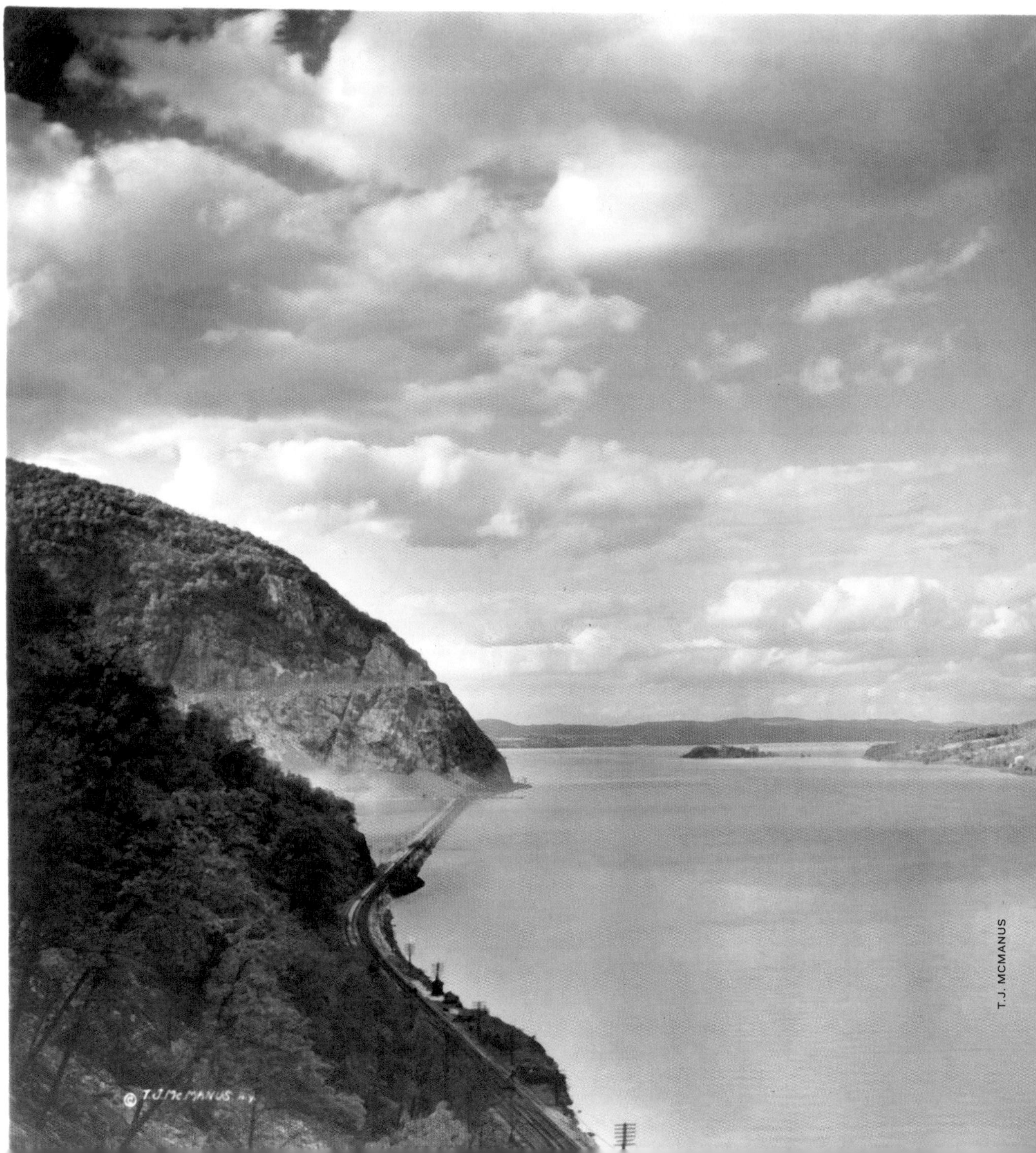

T.J. MCMANUS

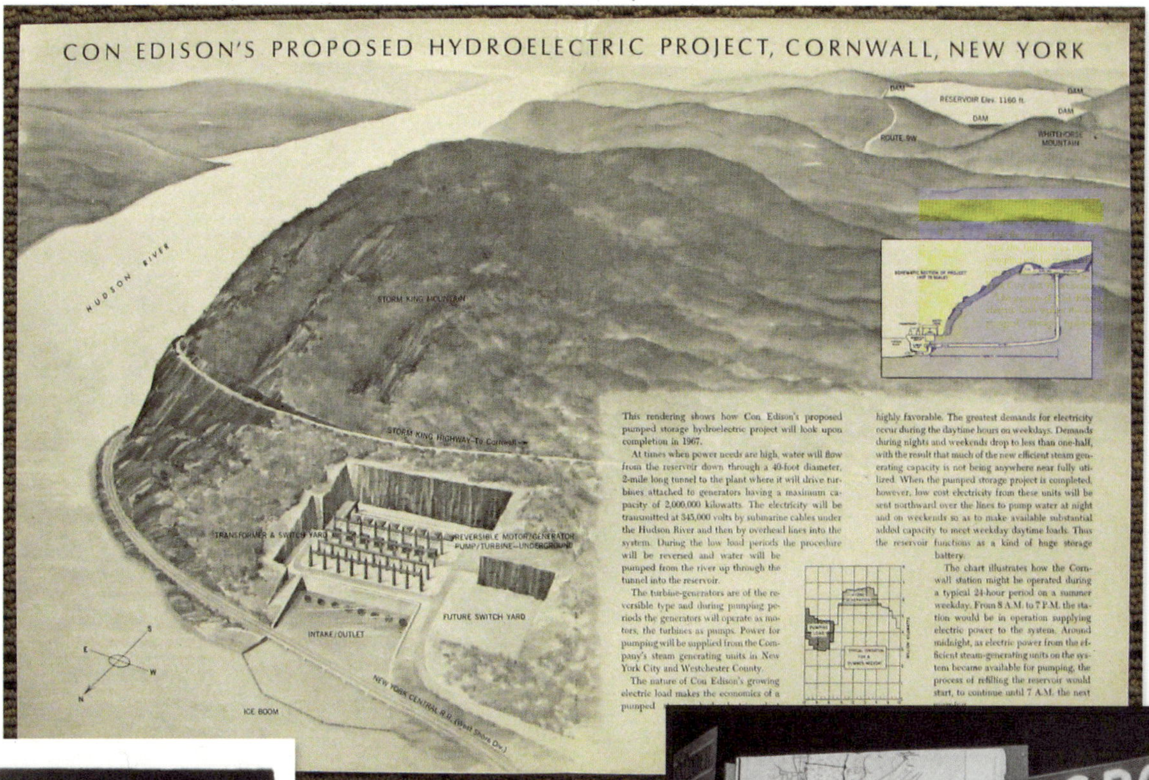

On behalf of our first client, the Hudson River Fishermen's Association, NRDC helped halt the construction of a hydroelectric plant at Storm King Mountain in New York. The Con Edison project would have decapitated the mountain and wreaked havoc on spawning grounds for the river's striped bass.

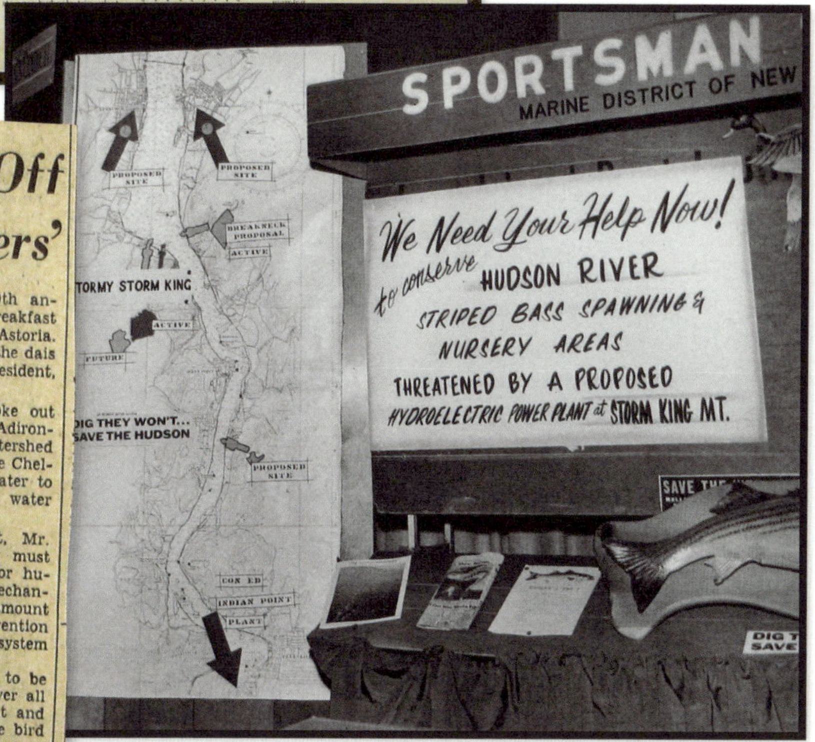

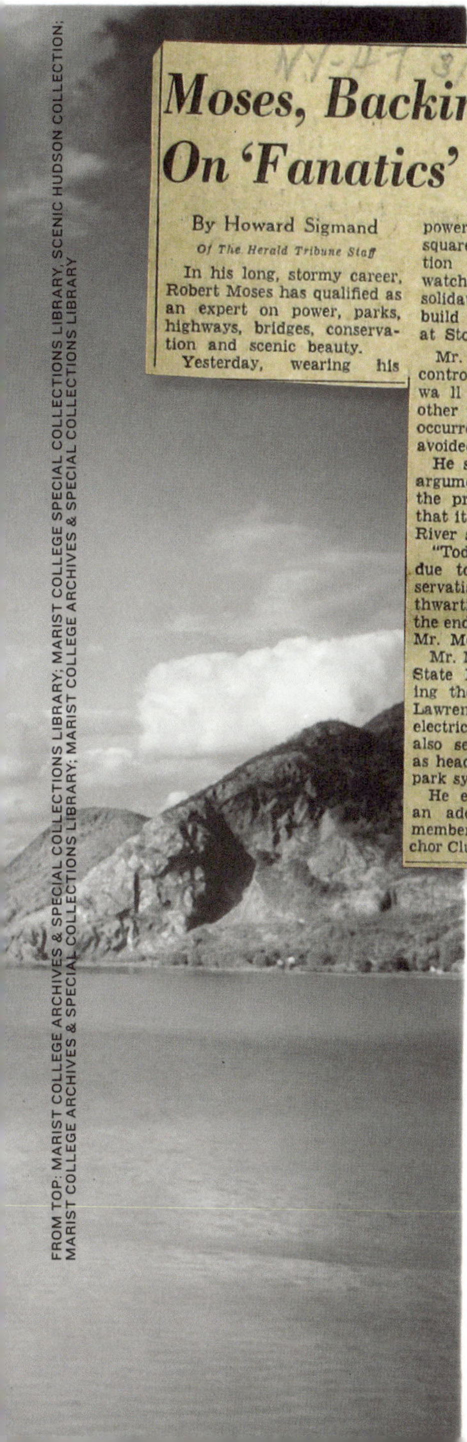

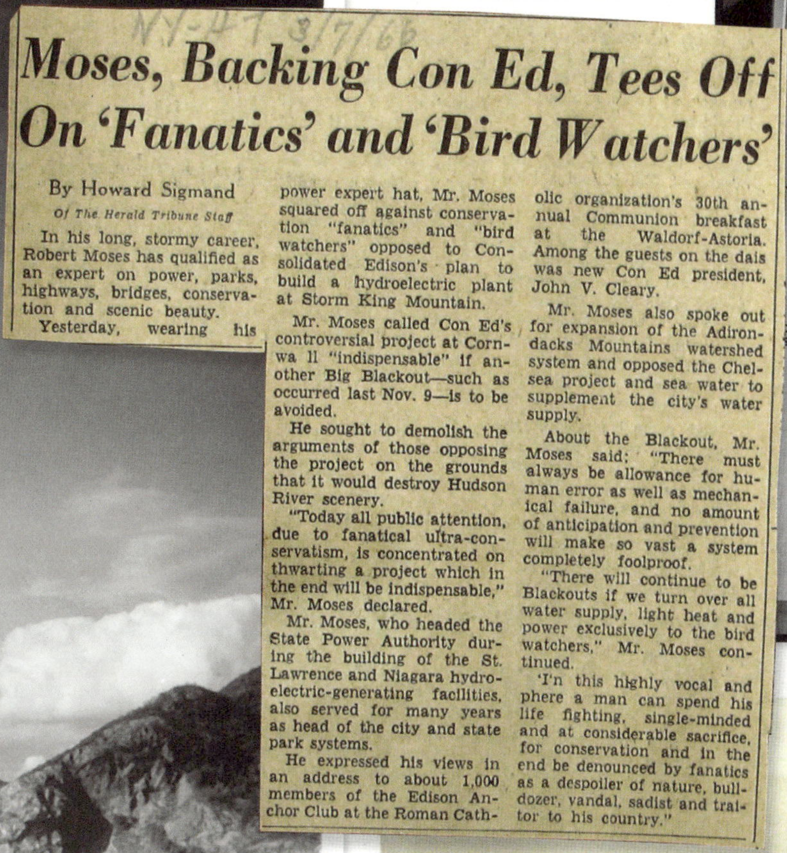

Moses, Backing Con Ed, Tees Off On 'Fanatics' and 'Bird Watchers'

By Howard Sigmand
Of The Herald Tribune Staff

In his long, stormy career, Robert Moses has qualified as an expert on power, parks, highways, bridges, conservation and scenic beauty.

Yesterday, wearing his power expert hat, Mr. Moses squared off against conservation "fanatics" and "bird watchers" opposed to Consolidated Edison's plan to build a hydroelectric plant at Storm King Mountain.

Mr. Moses called Con Ed's controversial project at Cornwall "indispensable" if another Big Blackout—such as occurred last Nov. 9—is to be avoided.

He sought to demolish the arguments of those opposing the project on the grounds that it would destroy Hudson River scenery.

"Today all public attention, due to fanatical ultra-conservatism, is concentrated on thwarting a project which in the end will be indispensable," Mr. Moses declared.

Mr. Moses, who headed the State Power Authority during the building of the St. Lawrence and Niagara hydro-electric-generating facilities, also served for many years as head of the city and state park systems.

He expressed his views in an address to about 1,000 members of the Edison Anchor Club at the Roman Catholic organization's 30th annual Communion breakfast at the Waldorf-Astoria. Among the guests on the dais was new Con Ed president, John V. Cleary.

Mr. Moses also spoke out for expansion of the Adirondacks Mountains watershed system and opposed the Chelsea project and sea water to supplement the city's water supply.

About the Blackout, Mr. Moses said: "There must always be allowance for human error as well as mechanical failure, and no amount of anticipation and prevention will make so vast a system completely foolproof.

"There will continue to be Blackouts if we turn over all water supply, light heat and power exclusively to the bird watchers," Mr. Moses continued.

"I'n this highly vocal and phere a man can spend his life fighting, single-minded and at considerable sacrifice, for conservation and in the end be denounced by fanatics as a despoiler of nature, bulldozer, vandal, sadist and traitor to his country."

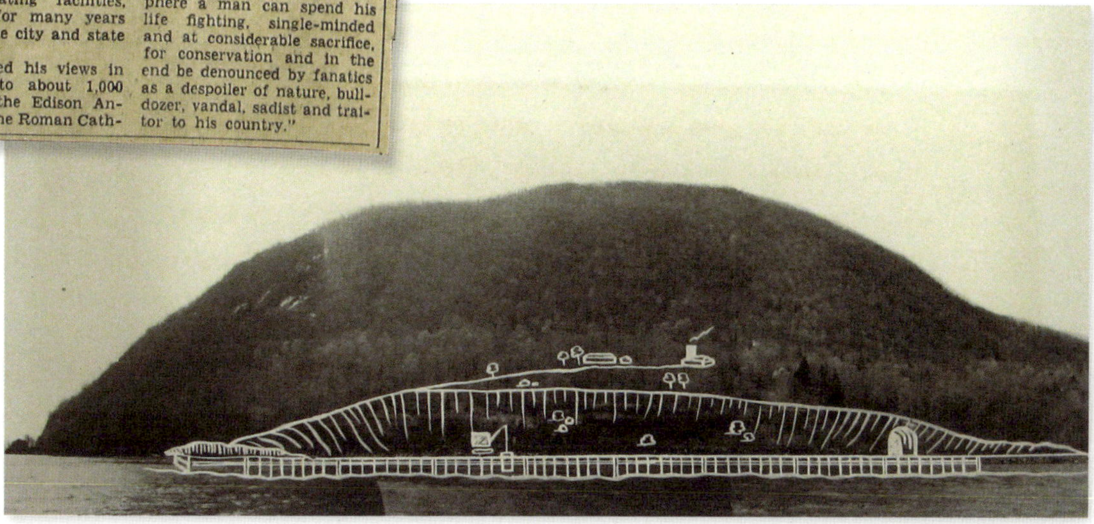

FROM TOP: MARIST COLLEGE ARCHIVES & SPECIAL COLLECTIONS LIBRARY; MARIST COLLEGE SPECIAL COLLECTIONS LIBRARY, SCENIC HUDSON COLLECTION; MARIST COLLEGE ARCHIVES & SPECIAL COLLECTIONS LIBRARY; MARIST COLLEGE ARCHIVES & SPECIAL COLLECTIONS LIBRARY

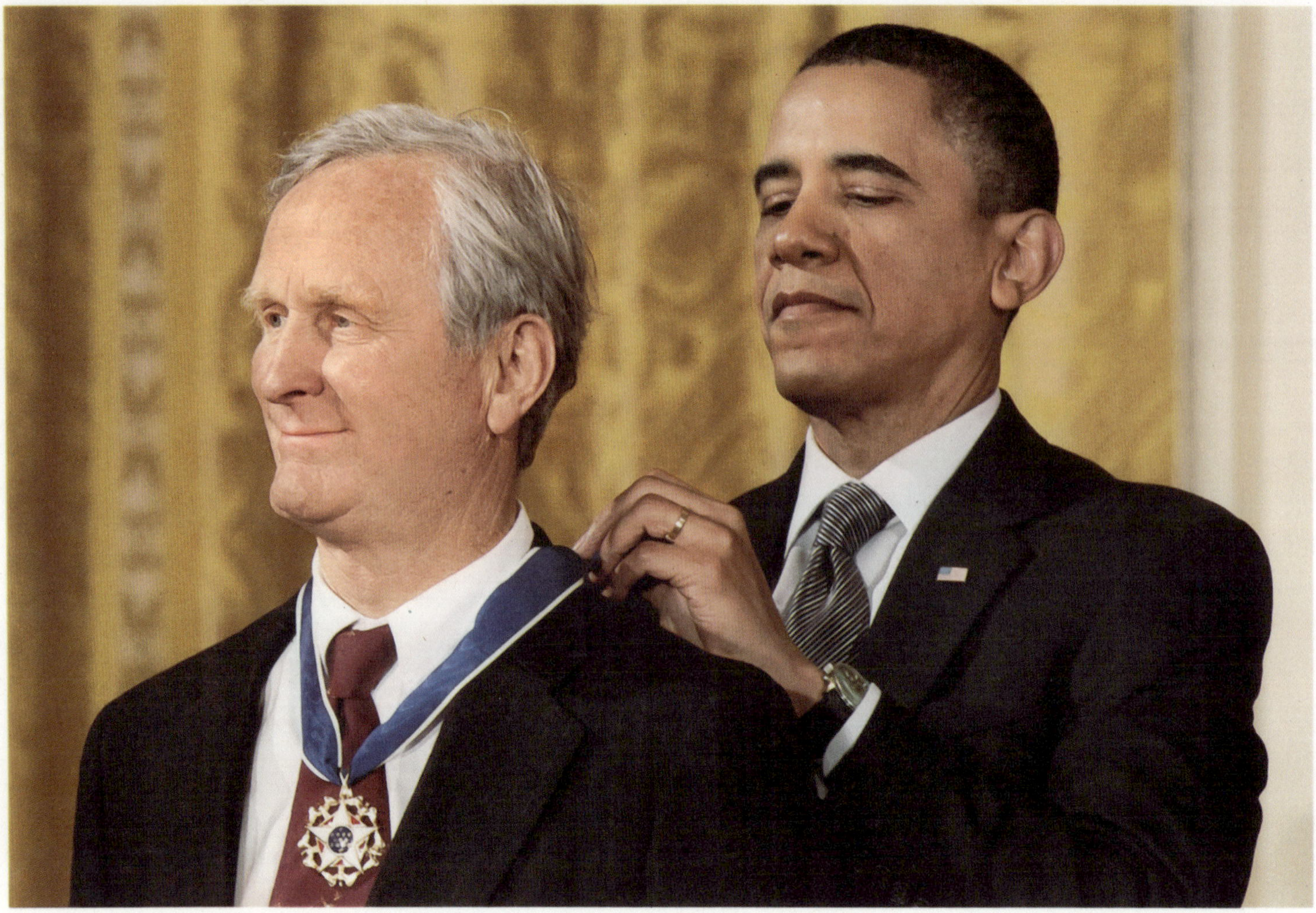

understood, standing together and partnering with diverse communities builds power for all.

As Storm King proved, saving the environment is a long-distance race. You never know where the finish line may be, but dropping out early is not an option. Take our fight to shield Canada's ancient forests from acid rain, for example. Forty years ago, when we took our first steps against the airborne pollution that was causing acid rain, how could we have imagined that the journey would lead us in time to an alliance with Nebraska farmers to oppose a pipeline that would carry filthy crude oil from the tar sands of Alberta, Canada, to the U.S. Gulf Coast, or to a partnership with a Latino community in Chicago, whose children were choking on the dust from the residue of that refined oil? Or that NRDC would progress to a consumer campaign against toilet paper made from Canada's virgin boreal forests, some of the most vital carbon sinks on earth? In nature, all things are connected. So in order to protect it, we'll follow the threads wherever they may lead and for as far as they take us.

That multipronged and decades-long fight, like many others detailed in this book, centers on the singular peril of climate change and our addiction to fossil fuels. But it also showcases the ever-evolving role NRDC plays in a movement whose emerging leaders, both inside and outside of the organization, remind me a lot of its founders 50 years ago. They're young, passionate, mad as hell, and not going to take it anymore.

The year 1970 was a pivotal moment in our history, and so is 2020. Even as scientists yell from the rooftops that the planet is roasting, corporations are bent on the reckless pursuit of the status quo—finding and burning ever more fossil fuels that are making the earth increasingly uninhabitable. A U.S. president is also waging the most shocking assault in history on our environment and our public health, attempting to cripple all the commonsense safeguards Americans have relied on for half a century. He claims climate change is a hoax, rejects the very notion of scientific knowledge, and is trying to turn respected public agencies into propaganda shops that spread falsehood, confusion, and lies.

And yet we remain hopeful. Because we know that rapacious corporations and presidential wrecking balls are just dark blips in the long sweep of history. We are here to diminish their mark. As the stories in this book demonstrate, NRDC has never been intimidated by the scale of the challenges that face us. With nothing less than the future of the planet at stake, there's no alternative but to dig in and fight back. The past 50 years have fully prepared us for what we're up against, and, once again, we're following the fight wherever it takes us and for as long as it takes to protect the planet and its people.

Top: In February 2011, President Obama awarded John Adams with the Presidential Medal of Freedom. Opposite: John and Patricia Adams canoe during a boat trip in southeast Alaska in 1997.

ANTHONY CLARK/NRDC

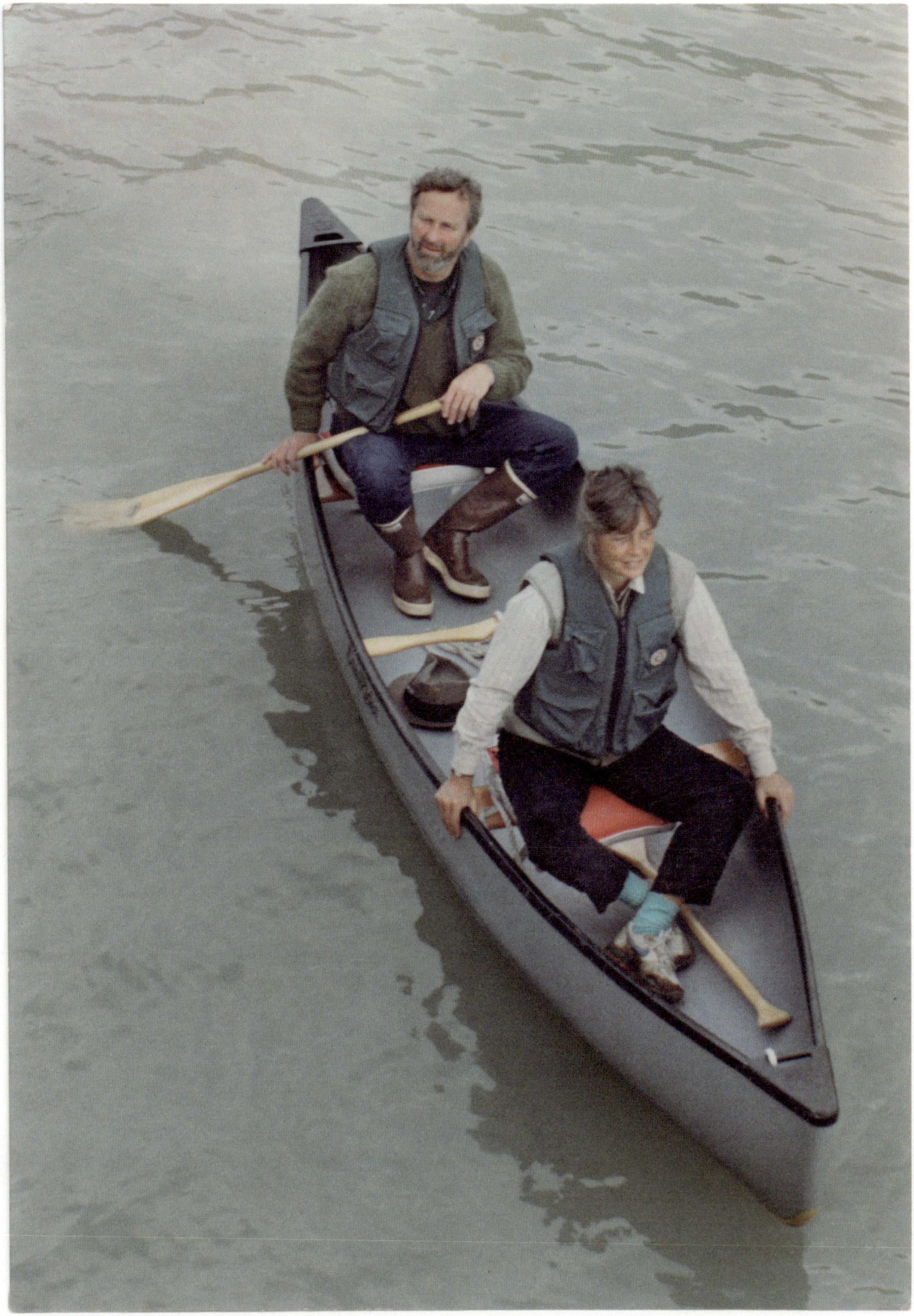

NRDC

ACKNOWLEDGMENTS

FIRST, I WANT TO RECOGNIZE Patricia, my life partner in building NRDC all these years.

We could never have gotten on our feet without the first chairman of our board, Stephen Duggan, and his wife, Beatrice "Smokey" Duggan, and others who were present at the creation, including Adele Auchincloss, Boris Bittker, Jim Marshall, Mike and Winsome McIntosh, John Robinson, Whitney North Seymour Jr., David Sive, and George Woodwell.

Our four board chairs since then—Bill DeWind, Fritz Schwarz, Dan Tishman, and Alan Horn—have led the organization from strength to strength. Over the decades, they have worked with an extraordinary array of trustees and other supporters, and I'm deeply grateful to every one of them.

Every successful organization is built on strong foundations. I thank our first decade of leaders for their contributions to NRDC in its formative stage and for their loyalty, friendship, and support over the past 50 years: Karim Ahmed, Dick Ayres, Roger Beers, Steve Blevins, Jane Bloom, Peter Borrelli, John Bryson, Faith Campbell, Ralph Cavanagh, Sarah Chasis, Bill Christie, Tom Cochran, David Doniger, Fran Dubrowski, David Goldstein, Eric Goldstein, Dick Hall, David Hawkins, Laura King, John Leshy, Stella Liang, Angus Macbeth, Al Meyerhoff, Lawrie Mott, Glenn Paulsen, Ricky Perera, Marc Reisner, Larry Rockefeller, Ross Sandler, Jacob Scherr, David Schoenbrod, Gus Speth, Tom Stoel, Ed Strohbehn, Pattie Sullivan, James Thornton, Johanna Wald, Jackie Warren, and Donna Wilcox.

Dozens more have devoted more than 25 years, almost their entire professional lives, to the organization: Evelyn Arévalo, Kaid Benfield, Gloria Bowman, Sharon Buccino, Hal Candee, Sheryl Carter, Lisa Catapano, Chuck Clusen, Kevin Curtis, Darlene Davis, Gail de Rita, Sarah Edwards-Schmidt, Deborah Faulkner, Barbara Finamore, Karen Garrison, Ashok Gupta, Sharon Hargrove, Allen Hershkowitz, Mark Izeman, Bobby Kennedy Jr., Kit Kennedy, Sandy Kolakowski, Dan Lashof, Niel Lawrence, Nancy Marks, Peter Miller, Stan Norris, Annie Notthoff, Matthew Perrin, Joel Reynolds, Abby Schaefer, Lisa Speer, John Steelman, Monique Waples, and Sami Yassa.

I'm deeply indebted to those who have succeeded me as president of NRDC: Frances Beinecke, an inspirational leader of the American environmental movement and a true friend for almost half a century; Rhea Suh, who left a special mark on the organization with her deep concern for social equity; and now Gina McCarthy, a towering figure in the protection of the environment and the fight against climate change and the perfect person to propel NRDC to new heights. And special thanks to Mitch Bernard, whose leadership coupled with his thoughtfulness has been vital.

Thanks to Linda Lopez, Stephen Mills, Jack Murray, Gina Trujillo, and Marie Weinmann, together with their staff, for building the power of a membership that numbers in the millions.

NRDC will certainly remain a *Force for the Future*, with Jennifer Bernstein and her team working vigilantly to grow funding; Bob Deans, Michelle Egan, Lisa Goffredi, and Jenny Powers guiding our important communications work; Ed Yoon leading the way for our Center for Policy Advocacy; and Mercedes Falber and her team focusing on diversity, equity, and inclusion as well as a commitment to keeping and recruiting the best of the best.

Special recognition to Susan Barbarisi, Mary Donnellon, Zelda Leslie, and Ann Roach, who have acted as my right hand and kept the ship on course.

Profuse gratitude to all those who made this book possible, including George Black, Christina Choi, Darcy Eveleigh, Virginia Lee, Melissa Mahony, Ronald Sequeira Jr., Alexander Spacher, and Kristen Walsh.

Countless other men and women of great expertise and deep commitment have made NRDC into the world's leading environmental organization and changed the world in the process. All I can say to them, and to our generous and indispensable donors who have made it all possible, is thank you, thank you, thank you.

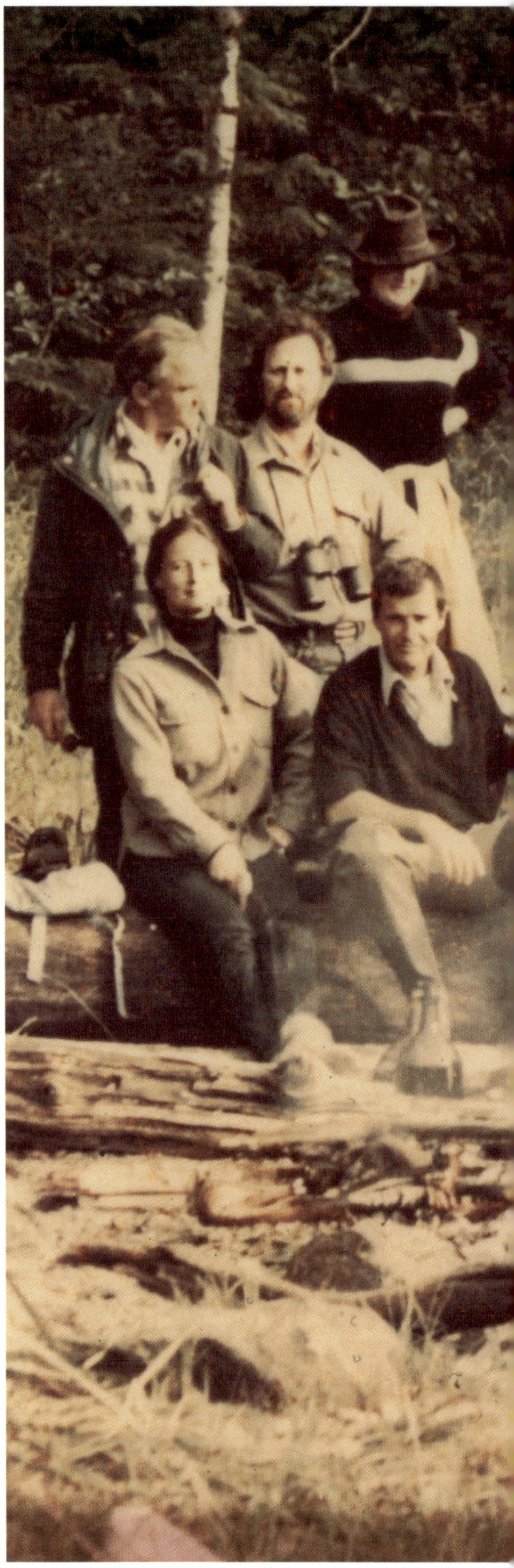

NRDC

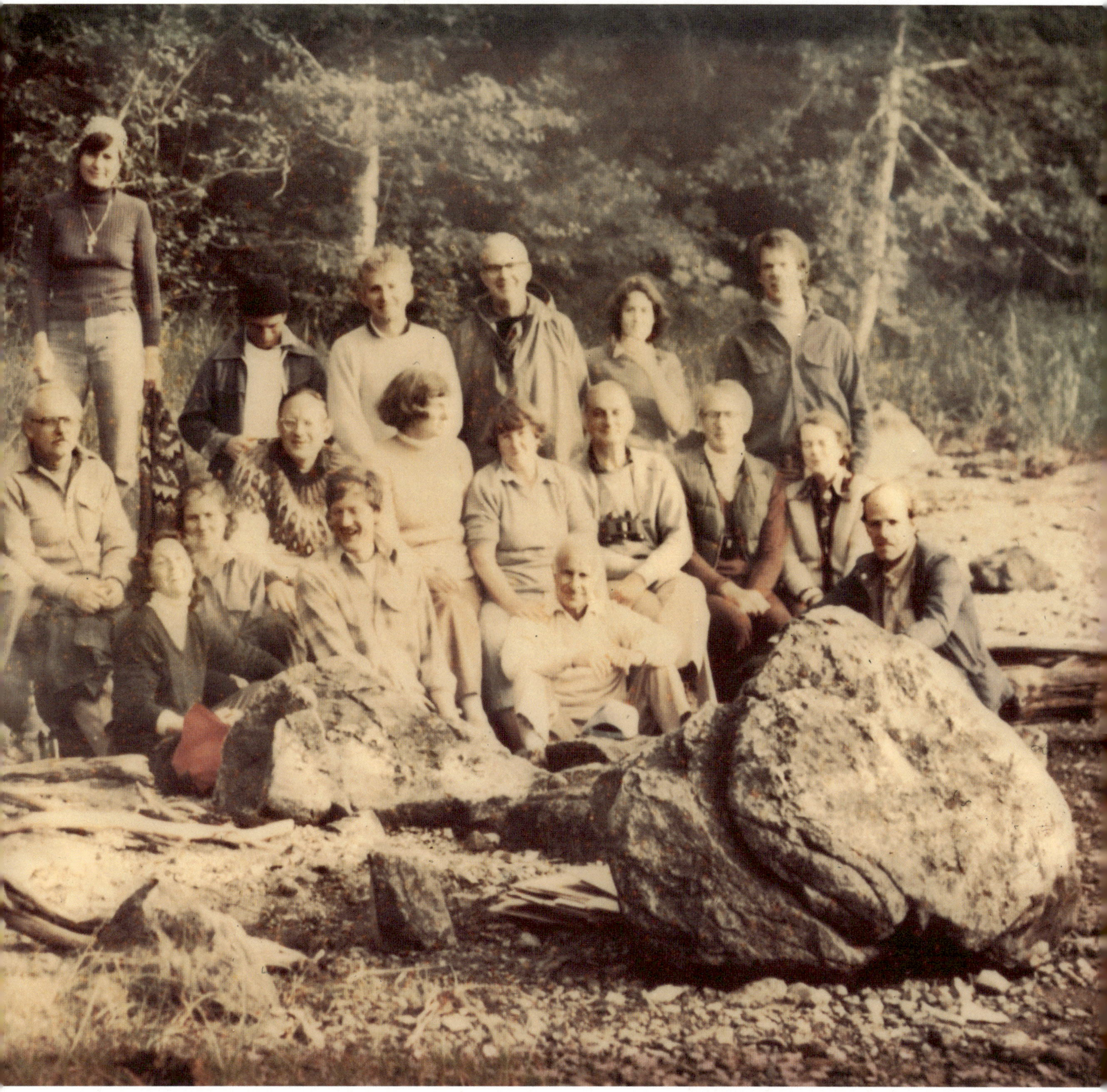

The first NRDC trip, organized by Mike McIntosh, to recognize the threats to Alaska's Tongass National Forest. Top row, from left: Hamilton Kean, John Adams, Adele Auchincloss, Hella McVay, unknown, Frank Parker, John Sawyer, Frances Beinecke, Tom McHenry. Second row, from left: Patricia Adams, Mike McIntosh, Donald Harris, Scott McVay, Baba Parker, Patricia Kind, Louis Auchincloss, Barney McHenry, Anne Sawyer, Larry Rockefeller. Front row, from left: Winsome McIntosh, Janet Harris, Ron Hawk, Philip Kind Jr.

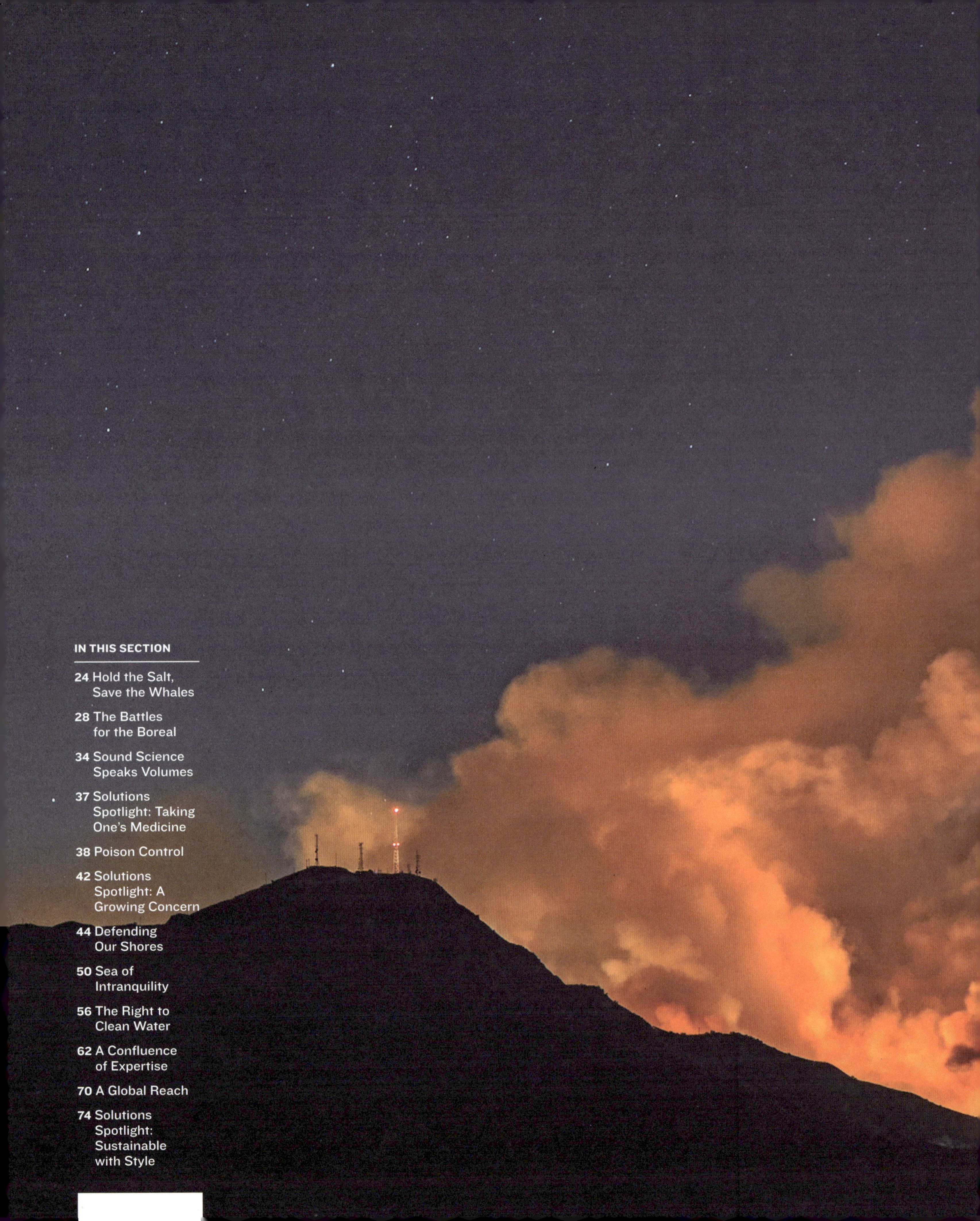

IN THIS SECTION

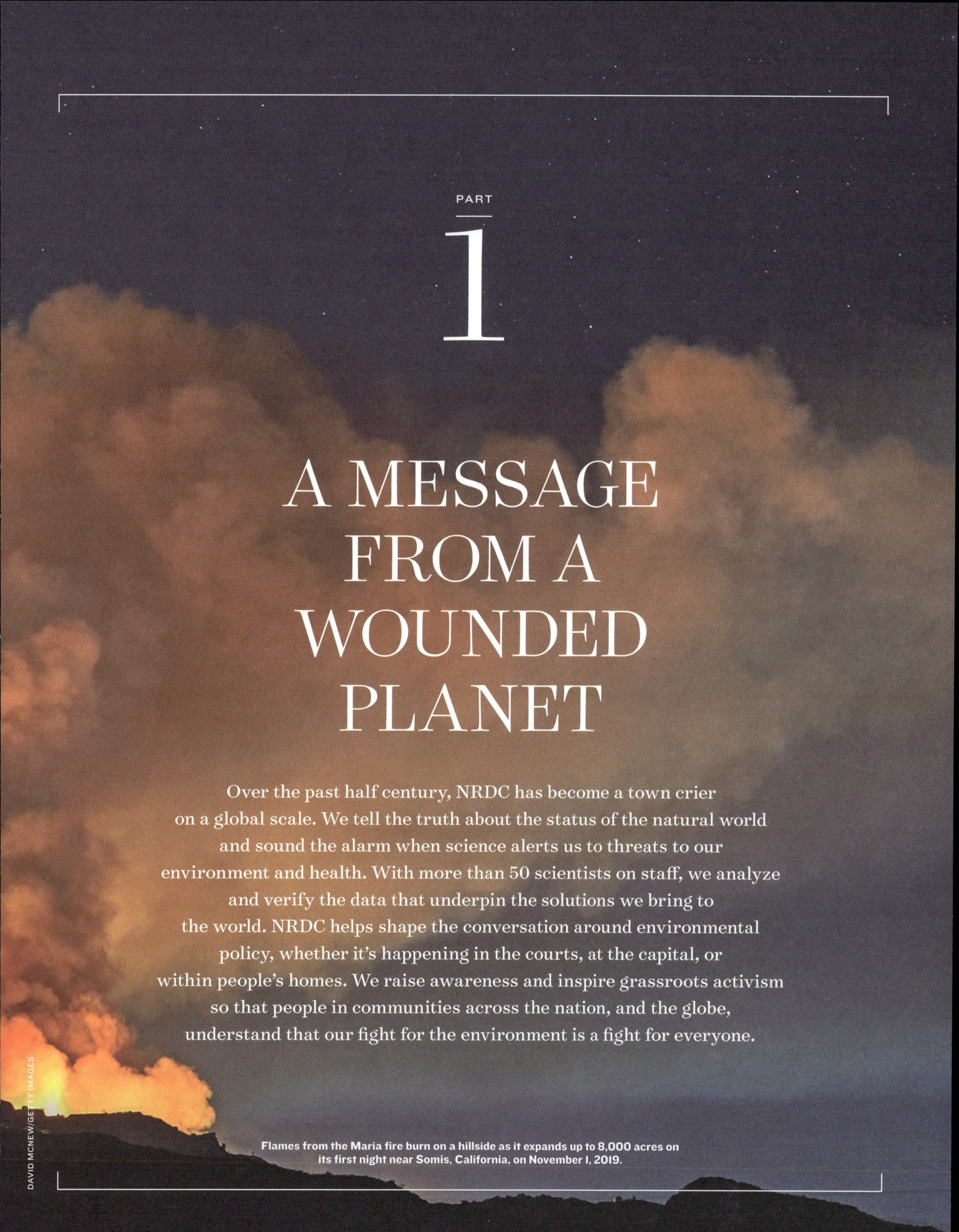

PART

1

A MESSAGE FROM A WOUNDED PLANET

Over the past half century, NRDC has become a town crier on a global scale. We tell the truth about the status of the natural world and sound the alarm when science alerts us to threats to our environment and health. With more than 50 scientists on staff, we analyze and verify the data that underpin the solutions we bring to the world. NRDC helps shape the conversation around environmental policy, whether it's happening in the courts, at the capital, or within people's homes. We raise awareness and inspire grassroots activism so that people in communities across the nation, and the globe, understand that our fight for the environment is a fight for everyone.

Flames from the Maria fire burn on a hillside as it expands up to 8,000 acres on its first night near Somis, California, on November 1, 2019.

DAVID MCNEW/GETTY IMAGES

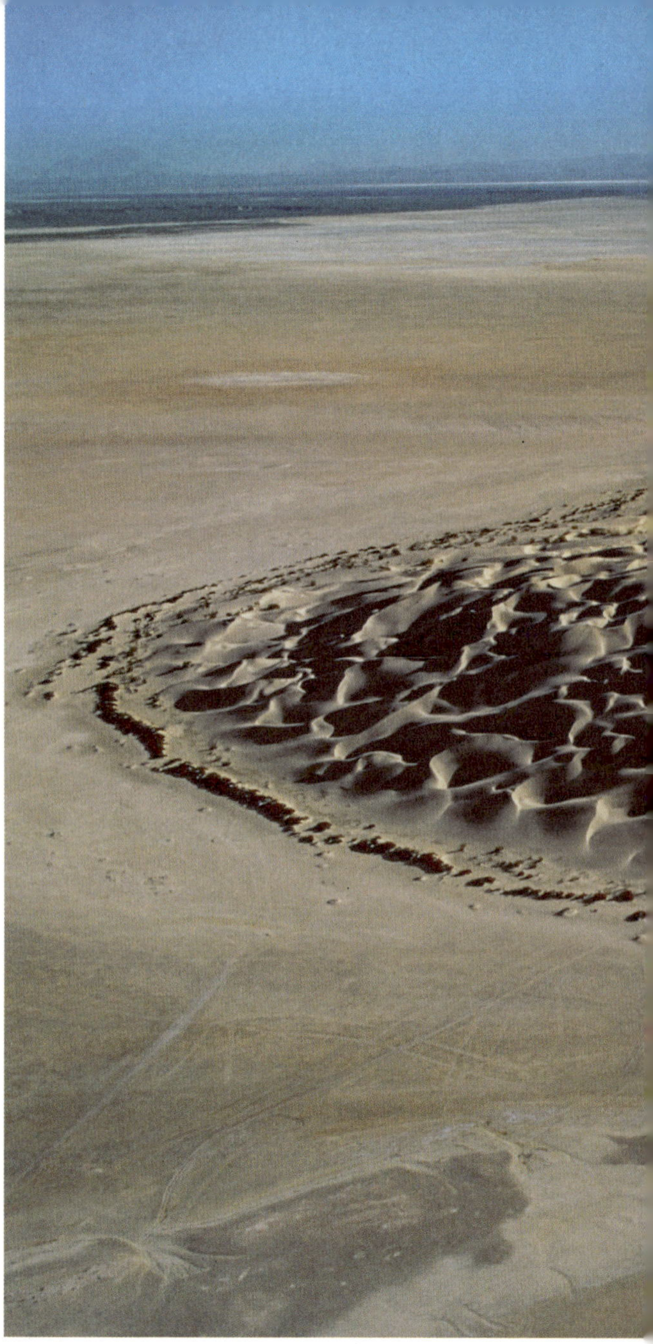

HOLD THE SALT, SAVE THE WHALES

IF YOU WANT TO PROTECT THE NATURAL wonders of the planet, you have to be ready to stand up to the biggest, most powerful adversaries, whether government or corporate, because they're the ones with the greatest capacity to do harm. Take, for example, the giant Japanese conglomerate Mitsubishi Corporation.

In 1994, our longtime international specialist Jacob Scherr received a call from a Mexican poet named Homero Aridjis, asking for help in blocking a threat to a special place on the coast of Baja California, the Laguna San Ignacio. The lagoon's clear, jade-green waters are the last place on earth where the world's 26,000 gray whales breed and birth their calves, undisturbed by human intrusion after their 5,000-mile migration from the Arctic.

Together with the Mexican government, Aridjis said, Mitsubishi was proposing to turn this critical breeding ground—designated just a year earlier as a UNESCO World Heritage site—into the biggest salt factory on earth, with a footprint larger than Washington, D.C. If built, the factory would each day release 22,000 tons of concentrated brine waste, laden with toxic chemicals, into Whale Bay, about six miles north of the lagoon's entrance. There were grand economic promises to tempt the Mexican government, of course: The company would invest $120 million in the project, which would potentially generate $80 million a year in hard currency revenues.

Jacob, in Frances Beinecke's words, is "a big-picture guy, a bit of a dreamer with an over-the-horizon view and an analytical mind that can grasp a problem, break it down, and imagine solutions that can work for everyone." In other words, the right person on the right issue at the right time.

He joined forces with Joel Reynolds, a senior attorney and director of our marine mammal team and now our western director. Together they designed a campaign unlike anything NRDC had done before, and the rest of the organization went to work. We attacked Mitsubishi on all fronts: with hard science; publicity and storytelling; economic pressure on investors; and alliances and partnerships with dozens of groups in Mexico, the United States, Europe, and Japan.

The whales of Laguna San Ignacio are a curious bunch, often emerging near boats to take a look at what is happening at the surface. Back in 1976, a local fisherman named Francisco "Pachico" Mayoral realized that some whales would even let him reach over and touch them. From there, Pachico and his family started an eco-friendly whale-watching business. This operation and other local ecotourism ventures, which still run today, also presented an opportunity to protect this wonderful, wild place by giving people an up-close look at what is at stake. Starting in 1997, NRDC began organizing trips to Laguna San Ignacio for scores of visitors, including noted marine activists like filmmaker Jean-Michel Cousteau and actors Pierce Brosnan and Glenn Close, who threw their influence behind our campaign after having the magical experience of seeing, at close quarters, the mother whales caring for their calves.

Adding to the passion of these supporters was the expertise of a group of 34 of the world's most renowned scientists, including nine Nobel Prize winners, who in 1999, with our assistance, published an open letter in the New York Times and other major newspapers. The authors succinctly described the globally recognized importance of the gray whale and its unique lagoon habitat and the magnitude of the "unacceptable risk" posed by the salt plant—preemptively undermining any corporate-financed "science" Mitsubishi might present.

We also tapped into the emerging potential of social media, creating a tool on our website that allowed our members to target individual Mitsubishi dealers by clicking on their zip code. Nothing disturbs a corporation more than threats to its bottom line, and the final item in our tool kit was a campaign to pressure mutual funds to boycott the company's stock,

The site of Mitsubishi's proposed salt mine, just six miles north of Laguna San Ignacio.

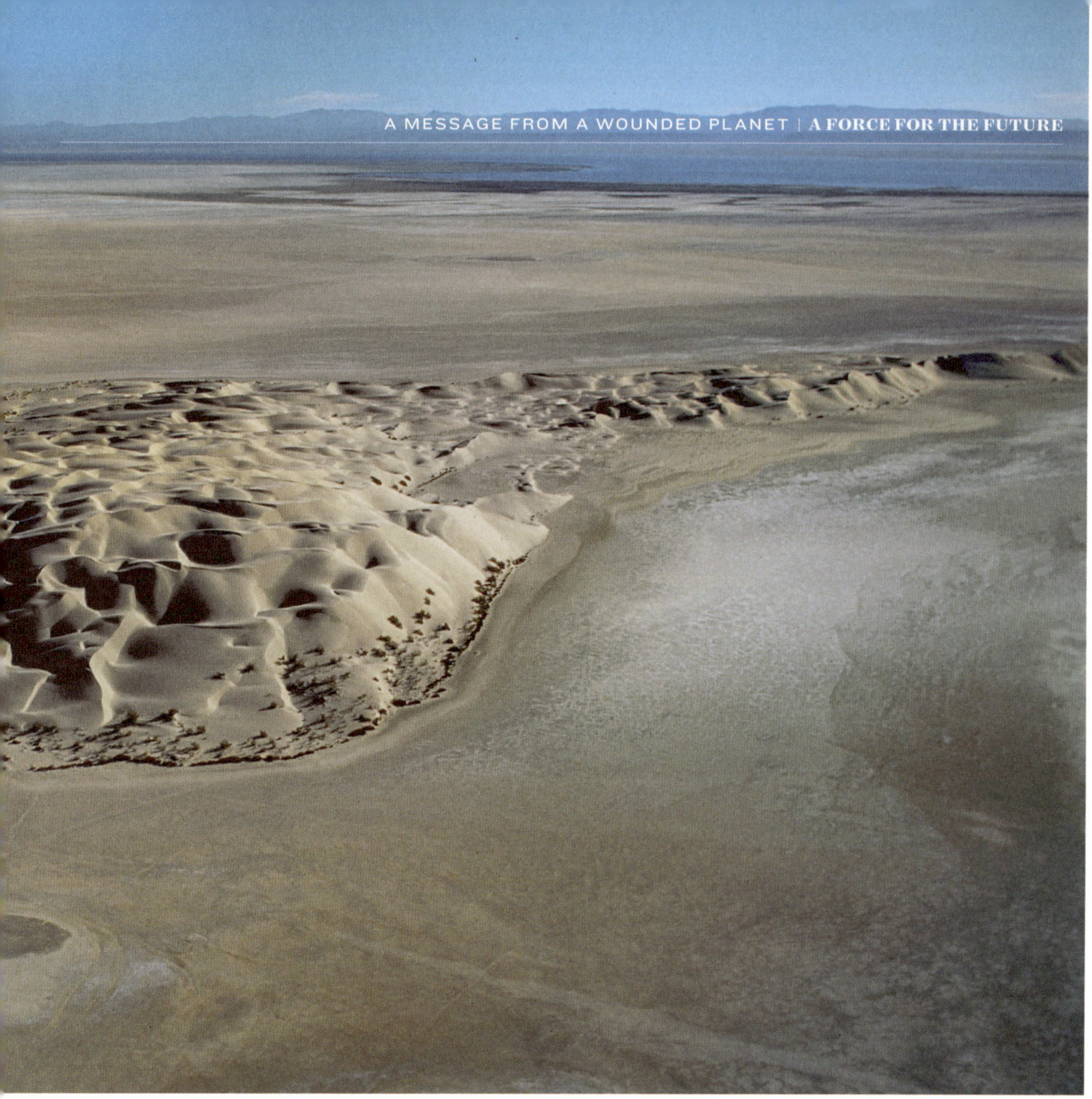

"Laguna San Ignacio is an extraordinary part of the world's natural heritage—important not just for gray whales but also for humanity's relationship to the creatures with which we share this planet. Its protection lies at the very heart of NRDC's work."

—**Joel Reynolds, senior attorney and Western director, NRDC**

which a group of 15 funds announced and vowed to maintain until Mitsubishi abandoned its saltworks project.

Reacting to the buzz that we and our partners created around the issue, Mexican President Ernesto Zedillo decided in 2000 to see what all the fuss was about and brought his family to Laguna San Ignacio. His wife, captivated by the scene before her, leaned out of their panga boat and kissed one of the whales on the head. Days later, Zedillo called a press conference and canceled the salt factory.

But that wasn't the end of the story. NRDC couldn't just declare victory and walk away. We had an obligation to the small communities around Laguna San Ignacio, which depend on its health for their livelihoods and are its natural guardians. Since 2000, we've worked together with our partners—including the residents themselves, through their communal ejidos—to secure protection for hundreds of thousands of acres of land around the lagoon. This enduring partnership has created a trust fund to promote sustainable development, education, local businesses, and ecotourism projects, so that new generations of local residents and visitors from around the world can enjoy Laguna San Ignacio while continuing to witness new generations of magnificent gray whales.

Joel Reynolds, who was instrumental in saving Laguna San Ignacio, continues to oversee our work for the lagoon, the local community, and the whales. Here, he guides NRDC members on a whale-watching trip to the lagoon.

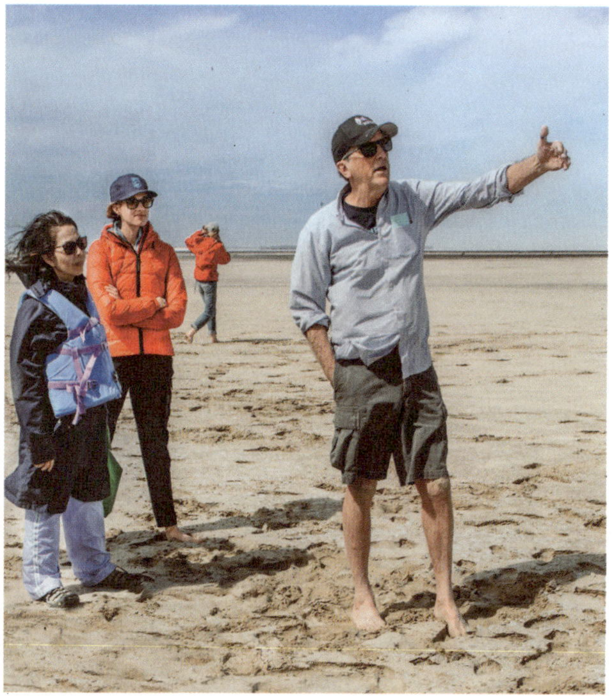

FROM TOP: JIM WARK/AIRPHOTO; HEIDI ZUMBRUN FOR NRDC

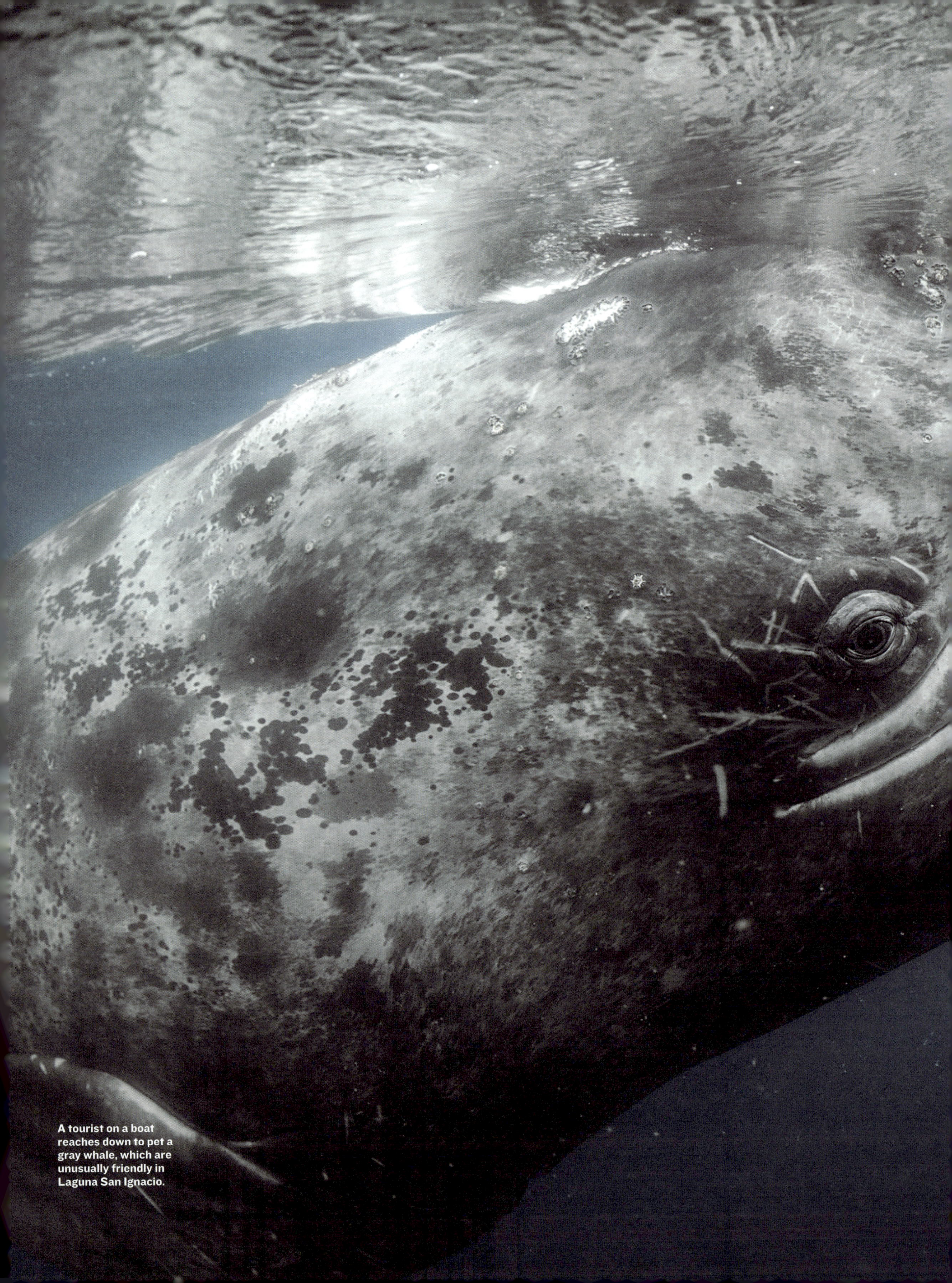

A tourist on a boat reaches down to pet a gray whale, which are unusually friendly in Laguna San Ignacio.

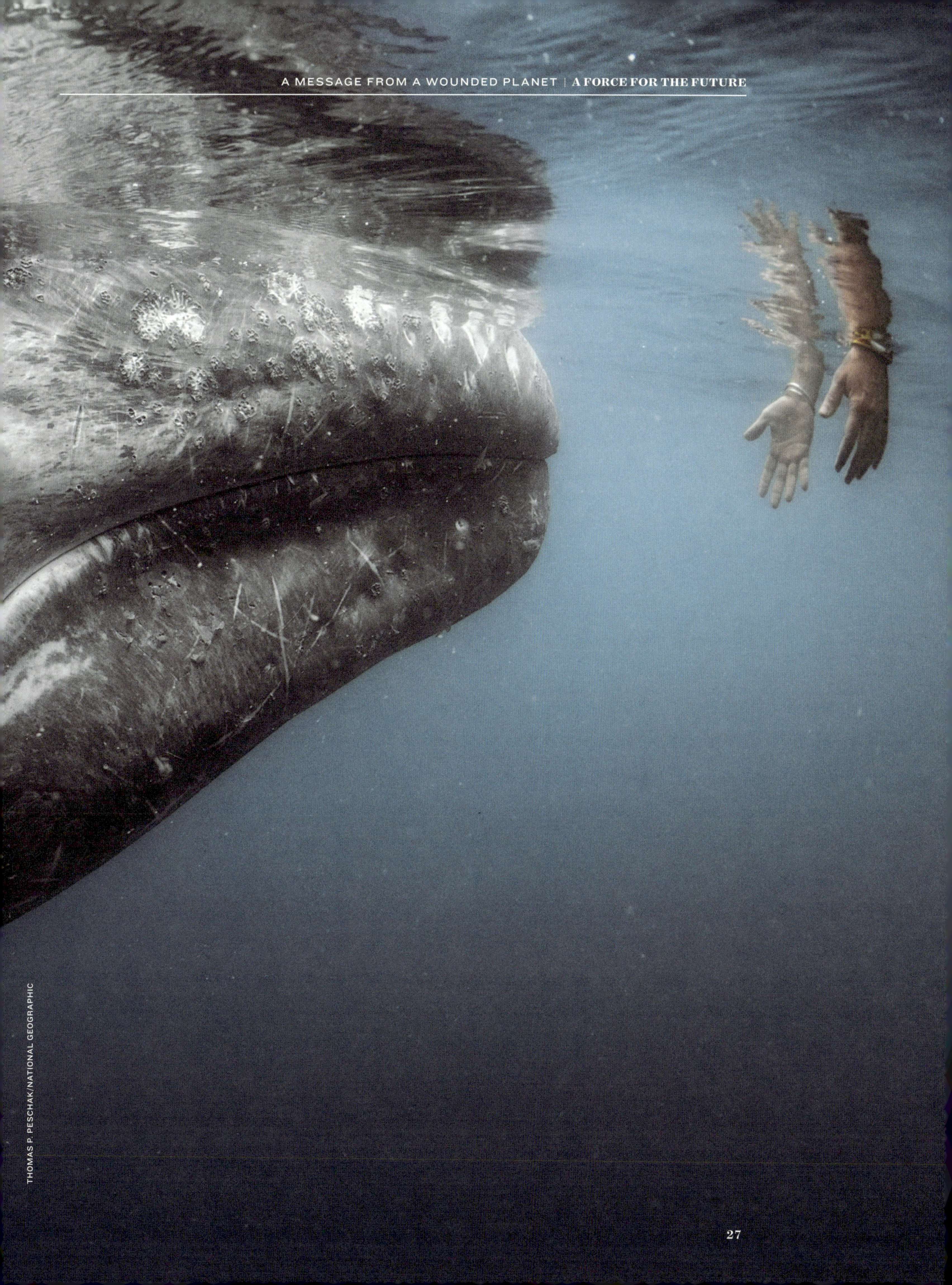

THOMAS P. PESCHAK/NATIONAL GEOGRAPHIC

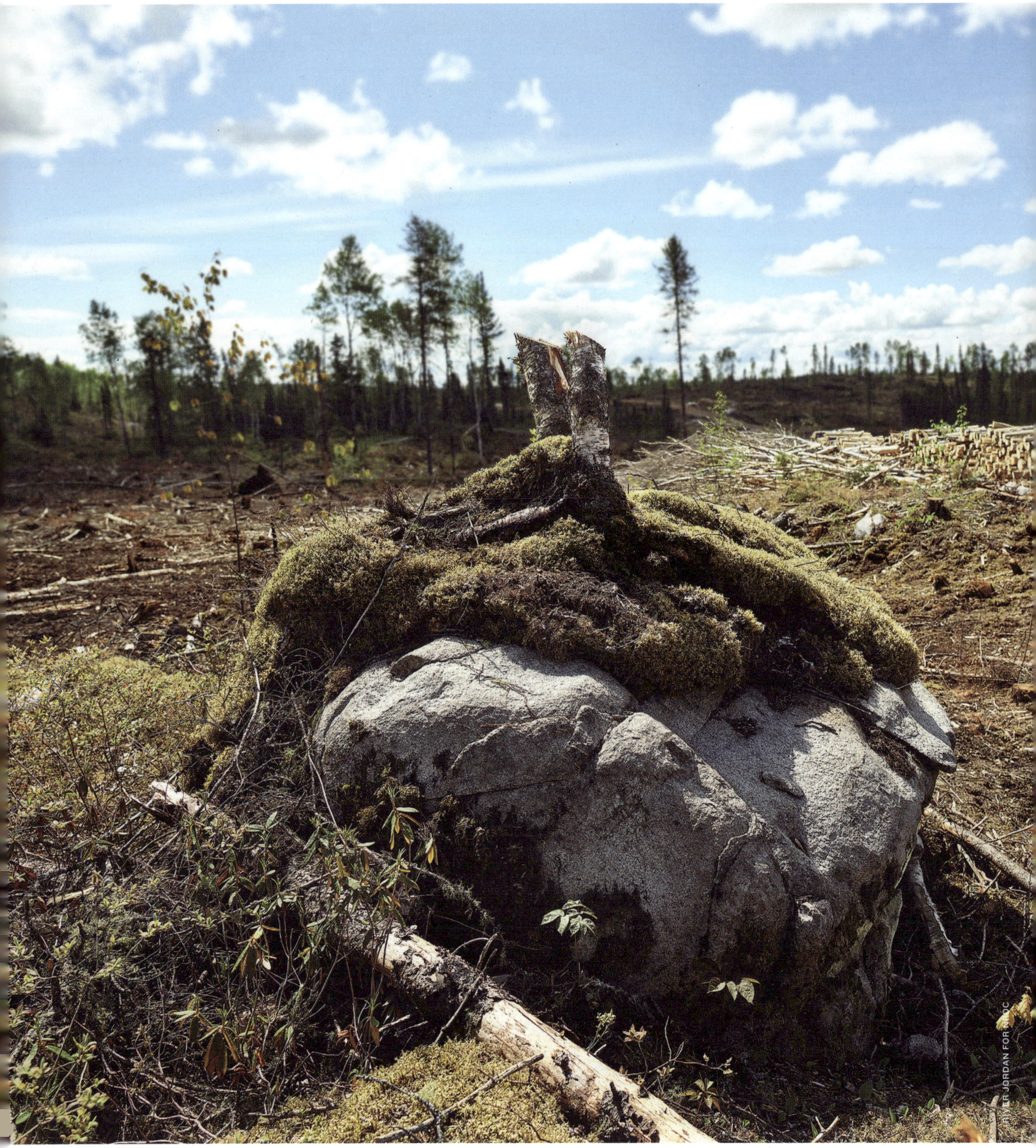

RIVER JORDAN FOR NRDC

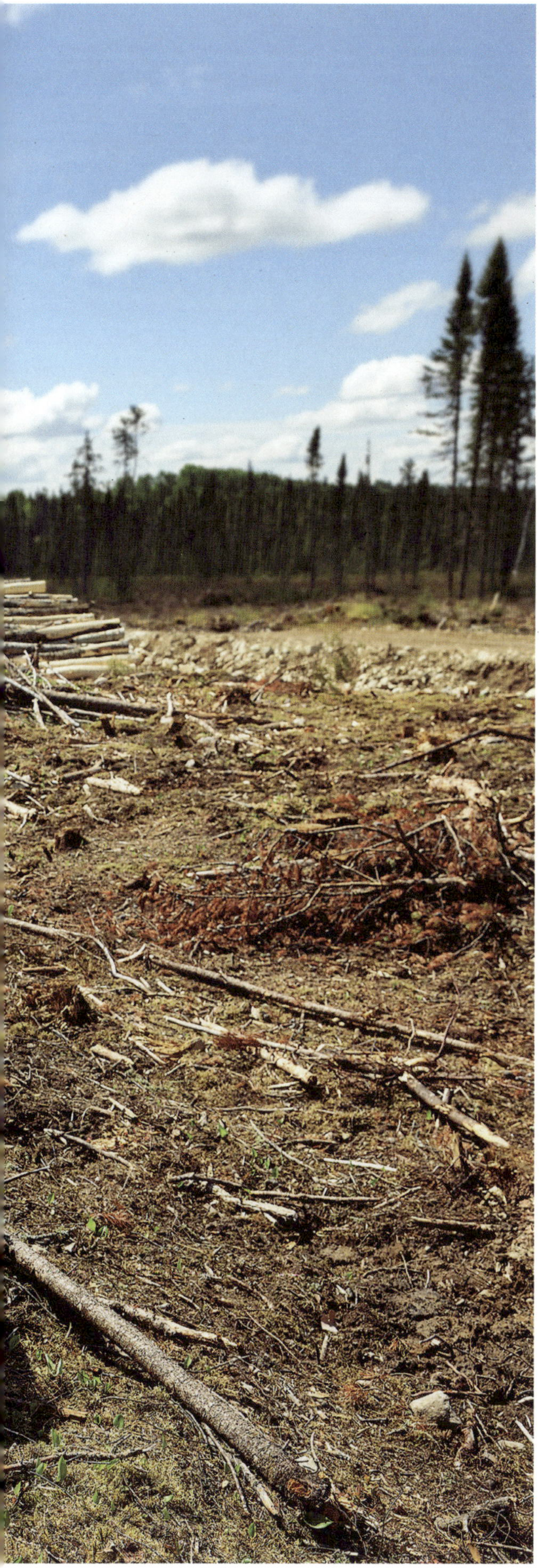

THE BATTLES FOR THE BOREAL

MOST PEOPLE KNOW THAT TREES take in carbon dioxide and expel oxygen. If you asked them to name the forests that store the most carbon, they would most likely guess the tropical rainforests, due to the headline-grabbing fires in the Amazon. The correct answer, however, is the high-latitude boreal forests of Canada, Russia, Scandinavia, and Alaska, which store almost twice as much carbon in their plant matter and soils as their tropical counterparts. Canada's boreal contains a quarter of the world's intact forests, spanning more than a billion acres. And that's where we focus our work. These woods to our north are a natural wonderland, rich in wildlife—wolves, lynx, caribou, grizzlies, and billions of migratory birds—and culture. About 600 First Nation communities continue to practice their ancestral ways of life here.

We've worked for decades to earn the trust of and partner with Indigenous communities in Canada. NRDC supported British Columbian First Nations in their efforts to protect the pristine forests of Clayoquot Sound and the Great Bear Rainforest (which gave us our logo, the spirit bear), and farther east in Quebec, we worked with the Cree Nation to block plans for a gigantic hydropower project in James Bay. So when the Athabasca Chipewyan and Mikisew Cree in the province of Alberta alerted us to a new threat to the boreal, we took their warnings seriously and got to work with them, too.

In the early 2000s, as oil prices skyrocketed, big fossil fuel companies began to ravage Alberta to extract heavy crude. It was the start of the tar sands boom, and NRDC decided that this was the place to draw a line in the sand in the fight against climate change.

Getting this exceptionally dirty crude oil to market required building pipelines, so that's what we had to stop. We were up against two huge Canadian corporations: Enbridge, the biggest pipeline company in the world, and TransCanada.

Between 1996 and 2015, the timber industry logged more than 28 million acres of Canada's boreal forest, an area roughly the size of Ohio.

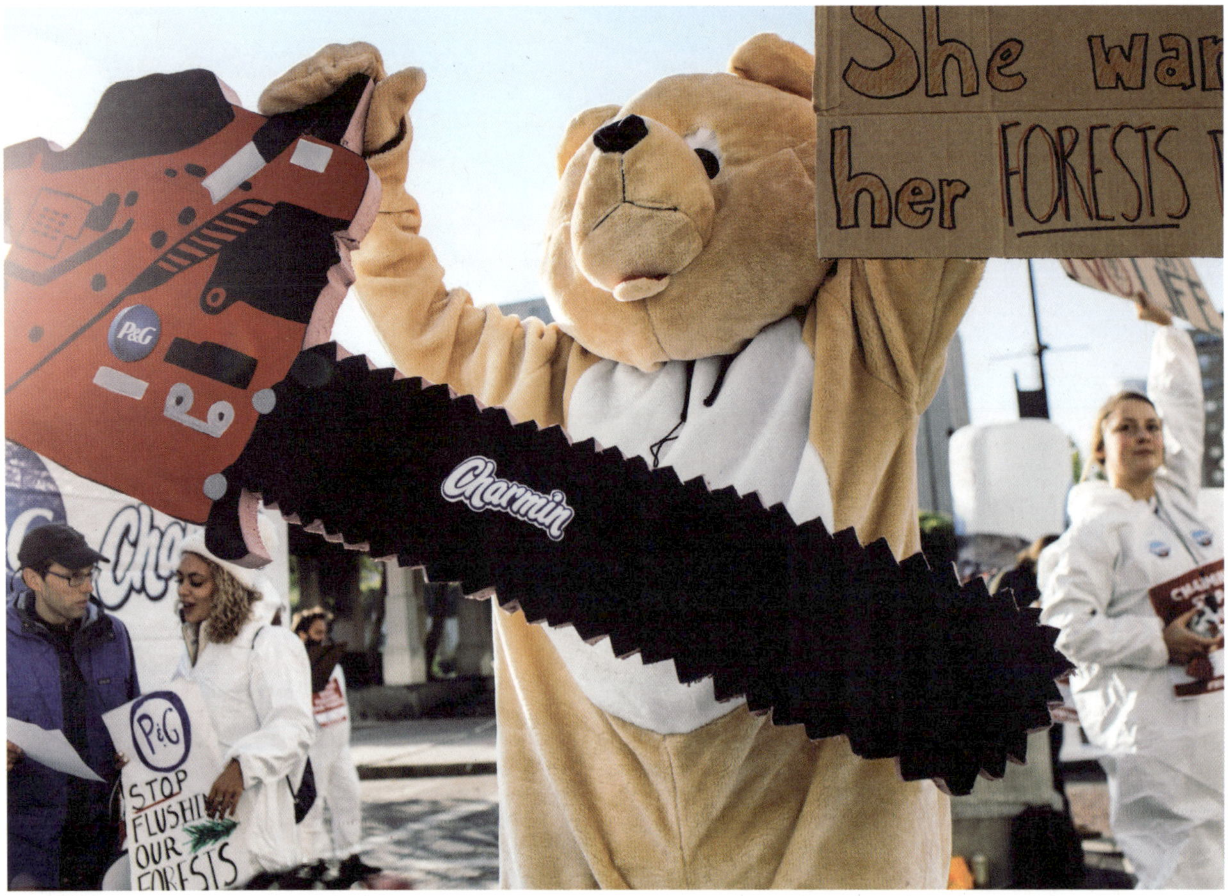

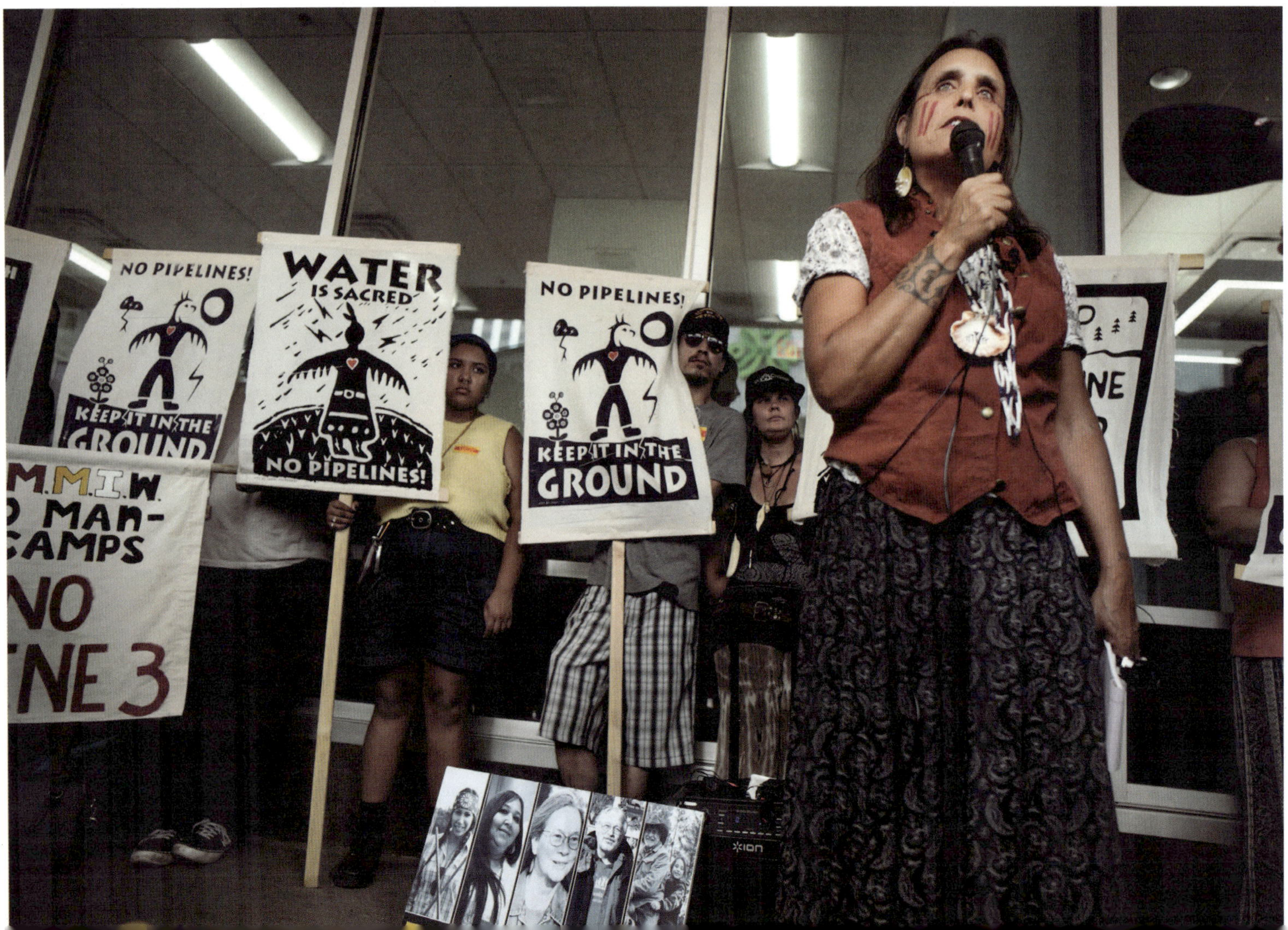

Top: Protestors, including NRDC staff, gather outside Procter & Gamble's headquarters in Cincinnati during the company's shareholders' meeting in October 2019. Bottom: Winona LaDuke, director of the nonprofit group Honor the Earth, speaking out in June 2018 against Enbridge's Line 3 tar sands pipeline, which would traverse northern Minnesota.

FROM TOP: ANDREW SPEAR FOR NRDC; RICHARD TSONG-TAATARII/STAR TRIBUNE VIA AP

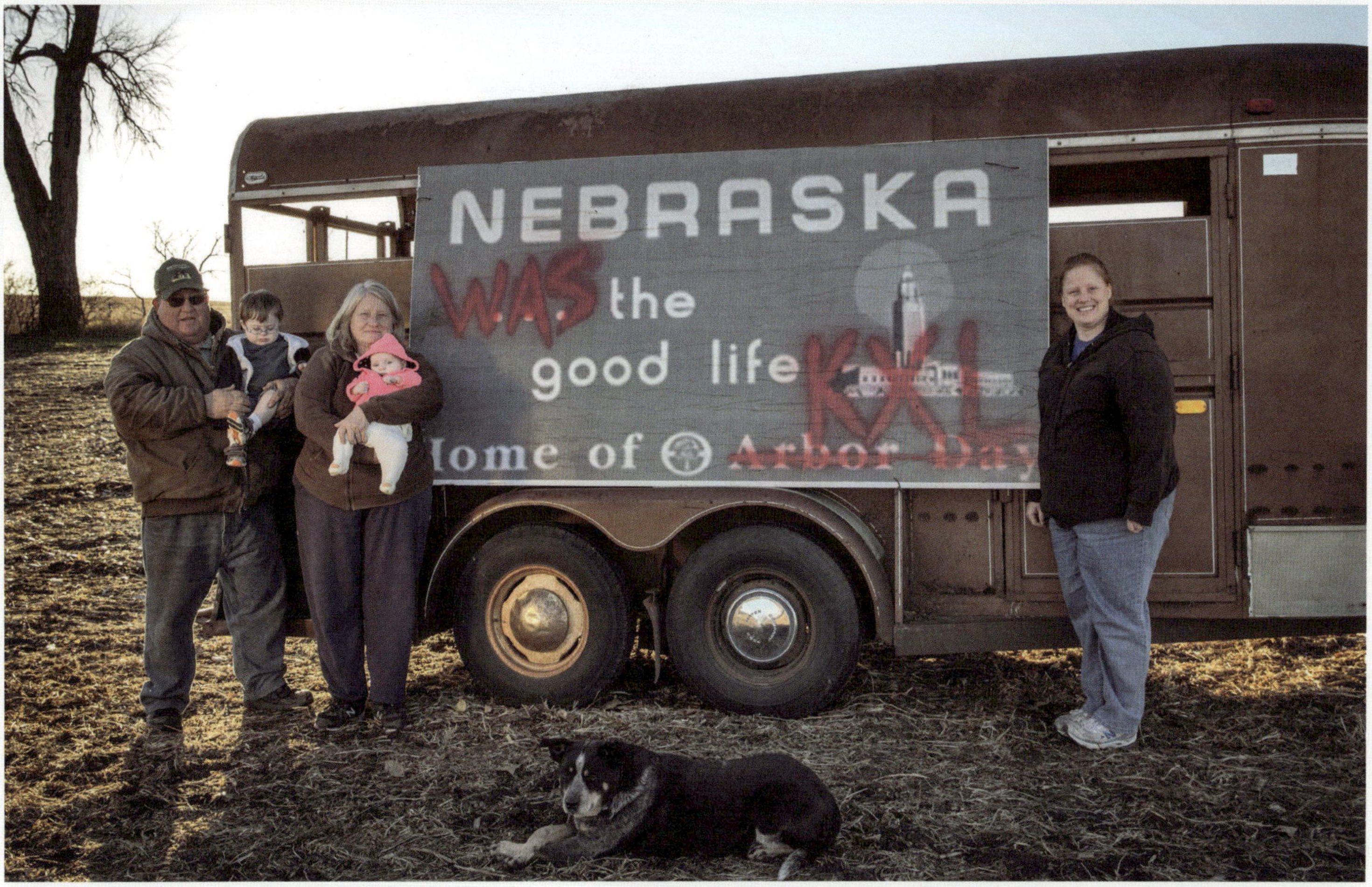

FROM THE FRONTLINES

Art Tanderup

"There's never a dull moment out on the prairie here when they're trying to shove a pipeline down your throat." Art Tanderup doesn't mince words when talking about the roller-coaster ride of a fight against the proposed Keystone XL pipeline—a battle he and his fellow Nebraskans have been waging for the past dozen years.

Soon after Art and his wife, Helen, retired in 2009, TransCanada began trying to claim portions of their 160-acre farm in Neligh—owned by Helen's family for more than a century—in its effort to build a dirty tar sands pipeline through the state. Their land, which is along the historic Ponca Trail of Tears, has since become a hub for the KXL resistance in Nebraska, a spot so locally well known that mail addressed simply to "Pipeline Fighters Village" has no trouble reaching them.

Nebraska landowners and Native Americans who are trying to preserve their properties and heritage have joined forces here. Together, they created four crop art installations in the Tanderups' fields that display massive #NoKXL messages visible from above, hosted the 2014 Harvest the Hope concert (featuring performances by Neil Young and Willie Nelson), and organize a sacred Ponca corn planting and harvest every year—all in an effort to raise awareness about the pipeline threat and build support for their resistance efforts. In 2018, the Tanderups also gifted 10 acres of their land to the Ponca Nation—both as a strategy to block KXL and because, Art says, "it was only right to give it back to them."

Through the years, the Tanderups have worked closely with NRDC and other national groups as well as local partners such as Bold Nebraska to challenge the pipeline on legal grounds. They have enjoyed several victories along the way, but the fight isn't over yet. "The support and help of the national environmental organizations that have come together on KXL has just been phenomenal," Art says. "Without them, it would be extremely difficult to get the message out there and to have the power to fight these court battles. So it's very much appreciated what NRDC has done."

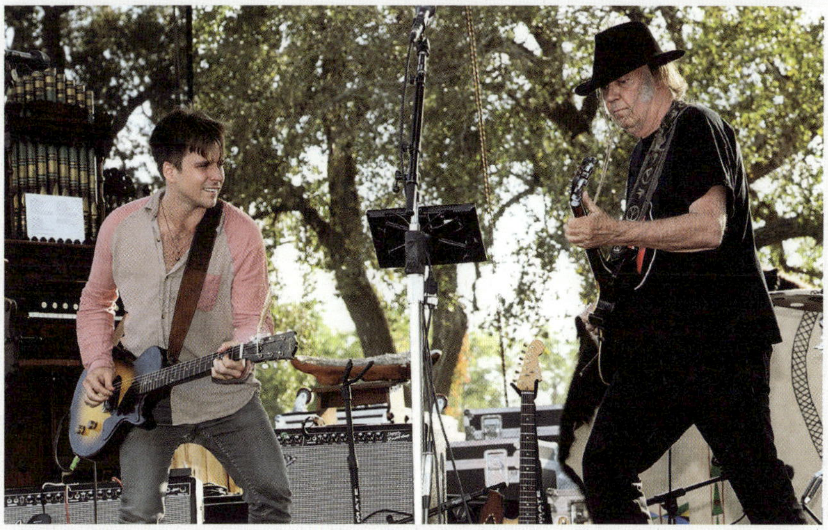

Top: Art and Helen Tanderup with their daughter, their grandchildren, and the family dog. Above: Lukas Nelson (left) and Neil Young at the Harvest the Hope concert on the Tanderup farm

FROM TOP: MARY ANNE ANDREI/BOLD NEBRASKA; GARY MILLER/GETTY IMAGES

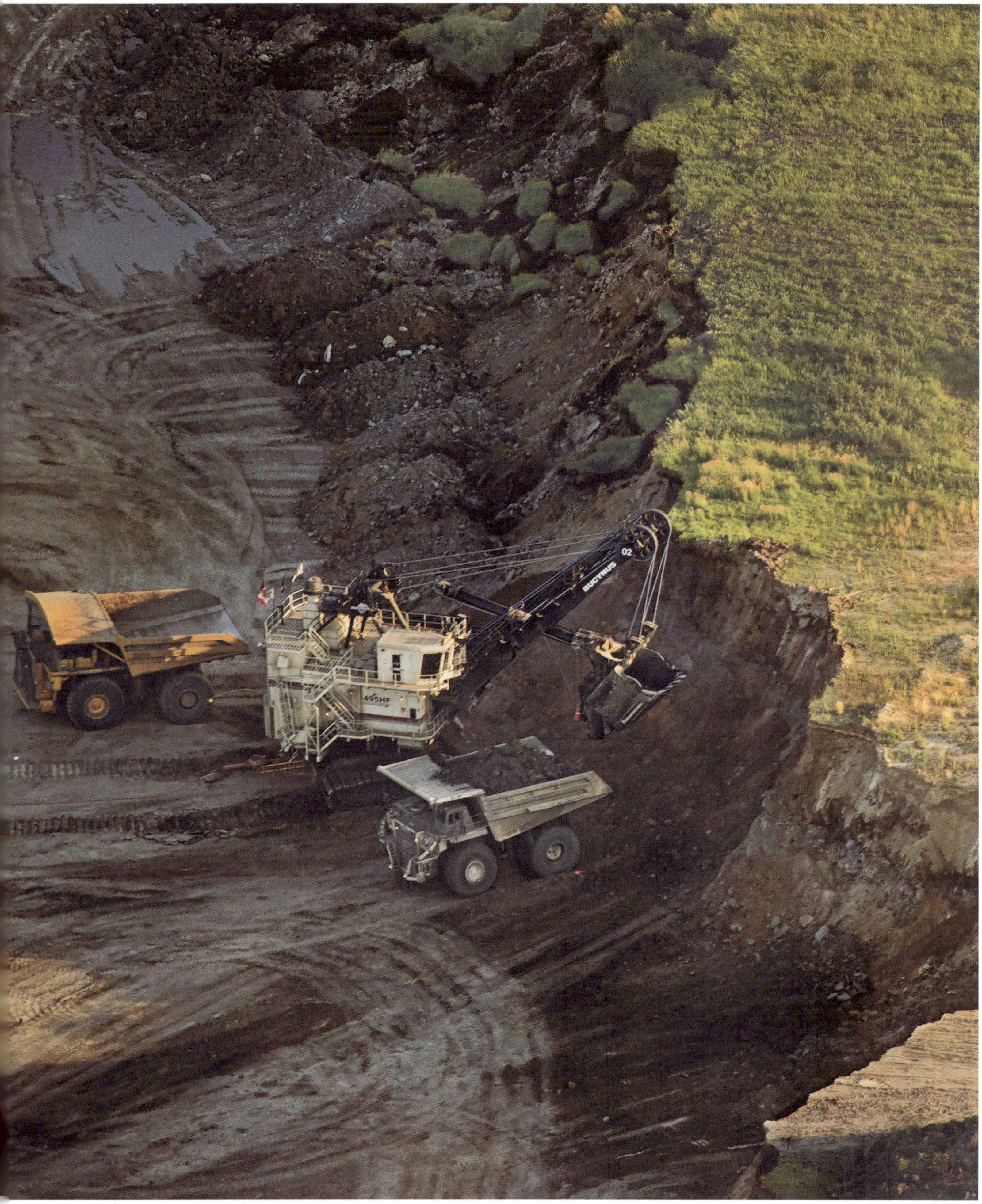

AARON HUEY/NATIONAL GEOGRAPHIC. OPPOSITE: JOE BRUSKY/OLB VIA FLICKR

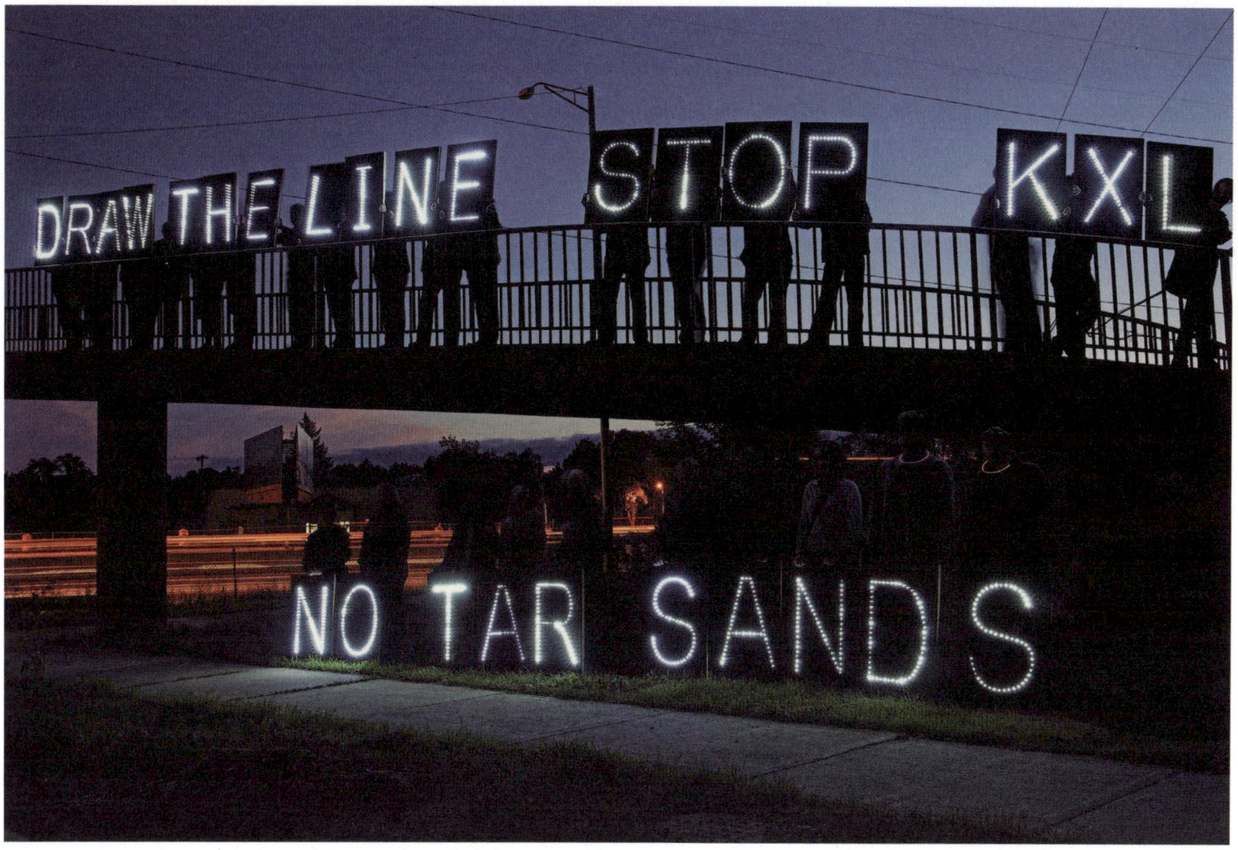

Whether spilled or burned, tar sands crude is a bad idea for the planet.

In 2008, TransCanada announced plans for a 1,700-mile pipeline called Keystone XL (KXL) that would cross the U.S.-Canada border and run all the way to refineries in Port Arthur, Texas. Was it safe? TransCanada had promised that its predecessor, Keystone 1, would "meet or exceed world-class safety and environmental standards," but in its first year of operation, it suffered 35 spills. Then, in 2010, an Enbridge pipeline ruptured in Kalamazoo, Michigan, pouring more than a million gallons of tar sands crude into local rivers and causing the second-biggest (and most expensive) inland spill in U.S. history.

That was when Susan Casey-Lefkowitz, then NRDC's Canada specialist and today our chief program officer, joined Anthony Swift, whose work would reshape the debate over pipeline safety. Having worked at the U.S. Department of Transportation, Anthony knew that a significant portion of the nation's 200,000-mile pipeline system was in poor condition. He also recognized that tar sands crude—actually diluted bitumen, or dilbit—was "a whole new beast." The crude is highly corrosive, and the Kalamazoo disaster revealed that it behaves differently from conventional oils. Soon after it's spilled, dilbit stops floating, so it can't be skimmed off the surface of a waterway; it sinks to the bottom and sticks to everything, making it much harder to remove. The Kalamazoo cleanup would end up taking six years and costing $1 billion.

KXL threatened to be even more disastrous, since the pipeline would run straight across the Ogallala Aquifer, the lifeblood of the midwestern farm states and already seriously depleted by irrigation. TransCanada promised that KXL would be the safest pipeline in the world, but NRDC's 2011 report, written by Anthony, ripped that promise to shreds. And our technical analysis of the risks of tar sands dilbit underpinned what became the signature climate campaign of the decade. Whether spilled or burned, tar sands crude was a bad idea for the planet.

NRDC galvanized local opposition to KXL, building unexpected partnerships with ranchers and farmers, folks who had not traditionally been allies of the environmental movement. We also worked assiduously with the media to brief them on the unique dangers of tar sands oil, and our close collaboration with InsideClimate News led to its special report, The Dilbit Disaster, which won a 2013 Pulitzer Prize.

In 2015, President Obama gave the thumbs-down to KXL, and tar sands production has slumped to just a third of what the industry projected. But Anthony, together with Josh Axelrod and the rest of the Canada team, is still on the case. The Trump administration is determined to revive KXL, and we won't quit until the threat to the planet and its people is gone for good.

Rampant clearcutting is also menacing the boreal forests and the Indigenous peoples who live within them—much of it for the sole purpose of providing Americans with cheap, soft toilet paper. So NRDC is taking on big paper companies like Procter & Gamble, Kimberly-Clark, and Georgia-Pacific, just as we took on the pipeline giants. This time we're doing it through a consumer campaign, with a scorecard that rates popular brands by their usage of virgin or recycled fiber. When the options are either to help turn one of the world's greatest carbon sinks into a carbon bomb or to simply switch TP brands, the choice is pretty clear cut.

Top: A protest held on Draw the Line National Day of Action Against Keystone XL in 2013.
Opposite: Mining trucks carry loads of tar sands oil in Fort McMurray, Alberta, Canada.

SOUND SCIENCE SPEAKS VOLUMES

THE FOUNDERS OF NRDC MAY ALL HAVE been lawyers, but since our earliest days, science has been at the heart of everything we do. If we were going to fight the threats to our natural environment and public health, we knew our legal work had to demonstrate a deep understanding of chemistry, biology, toxicology, atmospheric science, and many other disciplines. Likewise, the remedies we proposed would have to be grounded in sound science if they were to be realistic and effective. And so, over the decades, we hired the best scientists we could find.

In 2006, we decided it was time to up our game. The issues we worked on were becoming more diverse and complex, scientific knowledge in all fields was developing rapidly, and the solutions we were designing called for an ever-expanding skill set. So with a dedicated endowment and strategic guidance from physician and board member Tom Roush, we created the NRDC Science Center.

The center's director, Tina Swanson, is a biologist by training, and with her core team—Kim Knowlton, an expert in climate change's effects on public health, and Stacy Woods, a specialist in analytical design and statistical analysis—she has built what she calls a "force multiplier" for the organization.

The first thing the center did was to set up a two-year postdoctoral fellowship program. We started with two fellows, then expanded the program to four, nurturing and mentoring the next generation of environmental expertise. A good number of our fellows have become key staff members, like Kim and Sylvia Fallon, a geneticist specializing in the Endangered Species Act. Many others have gone on to important positions in federal and state government. Together, this rotating scientific talent pool, chosen to respond to the most pressing needs of our policy, advocacy, and litigation staff, has given us unparalleled flexibility. Say we need an expert on petroleum engineering who can calculate the life-cycle impact of a new gas-to-liquid power plant, or a hydrologist who knows how to figure out the precise effects of uranium leach mining on groundwater supplies. The Science Center will find them and put them to work. Furthermore, the Science Center sees that all NRDC's research goes through a rigorous internal peer review process, adding to the organization's credibility and authority.

"If you take it all collectively, we have the scientific capacity of a university," Tina says. Although other leading environmental groups also do superb original research, this model is unique to NRDC.

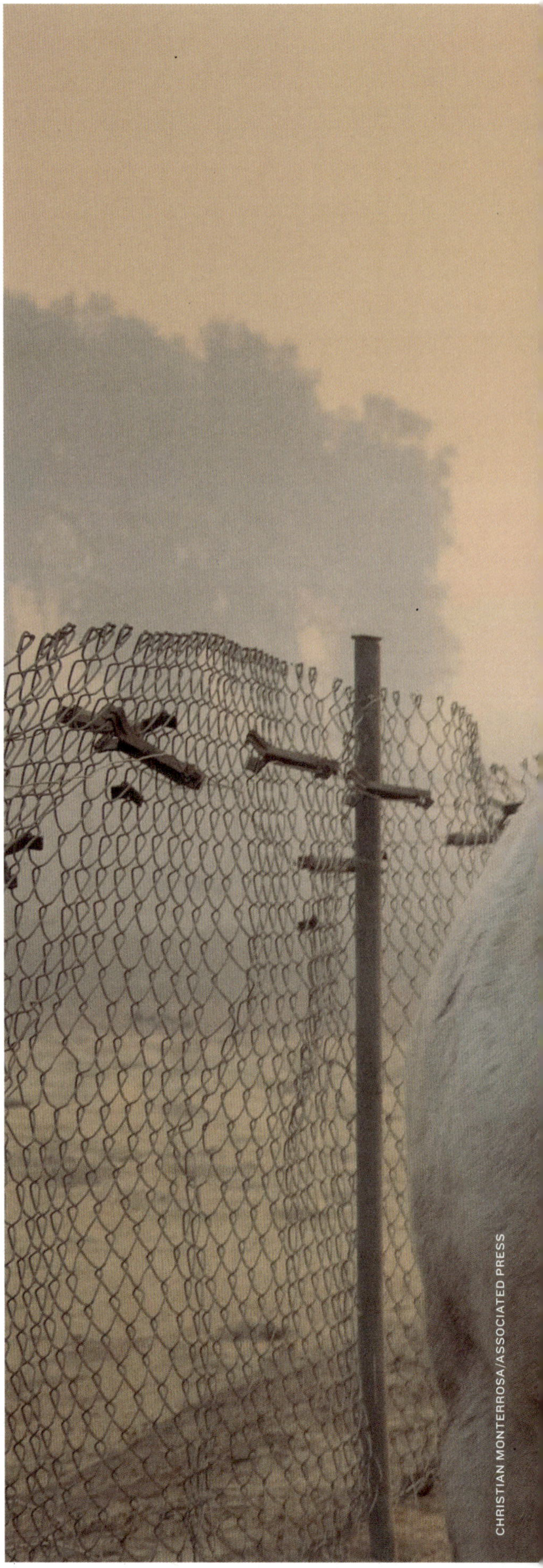

CHRISTIAN MONTERROSA/ASSOCIATED PRESS

A volunteer helps evacuate horses during California's Easy fire in 2019. According to a 2019 report by NRDC's Science Center, the health costs for climate-related events, including wildfires, in 2012 alone totaled $10 billion (in 2018 dollars).

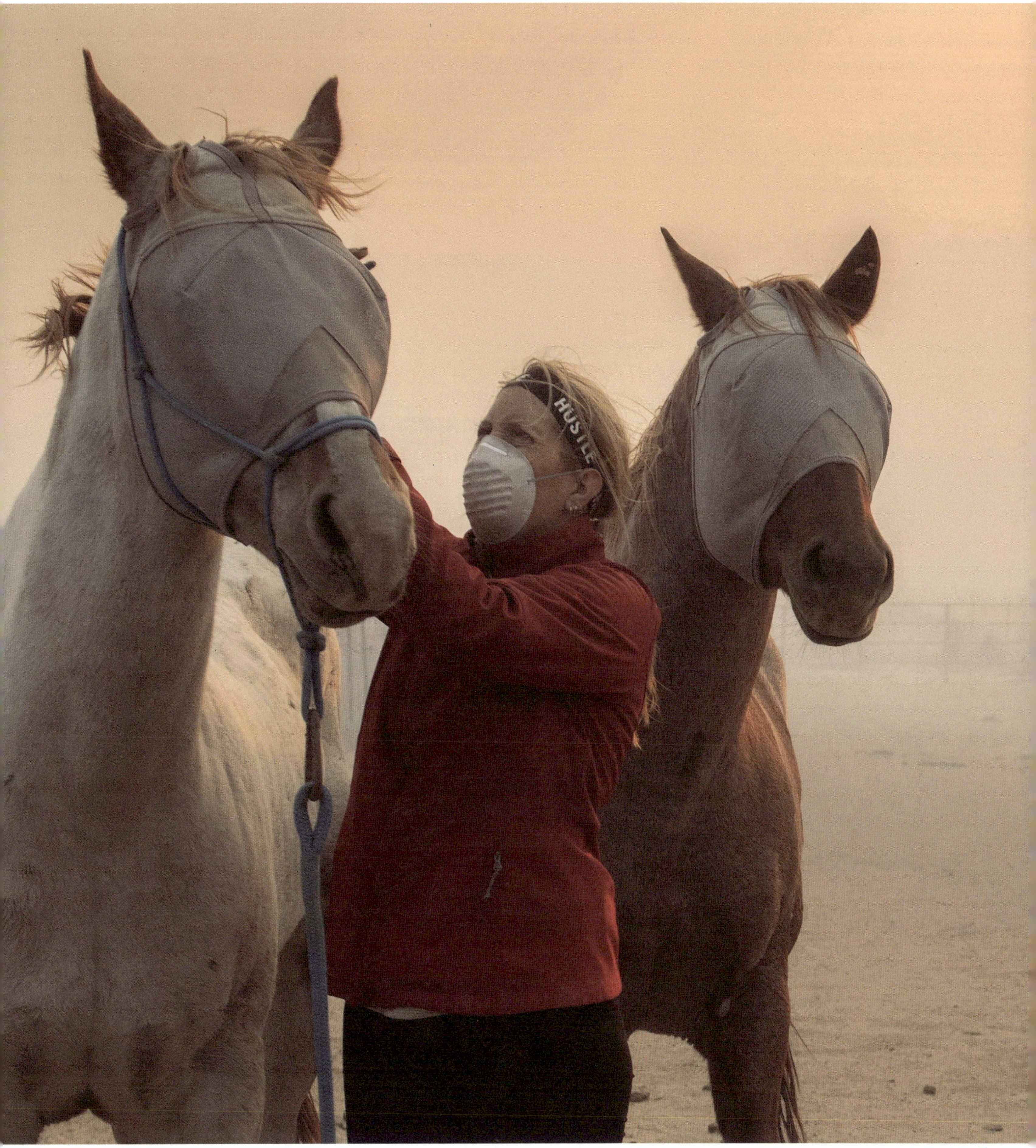
HUSTLE

"Science has always been the foundation for NRDC's advocacy, and it's thrilling to be part of our Science Center. We help bring versatile, talented scientists into NRDC's community to probe complex, multidisciplinary environmental health challenges."

—Kim Knowlton, senior scientist and deputy director of the Science Center

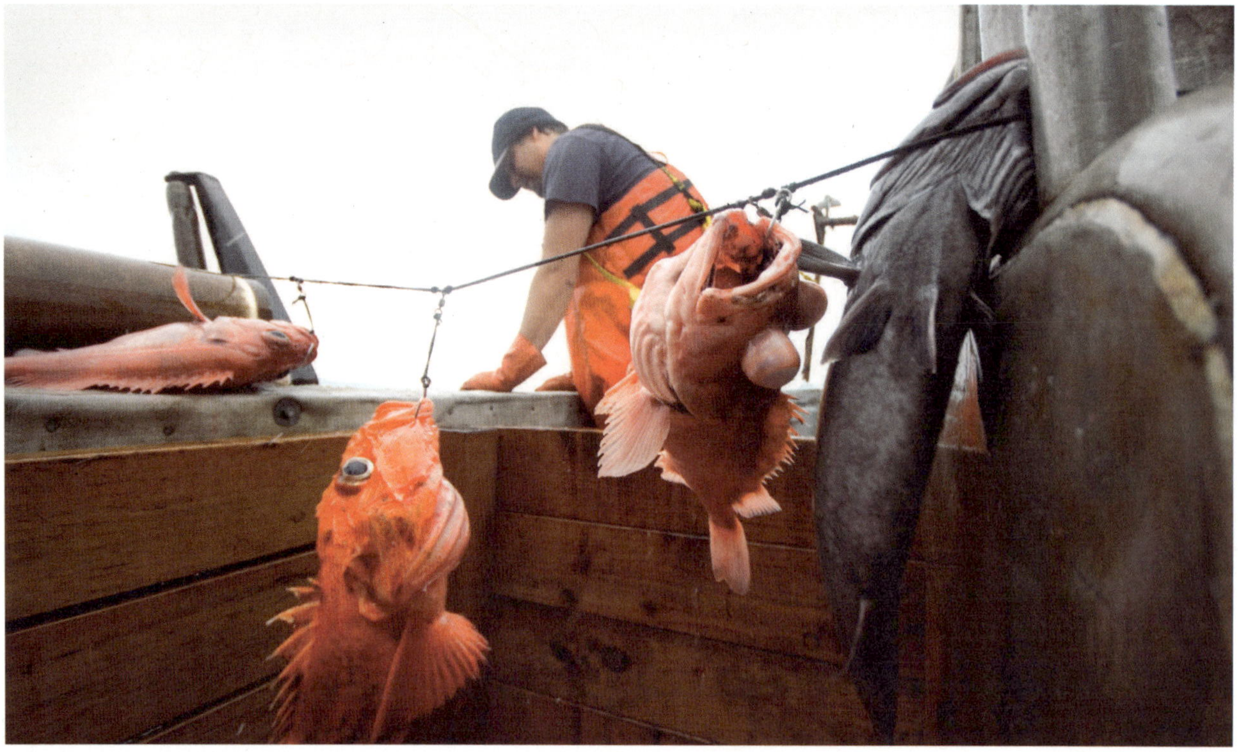

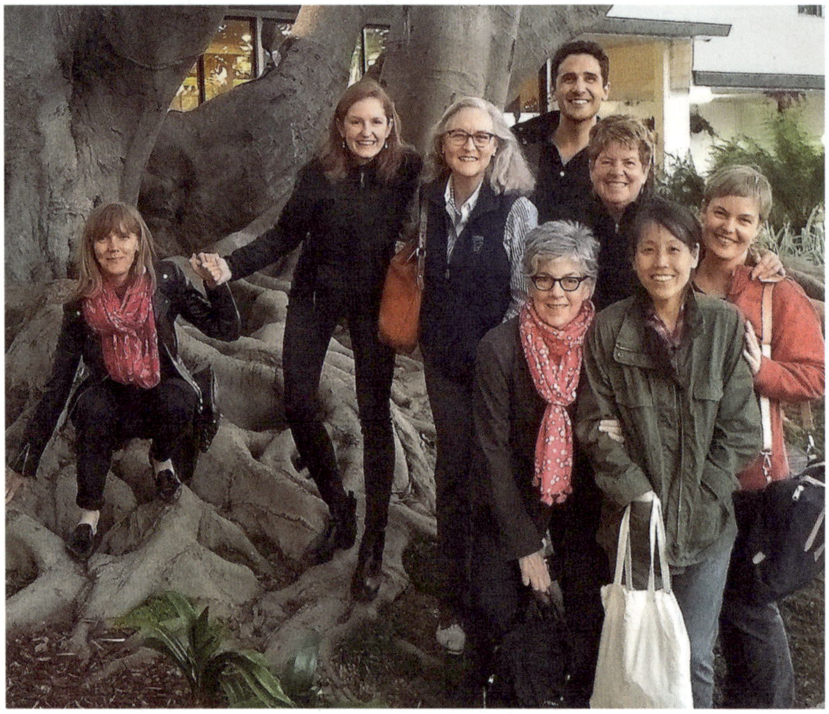

Kim Knowlton's research focuses on the link between climate change and public health, and she (above, first row, left) advocates for strategies to prepare for—and prevent—climate-related health impacts, especially in vulnerable communities.

The Science Center team, clockwise from far left: Pamela MacDougall, Kelsey Kane-Ritsch, Leslie Jones, Vijay Limaye, Christina Swanson, Stacy Woods, Yukyan Lam, Kim Knowlton. The team works on various research and tools, such as producing an open-source software package that uses available data to create computer simulations and suggest alternative management strategies for specific fish populations.

While we actively seek out partnerships in the academic world, there's nothing abstract about the science we do. We focus our research on identifying the knobs and levers that could advance practical, creative solutions to problems that have stymied others.

Examples abound. When U.S. National Marine Fisheries Service (NMFS) scientists were challenged to identify sustainable annual catch limits for commercially harvested species with very limited population data, the Science Center helped the Oceans team produce an open-source software package that crunches whatever data are available, creates computer simulations, and suggests alternative management strategies for specific fish populations. A number of government entities around the world, including NMFS and the state of California, now use the software as a management strategy evaluation tool, and the Marine Stewardship Council uses it as a risk assessment tool for fisheries with limited data.

Or take the challenge California will face when the owners of five million new electric vehicles plug them in to charge overnight. How can that be done without crashing an already overstressed electrical grid? A Science Center fellow, smart-grid expert Pamela McDougall, came up with an answer. By the way, if you are seeing a pattern of female-powered expertise here, it's no accident; one thing I'm especially proud of is how NRDC has broken through the "glass ceiling" in science, even in more traditionally male-dominated areas like engineering and data visualization.

With the Science Center now at the hub of all of NRDC's priority programs, its leader sums up its philosophy nicely. "We use science as a compass to point us in the right direction," says Tina, "as a map to show us how to get there, and as a gauge to measure how far we've come and how far we still have to go."

FROM TOP: BRIDGET BESAW/CAVAN VIA ALAMY; NRDC. OPPOSITE: STEPHANIE KLEIN-DAVIS/THE ROANOKE TIMES VIA AP

Solutions Spotlight

TAKING ONE'S MEDICINE

When you are fighting for something as important as food safety and the continued effectiveness of antibiotics, you have to get creative. Astonishingly, about two-thirds of all medically important antibiotics sold in the United States are given to livestock—mostly to healthy animals. This overused and unnecessary practice breeds drug-resistant bacteria, sometimes known as "superbugs," which can be very dangerous.

A Washington University study from January 2019 estimated that drug-resistant infections kill more than 160,000 Americans every year.

To confront this emergency, we began in classic NRDC fashion—with litigation. But lawsuits take time to work their way through the courts and don't always solve the problem, so we opened a second, third, and fourth front. We relentlessly pressed the issue in the press and on social media and won new laws in California, Maryland, and San Francisco.

In 2014, we opened a consumer awareness campaign aimed at convincing Foster Farms, the biggest chicken producer on the West Coast, to stop using antibiotics routinely on their animals. Then we pivoted to fast-food chains, like Subway and KFC, that buy large amounts of meat and poultry. To get their customers' attention, we launched petitions online, put up billboards on the streets, and had people dress up in chicken suits outside of restaurants.

At the start, in 2010, no major chicken company had publicly committed to ceasing routine antibiotic use. Our goal was to get at least half of the industry on board. The result—thanks to a team led by Jonathan Kaplan, Avinash Kar, Erik Olson, and Lena Brook—has been stunning.

Currently, according to industry estimates, more than 90 percent of chicken produced in the United States is raised without antibiotics deemed medically important by the U.S. Food and Drug Administration. In fact, the latest FDA data show that only 4 percent of such antibiotics sold for livestock is used on chickens. Next up: beef and pork.

A whopping 92 percent of U.S. chicken sold in 2018 was produced without the use of antibiotics considered medically important by FDA. Together with our allies, NRDC played a big role in driving this change.

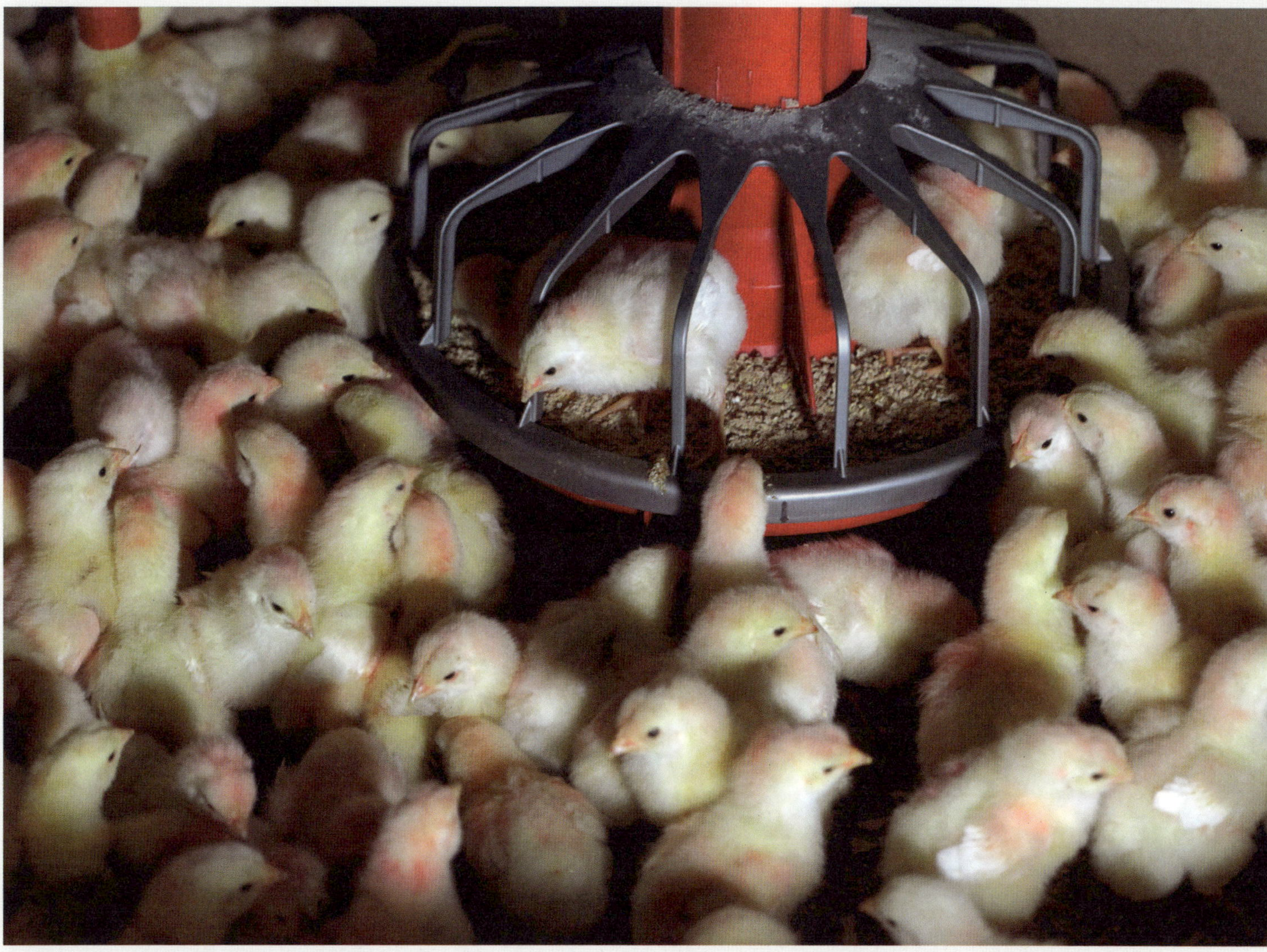

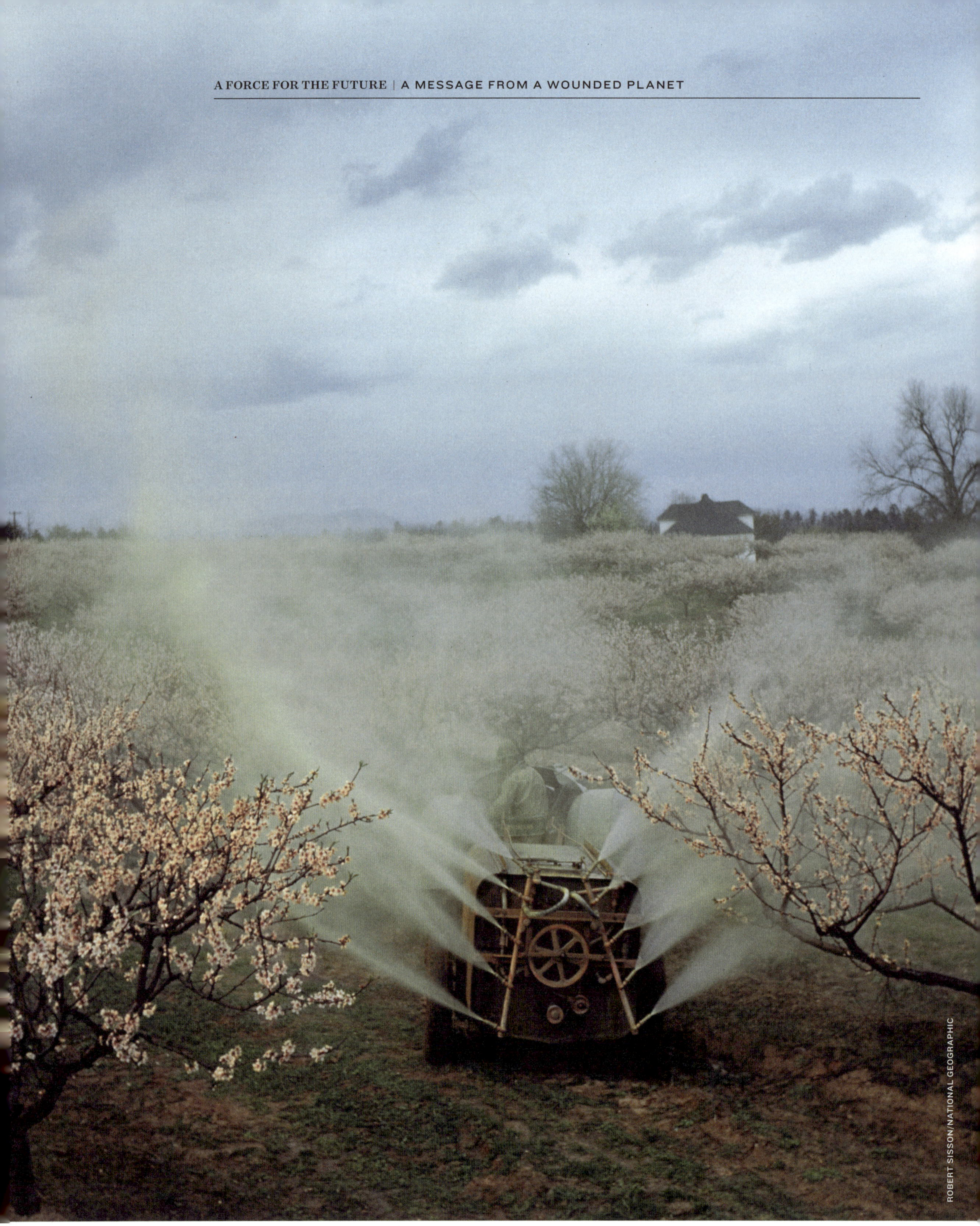

ROBERT SISSON/NATIONAL GEOGRAPHIC

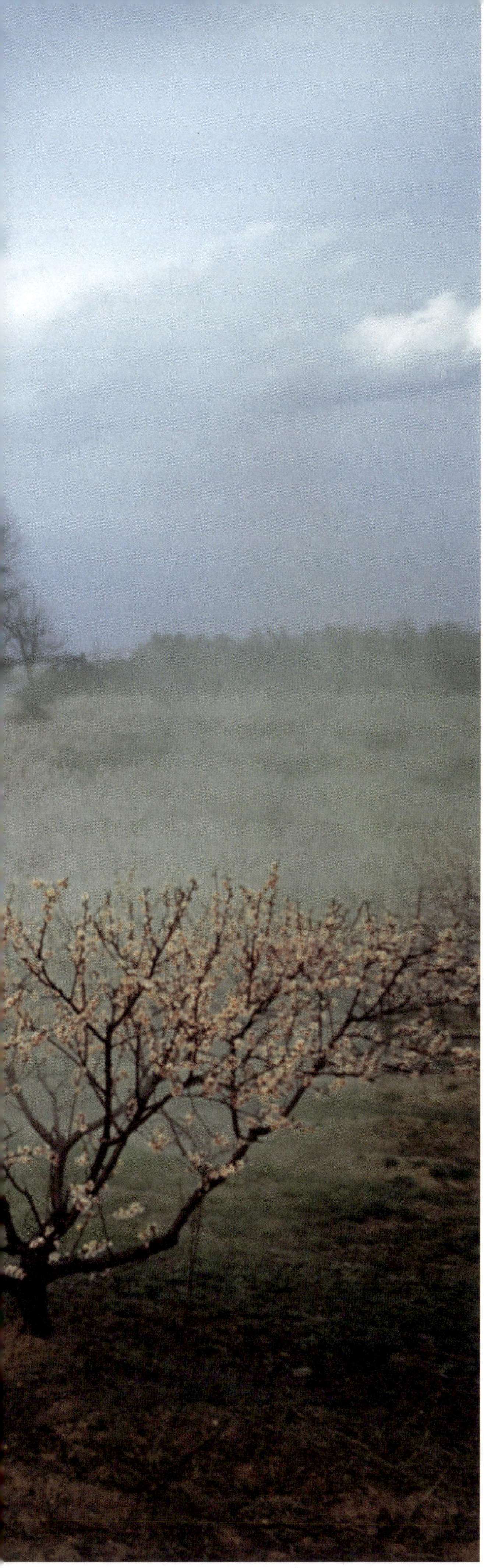

POISON CONTROL

WITH THOUSANDS OF POTENTIALLY hazardous chemicals on the market, it has always shocked me that the governing principle around their regulation has been "innocent until proven guilty." Manufacturers assure us their products are safe, and government action comes only after the negative health impacts of a substance become apparent. Imagine, then, how disturbing it was to discover two decades ago that one of our most widely used pesticides is adapted from World War II–era nerve agents. Patented by Dow Chemical, chlorpyrifos, which belongs to a class of chemicals called organophosphates, disrupts the transmission of messages between insects' nerve cells.

NRDC launched its first pesticide program back in 1982. We started with a focus on the exposure risks to farmworkers in California but then homed in on the growing body of scientific evidence suggesting that chemicals like chlorpyrifos can cause long-term damage to developing brains, from the time a child is in its mother's womb through its infancy and into childhood. In 1996, we played a central role in the passage of the Food Quality Protection Act, which mandated, among other things, that the EPA set standards for pesticide use based on "a reasonable certainty of no harm."

Four years later, we forced a ban on residential chlorpyrifos uses, such as indoor pest treatments and lawncare. But in 2006, the EPA reauthorized the chemical for use in agriculture. Whether in homes or on farms, disadvantaged communities tended to have the highest exposures: People living in low-income housing had bigger problems with domestic pests, and in California's Central Valley, Latino children attended schools that butted up against farm fields laden with chlorpyrifos.

NRDC has been serving as the "translator" of scientific research for a broad statewide coalition, Californians for

Scientists have found that commonly used pesticides are dangerous to humans and can cause cancer and neurological problems, such as learning disabilities. They are also harmful to pollinators, such as bees and butterflies.

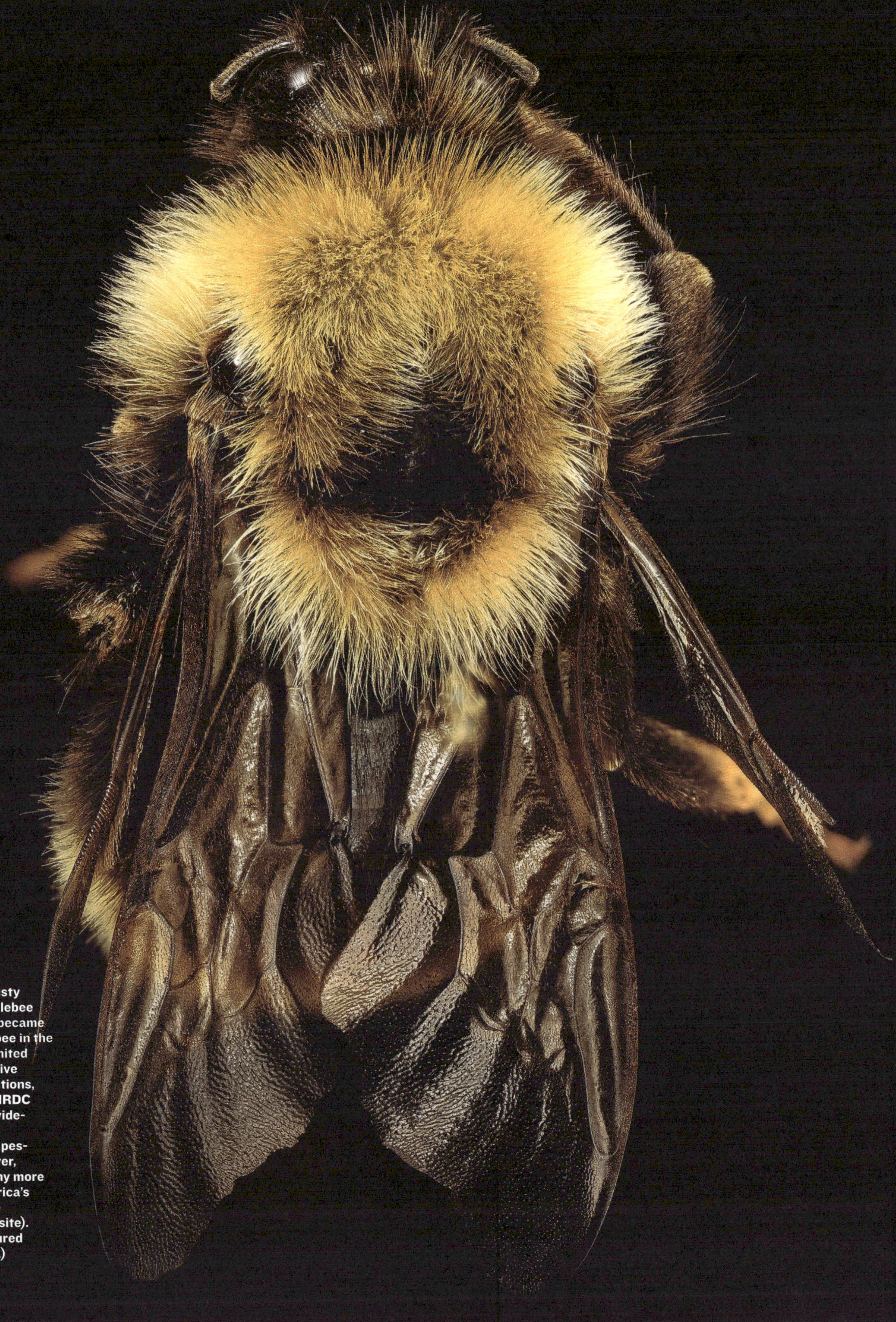

In 2016, the rusty patched bumblebee (shown here) became the first wild bee in the continental United States to receive federal protections, thanks to an NRDC lawsuit. The widespread use of neonicotinoid pesticides, however, threatens many more of North America's other wild bee species (opposite). (All bees pictured died naturally.)

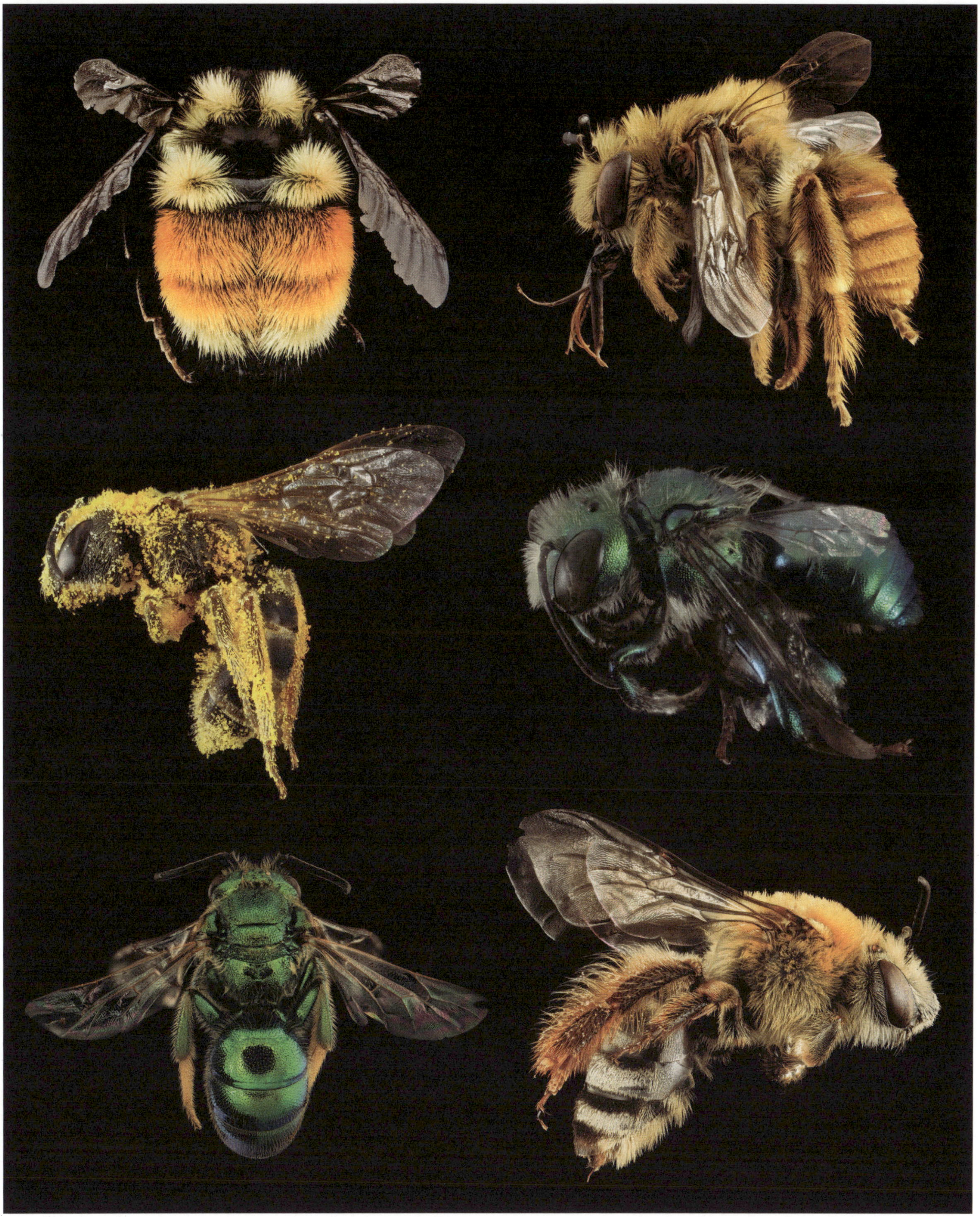

ALL BEE PHOTOS: USGS NATIVE BEE INVENTORY AND MONITORING PROGRAM

Pesticide Reform, and we've won a commitment from the state, which represents 20 percent of the U.S. chlorpyrifos market, to end virtually all use of the chemical by the end of 2020. Meanwhile, the EPA continues to kick the can down the road, claiming that there's still "uncertainty" about the health effects of chlorpyrifos. In August 2019, Earthjustice, representing NRDC and other groups, filed suit against the agency in federal court for the second time.

Other pesticides high on our priority list are weed killers (like glyphosate) and insecticides (like neonicotinoids, or "neonics"). Glyphyosate, marketed by Monsanto (now Bayer) as Roundup, has been deemed "a probable carcinogen" by the International Agency for Research on Cancer and is decimating the natural habitat of the iconic monarch butterfly. Meanwhile, neonics, the most widely used class of insecticides in the world, are devastating to bees—some formulations are 7,000 times more toxic to insects than DDT.

Enlist Duo, a combination of the pesticides glyphosate and 2,4-D, threatens the North American monarch butterfly. NRDC is fighting the use of the pesticide in and out of court.

Ominous phrases like "colony collapse disorder" have made Americans increasingly aware of the crisis facing pollinators. Three-quarters of all the world's crops depend on them, accounting for one in every three bites of food we eat. Most of the publicity shines on honeybees, but North America also has more than 4,000 species of native wild bees. In the final days of the Obama administration, the rusty patched bumblebee became the first wild bee in the continental United States to receive protection under the Endangered Species Act. The Trump administration, however, promptly halted the ESA listing for the bumblebee, whose numbers have dropped nearly 90 percent since the 1990s. Despite lobbying from powerful agribusiness interests, NRDC forced the administration to back down in one of our first of many legal victories against Trump.

While we continue to fight the feds' lax pesticide policies—suing the EPA to restrict the use of neonics, as well as for violating the law in approving the use of Enlist Duo, a dangerous herbicide containing glyphosate—Rebecca Riley, the legal director of NRDC's Nature Program, has also been at work with colleagues in our Midwest office to restore precious pollinator habitat. In Minnesota, we helped to pass a law compensating homeowners who replace their grass lawns with pollinator-friendly plants. In Illinois and Missouri, we've advanced legislation encouraging solar farm operators to turn the huge expanses of empty ground beneath their solar arrays into terrain primed for bees, butterflies, and other wildlife.

With a combination of science, law, and under-the-radar advocacy at the state level, we've been fighting on multiple fronts to save pollinators and eliminate harmful pesticides, simultaneously protecting the health of ecosystems, our food supply, and ourselves.

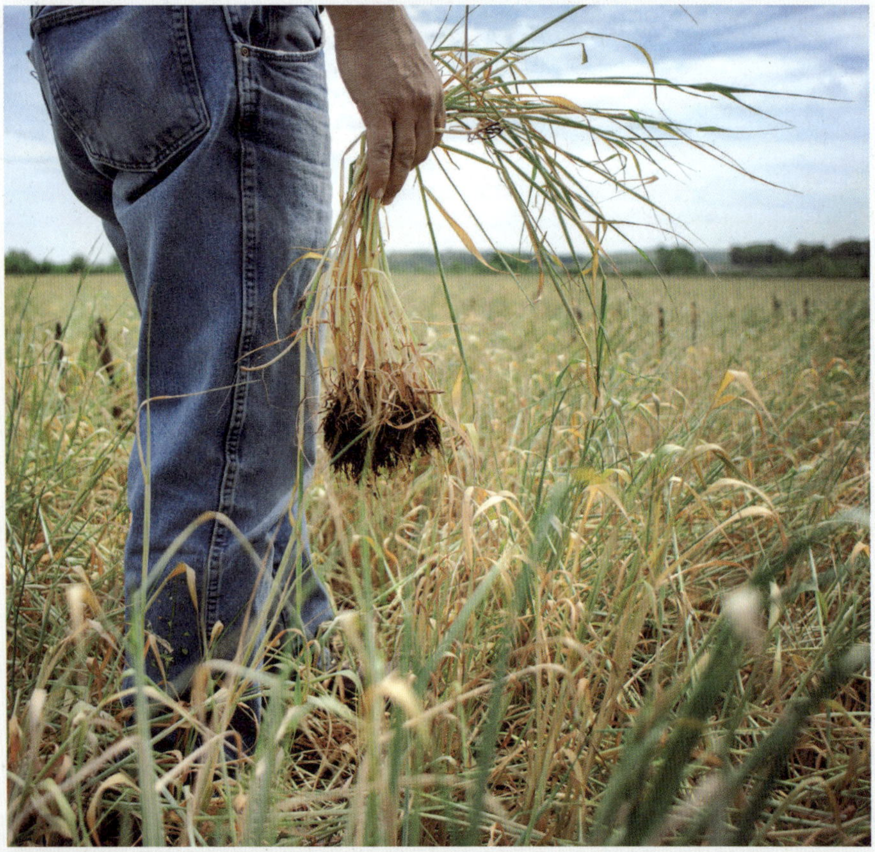

Solutions Spotlight

A GROWING CONCERN

Most of us don't think much about soil, but it's critical to water quality, the resilience of farmland in the face of climate change, and the economies of rural communities. Farmers care deeply about the health of their land, but the incentives built into our agricultural system too often prioritize increasing yield, by way of monocultures and chemical additives, over preserving soil quality.

But what if we could change those incentives, making farms healthy and productive for seasons to come? NRDC has been using the federal crop insurance program as a tool to do so. The program is the biggest of all farm subsidies and drives decisions about which crops to grow and which pesticides to use. We started in 2017 in Iowa, where corn and soybean crops dominate most farm fields. Working with local partners and the Iowa Department of Agriculture and Land Stewardship, our experts made a simple proposal: give farmers a $5-an-acre discount on their crop insurance if they plant off-season cover crops, such as cereal rye or oats, which help to protect the soil from erosion and boost its fertility. The initiative proved hugely popular, with farmers enrolling about 300,000 acres in its first two years. Since then, Illinois has followed suit, and NRDC is now planning to export the idea to other midwestern states.

ANGELA MAJOR/THE JANESVILLE GAZETTE VIA AP. OPPOSITE: MEDFORD TAYLOR/NATIONAL GEOGRAPHIC

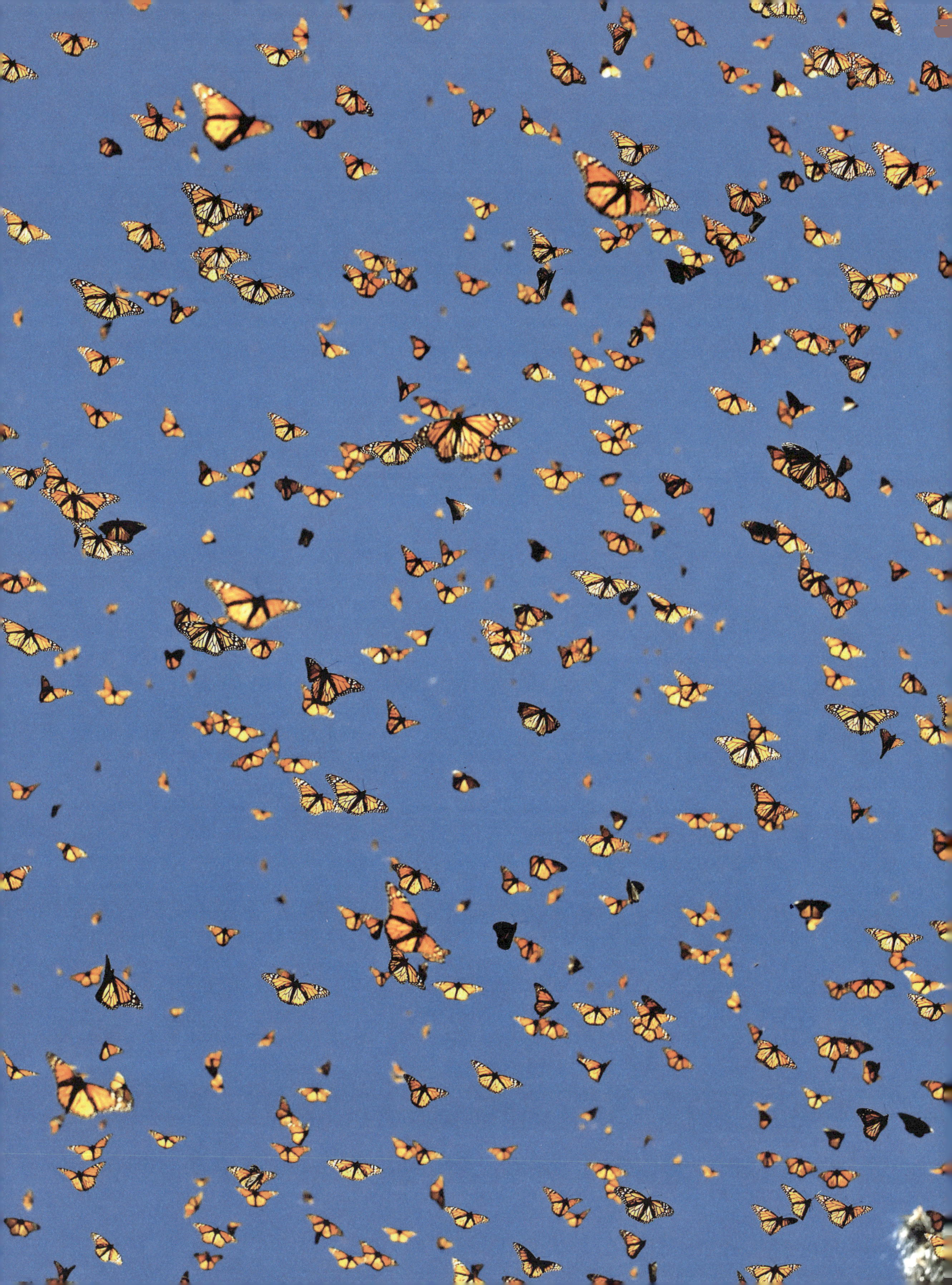

DEFENDING OUR SHORES

On the night of April 20, 2010, methane gas leaking from BP's Macondo oil well in the Gulf of Mexico engulfed the Deepwater Horizon drilling rig, igniting an explosion and fire that killed 11 of the workers on board. Two days later, the burning rig collapsed, rupturing a riser pipe from the well on the gulf floor, more than 5,000 feet below sea level.

As I digested the first news of the event, I wondered: Could this be as bad as the 1969 Santa Barbara spill, when an offshore rig blackened the waters and beaches along the California coast with four million gallons of oil? Or the Exxon Valdez tanker crash in Alaska 20 years later that sent 11 million gallons into Prince William Sound? BP's blowout turned out to be much worse. The well spewed a previously unimaginable amount of oil into the Gulf of Mexico for 87 days. Estimates vary, but at least 130 million gallons of crude filled the gulf, sullying more than 1,300 miles of shoreline habitat including wetlands and beaches. President Barack Obama called it "the worst environmental disaster America has ever faced."

The catastrophe was shocking, but it wasn't a surprise—merely an accident that had been waiting to happen. Over the preceding decade, our country's gluttonous appetite for oil had been fed by tens of billions of dollars in tax incentives and subsidies. And the government had reduced its oversight agencies to essentially rubber stamps for the industry, supporting the industry's push to drill in ever deeper and more hazardous places. The Macondo well was almost a mile beneath the sea surface in an area plagued by tropical storms.

Opposition to offshore drilling has been a signature cause for NRDC since our earliest days, and we responded to the BP disaster on all fronts. Our oceans and public health teams were on the scene of the devastation almost immediately, while our climate and energy experts began to shape new energy strategies that could end our ruinous addiction to oil.

This preventable disaster was a human as well as an environmental tragedy, striking a region that was still reeling from 2005's Hurricane Katrina and the economic recession that hit three years after that. BP's blowout ravaged one of the

A large plume of smoke rises over the Gulf of Mexico the day after BP's Deepwater Horizon oil rig exploded in April 2010.

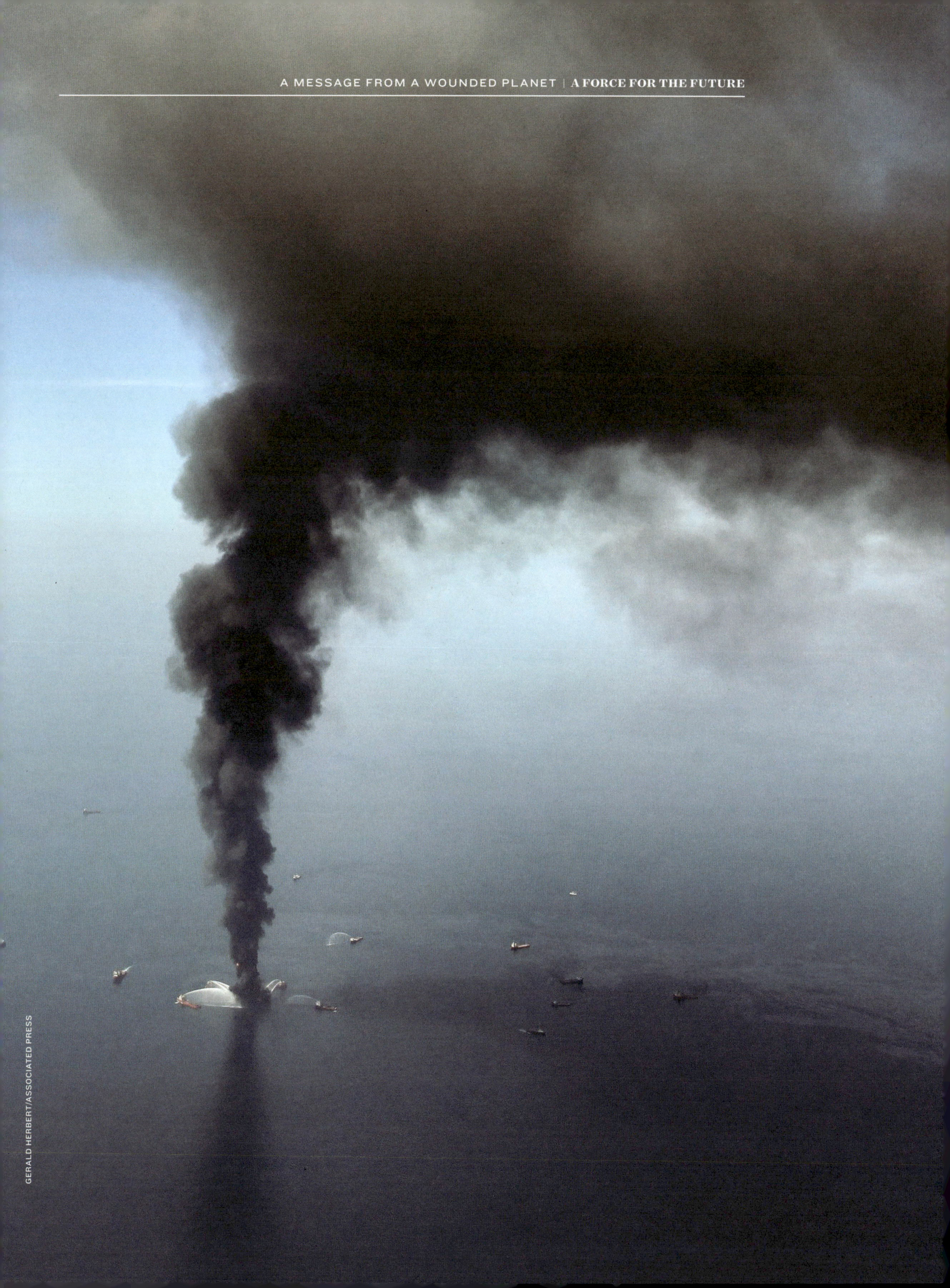

GERALD HERBERT/ASSOCIATED PRESS

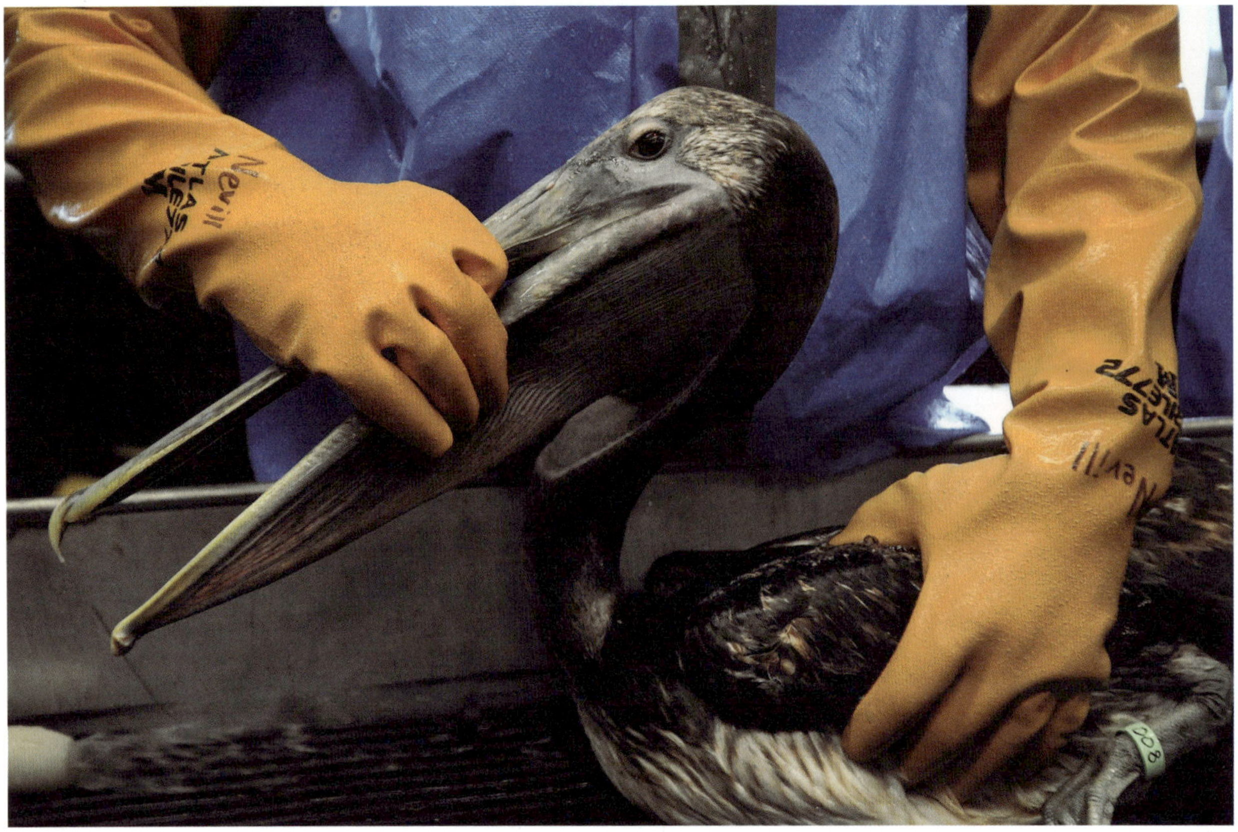

"One bad spill was enough to shut down three major industries—on which the economy of an entire region depended—overnight. And 10 years later, we still don't know what the full ecological impact was. Now oil companies want to expand into new waters. The industry has the technology to go anywhere—to the ends of the earth—and is willing to do so. The solution is clear: We need to stop Big Oil in its tracks."

—**Frances Beinecke, former NRDC president (2006–2015)**

most productive fisheries on the planet, and thousands of jobs were affected as more than a third of the gulf had to be closed to fishing for long periods of time. "It was like a Book of Job that doesn't end," said one community leader, Derrick Evans.

NRDC's communications team worked overtime to bring these human experiences to the world. In July 2010, we opened the Gulf Resource Center in the fishing community of Buras, Louisiana. Flanked by levees, Buras was submerged for weeks after Katrina, and its population, once 15,000, had fallen to less than 1,000. The center provided a gathering space for local residents, community groups, and visiting journalists, giving people direct access to our scientific and public health experts. *In Deep Water,* which we published that September, captured many of their stories. Authored by our executive director at the time, Peter Lehner, it was the first book to give a full account of the disaster.

In Deep Water asked three big questions: What happened? Why did it happen? And where do we go from here? Those were the same questions that a bipartisan commission appointed by President Obama attempted to answer. The greatest possible tribute to NRDC's central role in responding to Deepwater Horizon was that our president at the time, Frances Beinecke, was named as one of the commission's seven members. In a group of distinguished academics, oceanographers, engineers, and former government officials, Frances stood out as the only representative of a nongovernmental green organization.

The commission's report showed in scathing detail how the calamity in the gulf was not an anomaly but a systemic failure, one that could happen again unless we sever the cozy relationship between the oil industry and federal regulators, strengthen and undertake fundamental reforms in government oversight, ensure that sound science dictates decisions about where and how to drill, and dramatically increase safety practices throughout the industry.

"One of the abiding strengths of this country is our ability to learn from our mistakes," Frances told CNN in 2011. Sadly, the Trump administration seems not only deaf and blind to those lessons but hell-bent on repeating the mistakes from which they stemmed—which is why the fight against reckless offshore drilling will remain one of NRDC's most urgent priorities for however long it takes to end it.

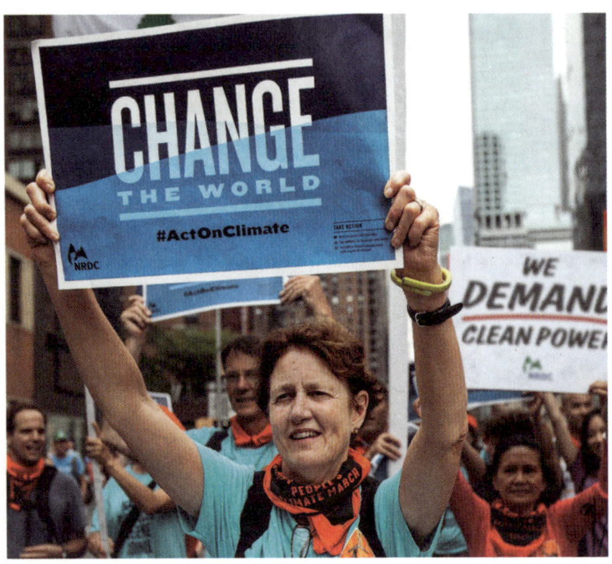

In 2010, President Obama appointed Frances Beinecke to the National Commission on the BP Deepwater Horizon Oil Spill and Offshore Drilling. Here, Frances joins the 2014 Peoples Climate March in New York, which brought more than 400,000 protesters to the streets.

FROM TOP: JO-ANNE MCARTHUR/REDUX PICTURES; NATALIE KEYSSAR FOR NRDC

FROM THE FRONTLINES

Kindra Arnesen

When Deepwater Horizon exploded and spewed oil into the Gulf of Mexico, Kindra Arnesen and her family hadn't yet recovered from the damage Hurricane Katrina brought to their home in Plaquemines Parish, Louisiana, five years earlier. On that April day in 2010, Kindra, the wife of a fisherman who spent many years working on boats herself, remembers immediately worrying about the rig's workers. "My first thoughts were never about what the chemical impact was going to be," she says. "We trusted our elected officials. We trusted the EPA." But soon the toxic aftermath of Deepwater Horizon would consume Arnesen's life.

Brown sludge started washing up on her community's shoreline almost immediately. Then her Plaquemines neighbors started becoming sick—including her husband, David, who had helped with some cleanup operations. Kindra resolved herself to fighting to make things right.

By chance, she met Rocky Kistner, a communications specialist who was helping set up the NRDC Gulf Resource Center in the nearby fishing town of Buras. Rocky helped amplify her story and bring Kindra's passion to the fore. She is now one of the Gulf's fiercest advocates. Fed up with the lack of response from local meetings, Kindra traveled with NRDC advocates to Washington, D.C., to demand answers. "That's where I cut my teeth in D.C.," she says. "It gave me the opportunity to learn a lot about the comings and goings in D.C. and opened my eyes to a whole different world. NRDC afforded me an outlet for my voice and I'll be forever grateful for that."

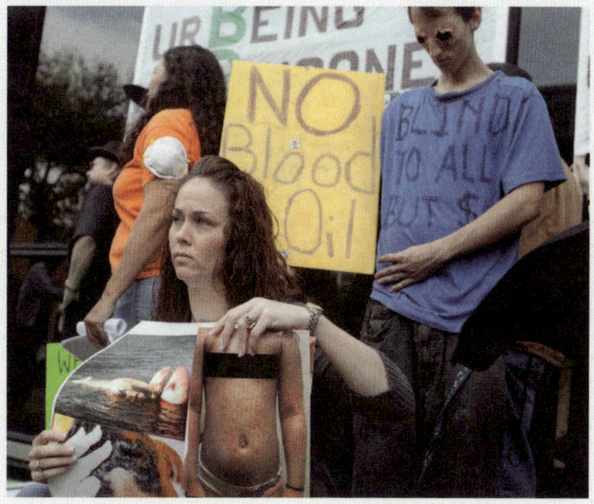

At a 2012 protest in New Orleans, Kindra Arnesen holds up pictures of people and animals sickened since the Deepwater Horizon oil disaster.

Opposite, top: Rescue workers help an oil-covered brown pelican. Below: A worker picks up globs of oil with an absorbent snare on Queen Bess Island in Plaquemines Parish, Louisiana.

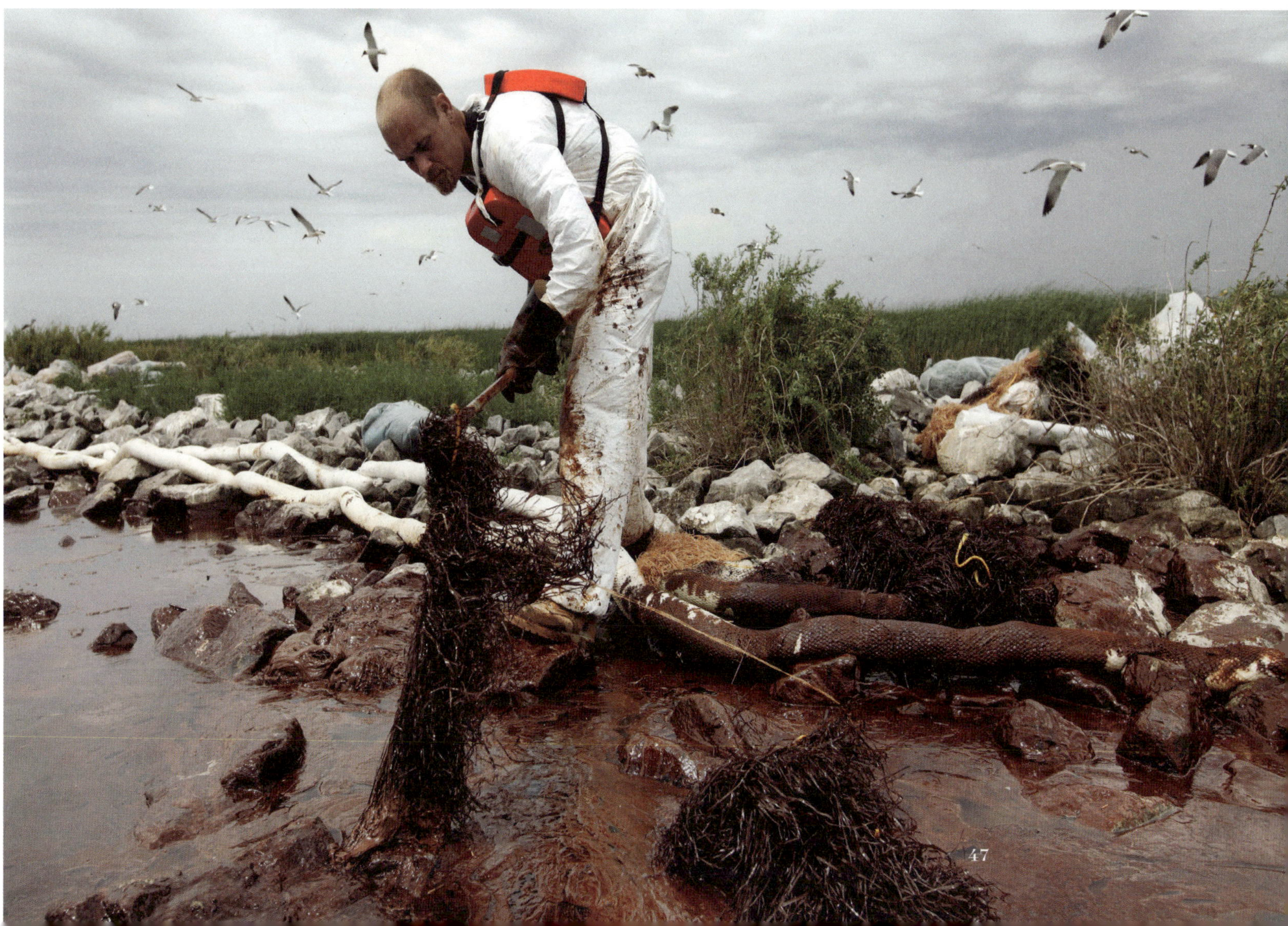

FROM TOP: JULIE DERMANSKY; GERALD HERBERT/ASSOCIATED PRESS

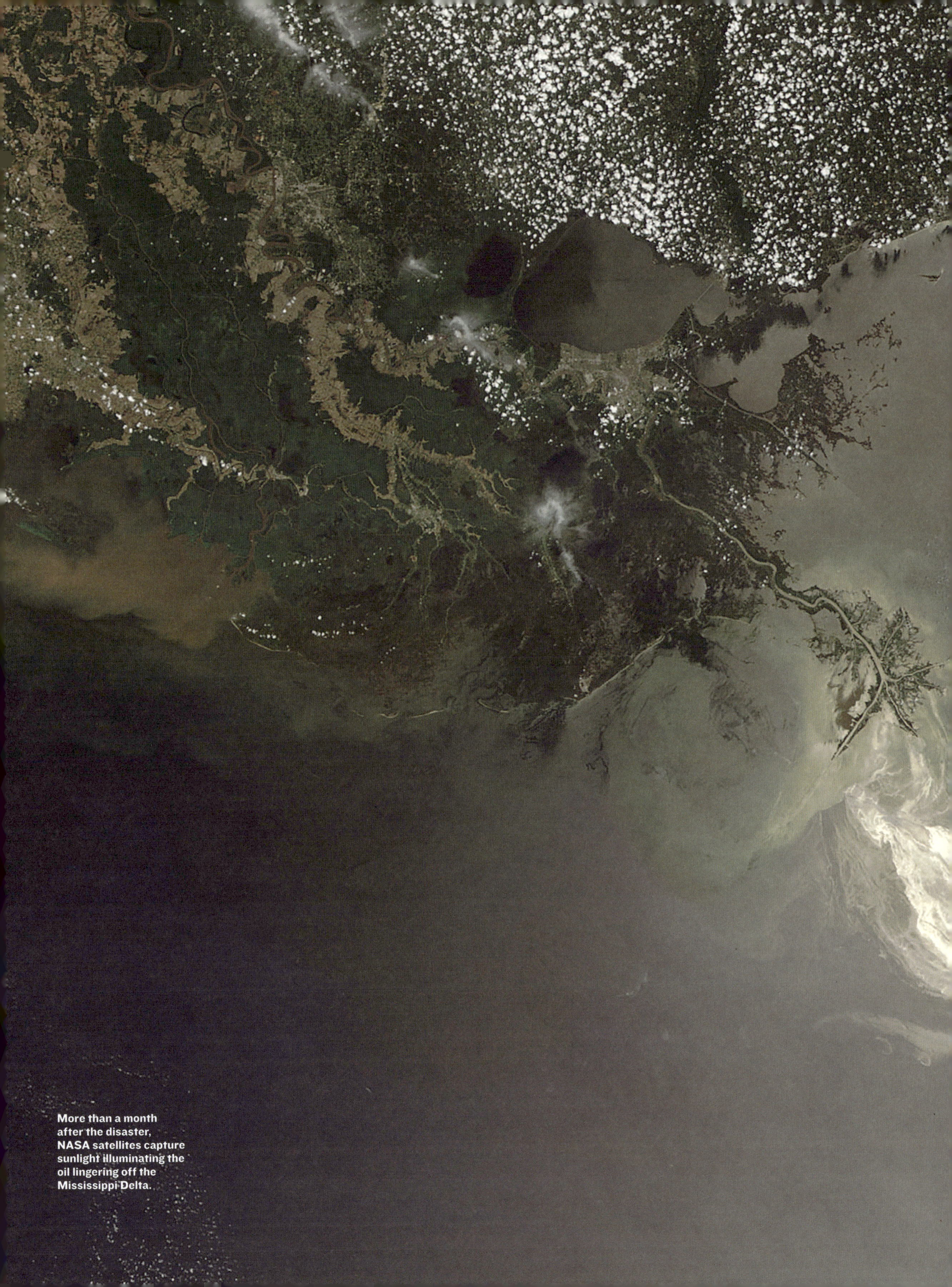

More than a month after the disaster, NASA satellites capture sunlight illuminating the oil lingering off the Mississippi Delta.

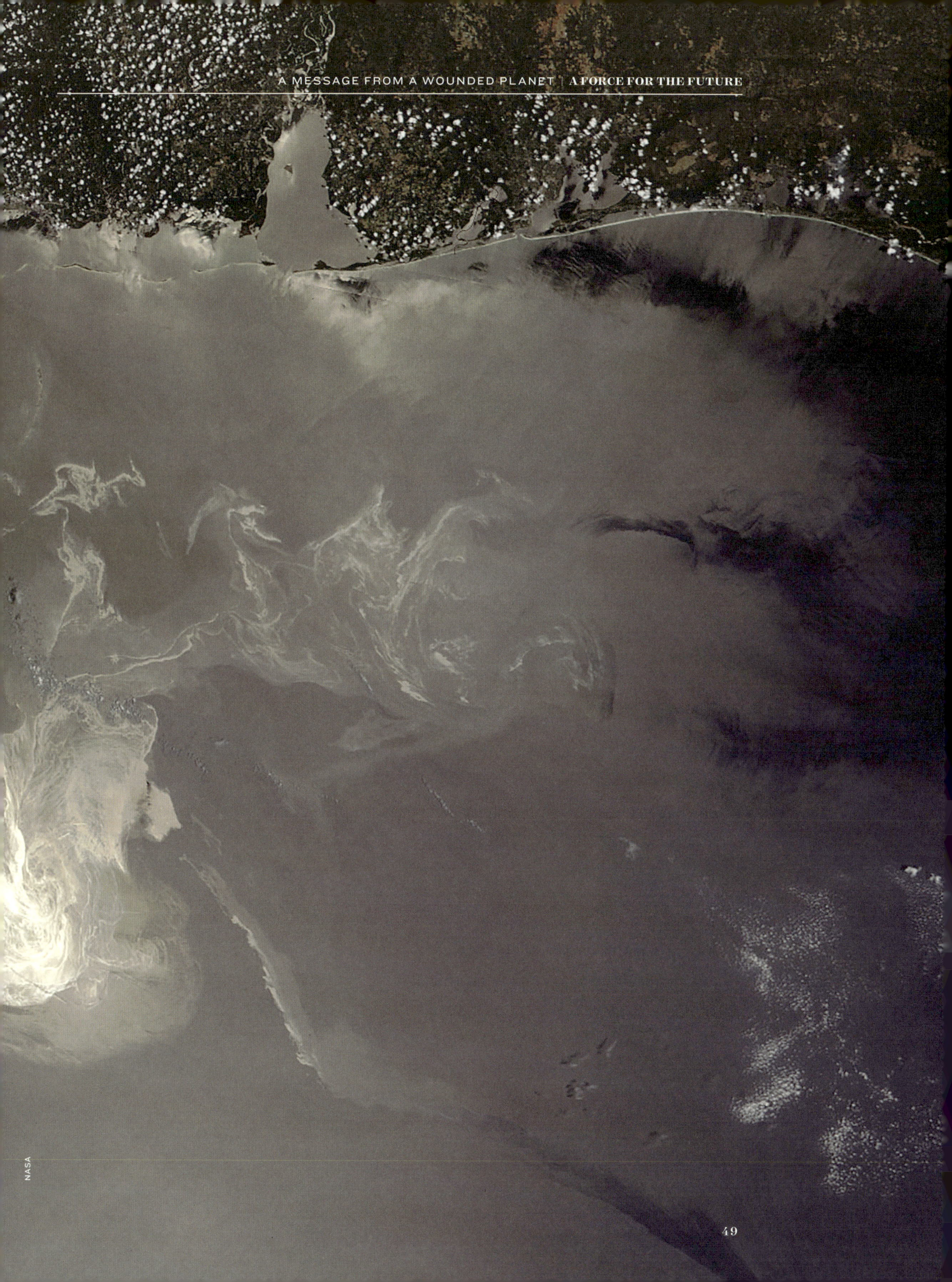

NASA

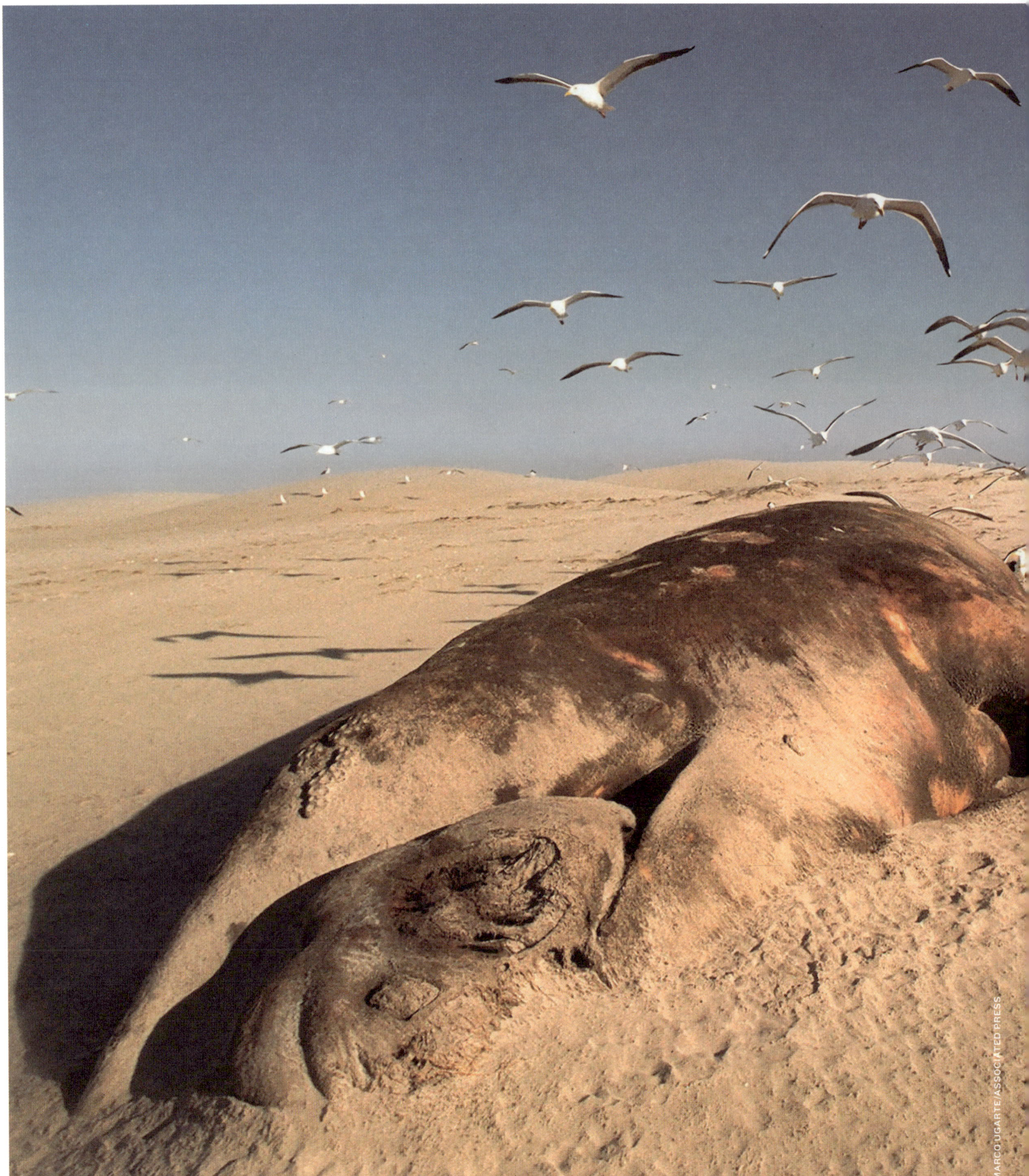

MARCO UGARTE/ASSOCIATED PRESS

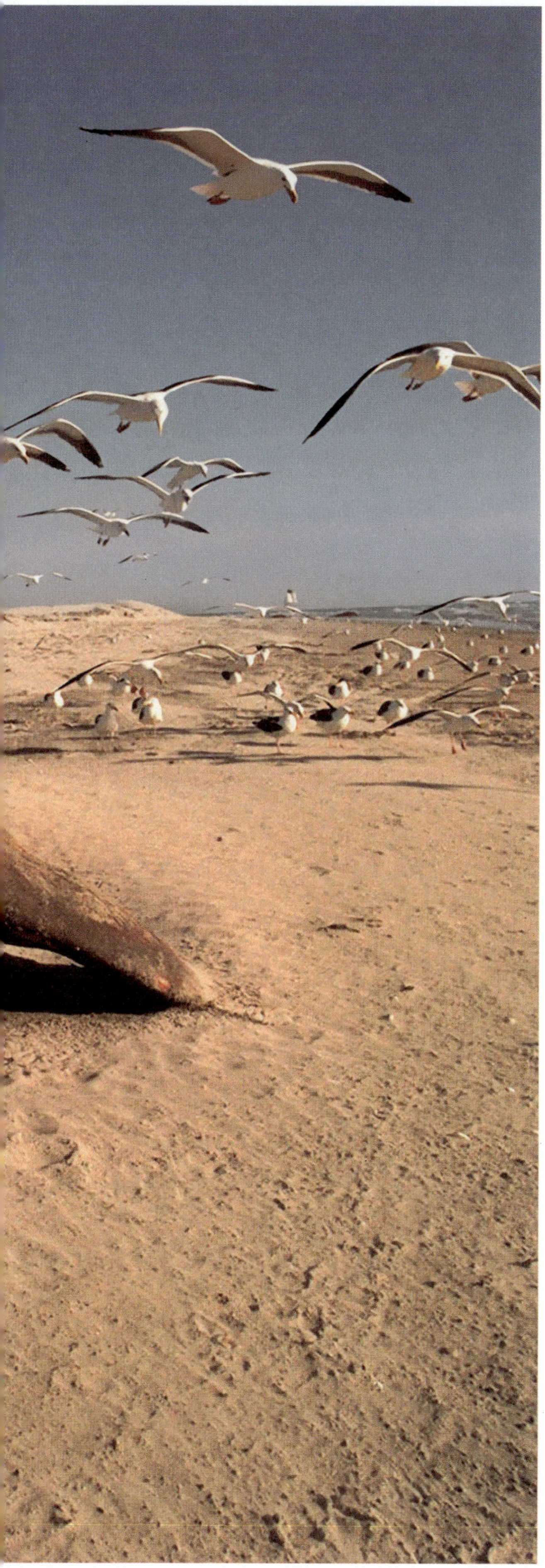

SEA OF INTRANQUILITY

OVER THE DECADES, NRDC HAS ENJOYED countless victories, but we'd never won an Emmy. That changed in 2017, the year we won two, including the award for best nature documentary. *Sonic Sea*, codirected by Daniel Hinerfeld of our Santa Monica office and narrated by the Oscar-nominated actress Rachel McAdams, featured the world-renowned oceanographers Jean-Michel Cousteau and Sylvia Earle. The documentary drew on two decades of work by our marine mammal specialists, Joel Reynolds and Michael Jasny, who have carved out a unique place for NRDC in combating the destructive effects of ocean noise.

For cetaceans—whales, dolphins, and porpoises—the sea is a complex, finely tuned soundscape of clicks and buzzes, whistles and songs. The animals rely on these acoustic signals to help guide their migrations, maintain social relationships, find food and mates, and avoid predators. Without this communication, they cannot survive.

The 1980s and '90s saw a spate of unusual mass strandings of marine mammals, involving deep-diving whales that are seldom seen near shore. In many cases, the fatal events coincided with naval exercises by U.S. and NATO warships, and evidence mounted that the culprit was active military sonar, designed to detect enemy submarines, that could light up hundreds of square miles of sea with sound. Necropsies on many of the beached whales showed signs of severe decompression sickness—"the bends"—suggesting that they had surfaced or submerged rapidly in a desperate attempt to flee the threatening noise.

In the words of author Charles Siebert, writing about the issue in the *New York Times Magazine,* NRDC's years of litigation against military sonar marked "a turning point" in the long, fraught relationship between humans and whales. We had to take on the U.S. Navy, which wasn't easy, for judges had to weigh legitimate national security interests against the requirements of the Endangered Species Act, the Marine Mammal Protection Act, the Coastal Zone Management Act, and other environmental laws. But we had remarkable success, winning cases against the government's failure to

A dead gray whale lies with her baby on the beach at Ojo de Liebre in Baja California, Mexico, March 1999.

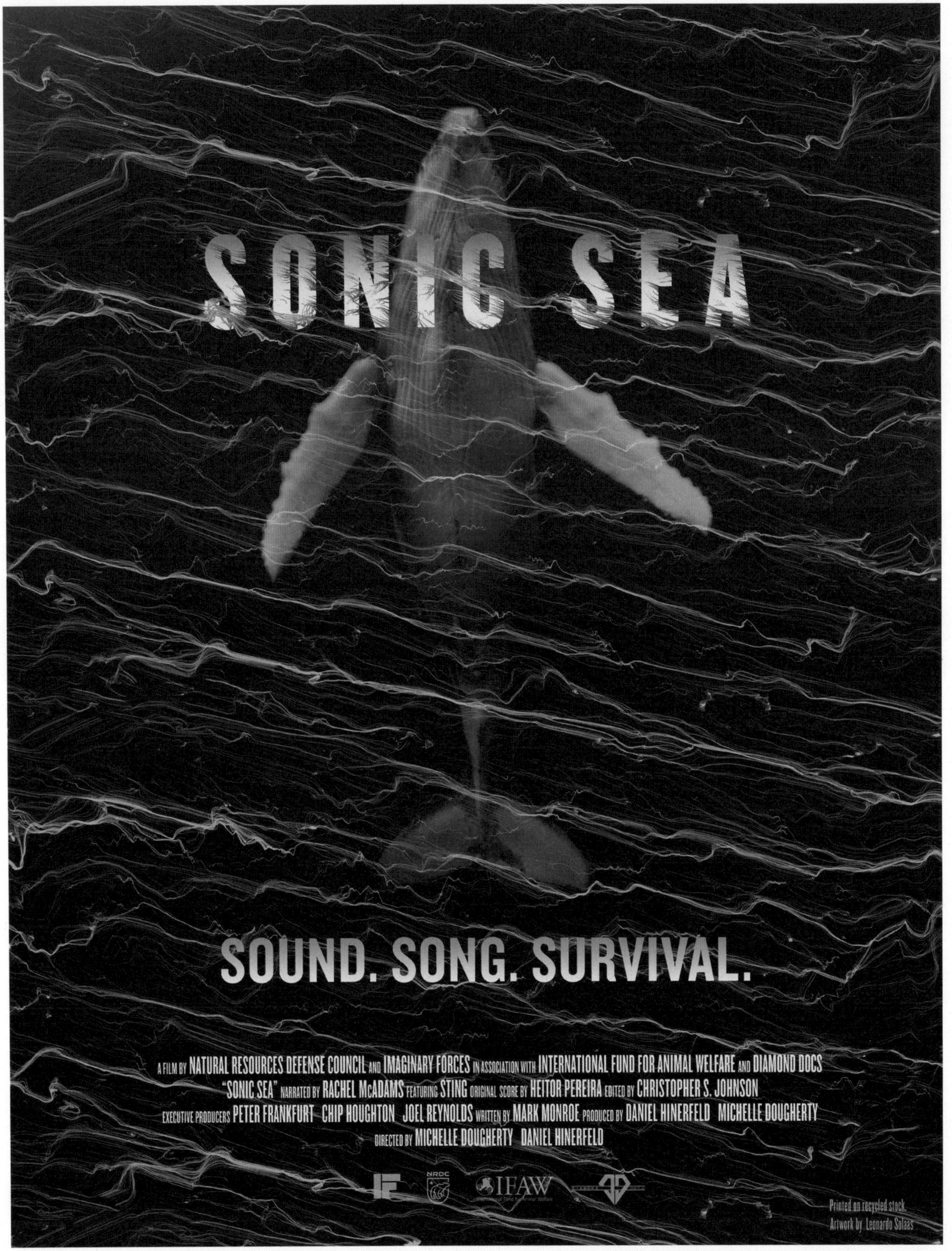

ARTWORK BY LEONARDO SOLAAS FOR NRDC

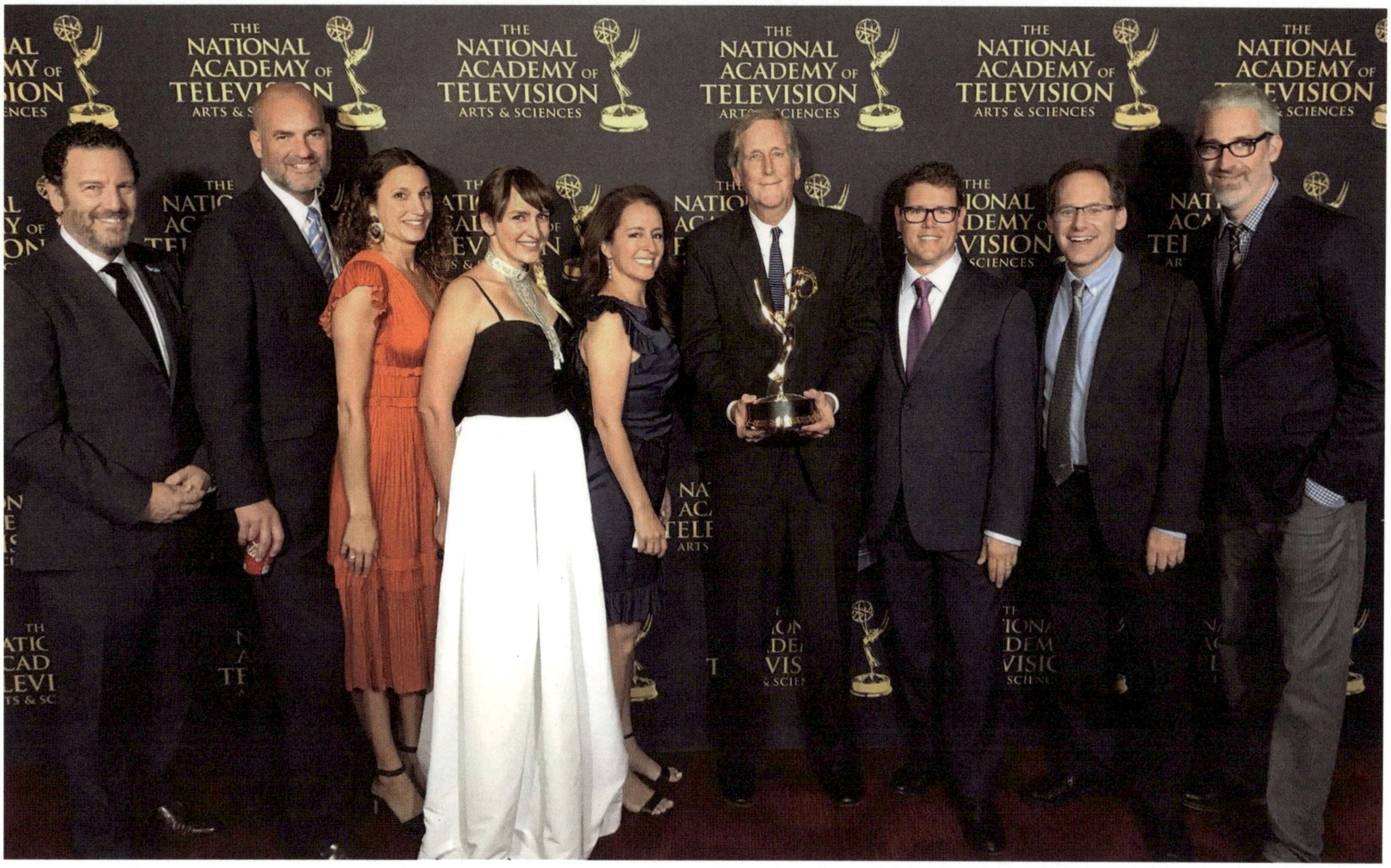

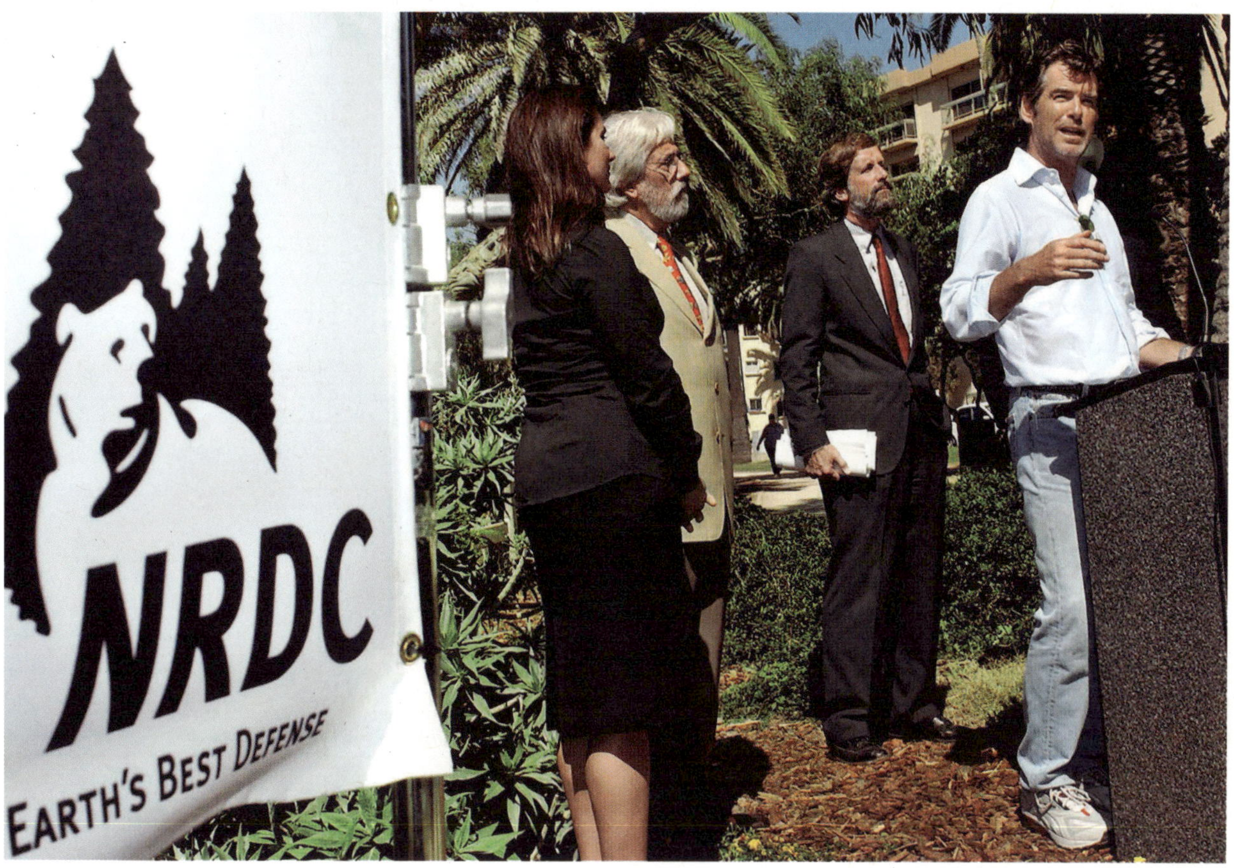

FROM TOP: NRDC; RIC FRANCIS/ASSOCIATED PRESS

Opposite: A *Sonic Sea* film poster.
Top: NRDC's Joel Reynolds (center, holding Emmy) and Daniel Hinerfeld (third from right), pose with the rest of the documentary team shortly after winning the award in 2017.
At left: Actor Pierce Brosnan announces a settlement in NRDC's lawsuit in 2003 against the U.S. Navy to protect marine mammals. Standing behind him are his wife, Keely, diver Jean-Michel Cousteau, and Reynolds.

protect marine mammals from military sonar and forcing the U.S. Navy to agree to prepare environmental impact statements for all future training exercises.

In 2006, we got a temporary restraining order against the world's largest multinational maritime exercise, Rim of the Pacific, which takes place every two years in waters off Hawaii, and won six additional safeguards for marine mammals. Then in 2008, NRDC's challenge to a two-year series of naval training exercises off the California coast went all the way to the Supreme Court. Although the justices struck down two of the six new safeguards, they left four intact.

One of our most recent courtroom victories on this issue, in 2015, obliged the U.S. Navy to halt the use of sonar and explosives in sensitive waters off southern California and Hawaii. NRDC is now working to conserve those areas into the future and to establish similar protective zones in the Atlantic, the Gulf of Alaska, and the Pacific Northwest.

Our work embodies our belief that environmental protection and naval readiness can go hand in hand, as our laws provide. The navy itself has been clear: Putting important habitat off-limits as NRDC's litigation has done has had no impact on sailor safety or naval readiness. As a result of this work, in fact, the U.S. Navy has become a world leader in marine mammal research and is helping to map out key whale habitat around the country. The navy is also doing more to protect marine mammals and their habitats from powerful sonar and explosives during routine training exercises, although more effort is needed.

But the crisis of ocean noise extends far beyond sonar. At any given time, 60,000 tankers, container ships, and other commercial vessels are crisscrossing the world's oceans, each adding to the underwater din. Seismic survey vessels, meanwhile, probe for oil and gas deposits beneath the seabed, using high-powered airguns that blast loud bursts of compressed air about five times a minute for weeks and months on end. After more litigation, NRDC reached a landmark settlement agreement for the Gulf of Mexico, the world's most heavily prospected body of water, that includes closure areas for threatened species and funding for safer alternatives to airguns. We're now pressing for a long-term cap on oil and gas exploration in the gulf and for a complete prohibition of those activities off the East Coast, where the endangered right whale is fighting to survive.

We know that litigation alone won't bring the solutions the ocean and its inhabitants need. Changing the behavior of a giant global industry like commercial shipping calls for a blend of technological innovation, international cooperation, regulation, and economic incentives. In 2014, we persuaded the International Maritime Organization to establish guidelines for commercial vessels to operate more quietly. We're now working with ports, shipping lines, and regulators in North America and Europe to actually begin quieting vessels and to help silence the cacophony we've created under the sea.

Below: People inspect the remains of four sperm whales beached on the Dutch island of Ameland in November 1997. Opposite: A California sea lion.

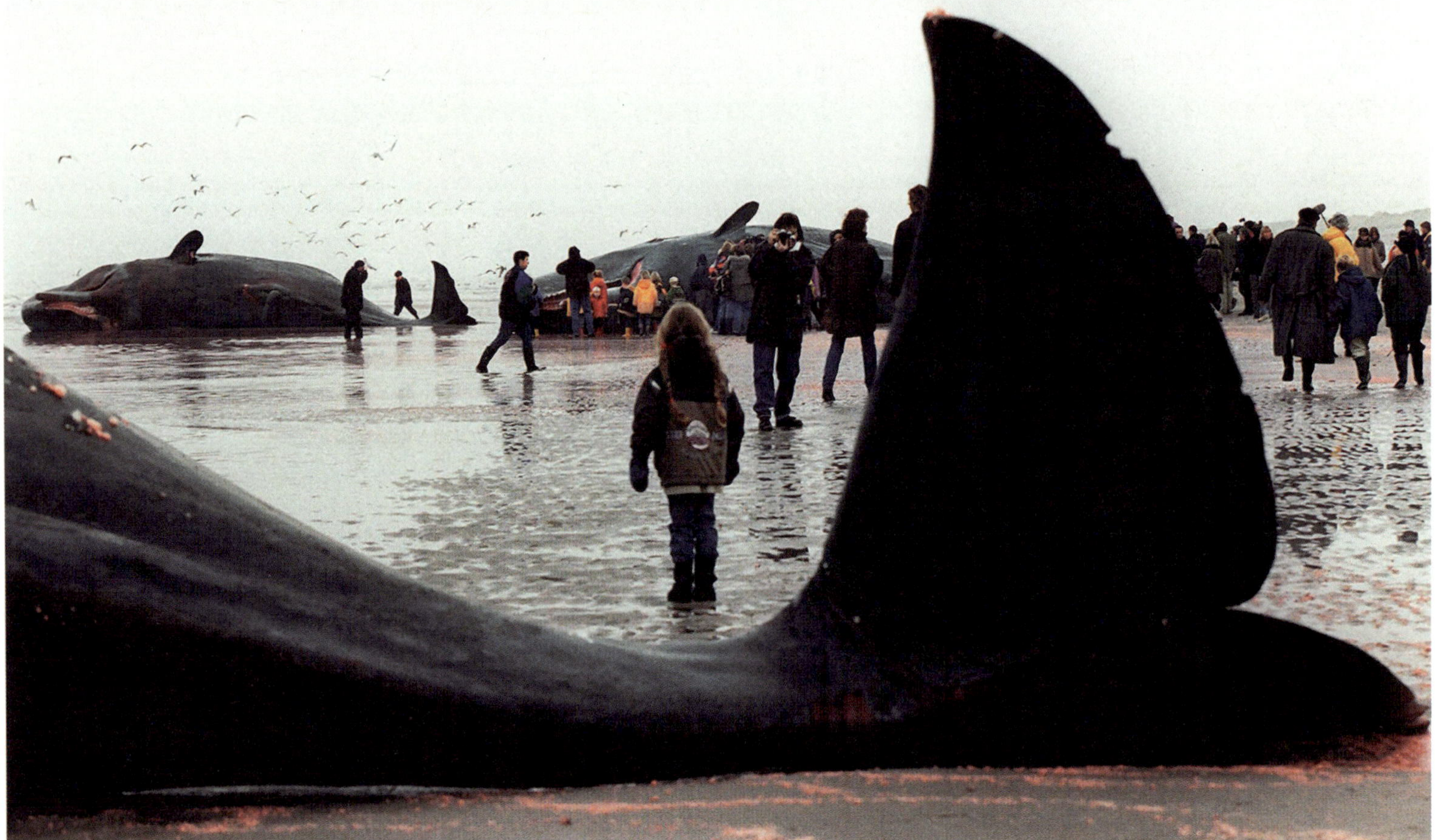

KAREL ZWANEVELD/ASSOCIATED PRESS. OPPOSITE: KONRAD WOTHE/MINDEN PICTURES

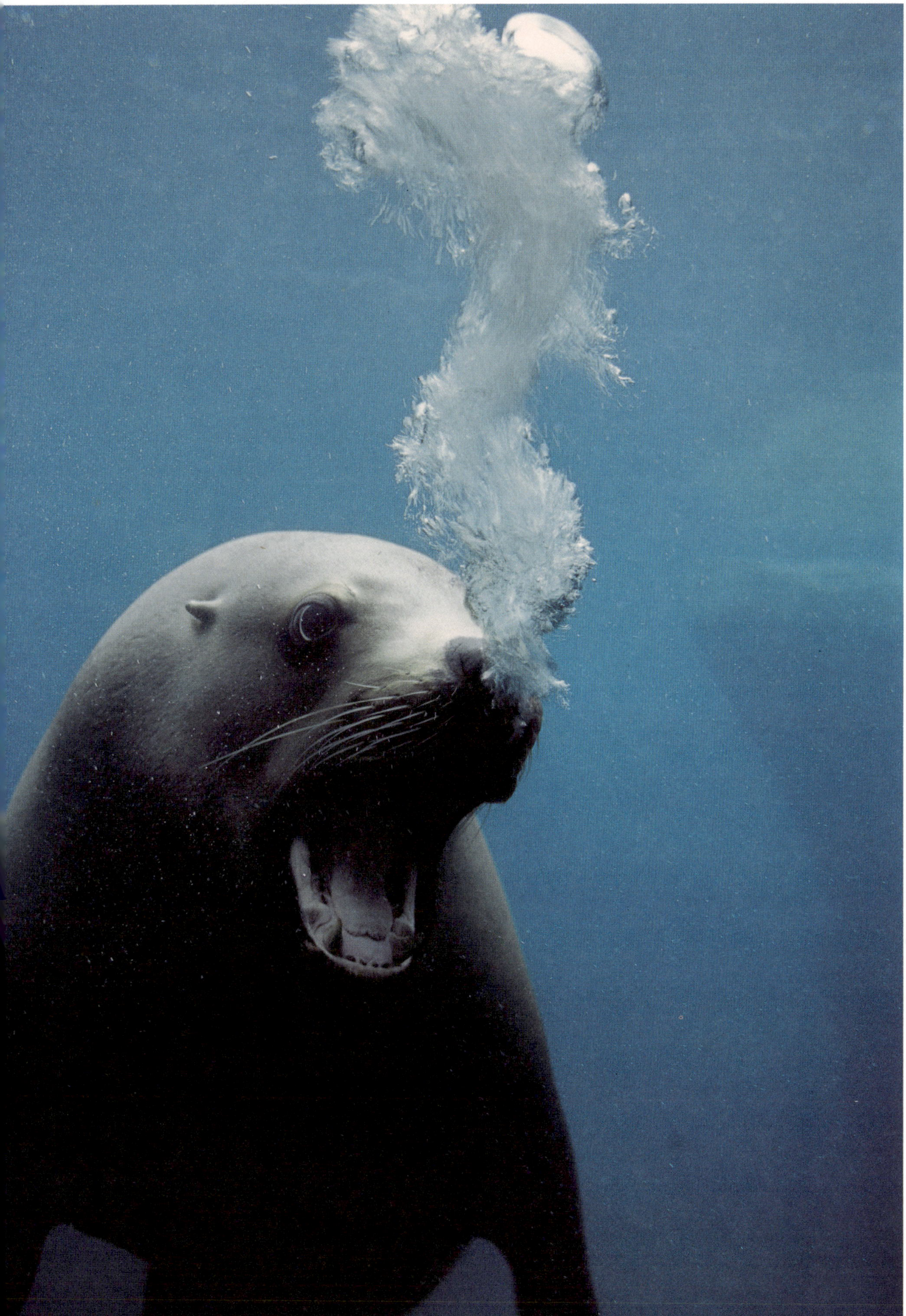

Our work embodies our belief that environmental protection and naval readiness can go hand in hand.

THE RIGHT TO CLEAN WATER

NOTHING DEFINED RHEA SUH'S TENURE as NRDC's third president better than her response to the outrageous levels of lead found in the Flint, Michigan, water supply. By the time the contamination came to light in 2015, the people of Flint had been drinking, bathing, and cooking with lead-contaminated water for more than a year. Flint encapsulated everything Rhea cares about most passionately. The crisis was a dramatic illustration of how the impacts of environmental violations fall disproportionately on already disadvantaged communities. And as the mother of a young child herself, Rhea was acutely aware of the special threat that lead, a potent neurotoxin, poses to the brain during fetal development, infancy, and early childhood. So when this public health crisis erupted, as well as when a similar one emerged in Newark, New Jersey, soon after, NRDC went to work to fight this textbook case of government recklessness and environmental racism.

Flint, famous as the birthplace of General Motors, is now a city in economic decline, with nearly half of its populace living below the poverty line. In 2014, facing a fiscal emergency, state-appointed officials running the city decided to save money by switching the city's water supply from the Detroit municipal system to the Flint River. Local residents, the majority of whom are Black, soon began complaining that their tap water was discolored, evil-smelling, and undrinkable. For months, city and state officials denied there was a problem. But in fact, the inadequately treated river water had been corroding old lead pipes, and tests showed that the number of children with high levels of lead in their blood had more than doubled since the city changed the water supply.

In the summer of 2015, the American Civil Liberties Union of Michigan turned to NRDC as the ideal organization to investigate this burgeoning public health crisis. Dimple Chaudhary, an attorney in our Washington, D.C., office, led our legal team, and NRDC and its local partners sued the city of Flint and the state of Michigan under the 1974 Safe Drinking Water Act. A group of young NRDC lawyers went up against the cream of Michigan's legal establishment. But when NRDC and its partners won a $97 million settlement that forced the city to remove its lead water pipes, our opponents were left staring at their shoes. "Dimple is a role model for the younger generation of NRDC lawyers," says her colleague Sarah Tallman. "She owned this case."

But the real heroes were the local people in Flint who were

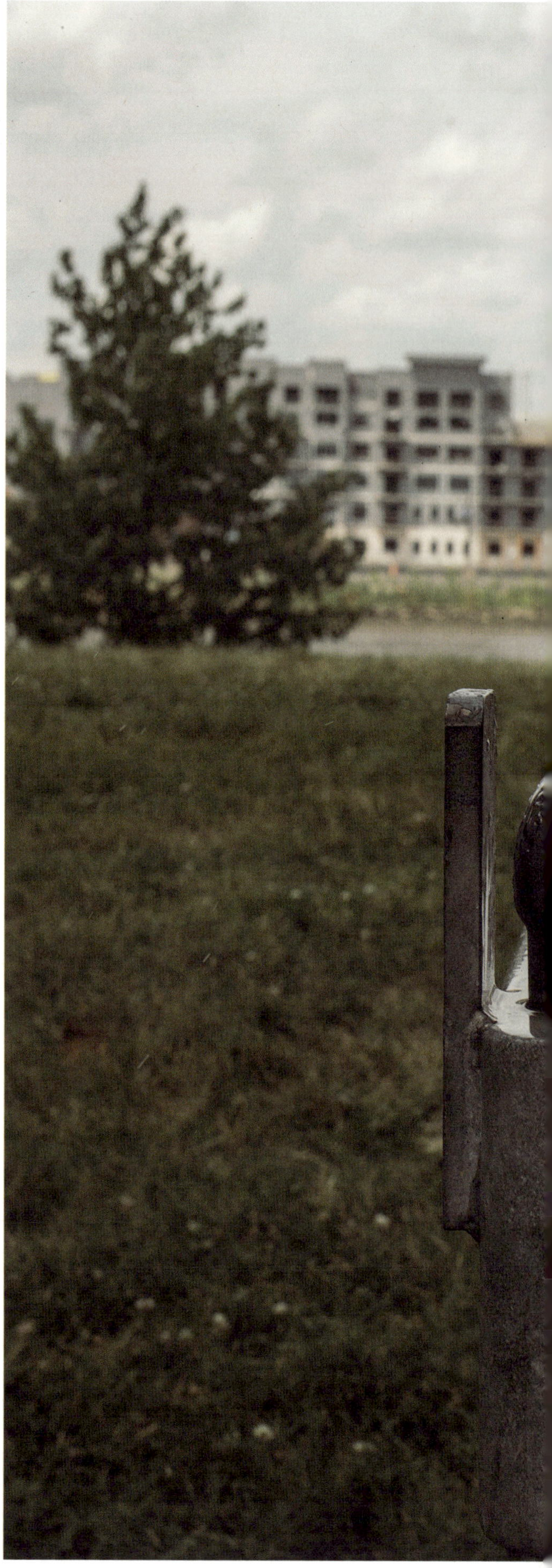

A child drinks from a fountain at the Essex County Riverfront Park in the Ironbound neighborhood of Newark, New Jersey.

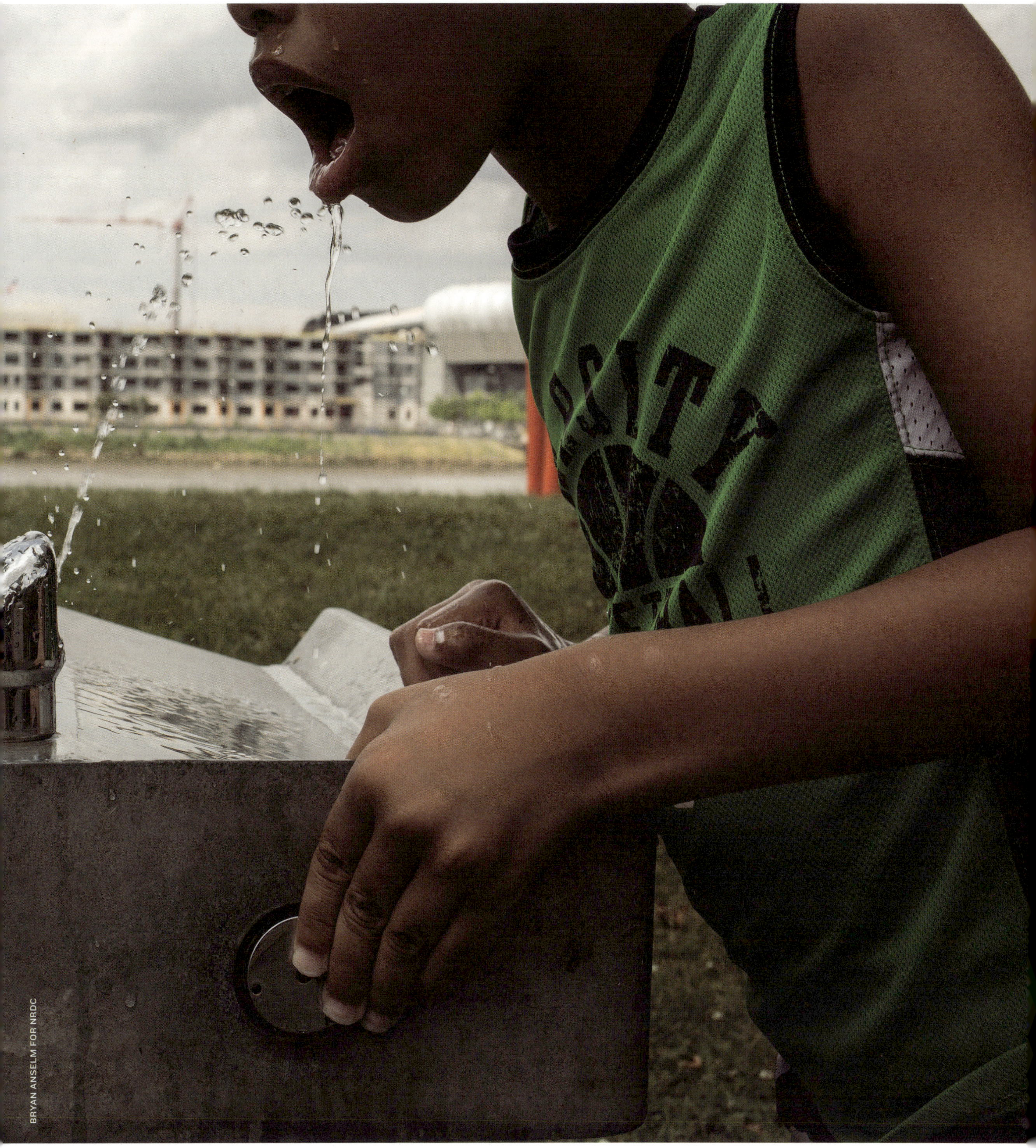

BRYAN ANSELM FOR NRDC

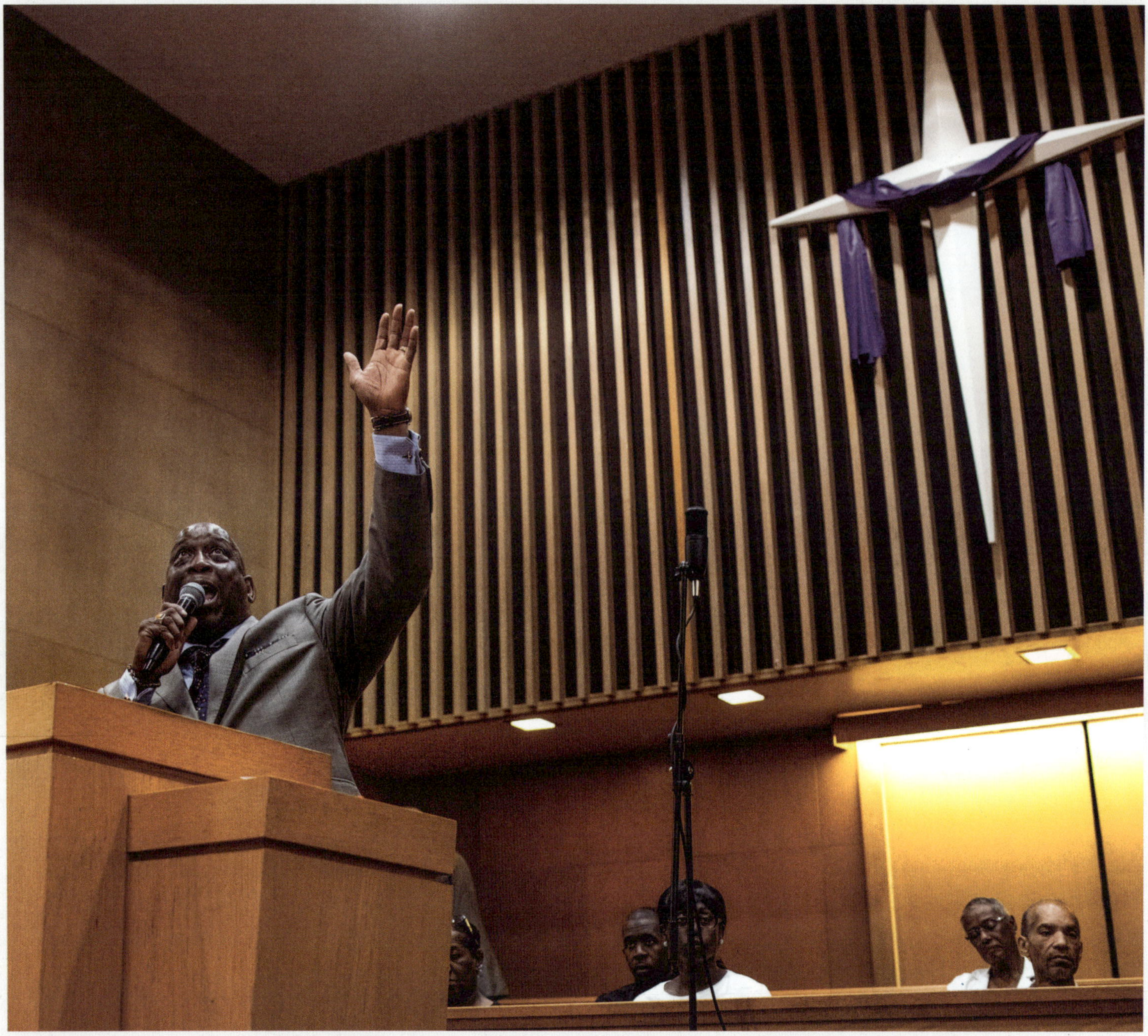

FROM THE FRONTLINES

Pastor Allen Overton

Pastor Allen Overton believes that church leaders' responsibility to their parish goes beyond their Sunday morning sermons. "We have a prophetic voice that needs to be utilized in community affairs—and in world affairs," he says. "We have to speak out against injustice, because injustice anywhere is injustice everywhere." So when the pastor learned about the water crisis in his hometown of Flint, Michigan, he knew he had a duty to raise his voice.

Together with Concerned Pastors for Social Action, Pastor Overton, who leads Flint's Christ Fellowship Missionary Baptist Church, joined forces with fellow Flint resident Melissa Mays, NRDC, and ACLU of Michigan to file the 2016 lawsuit against the city of Flint and Michigan state officials for unlawfully exposing the community to lead-contaminated drinking water. The case led to a $97 million settlement requiring Michigan to pay for the removal of all of Flint's lead and galvanized steel service lines within three years.

"I've got to admit that NRDC was the best group of people that we've ever come across to support our mission here," Pastor Overton says. "Nobody has helped us more than the people at NRDC. They took on the challenge of getting the pipes removed, and they didn't quit until they did just what they set out to do. I am honored and privileged to have had the opportunity to spend time with them and to do the work that we were able to do together."

Pastor Overton gives his morning sermon at his church.

BRITTANY GREESON FOR NRDC

the first to resist—mothers, pastors, community activists—and our team took its cues from them, putting the voices of residents and clients first. Our team went door-to-door to listen to people's real-life experiences and brought those stories before the judge: of elderly people forced to lug home heavy cases of bottled water in the depths of winter; of parents tormented by guilt at exposing their children to serious health, mental, and behavioral risks.

When the city dragged its feet on the settlement, we took Flint back to court; when it wasted settlement funds on a scattershot approach to locating the underground pipes, we worked with data scientists to show the city where it should look, using criteria such as the age, value, and location of homes. Meanwhile, the pressure we brought to bear on the state of Michigan forced it to enact the most progressive lead and copper rule in the nation, committing itself to removing all lead pipes in the state over the next 20 years.

Flint was a stunning breach of public trust, but it is far from an isolated case: A 2016 NRDC study showed that thousands of community water systems were violating federal safety standards and that nationwide more than six million lead service lines need replacing. So when, less than two years later, another Flint-style crisis surfaced in Newark, New Jersey, a concerted push by NRDC's communications and advocacy teams brought the injustice to the front pages. Again, the government of a low-income and predominantly Black and Latino city was made to fix a problem it had denied for too long. (The city's mayor attacked NRDC as a bunch of interfering outsiders, a rich irony since our local partner was the Newark Education Workers Caucus, a group of local educators.) When filters failed to get the lead out of people's tap water, Newark agreed to replace 18,000 lead service lines within 30 months.

The woeful stories of Flint and Newark confirmed Rhea's view that clean, safe, affordable drinking water should be a signature issue for NRDC. We have a national emergency on our hands, and it requires a national solution—clearer laws, stronger enforcement, and true accountability for offenders. In the past few years, NRDC has emerged as a leader in that fight and as an ally to those who have been denied a basic human right.

Scenes from the water crises of Flint and Newark.

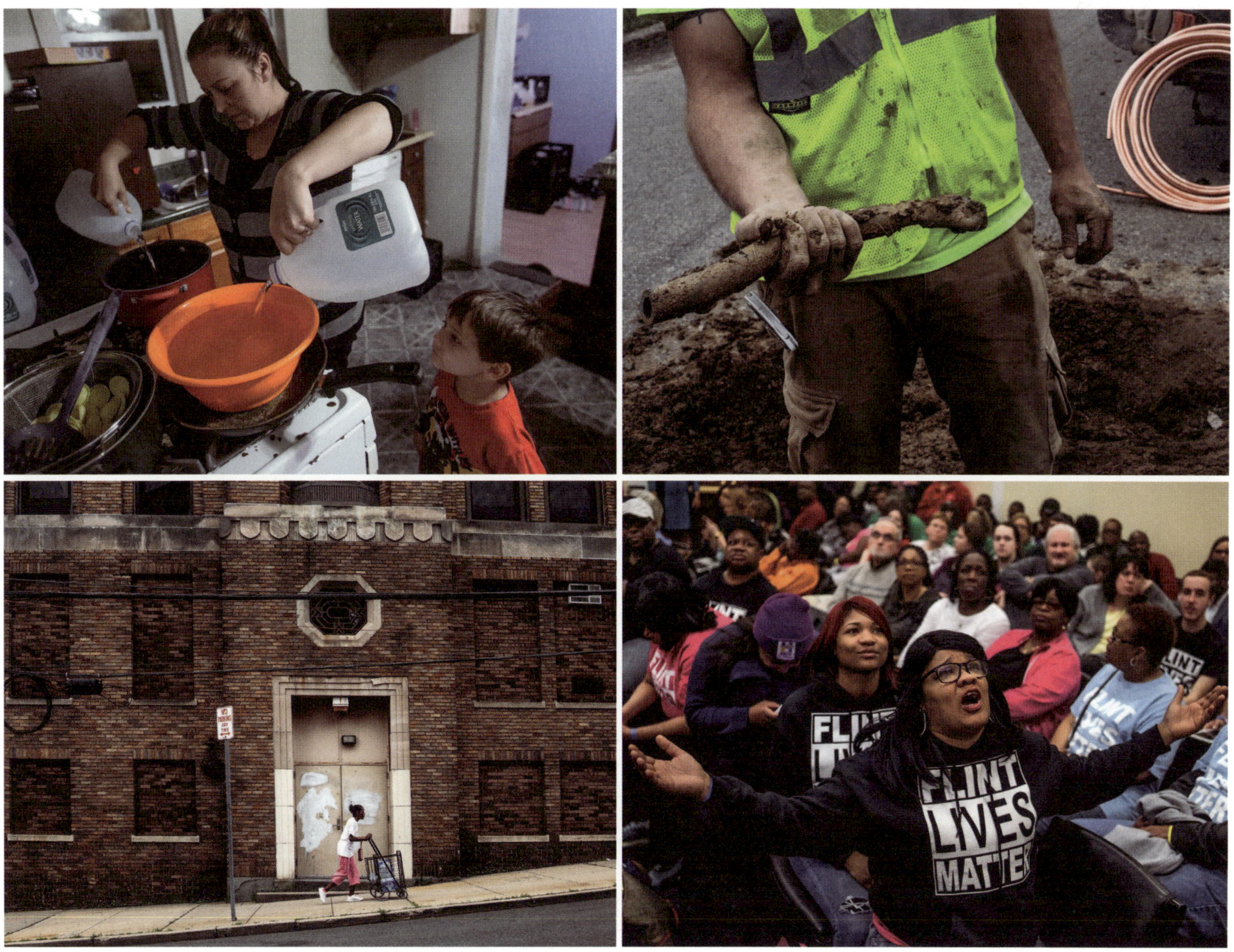

CLOCKWISE FROM TOP LEFT: RYAN GARZA/DETROIT FREE PRESS VIA ZUMA WIRE; BRITTANY GREESON FOR NRDC; JAKE MAY/THE FLINT JOURNAL-MLIVE VIA AP; DEMETRIUS FREEMAN FOR NRDC

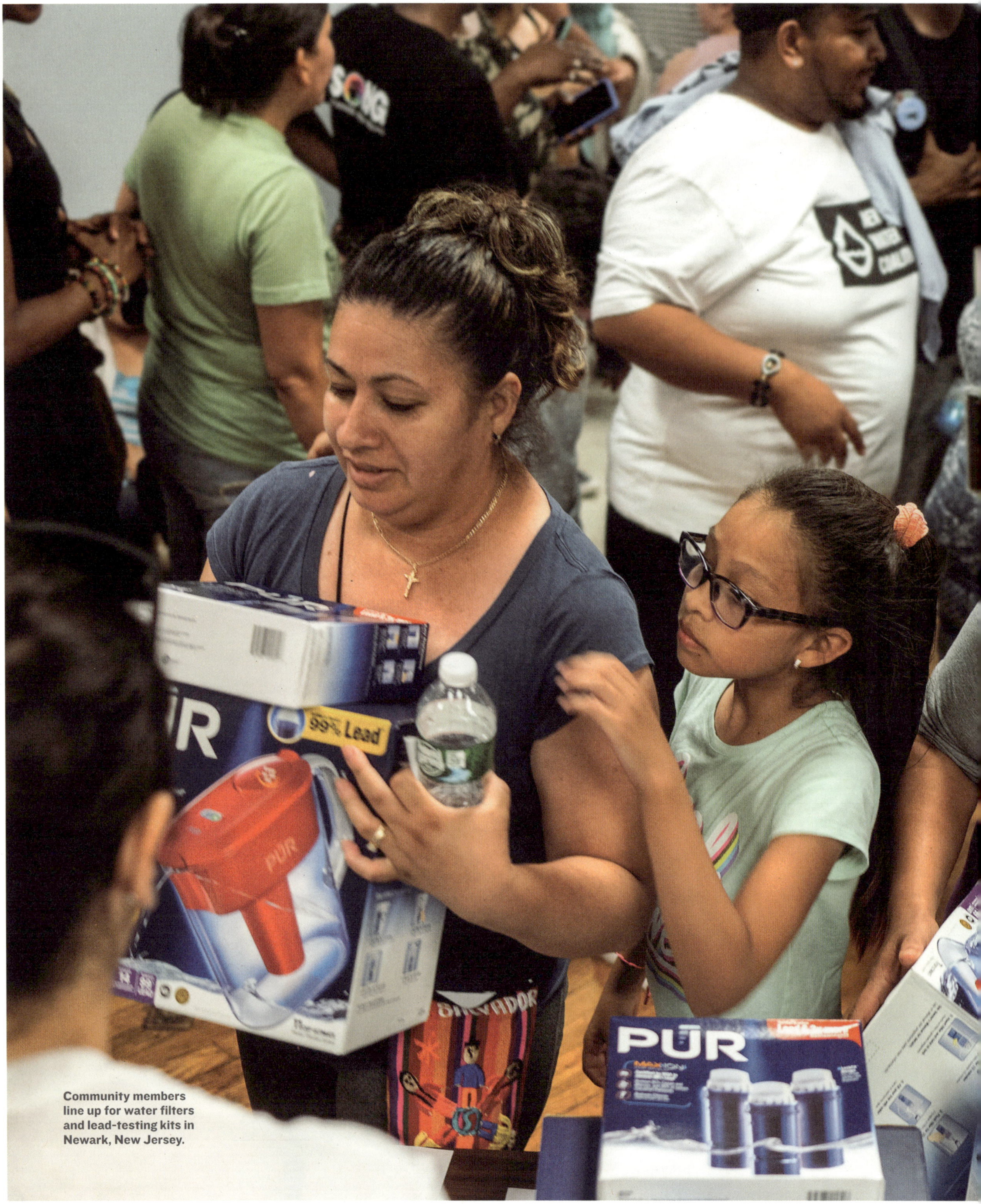

Community members line up for water filters and lead-testing kits in Newark, New Jersey.

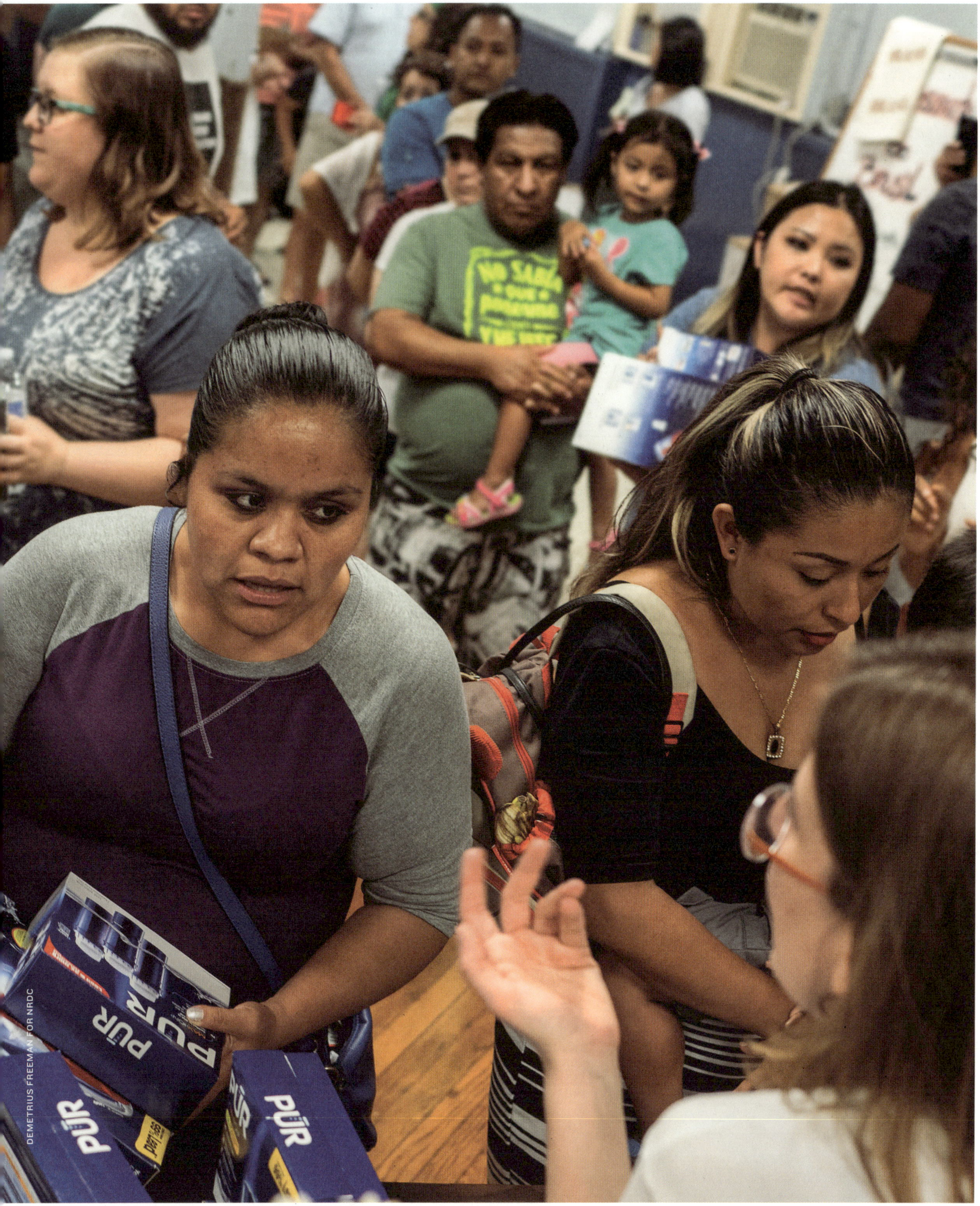

DEMETRIUS FREEMAN FOR NRDC

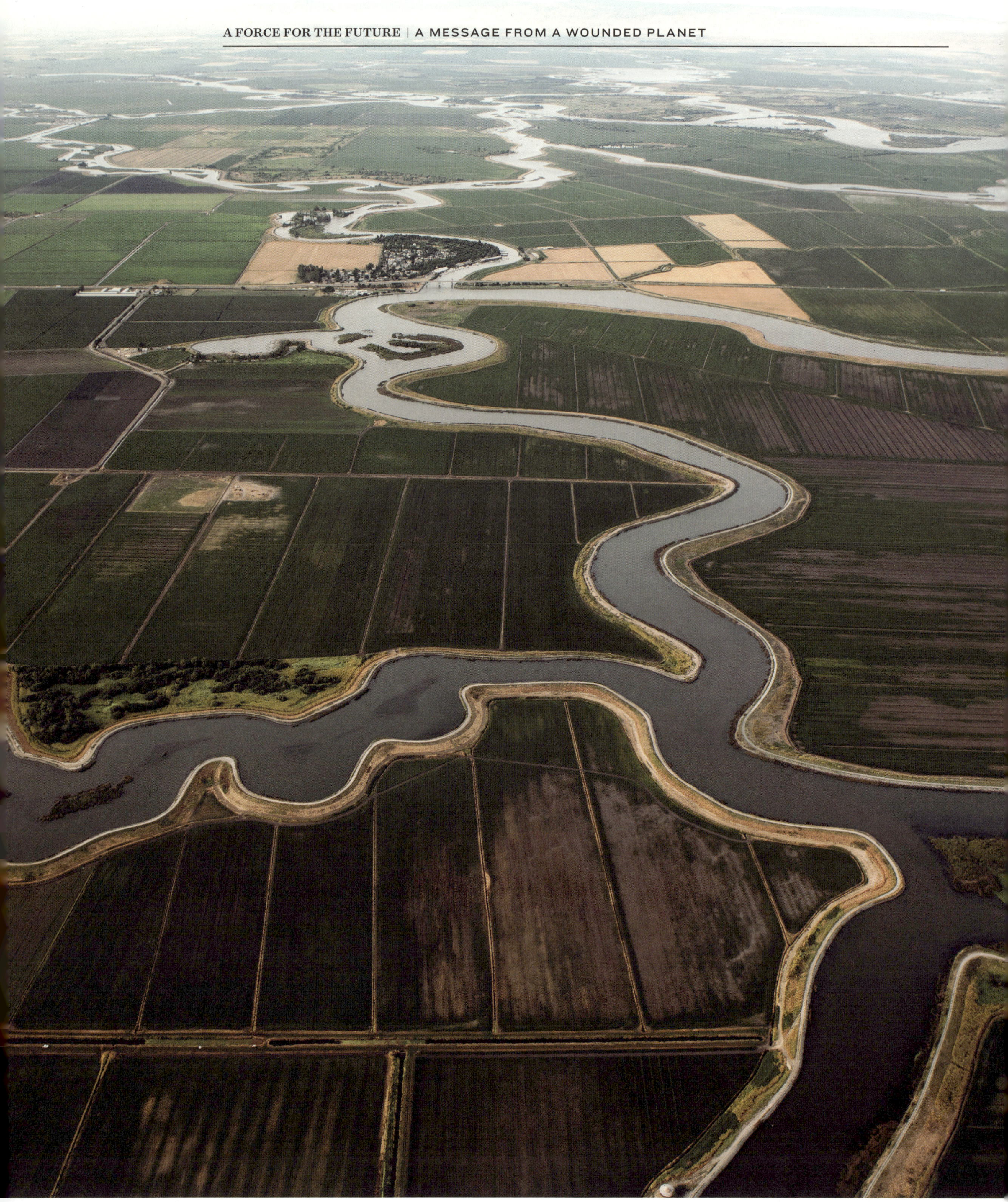

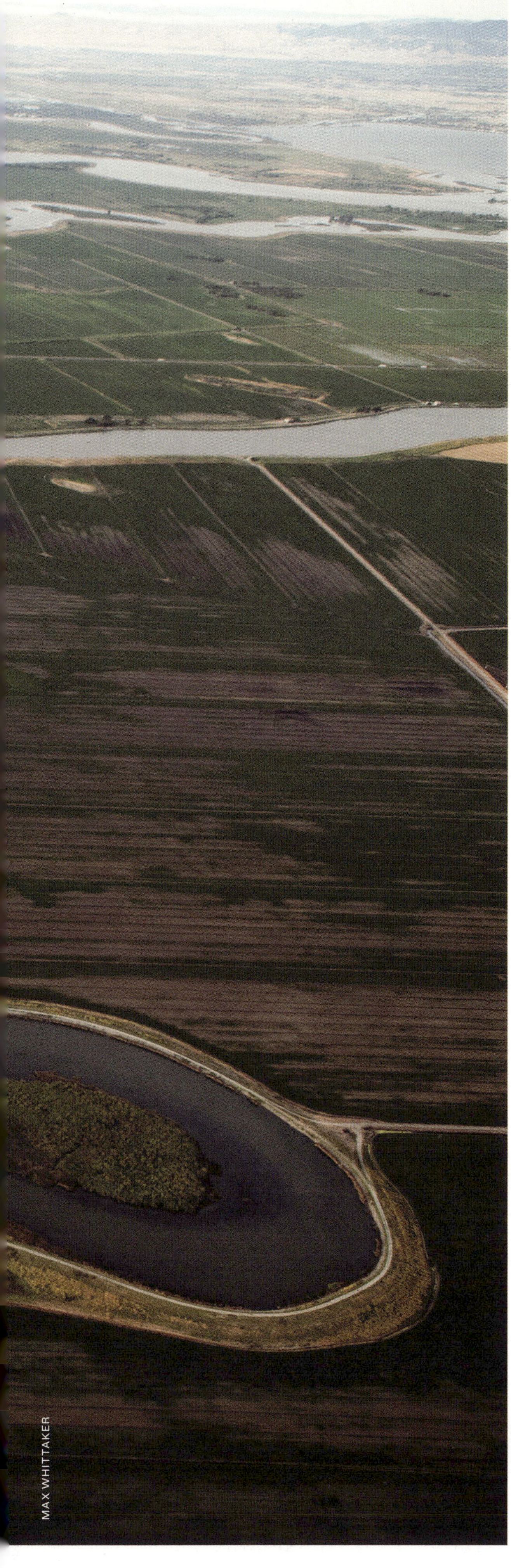

MAX WHITTAKER

A CONFLUENCE OF EXPERTISE

NRDC'S MARC REISNER PUBLISHED A book in 1986 called *Cadillac Desert*. An enduring classic, it lays bare the myth on which the West was founded: that a naturally arid region could guarantee in perpetuity as much water as people demanded, at low cost, and without destroying the environment.

Exhibit A for this fallacy is the San Joaquin River. The river rises in the Sierra Nevada near Yosemite National Park and runs for 350 miles before meeting the Sacramento River to form the San Francisco Bay Delta, the largest estuary on the West Coast. Nearly two-thirds of the state's population and a third of its irrigated farmland depend in part on diversions from the delta. It is California's most critical water resource.

The myth of endless cheap water has always been sustained by nature-defying engineers. The New Deal–era Central Valley Project helped transform desert into productive farmland, and the creation of the 319-foot Friant Dam, near Fresno, in the early 1940s diverted all of the San Joaquin's flow to farms. In most years, the river ran dry for nearly 60 miles. The delta itself was reengineered by giant pumps, levees, and purification plants that provided drinking water for millions—while turning wildlife-rich marshes into farmland and decimating one of the richest salmon fisheries in the West.

Environmental organizations had usually shied away from confronting the entrenched agricultural interests in the Central Valley, but NRDC stepped up in 1988 with a lawsuit against the U.S. Bureau of Reclamation based on its violations of the Endangered Species Act. While we wanted farmers to get a fair shake, our bottom line was that any settlement had to restore a living river and its native salmon runs to the benefit of local communities, the environment, and the fishing industry. The lawsuit took 18 years, but in the end we won a landmark agreement, resulting in one of the biggest river restoration projects in the country. Then, in 2009, President Obama signed the San Joaquin River Restoration Settlement Act, engineers opened the gates

An aerial photograph of the San Joaquin Bay-Delta.

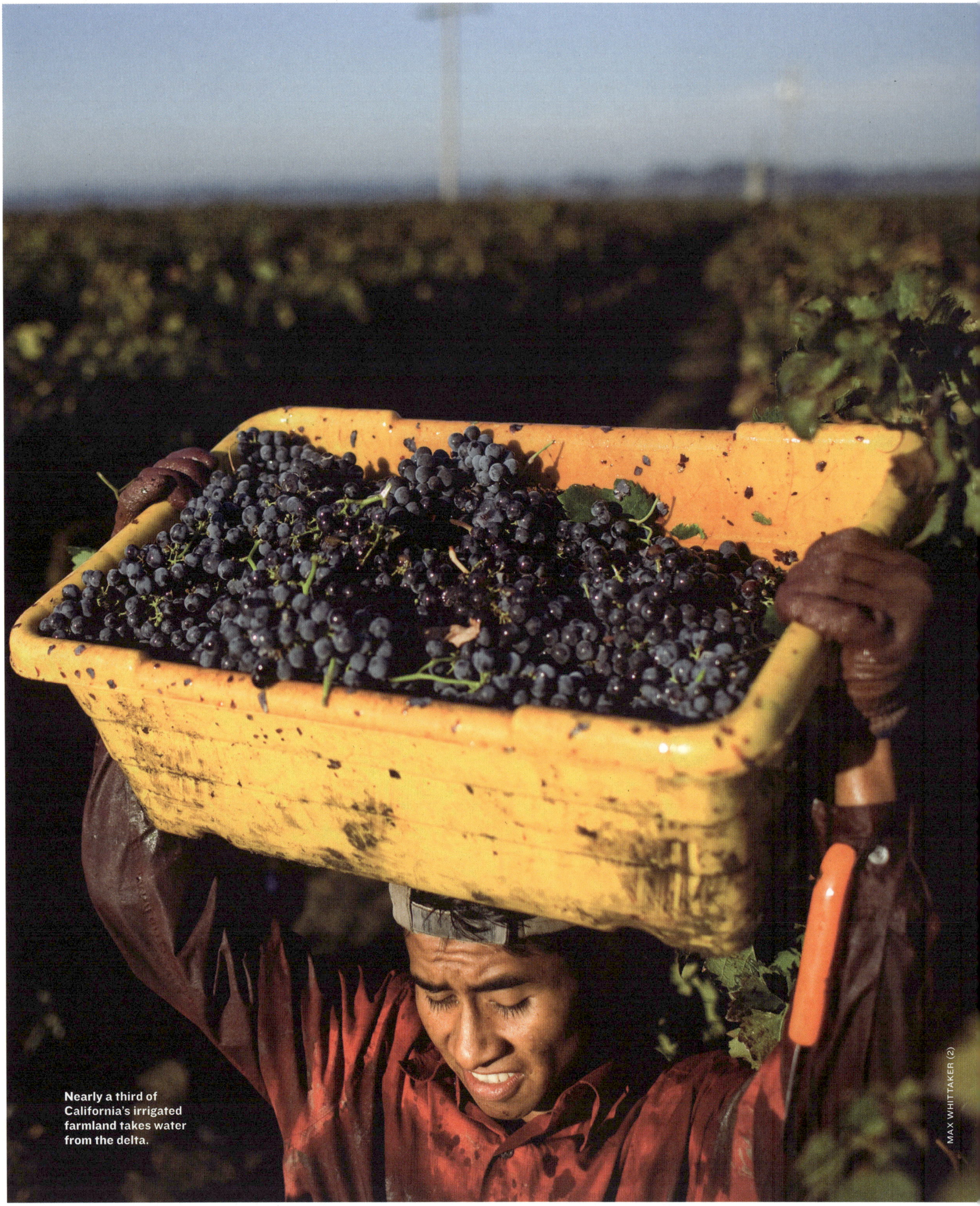

Nearly a third of California's irrigated farmland takes water from the delta.

MAX WHITTAKER (2)

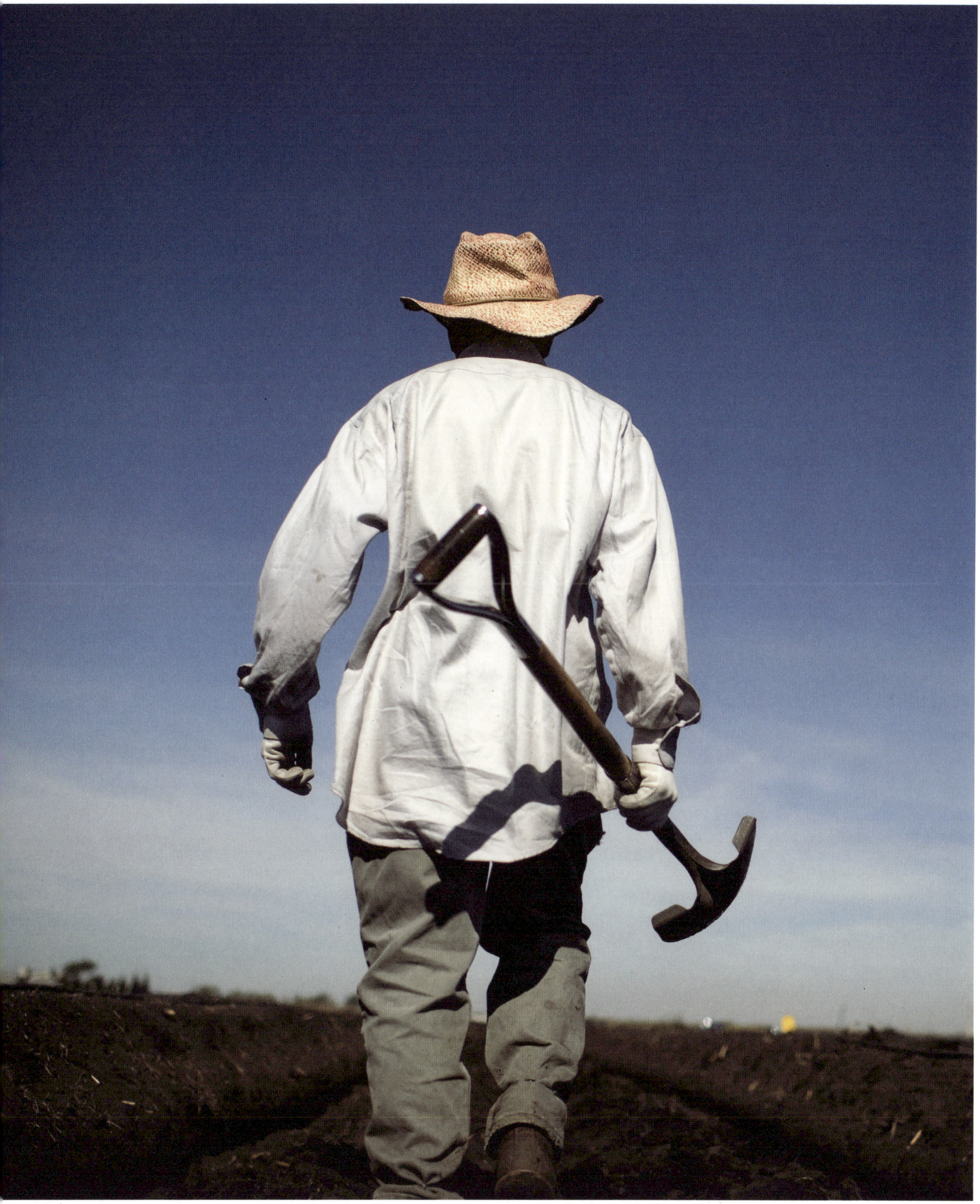

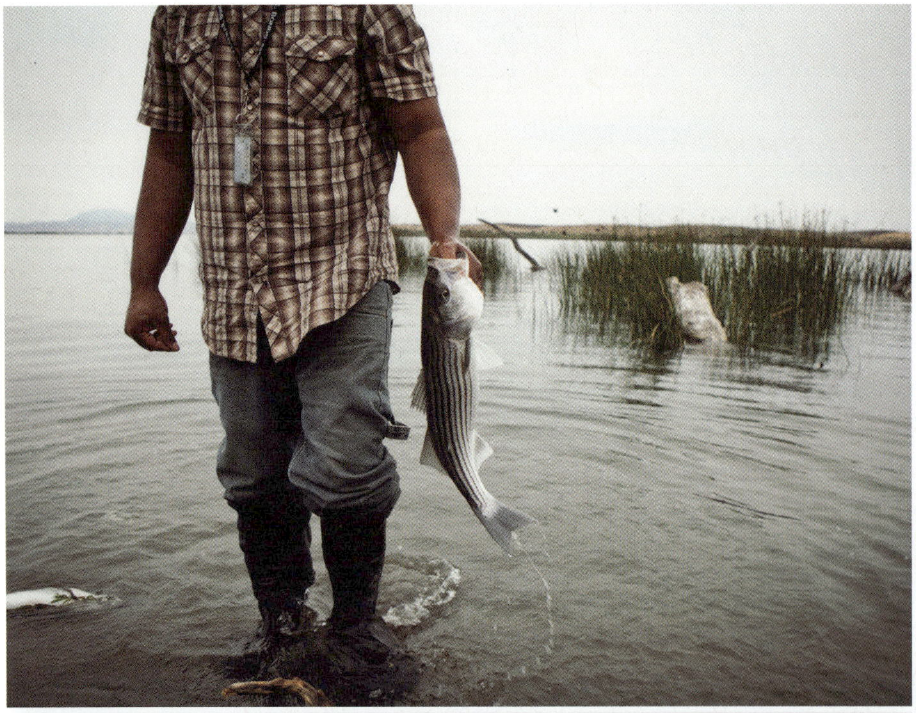

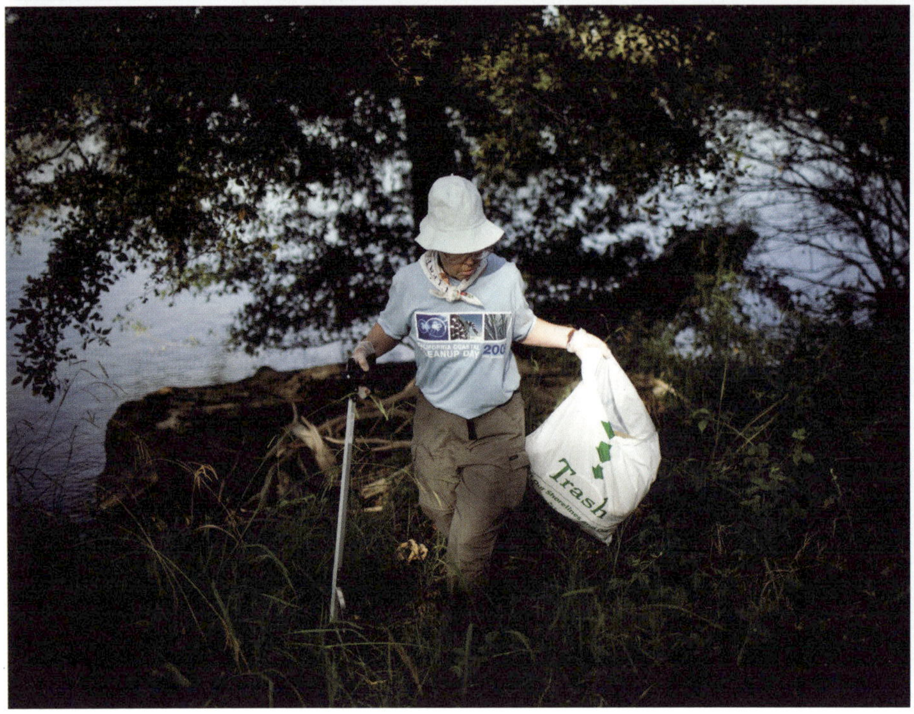

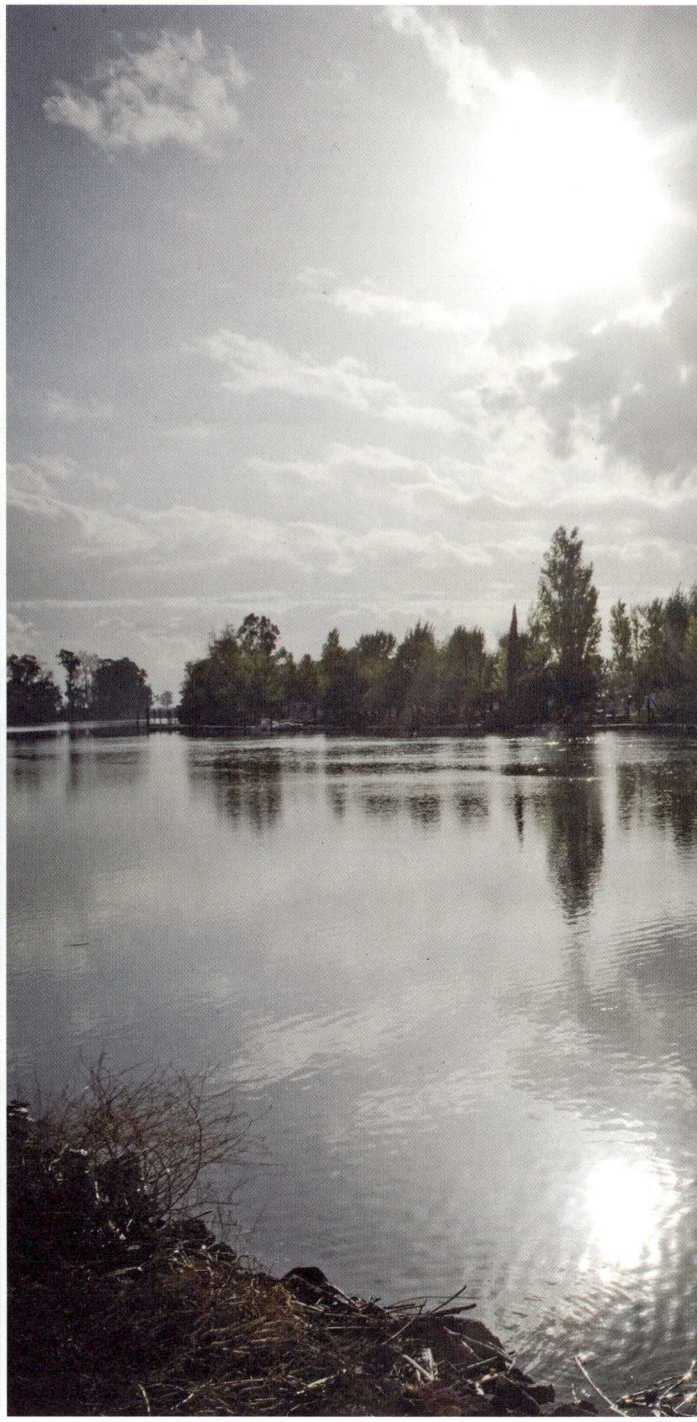

The Bay Delta's waterways are home to more than 20 species of fish—including Chinook salmon, steelhead trout, and American sturgeon—and help sustain thousands of fishing jobs.

MAX WHITTAKER (3)

of the Friant Dam, and, for the first time in decades, water flowed year round all the way down the San Joaquin River to the delta. In 2019, hundreds of salmon returned to their historic spawning grounds below Friant Dam.

But persistent drought, rising sea levels, and relentless development brought more severe pressures on the delta. Once again, politicians argued that engineers could solve the problem. In 2013, Governor Jerry Brown proposed a $15 billion scheme called California WaterFix that would have built two huge underground tunnels to redirect the Sacramento River, causing further damage to the delta. It took another four lawsuits and political opposition from fishermen, delta communities, and conservation groups, but NRDC and our partners eventually killed that plan in another historic victory in May 2019. Even so, in the words of Doug Obegi, who heads NRDC's river restoration work in California, "we've won many battles, but we're still in a war."

While other drought-threatened parts of the state have invested heavily in water efficiency—notably Los Angeles, long criticized for its thirsty lawns and swimming pools—most agricultural interests still insist on their traditional prerogatives. And now the Trump administration is at their beck and call. The current Interior Department has been eviscerating protections for the Bay Delta, demanding increased water

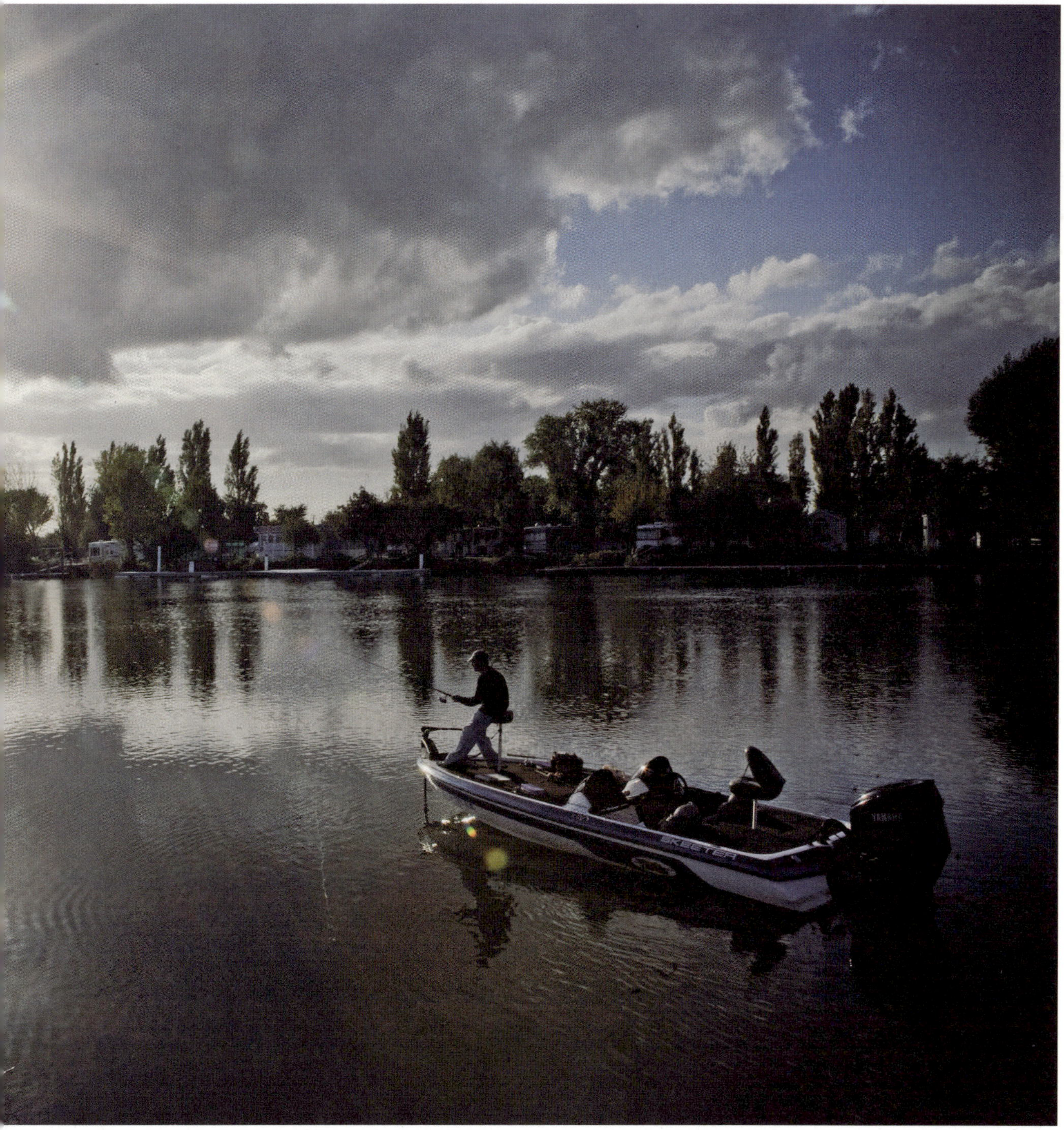

Our bottom line was that any settlement had to restore a living river and its native salmon runs to the benefit of local communities, the environment, and the fishing industry.

diversions for farmers and riding roughshod over scientific studies that show the likely devastating impacts such diversions would have on endangered species like the delta smelt and winter-run Chinook salmon. Most flagrantly, the same private interests that failed to get their way in court now plan to prevail by using the muscle of the federal government. To replace his disgraced secretary of the Interior, Ryan Zinke, Trump chose none other than David Bernhardt, who is a former lobbyist for California's Westlands Water District, the biggest agricultural water district in the nation.

We began our fight for the Bay Delta more than 30 years ago, and we'll stick with it for another 30 if necessary. When you take on an issue of this magnitude and complexity, that's the kind of enduring commitment it takes. Winning a lawsuit, even a historic one, can prove to be a pyrrhic victory unless your legal skills are bound with expert advocacy and the flexibility to withstand radical changes in federal policy and to develop sound policy alternatives. In this case, our approach was based on a firm grasp of such diverse disciplines as aquatic biology, hydraulic engineering, water efficiency, and agricultural economics. I don't believe that any organization but NRDC could have risen to the challenge to save the San Joaquin River and the Bay Delta.

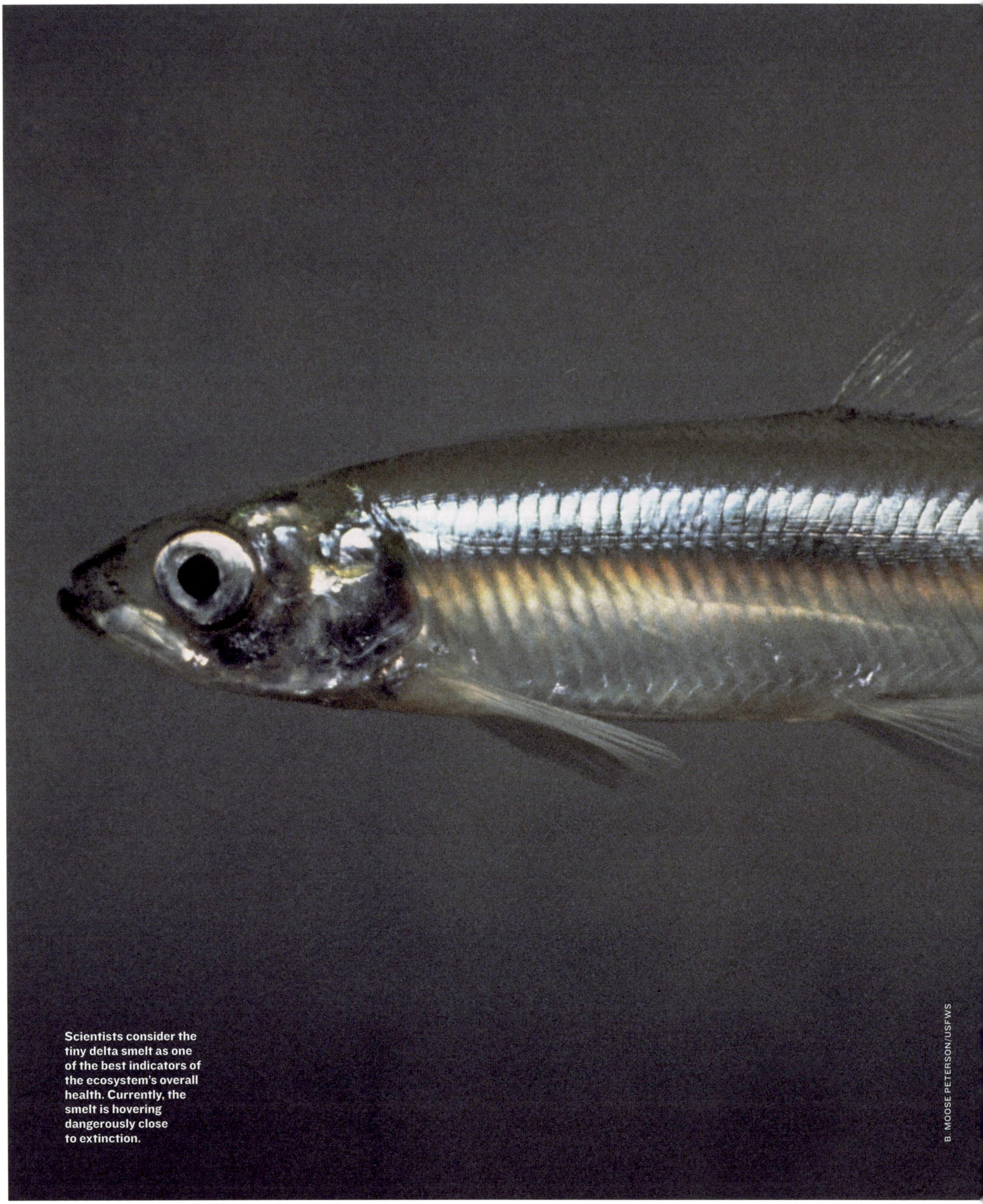

Scientists consider the tiny delta smelt as one of the best indicators of the ecosystem's overall health. Currently, the smelt is hovering dangerously close to extinction.

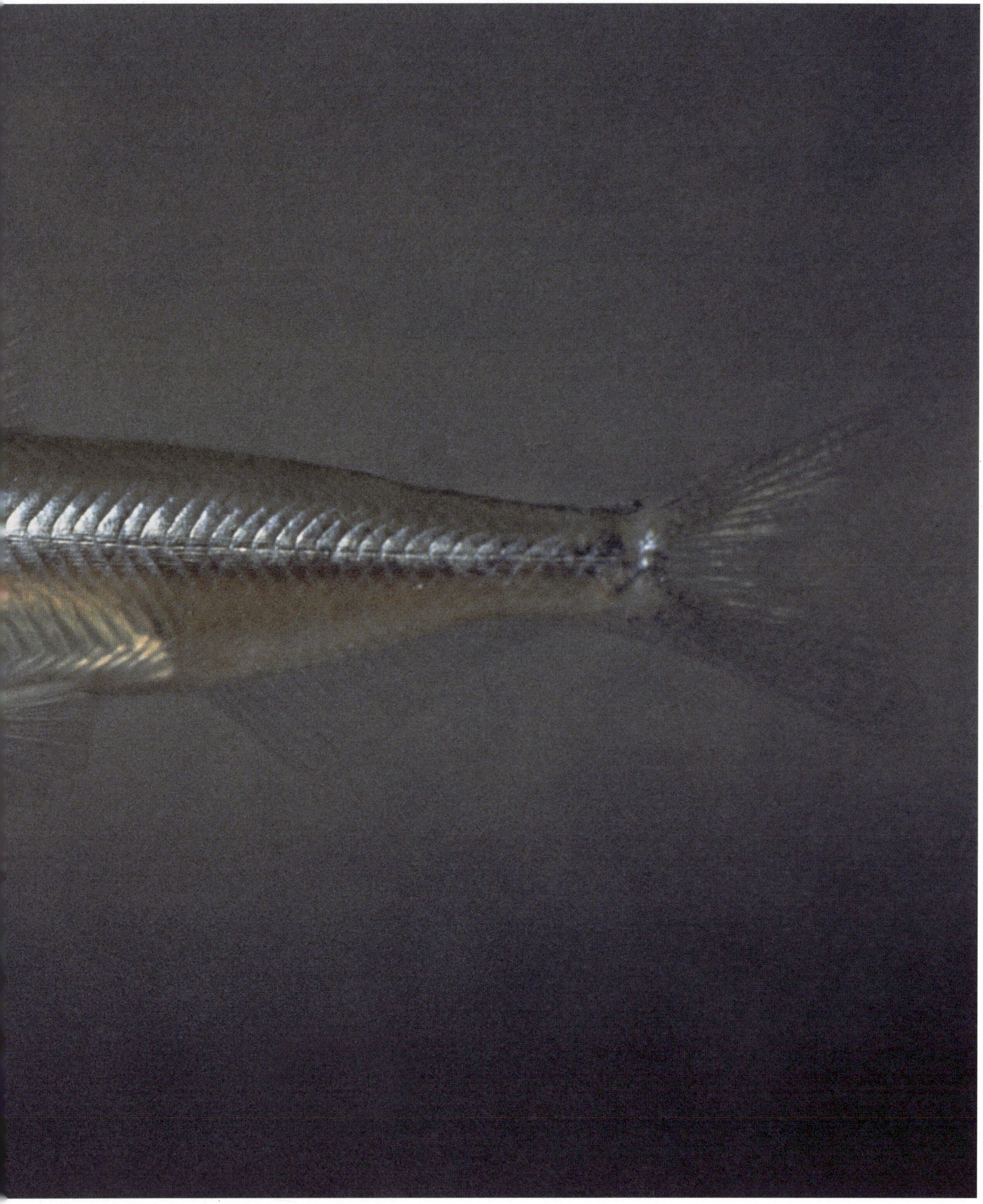

A GLOBAL REACH

TWENTY-FIVE YEARS AGO, THE IDEA that a U.S.-based organization could be effective in promoting environmental agendas in China and India—two countries that together account for more than a third of the world's population—seemed outlandish. But Barbara Finamore, the senior strategic director of our Asia work, knew the opportunity for collaboration would be too great to pass up. In 1996, she set up our first international project in China.

Three things guided our thinking about China. First, China's environmental problems were mounting, and the country would benefit from learning how other countries have tackled their own pollution. Second, NRDC had a unique track record of developing environmental laws and enforcement approaches in the United States. Third, China was keen to improve energy efficiency in its industries and buildings, which meant there was great potential to shrink the country's carbon footprint. Barbara and her small team began introducing advanced energy efficiency and environmental policies to China. Ten years later, NRDC opened an office in Beijing, which today employs nearly 50 people.

We've accomplished a lot since then. We helped develop China's first green building codes and demand-side policy for the grid. We facilitated a pioneering partnership on energy efficiency between California and the Jiangsu province. We supported advancements in greening supply chains in China and policies that help make cities more sustainable. But perhaps most significantly, we introduced environmental regulatory and transparency practices that helped China improve its air and water laws, as well as their enforcement.

In 2012 and 2013, notorious smog events covered broad swaths of China. That's when NRDC began a new project targeting China's coal consumption, which is not only the main contributor to the country's air quality problems but also the world's largest single source of carbon emissions. After working with leading Chinese researchers and institutions to develop policy recommendations and road maps for capping China's coal use, NRDC was happy to see the government adopt its first-ever binding coal cap target. In 2013, coal accounted for more than 67 percent of China's energy mix and half of the world's consumption. But now, just a handful of years later, the country is on track to slash the share of coal in its total energy consumption to 58 percent by the end of 2020. And China is just getting started, as we are continuing our efforts at the national and provincial levels. Some of our other essential work involves

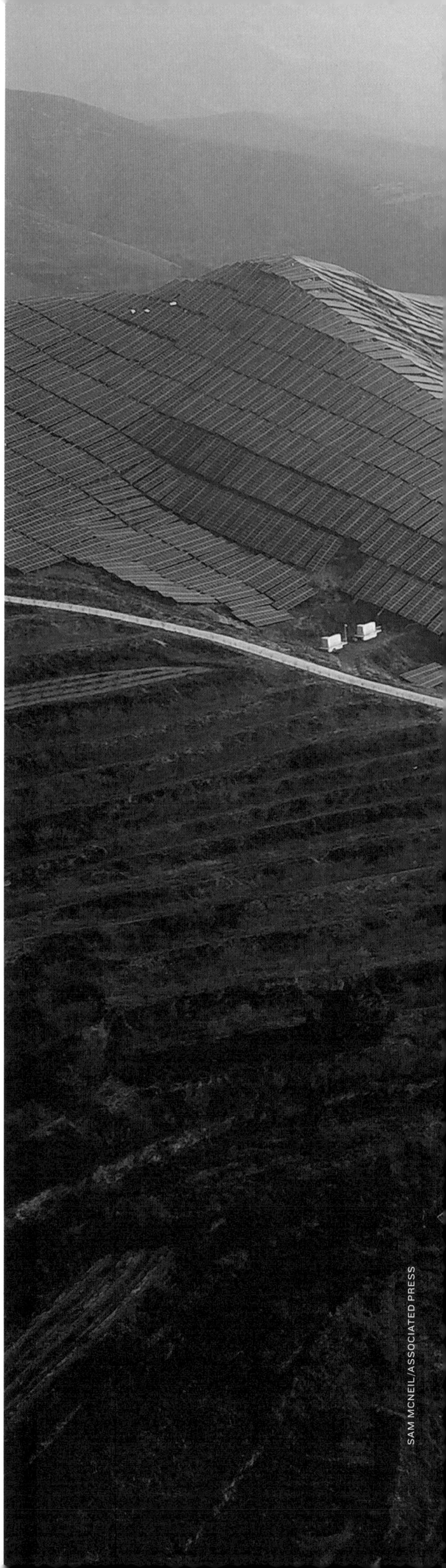

SAM MCNEIL/ASSOCIATED PRESS

A solar farm in Ruicheng County in central China's Shanxi Province, 2019.

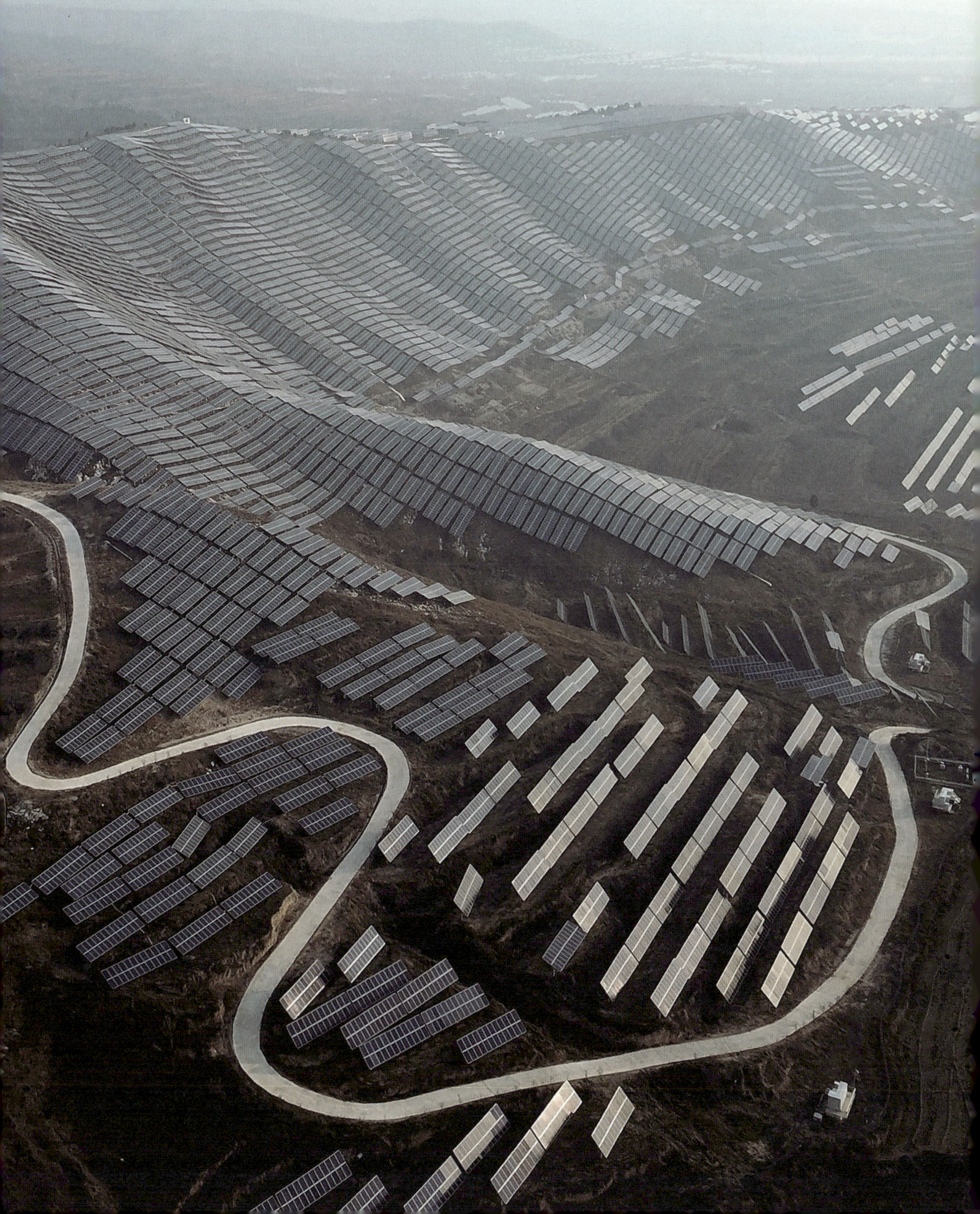

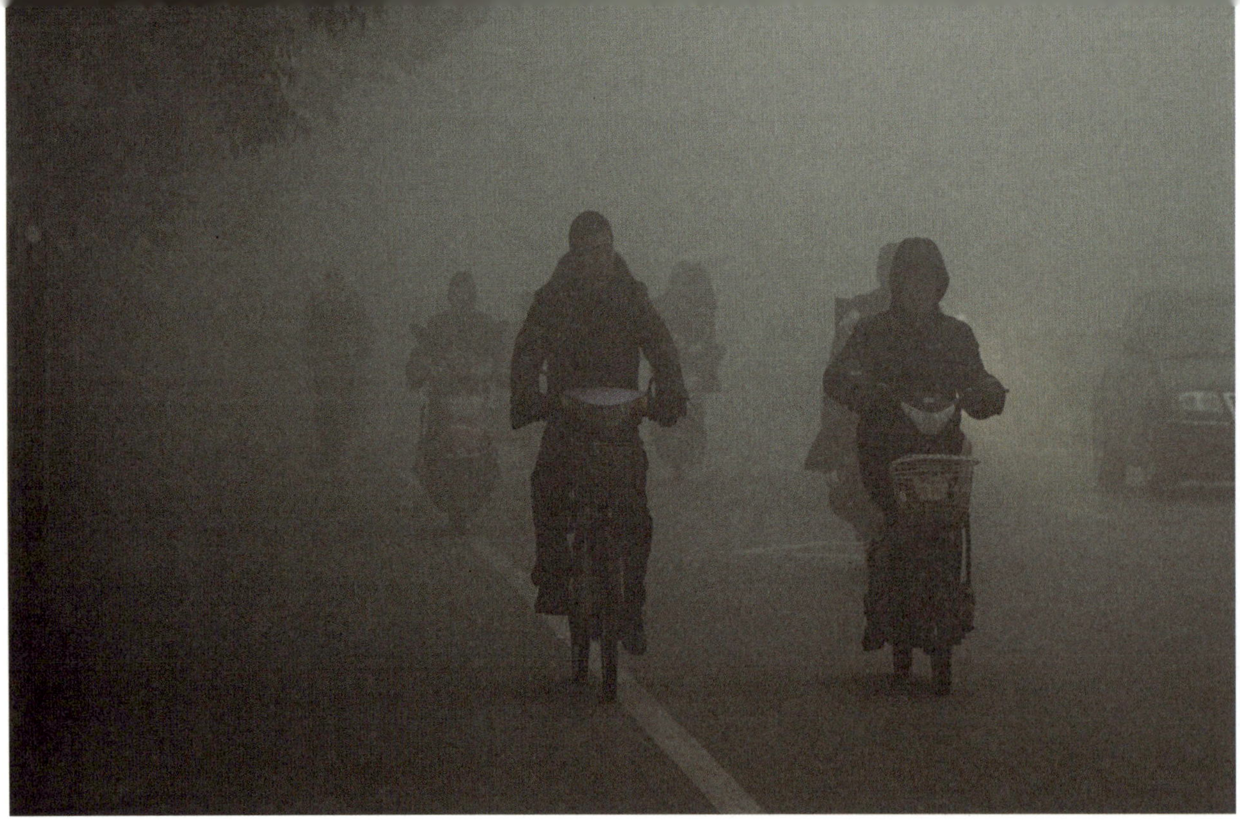

"In the 25 years since NRDC's China Program launched, China has made huge strides in environmental and climate action—and we are proud of having been there to provide essential support to its progress."

—JingJing Qian, senior director of the China Program

promotion of China's development of a national parks system, its implementation of pollution controls at ports, and its expansion of renewable energy storage capacity with the help of the world's biggest fleet of electric vehicles, already three million strong. We're proud of the role NRDC has played in China's impressive green transformation.

Meanwhile, in India, we launched a program to promote renewable energy in 2008. This presented a different kind of challenge than in China—and different opportunities. Although India has rapidly expanded its solar power market, coal still fuels 70 percent of its power supply, charging its fast-growing economy and delivering electricity to 300 million of its citizens who have no reliable access to it.

As in China, we are working on several fronts at once. Our India Program, founded by senior director Anjali Jaiswal, works with national, state, and local governments on market incentives for solar and wind power while combating soaring air pollution. The team also works to help scale energy efficiency codes for commercial buildings and household appliances—notably air conditioners.

Air-conditioning is a powerful symbol of the dilemma India faces. Demand for air conditioners has soared with rising incomes, yet the AC boom has aggravated the very problem to which it's responding. While cutting harmful carbon emissions is the ultimate answer to the climate crisis, extreme heat waves show that we also need to urgently mitigate the conditions that are already taking a devastating toll on public health.

Take the city of Ahmedabad, in the state of Gujarat, where India's prime minister, Narendra Modi, served for 13 years as chief minister. Ahmedabad's seven million residents have struggled to cope with temperatures that have reached 122 degrees Fahrenheit. After extreme heat took more than 1,000 lives in 2010—infants, the elderly, and low-wage, outdoor workers being the worst affected—the city began drafting countermeasures in collaboration with NRDC, the Indian Institute of Public Health Gandhinagar, and other groups.

In partnership with NRDC, Ahmedabad launched its Heat Action Plan in 2013 and has updated it annually. Its main strategy is the idea of preparedness—sharing knowledge about heat-related health risks and how to avoid them, readying local hospitals to deal with emergencies, and giving citizens red alerts via text messages to warn that dangerous temperatures are imminent. The plan couples this with low-cost, practical measures like "cool roofs," especially in vulnerable slum areas—reducing temperatures indoors by, for example, coating rooftops with reflective paint or covering them with wet jute sacking. "The Ahmedabad Heat Action Plan is a terrific example of how a model program can be scaled up," says former NRDC president Frances Beinecke, who has been deeply involved in our India work. Similar schemes are now in place in 100 cities and 23 states, helping to protect an estimated 700 million people.

We've drawn many lessons from our experiences so far in Asia. They've shown us that no challenge is too big to take on if you're willing to put in the years of spadework needed to build trust and credibility and to be guided by the two simple questions we asked in China a quarter century ago: "What do you need, and what can we do to help?"

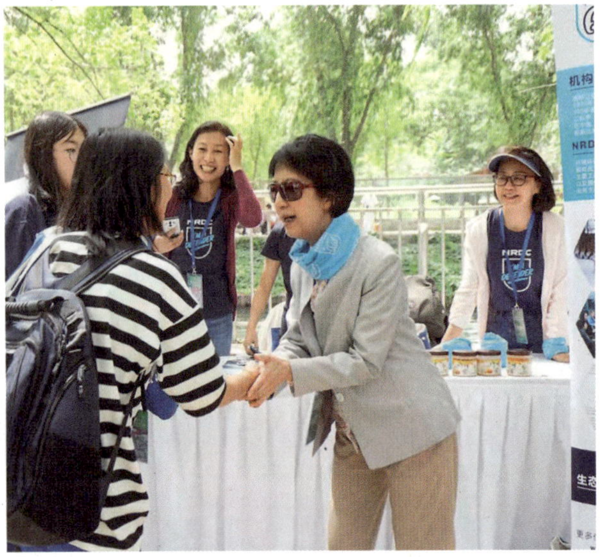

Since joining NRDC in 2002, JingJing Qian has worked to promote energy efficiency, clean energy use, and stronger environmental policy in China. Here, she and her team greet visitors at an NRDC event.

FROM TOP: ASSOCIATED PRESS; NRDC. OPPOSITE: ABBIE TRAYLER-SMITH/PANOS PICTURES/REDUX

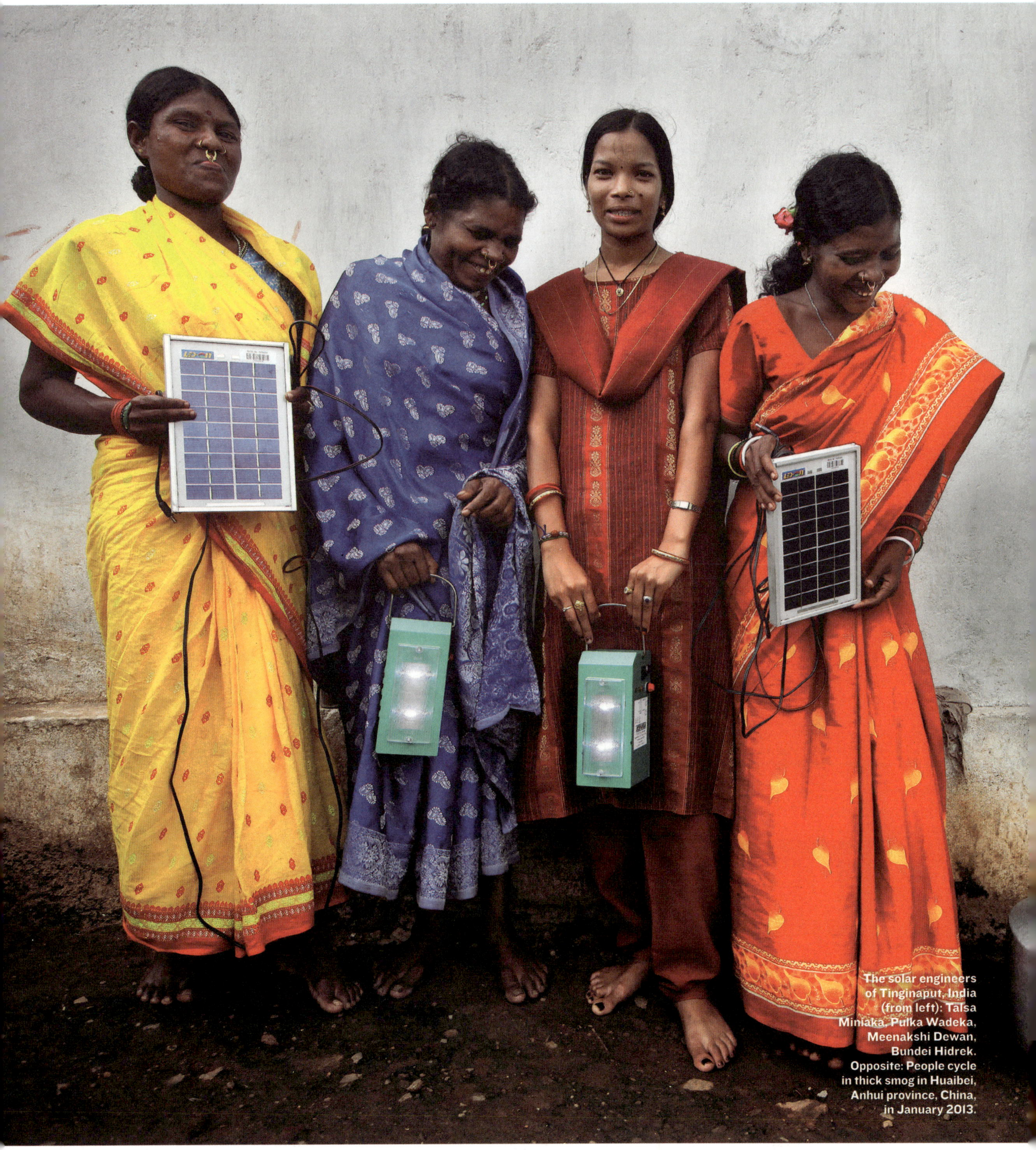

The solar engineers of Tinginaput, India (from left): Talsa Miniaka, Pulka Wadeka, Meenakshi Dewan, Bundei Hidrek. Opposite: People cycle in thick smog in Huaibei, Anhui province, China, in January 2013.

Solutions Spotlight

SUSTAINABLE WITH STYLE

Linda Greer, a senior scientist with NRDC from 1990 to 2018, is both a toxicologist and a virtuoso of win-win politics. Her trademark approach was showing polluting industries that shrinking their environmental footprint is also an excellent way of saving money.

In a globalized economy defined by the outsourcing of manufacturing to countries with lax environmental standards, Linda turned her attention to China and the apparel industry, which was discharging into waterways vast amounts of wastewater laden with toxic chemicals used for treating, dyeing, and rinsing fabric. Worse, manufacturers often didn't even know which mills were part of their supply chain.

Our answer was Clean by Design, a program created in 2009 by Linda and NRDC trustee Anna Scott Carter, who had years of experience with fashion industry giants like Ralph Lauren and Giorgio Armani. The program's signature list of 10 best practices demonstrated how simple measures—like reducing leaks, recycling rinsewater, and insulating steam pipes—could save the industry millions of dollars through reduced water and energy consumption.

Clean by Design has won converts in all parts of the industry, from mass-market giants like Puma and Levi-Strauss to luxury brands like Burberry to big-chain retailers such as H&M, Gap, and Target. "What makes Linda's work so revolutionary," said designer Stella McCartney, "is that it is simple and yet highly effective. I jumped—no, dived—at the chance to be part of it."

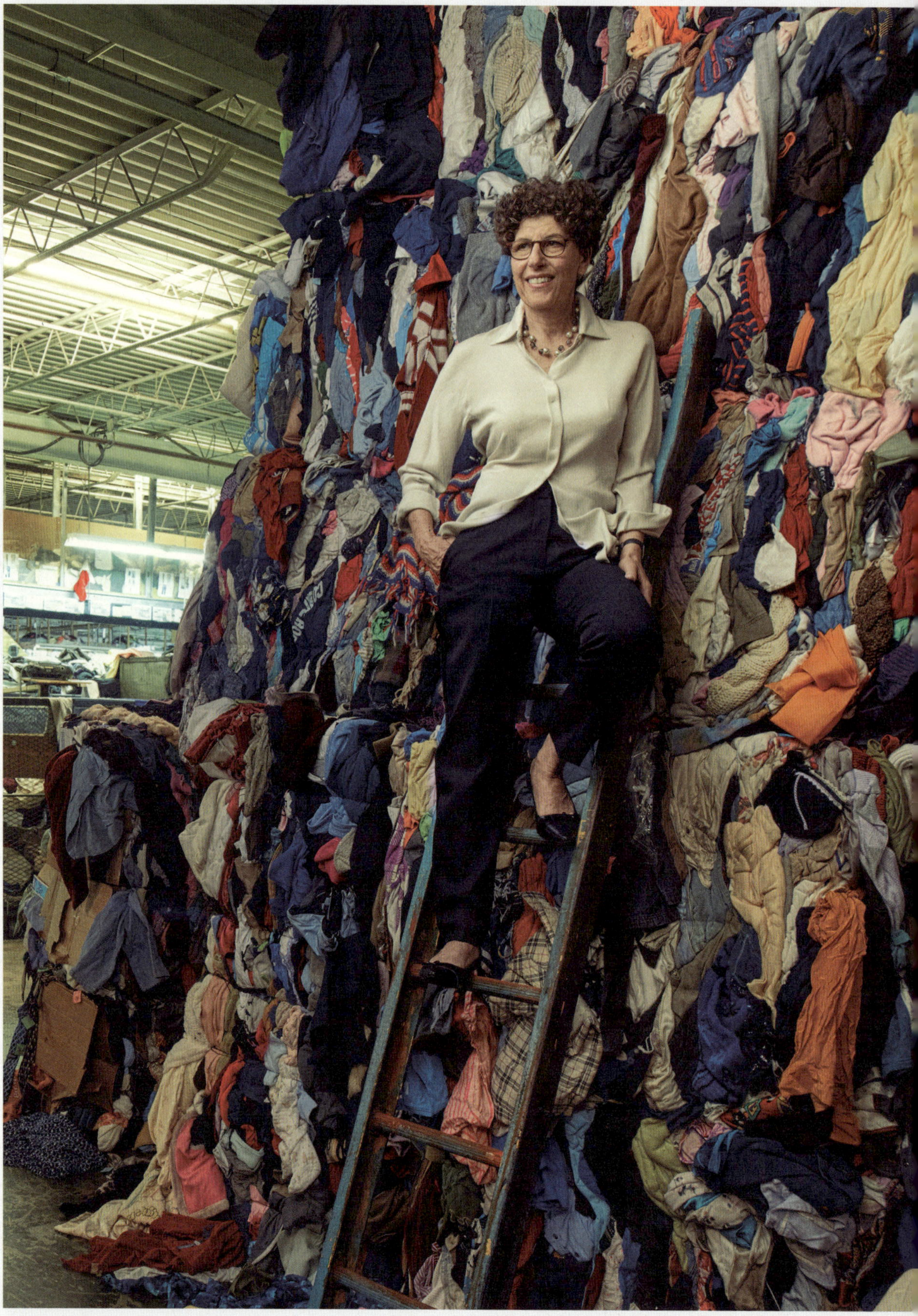

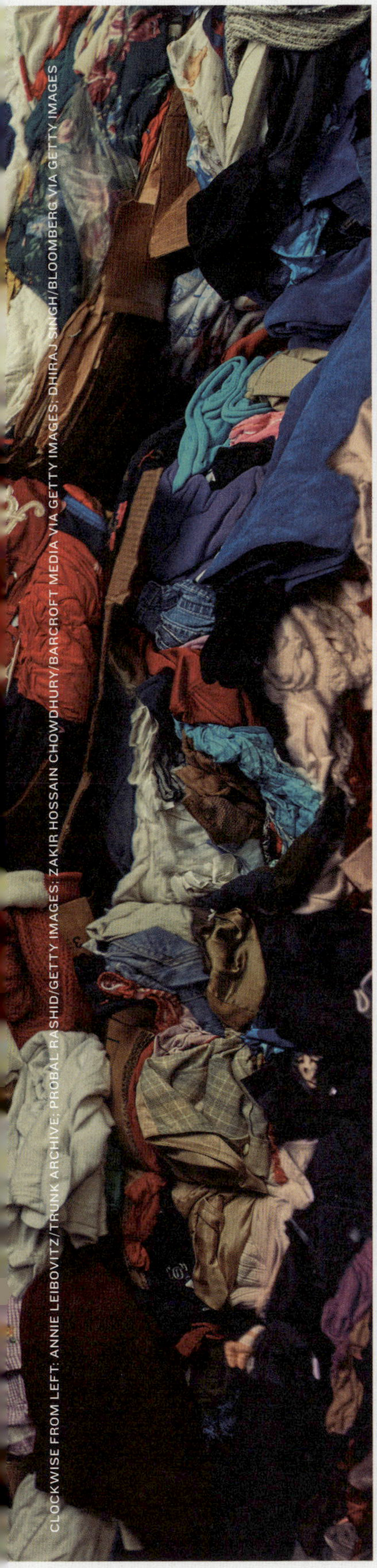

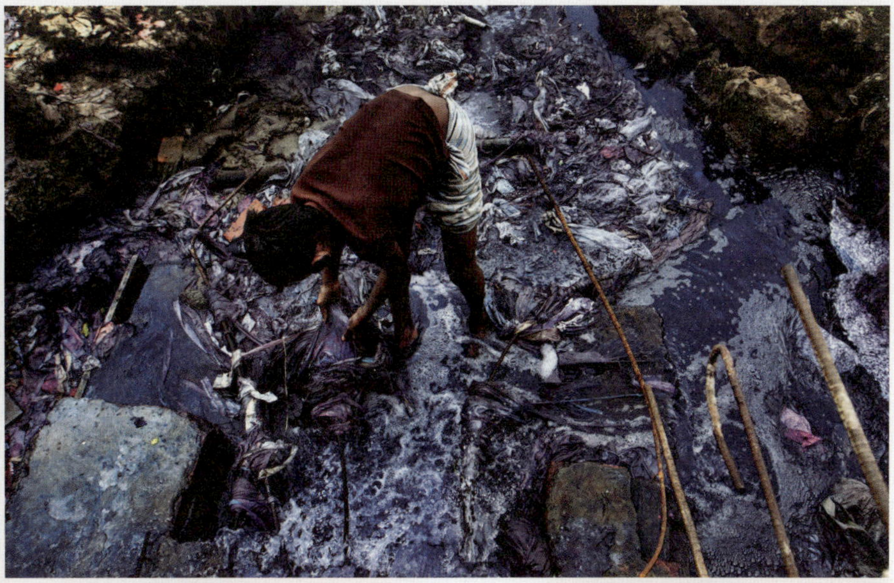

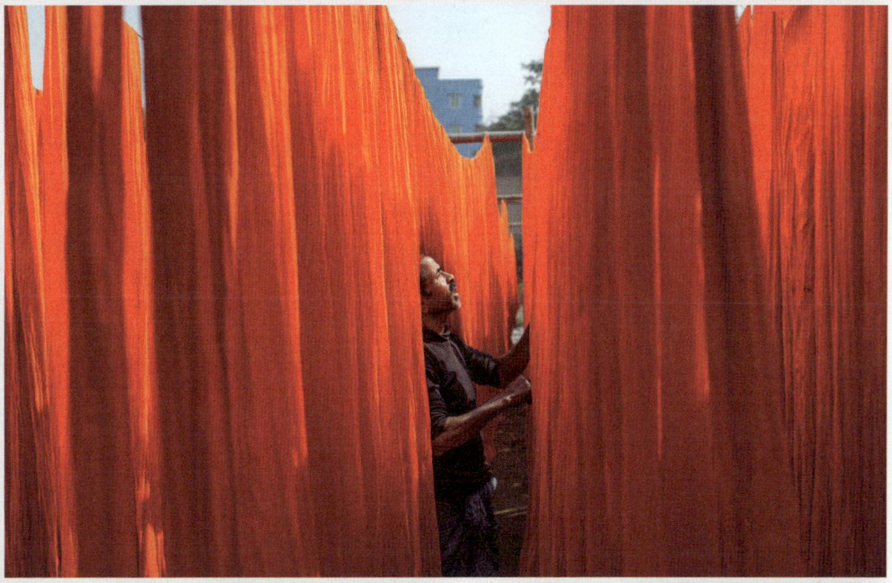

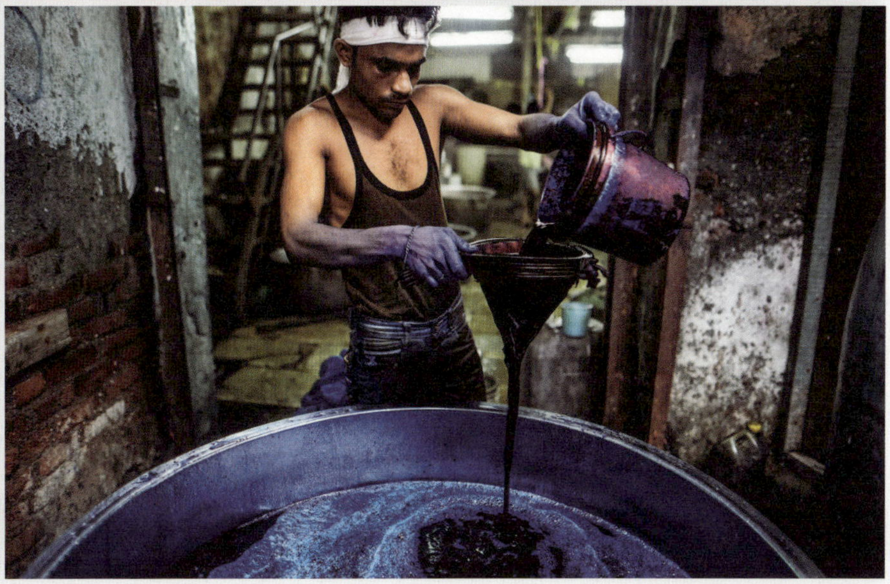

Far left: Linda Greer at 2ReWear, a textile-recycling company in Clifton, New Jersey. Top right: A nine-year-old boy in Bangladesh collects pieces of cloth he hopes to sell from the liquid waste of the dyeing industries—which are released directly into the Turag River. Middle right: A worker in Bangladesh inspects fabrics after they are dyed. Bottom right: A worker pours dye into a metal vat while preparing to dye fabric in a workshop in the Dharavi slum area of Mumbai, India.

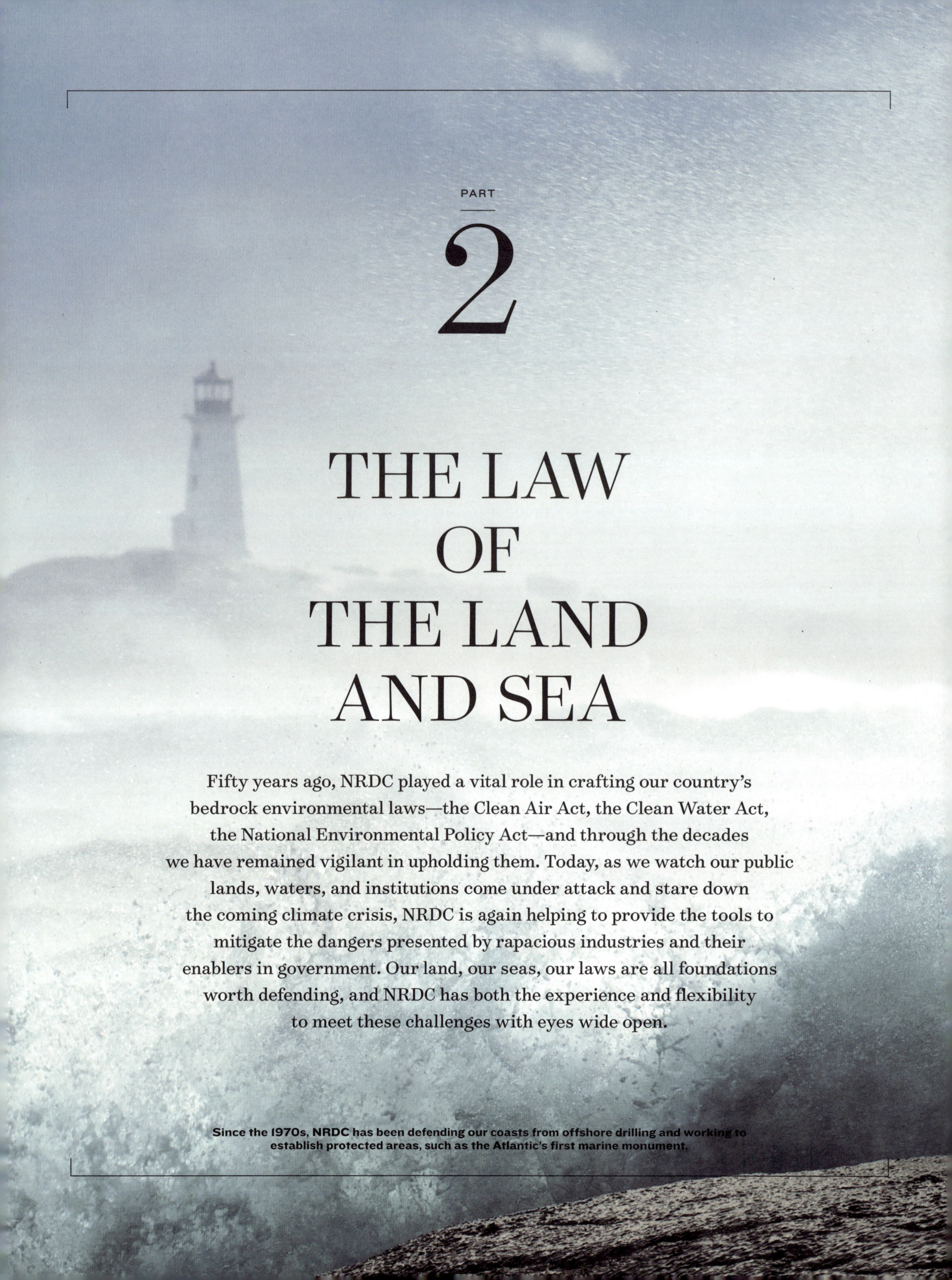

PART

2

THE LAW OF THE LAND AND SEA

Fifty years ago, NRDC played a vital role in crafting our country's bedrock environmental laws—the Clean Air Act, the Clean Water Act, the National Environmental Policy Act—and through the decades we have remained vigilant in upholding them. Today, as we watch our public lands, waters, and institutions come under attack and stare down the coming climate crisis, NRDC is again helping to provide the tools to mitigate the dangers presented by rapacious industries and their enablers in government. Our land, our seas, our laws are all foundations worth defending, and NRDC has both the experience and flexibility to meet these challenges with eyes wide open.

Since the 1970s, NRDC has been defending our coasts from offshore drilling and working to establish protected areas, such as the Atlantic's first marine monument.

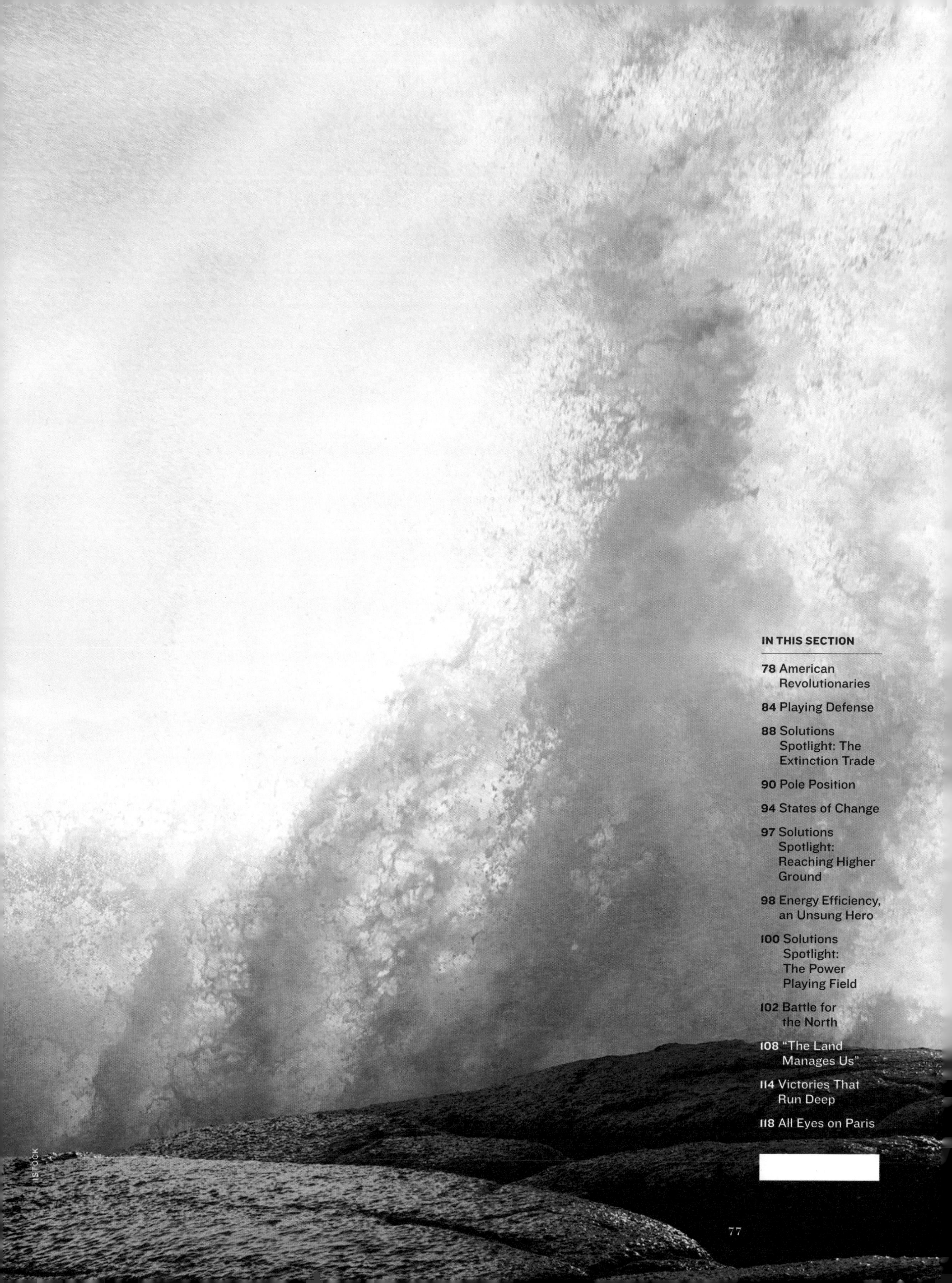

ISTOCK

IN THIS SECTION

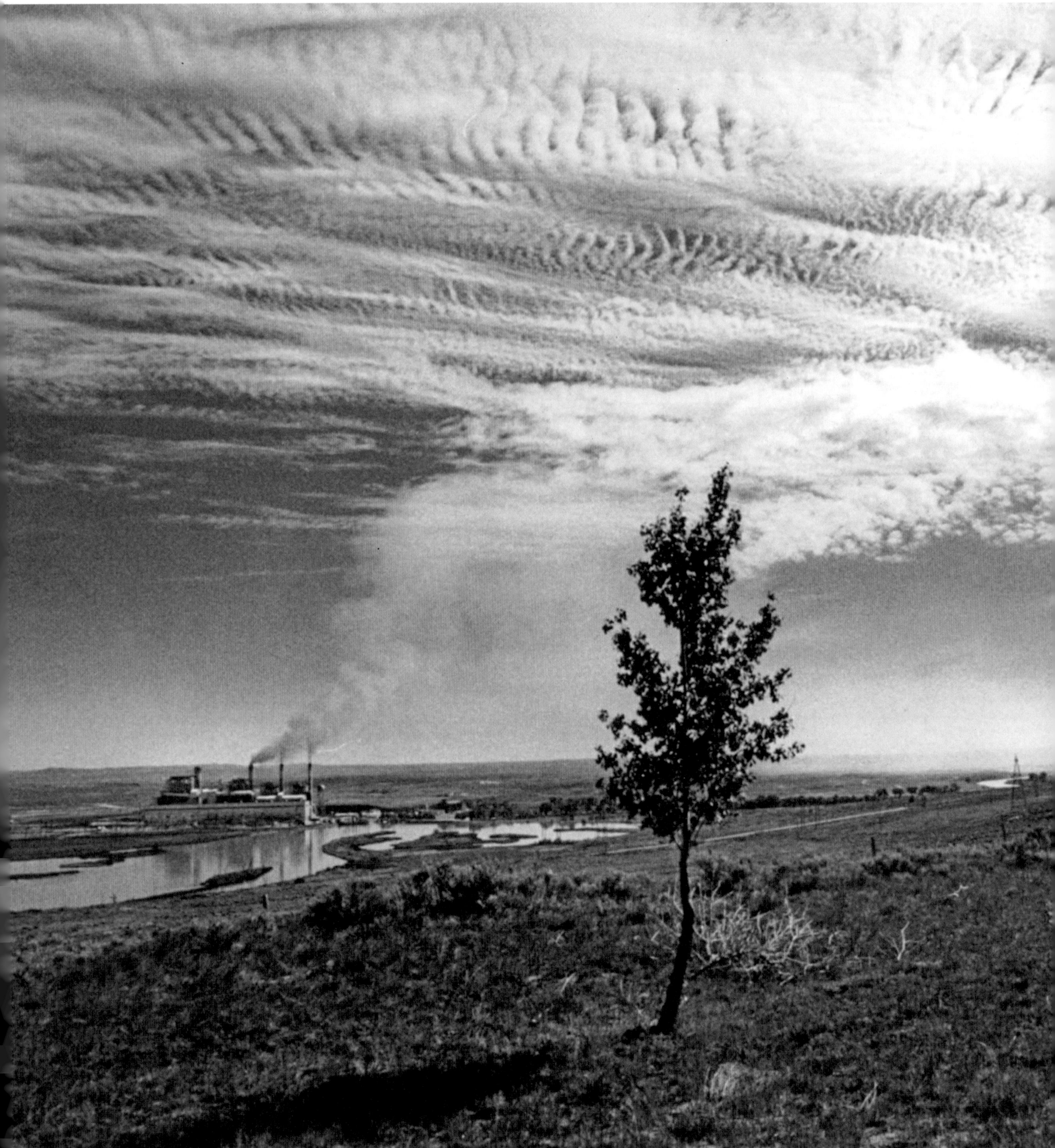

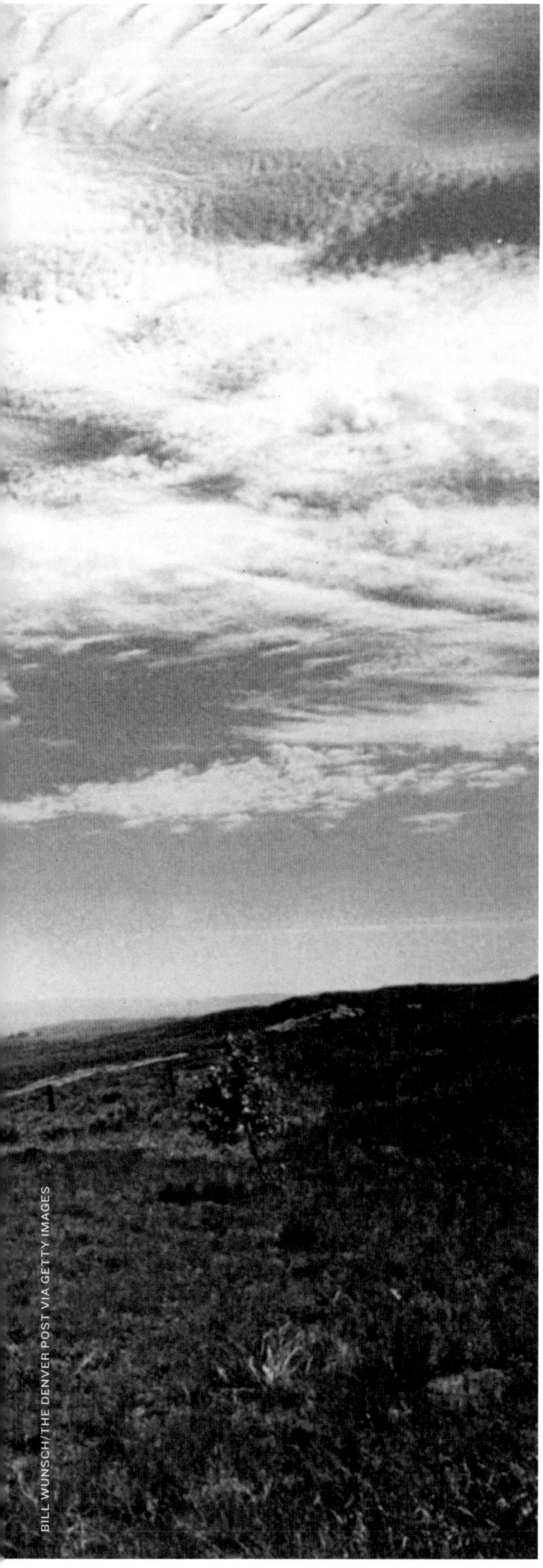

AMERICAN REVOLUTIONARIES

NRDC USES EVERY POSSIBLE LEGAL TOOL on the books to protect our environment. But two pieces of legislation in particular lie at the heart and soul of our mission: the 1970 Clean Air Act and the 1972 Clean Water Act, including the acts' respective amendments, which NRDC has been instrumental in crafting.

On its passage 50 years ago, the Clean Air Act required the newly established EPA to set air quality standards that would protect human health and demanded a plan from all 50 states on how they would comply. Two years later, the Clean Water Act set the ambitious (yet still unmet) goal of eliminating waterborne pollutants by 1985 and instituted a strict permitting system for pollutant dischargers. Both acts encourage ordinary citizens to bring suit against polluters and to challenge EPA actions that don't follow the law. NRDC has capitalized on that to the fullest, targeting both dirty industries and the EPA itself.

From the beginning, we established a clear division of labor. Dick Ayres and David Hawkins took on clean air while Gus Speth and Ed Strohbehn handled clean water. Within our first three years, NRDC had won dozens of cases. In the process, we'd proved to government agencies that we knew as much—and often more—about the relevant science as they did. They also came to know that NRDC would hold them accountable not only for failure to enforce the new rules but also for writing them properly in the first place. One EPA official joked that we were "like the American Revolutionaries—behind every tree."

I'll single out just a couple of these early cases, which I've chosen for two reasons. One is that they set the template for the two-pronged "write and enforce" approach, which has underpinned countless other cases we've fought over the past half century. The other is that they set the stage directly for the battles we've now had to refight during the Trump administration.

In two lawsuits in 1971 and 1972, we took on the powerful Tennessee Valley Authority (TVA), the nation's biggest utility. TVA was popular with the public because it provided millions of customers with low-cost electricity—something it accomplished by burning cheap, dirty, high-sulfur coal in its power plants. The TVA's stratagem for avoiding the

Coal-fired power plants like this one near Glenrock, Wyoming, experienced a building boom in the 1970s, to the detriment of the country's air quality.

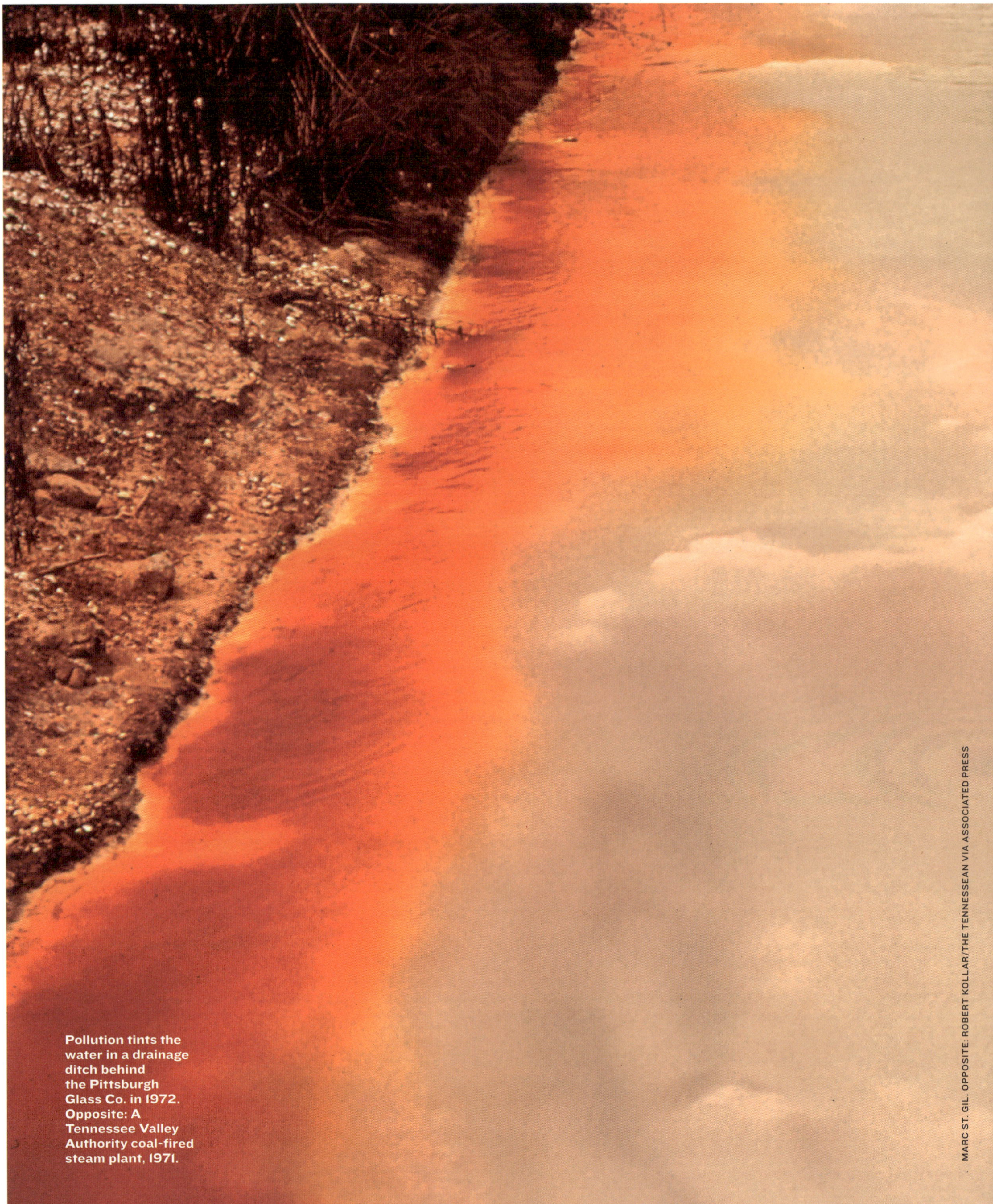

Pollution tints the water in a drainage ditch behind the Pittsburgh Glass Co. in 1972. Opposite: A Tennessee Valley Authority coal-fired steam plant, 1971.

MARC ST. GIL. OPPOSITE: ROBERT KOLLAR/THE TENNESSEAN VIA ASSOCIATED PRESS

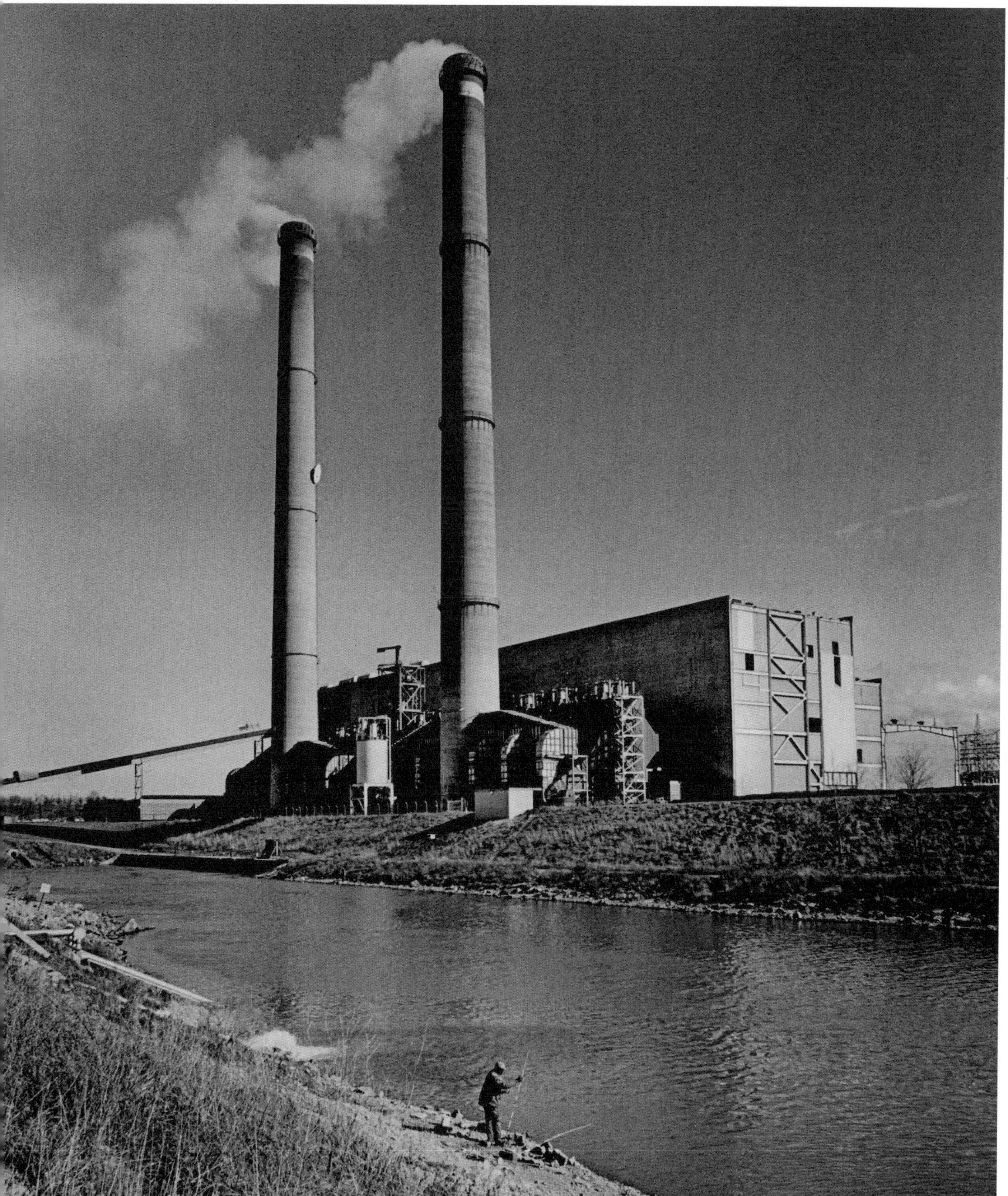

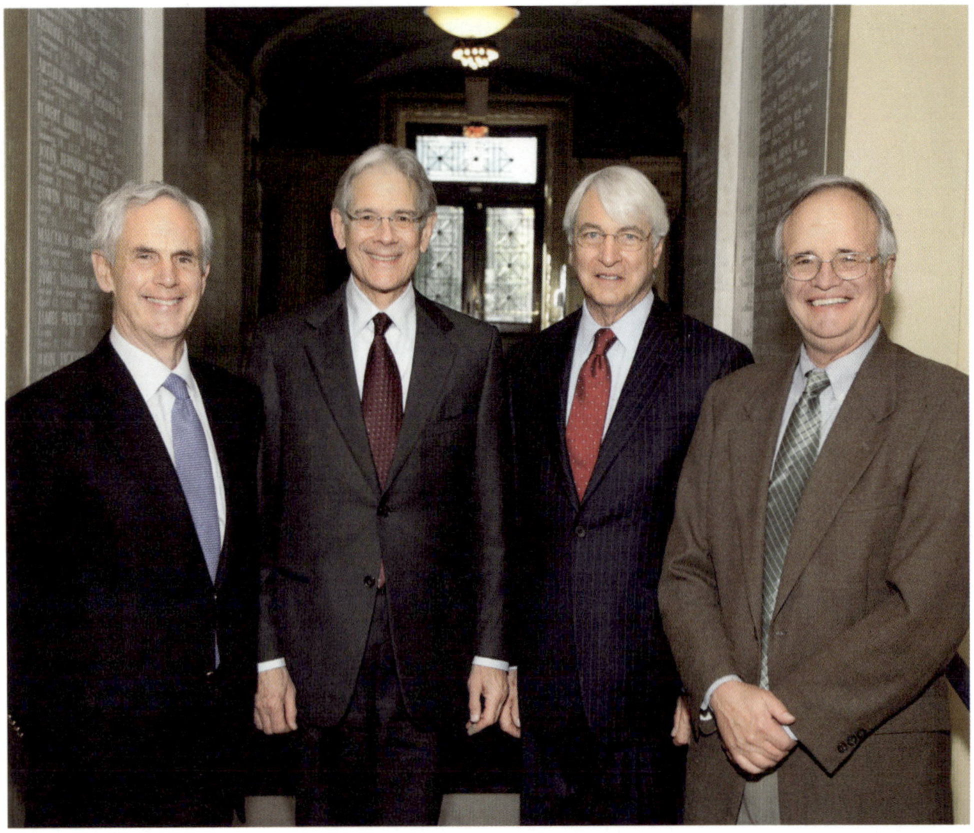

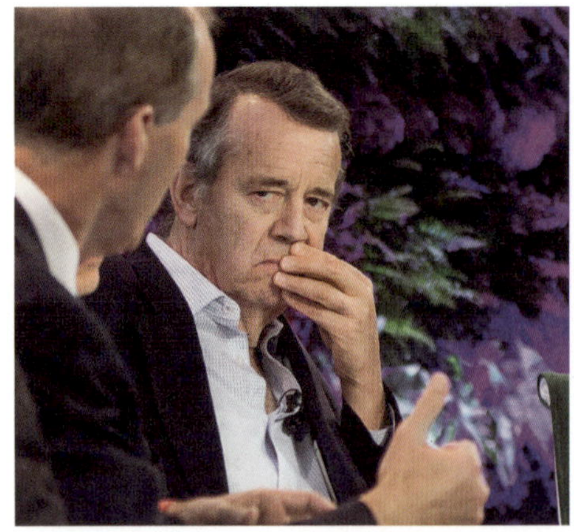

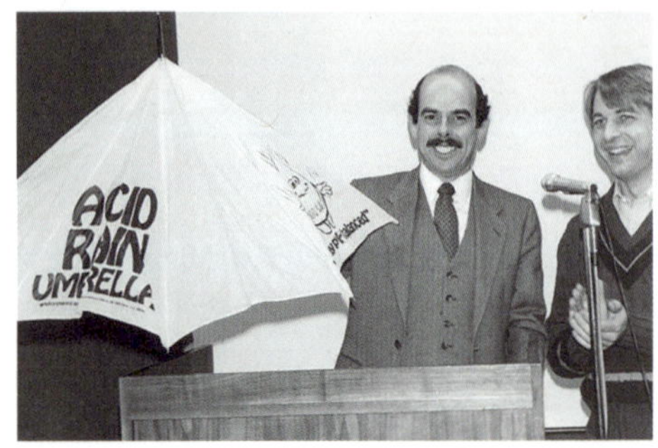

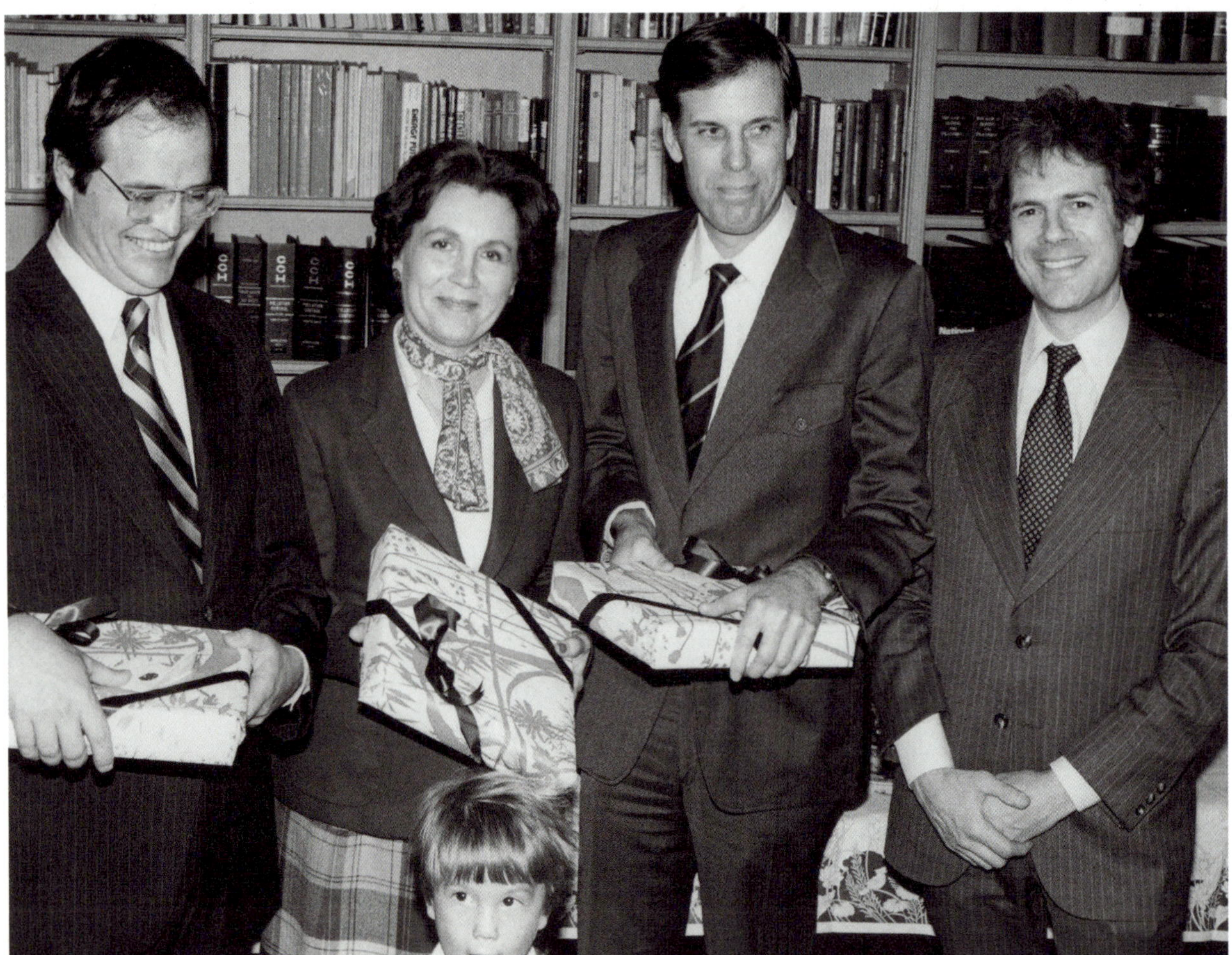

Top left, from left: NRDC cofounders John Bryson, Ed Strohbehn, Dick Ayres, and Gus Speth at a 2010 reunion at Yale. Top right: David Hawkins speaks on a *Fortune* magazine panel about renewable energy in 2013. Top right, bottom: Congressman Henry Waxman (left) and Ed in the 1980s. Bottom, from left: Gus, who was serving as chairman of the Council of Environmental Quality at the time of this photo in 1981, with council members Jane Yarn and Robert Harris, and Ed, who was the council's executive director at the time. (Gus's son, Jim, makes a cameo.)

CLOCKWISE FROM TOP LEFT: HAROLD SHAPIRO/YALE UNIVERSITY; STUART ISETT/FORTUNE BRAINSTORM GREEN; NRDC (2)

pollution-control technologies mandated by the Clean Air Act was to build towering smokestacks, more than 500 feet tall, and to make a spurious claim that the height of the stacks would improve air quality by dispersing pollution over a wider area. Our response was a successful lawsuit based on new science that showed how harmful emissions of sulfur dioxide and nitrogen oxides turn into even more toxic acids before falling to earth. This was the first time any environmental organization had tackled the problem of acid rain.

Prevailing in court was not enough, however. Dick and David began to focus on loopholes within the Clean Air Act that needed to be fixed. Thanks largely to their work, the act underwent two rounds of extensive amendments, the first in 1977 and the second in 1990.

Even more powerful than the TVA was the agency we went up against in our first landmark case under the Clean Water Act: the U.S. Army Corps of Engineers. The goal of the act was to make the nation's waters "fishable and swimmable" and clean enough for aquatic life to thrive, but the Corps considered it to only apply to "navigable waters," which meant that, since you can't sail a boat through a swamp or down a small seasonal stream, these waters were exempt. However, by the 1970s, scientists had demonstrated clearly that these wetlands, a traditional dumping ground for industry, were critical for flood control, for filtering out pollution, and for countless birds, amphibians, and other wildlife.

Our 1975 victory in *NRDC v. Callaway*—Howard H. "Bo" Callaway was the secretary of the army at the time—was a milestone in environmental law because it recognized that the act covered all kinds of waters broadly. Important amendments to the Clean Water Act two years later deliberately maintained that coverage. By that time, NRDC had become the acknowledged national leader of the fight for clean water as well as clean air.

What echoes down the years from those early victories, however, is how history repeats itself. The Ford administration's response to *NRDC v. Callaway* was to issue dire warnings that every farm pond in America was at risk from unelected, overzealous bureaucrats. President Trump repeated this message almost verbatim when he vowed to revoke the Obama administration's 2015 Clean Water Rule, a story I'll tell later in this book.

FROM THE FRONTLINES

Daniel Mundy Jr.

New York City firefighter Daniel Mundy Jr. has lived his whole life on Jamaica Bay—the 25,000-acre span of marshes, meadowland, beaches, and dunes tucked inconspicuously into the city's outer boroughs. His father has too. "As a kid, you got into your little boat in the morning, and as long as you had a half tank of gas or more, you were good to go explore for the whole day," Daniel remembers. "We were intimately aware of every turn in every marsh, and that's why we started to see the changes first. The pollution became so obvious."

In the early 1990s, the city began dumping improperly treated, nitrogen-rich wastewater into the bay. "At the time, nitrogen was just this natural thing—you put it on lawns as fertilizer," Daniel says. "It wasn't on anyone's radar as a problem." But those skyrocketing nitrogen levels caused big issues for the bay: reduced oxygen in the now rust-colored water, algal blooms, dead zones, massive fish die-offs, and receding wetlands. Suddenly, Jamaica Bay—once a bastion of biodiversity serving as a habitat to sea turtles, porpoises, more than 80 fish species, and one in every five kinds of North American birds—became inhospitable.

Determined to bring the bay back to life, Daniel and his father launched the nonprofit Jamaica Bay Ecowatchers and soon partnered with NRDC and other local conservation groups to tackle the wastewater problem. Backed by science and the Clean Water Act, the group took city and state officials to task in a yearslong negotiation that eventually culminated in a legal settlement. Facing the pressure of litigation, the city finally committed to installing innovative pollution-control measures at its waste treatment plants and to setting aside $15 million for marsh restoration and improved water-quality monitoring in the bay.

Today, Jamaica Bay is once again a refuge for wildlife as well as New Yorkers looking to reconnect with nature. "None of this would've been possible without the personal commitment of NRDC's lawyers," Daniel says. "I now regularly see the Department of Environmental Protection boats coming into the bay, and they're busy testing the water, right where we required them to."

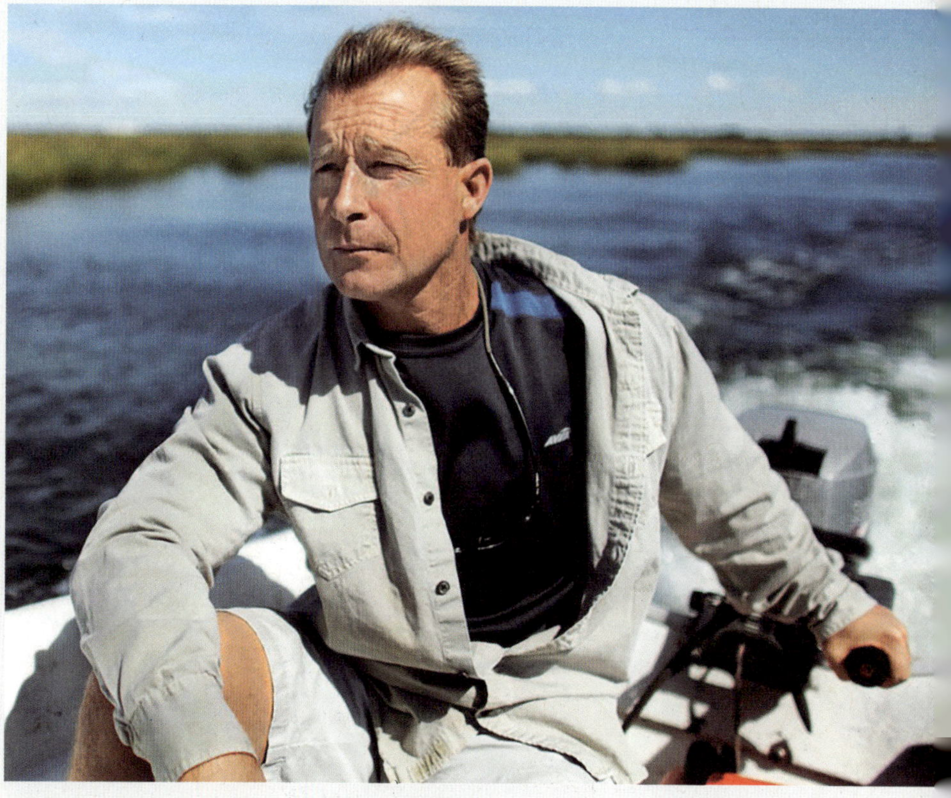

Daniel Mundy Jr. on Jamaica Bay, New York.

KRISTEN LUCE

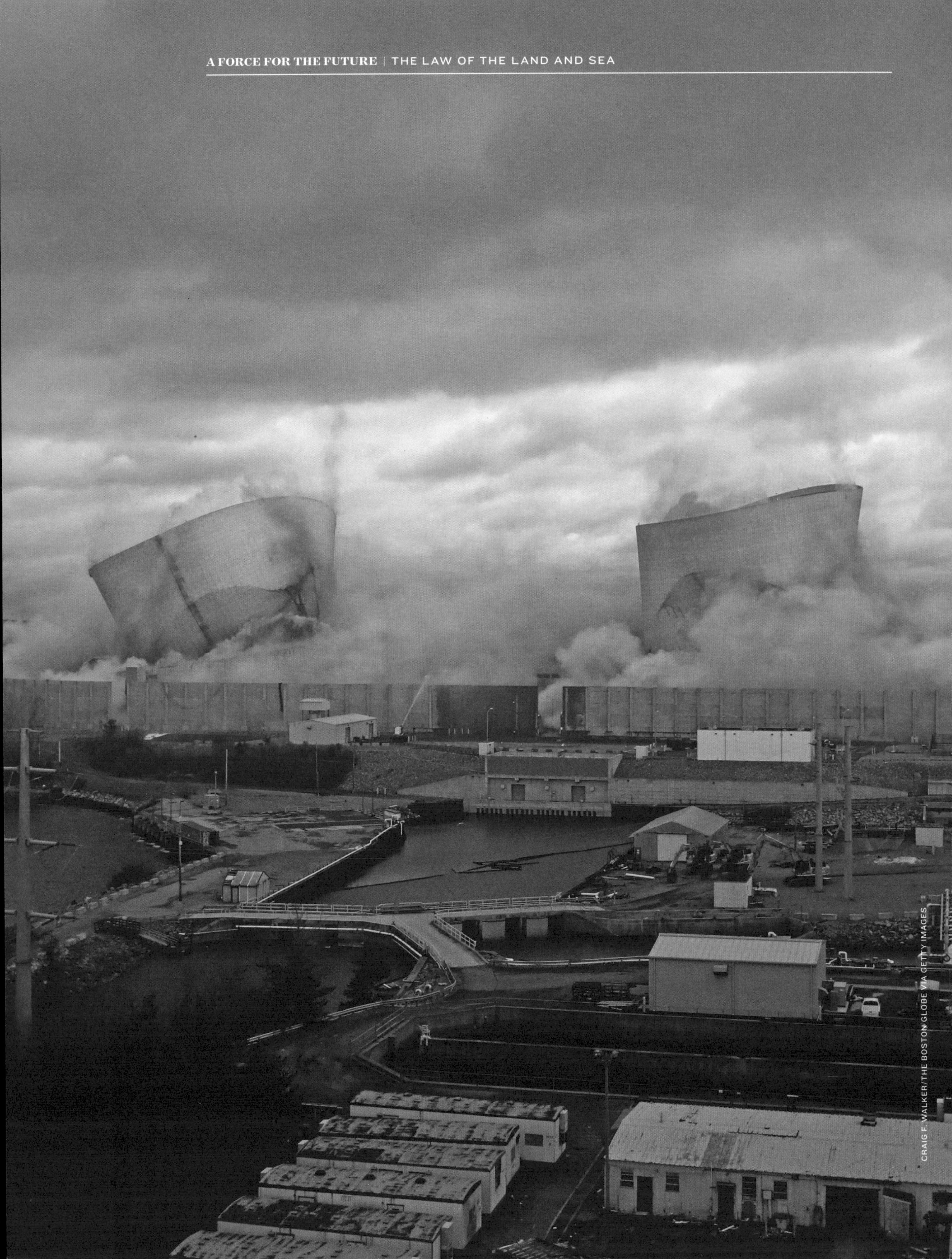

CRAIG F. WALKER/THE BOSTON GLOBE VIA GETTY IMAGES

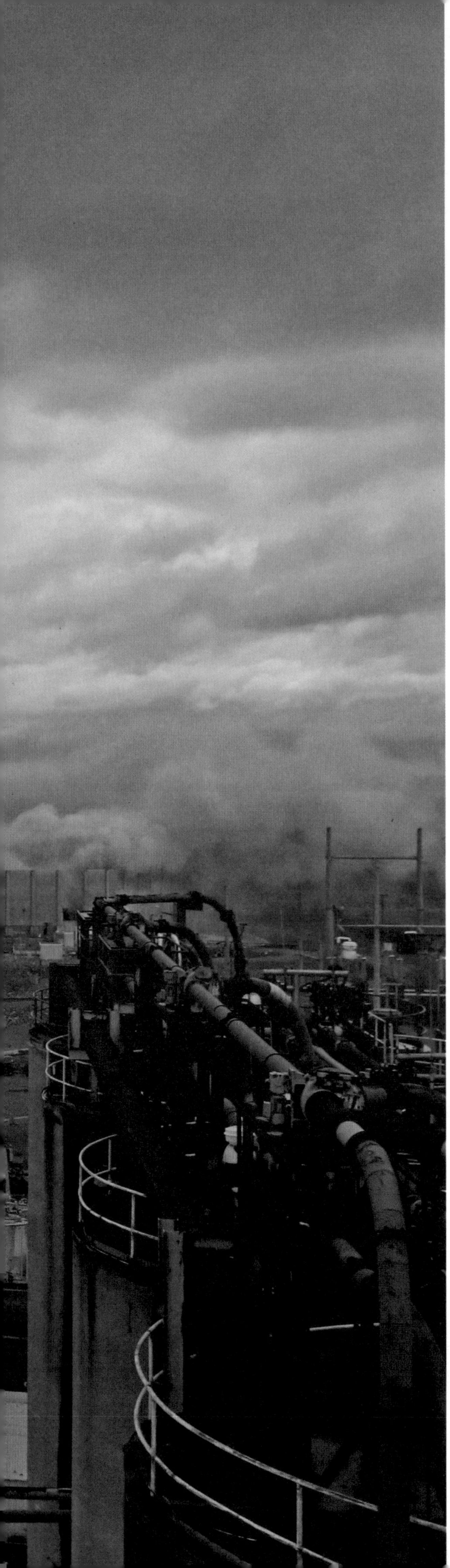

PLAYING DEFENSE

IN DECEMBER 2019, NRDC FILED ITS 100TH lawsuit against the Trump administration. That's roughly one for every 10 days of the administration. As of February 2020, 62 have been resolved, and we've lost only six. In many cases, the administration's arguments so flagrantly favored ideology and special interests over scientific fact and legal logic that the judges virtually laughed them out of court.

President Trump's first EPA administrator, Scott Pruitt, did many bad things, but he often did them badly. His successor, former coal lobbyist Andrew Wheeler, has proved to be smarter—or, if you prefer, more cunning. His sights are set on crippling two of the signal accomplishments of the Obama administration: the Clean Power Plan and the Clean Water Rule.

Announced in 2015, the Clean Power Plan set the first national standards for reducing carbon pollution from its largest source: coal-fired power plants. Its goal was to cut emissions by 32 percent by 2030 while stimulating the growth of a clean energy economy. To do so, the plan set reasonable state-specific targets and offered flexible options for meeting them. With its decades of scientific, technical, legal, and policy expertise, NRDC helped show that the plan was both feasible and affordable.

Polluters routinely cry wolf over having to comply with responsible public oversight. But David Doniger, the senior strategic director of NRDC's Climate & Clean Energy Program, points to the Clean Air Act as "the single-most cost-effective statute across the entire federal government." Agreed, industry invested billions to comply, but, by EPA calculations, the act has yielded $22 trillion in public benefits, including the prevention of 240,000 premature deaths and other healthcare costs, the reduction of crop damage, and improvements in visibility.

Faced with hard facts like these, the Trump administration instead doubled down on coal. In August 2018, it rolled out the so-called Affordable Clean Energy plan, a do-nothing replacement for the Clean Power Plan. Trump's new plan sets no requirements for power plants to cut carbon pollution but gives the oldest and dirtiest plants many ways of avoiding any reductions in their harmful emissions. It also weakens the limits on carbon pollution from new coal plants, using standards based on decades-old technology. This scheme was sold to the public in the name of cleaner energy and improved efficiency. Wheeler's former clients were thrilled.

Meanwhile, the goal of the 2015 Clean Water Rule was to clarify requirements of the 1972 Clean Water Act after a pair of Supreme Court rulings left confusion about exactly which waters warranted protection under the act. After careful

Two concrete cooling towers were demolished in April 2019 at the former Brayton Point Power Station in Massachusetts, once the largest coal-fired power plant in New England.

analysis of more than 1,200 peer-reviewed publications, President Obama's rule was based on a clear scientific understanding of how the country's entire hydrologic system works—notably our wetlands, the very issue on which we'd fought the Army Corps of Engineers 40 years earlier.

Repeal of the rule, and its replacement in January 2020 by Trump's so-called Navigable Waters Protection Rule (which we call the "Dirty Water Rule"), would return many waters to the bad old days before the Clean Water Act, when factories, the agricultural industry, and real estate developers routinely dumped pollutants into streams and wetlands. The most jaw-dropping part is that the administration says it has no idea how many water bodies its changes will affect or what the public health and environmental consequences will be. According to prior EPA studies and NRDC's own analysis, Trump's Dirty Water Rule will compromise the health of nearly two million miles of streams and about half of our wetlands and threaten drinking water sources for tens of millions of Americans.

Needless to say, NRDC is fighting these rollbacks on all fronts. Trump's assault on the environment may be unprecedented, but it's also a movie we've seen before. We stymied the worst excesses of the Reagan and Bush years with far fewer resources than we have today, which now includes hundreds of the best lawyers, scientists, and policy advocates in the nation. They unite the skills of three generations, inspired by the veterans of our clean air work, like the two Davids—Doniger and Hawkins (who says he won't retire until the last coal plant is retired). Our principal clean air advocate, John Walke, our principal clean water advocate, Jon Devine, and the codirectors of our superb litigation team, Aaron Colangelo and Michael Wall, represent NRDC's second generation. And the attorneys leading the courtroom battles to save the Clean Power Plan and the Clean Water Rule, such as Ben Longstreth, Lissa Lynch, Cassie Rahm, Jolie McLaughlin, and Michelle Wu, embody a new generation of rising stars. With talent like this in our ranks, it's no wonder that our confidence remains undimmed, even in the darkest of times.

Wetlands cover roughly 110 million acres of the United States. They filter pollution, replenish groundwater, and provide habitat for wildlife. Protecting these ecosystems is critical to the health of our environment, and ourselves.

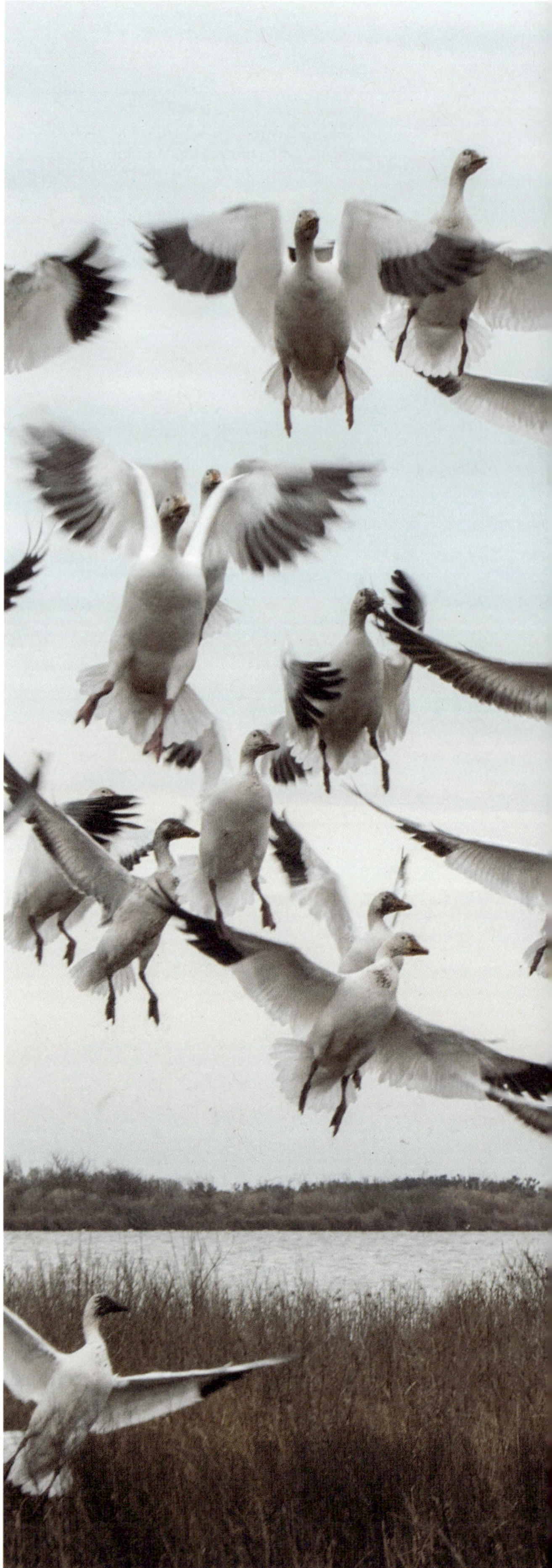

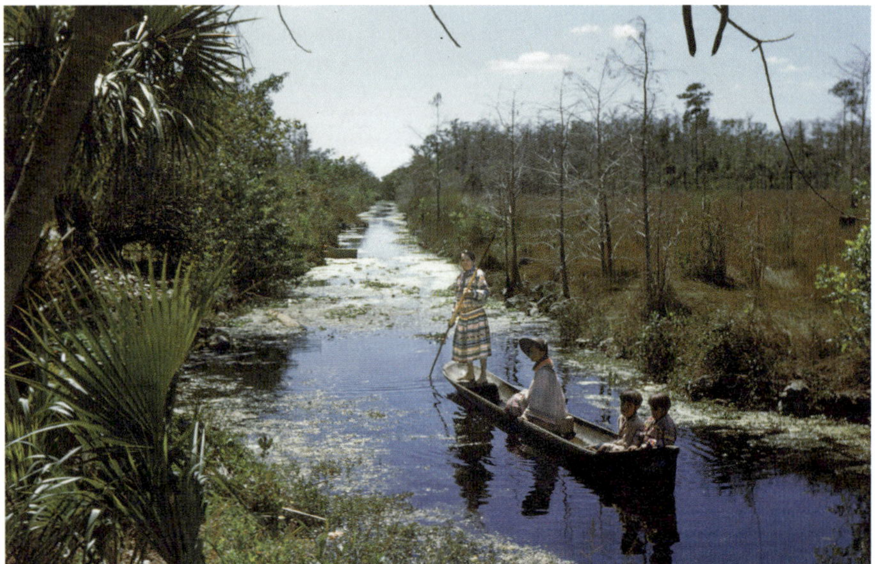

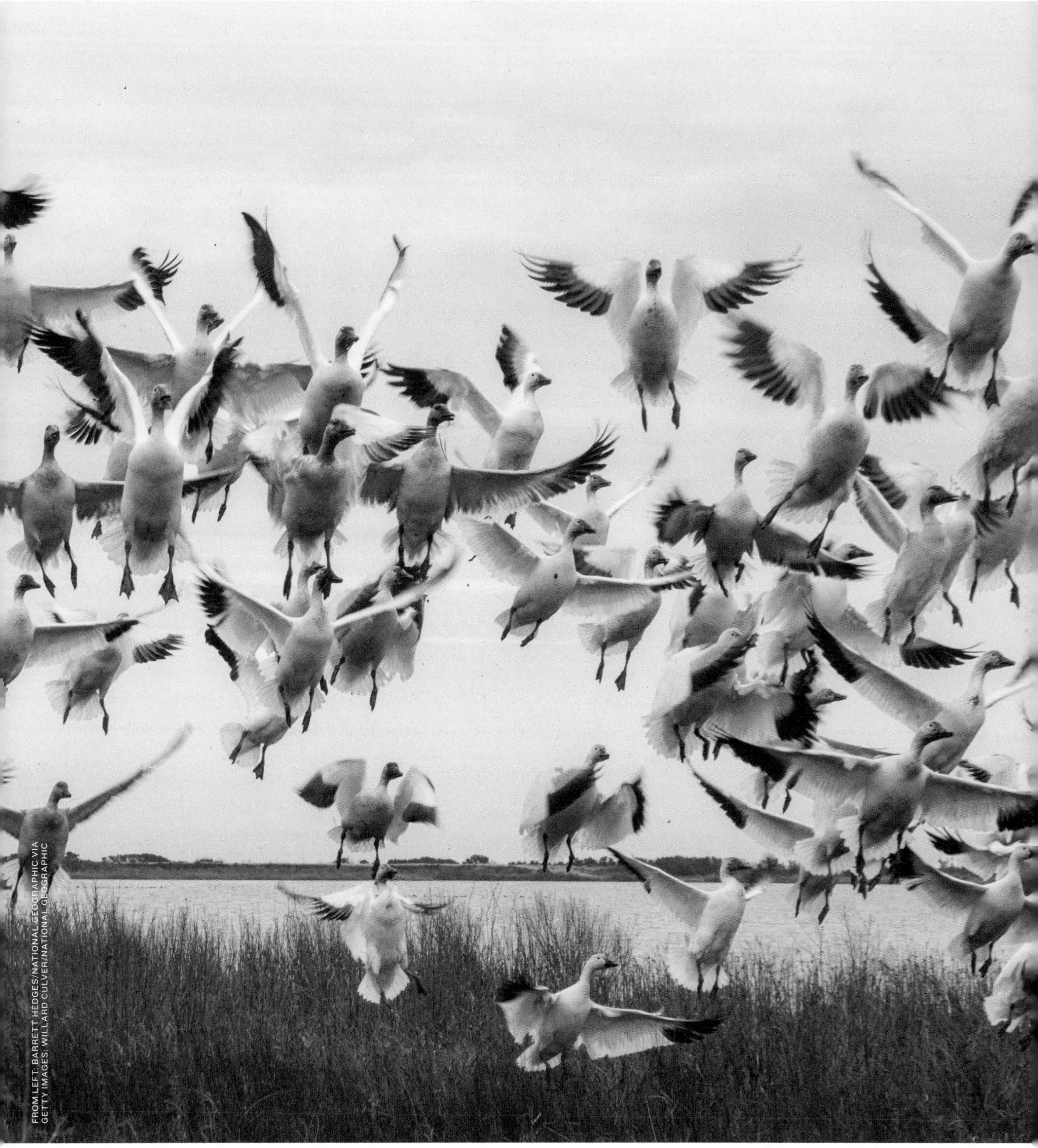

FROM LEFT: BARRETT HEDGES/NATIONAL GEOGRAPHIC VIA GETTY IMAGES; WILLARD CULVER/NATIONAL GEOGRAPHIC

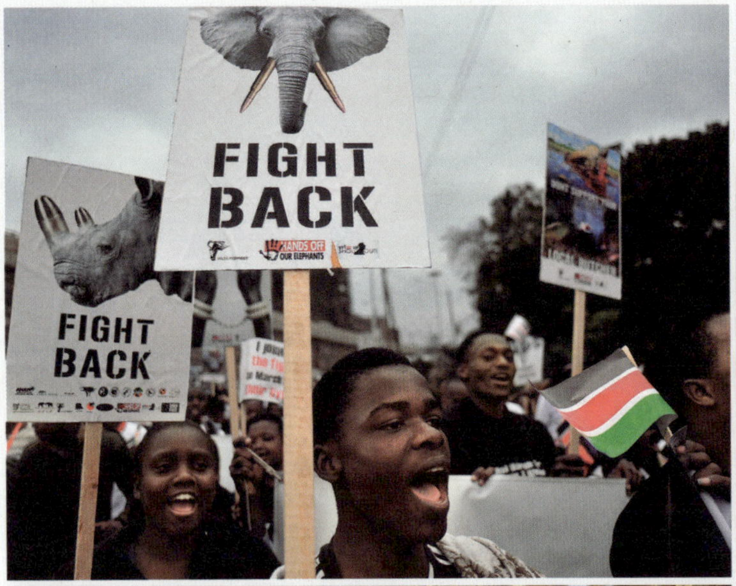

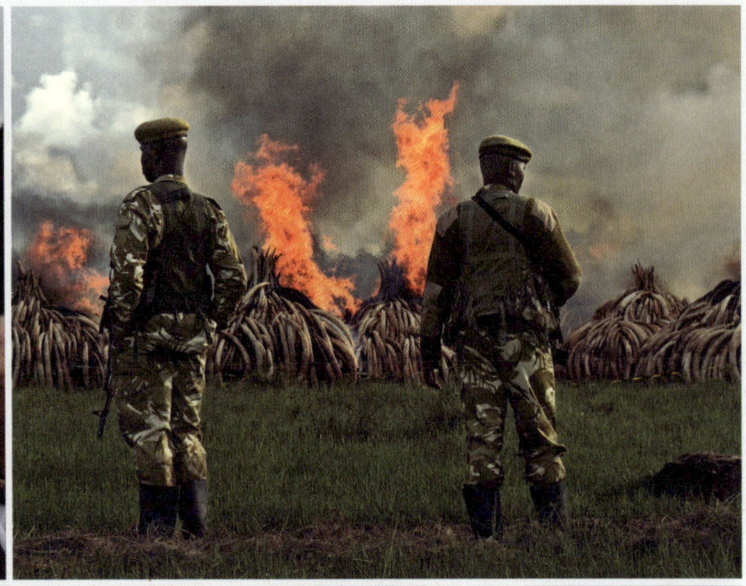

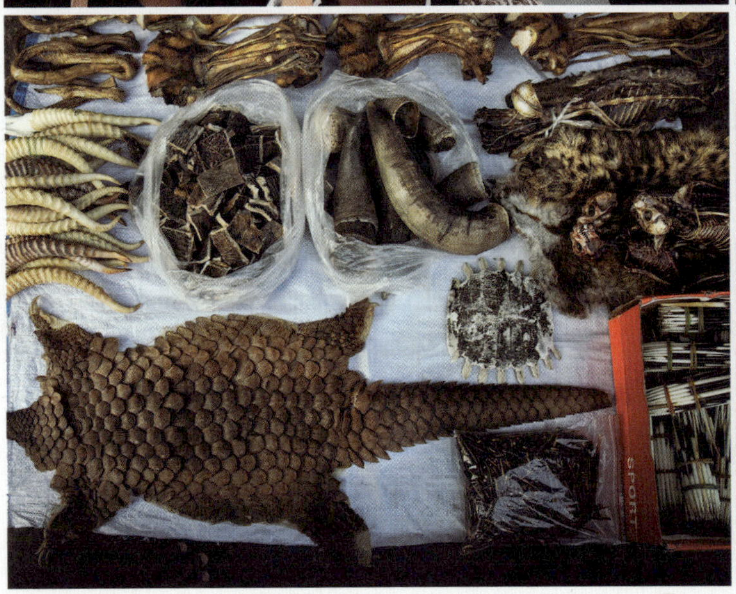

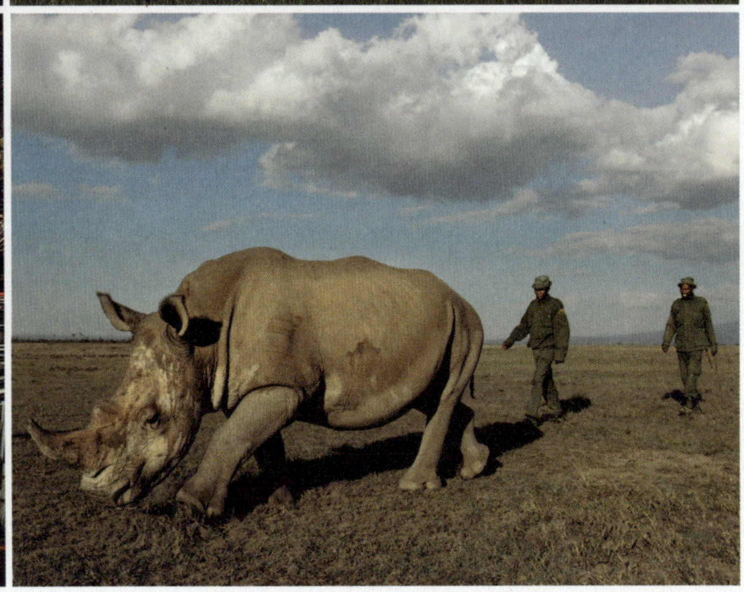

CLOCKWISE FROM TOP LEFT: SIMON MAINA/AFP VIA GETTY IMAGES; CARL DE SOUZA/AFP VIA GETTY IMAGES; KAREL PRINSLOO/ASSOCIATED PRESS; TAYLOR WEIDMAN/GETTY IMAGES.

Solutions Spotlight

THE EXTINCTION TRADE

We are currently experiencing the sixth mass extinction event in the planet's history, with species vanishing at rates faster than at any time since the dinosaurs disappeared some 60 million years ago. Our world has lost 60 percent of its vertebrate species since 1970. In addition to habitat loss and degradation, a leading driver of this decline is direct exploitation of species, including the illegal international wildlife trade.

Trophy hunters and poachers target charismatic species for their heads, hides, bones, and tusks. Over the years, working with partners like the Center for Biological Diversity, we have made great strides in gaining federal and state restrictions on these lucrative markets. But since 2017, the Trump administration has forced us to switch into defense mode.

There's no better symbol of the administration's destructive approach to our biodiversity problem than its formation of the International Wildlife Conservation Council, which Trump stuffed with lobbyists from the "thrill-kill" community. We argued that this is illegal since such taxpayer-funded advisory panels should serve the public interest. In September 2019, a federal district court agreed that the administration had failed to "provide a reasoned explanation for the council's creation." The following February, Trump's pro-trophy hunting council was officially extinct.

We've also sued to curb the import and domestic sale of thousands of giraffe parts, forcing the U.S. Fish and Wildlife Service to acknowledge that regulation is essential if we're to protect these magnificent animals from oblivion. And as we continue the fight, we'll remind people that the innocuous phrase "wildlife trade" is all too often a euphemism. Let's call it what it really is: wildlife crime.

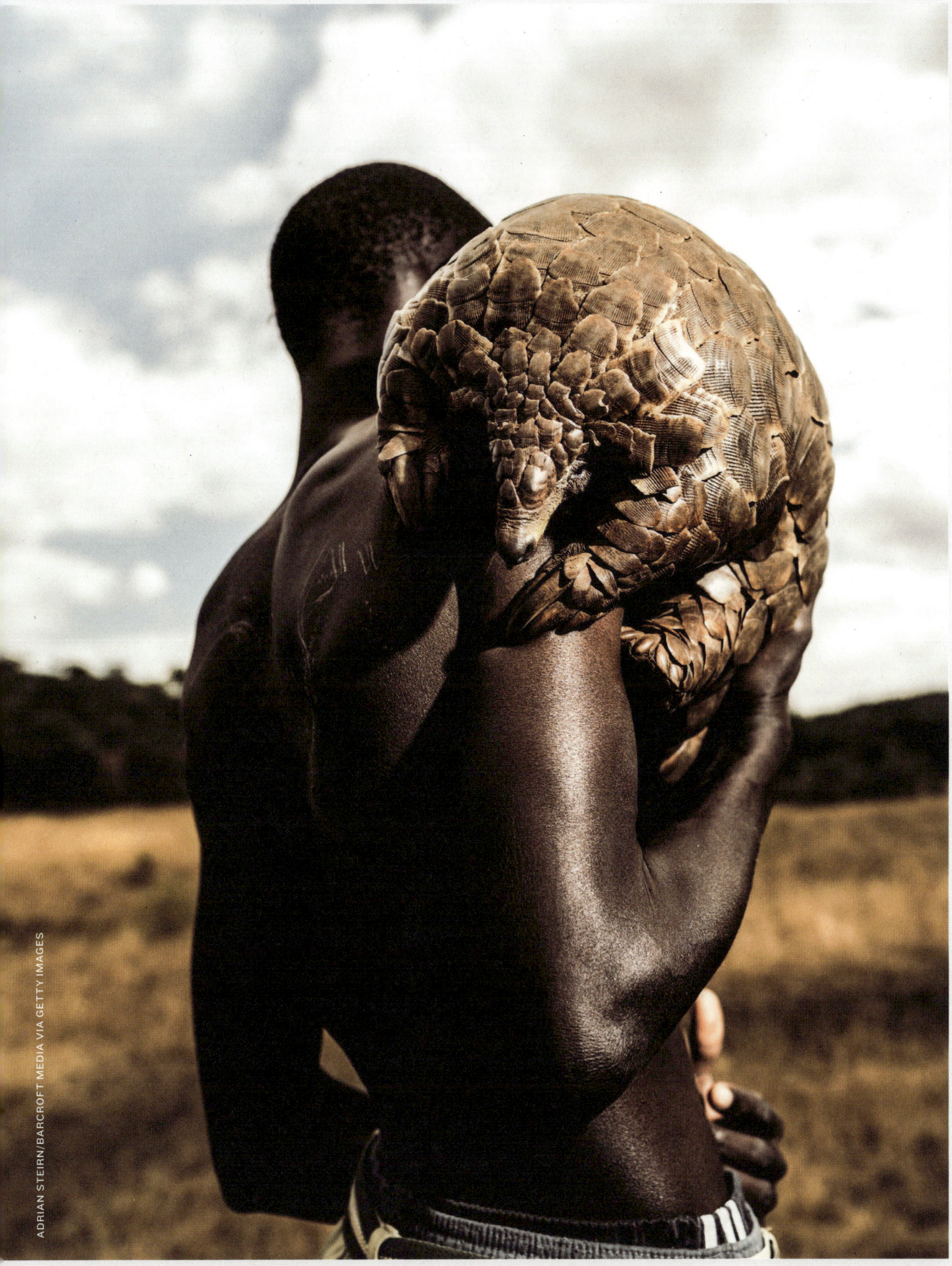

ADRIAN STEIRN/BARCROFT MEDIA VIA GETTY IMAGES

A wildlife rehabilitation worker in Zimbabwe holds a pangolin, the most heavily trafficked animal in the world—and as a result, one of the most endangered.

POLE POSITION

IF CALIFORNIA WERE AN INDEPENDENT nation, it would have the world's fifth-largest economy. This economic muscle, backed by enlightened political leadership, has often made the state a trailblazer for national and even international policy—nowhere more than in the fight for clean air and against carbon pollution. "What happens in California doesn't stay in California," says Annie Notthoff, NRDC's advocacy director in San Francisco.

By the 1950s, California, a state known for its iconic American love affair with the automobile, was suffering the consequences of that relationship in the form of deadly smog. Long before federal regulators acted, and long before we understood that transportation is the single-biggest source of climate pollution, California enacted the nation's first rules to reduce harmful tailpipe emissions. Because of California's poor air quality, Congress carved out a unique provision in the Clean Air Act that allowed the state to set its own standards—stricter than those in the federal law. Other states struggling with air pollution were free to join California if they wished, and 13 have done so. Today, those states with stronger emissions standards account for nearly 40 percent of the U.S. auto market.

In 2002, Roland Hwang, now the managing director of NRDC's Climate & Clean Energy Program, worked closely with then state assemblywoman Fran Pavley to draft California's landmark clean cars bill, which authorized the California Air Resources Board to set strong greenhouse gas emissions standards for all new cars and light trucks. Its crucial argument, accepted five years later by the Supreme Court, was that carbon dioxide was a pollutant as defined by the Clean Air Act. The implications were revolutionary.

Widely recognized today as a leader in the automotive revolution, Roland helped broker the so-called clean cars peace treaty in 2010. In the agreement, automakers, labor unions, environmentalists, and states reached consensus

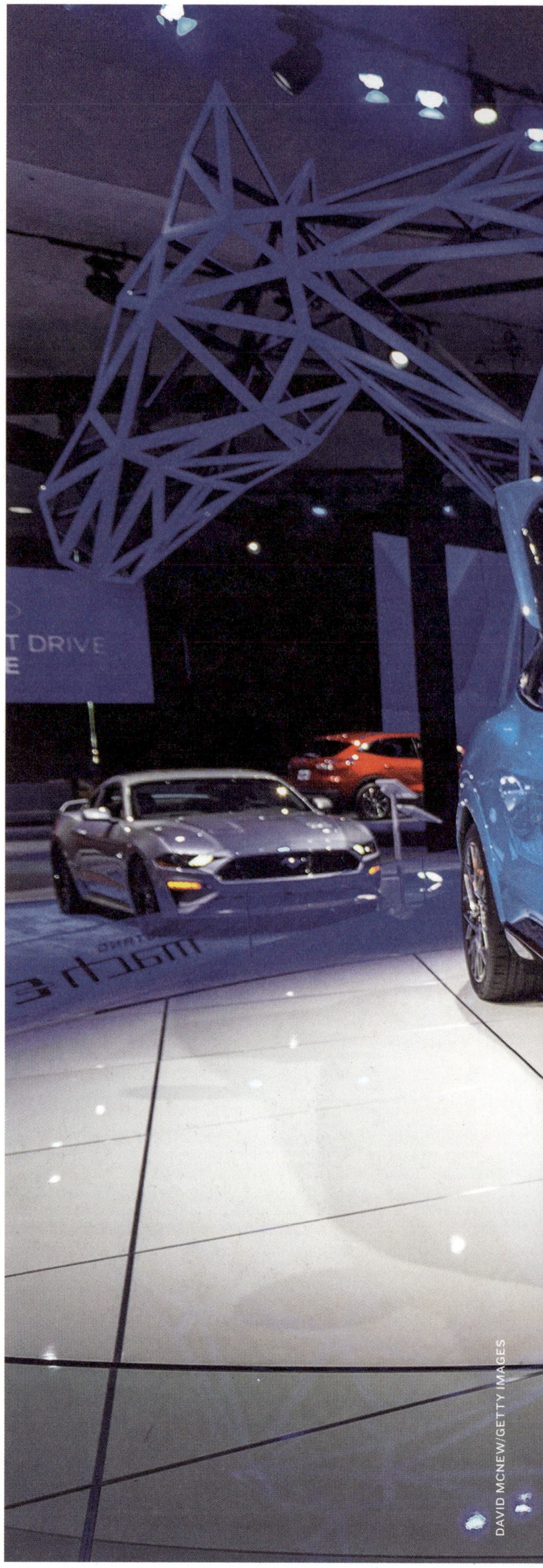

Automakers will introduce 80 new models of electric, plug-in hybrid, or fuel cell vehicles by 2021. Here, the 2019 Automobility LA show displays an electric Ford Mustang Mach-E.

DAVID MCNEW/GETTY IMAGES

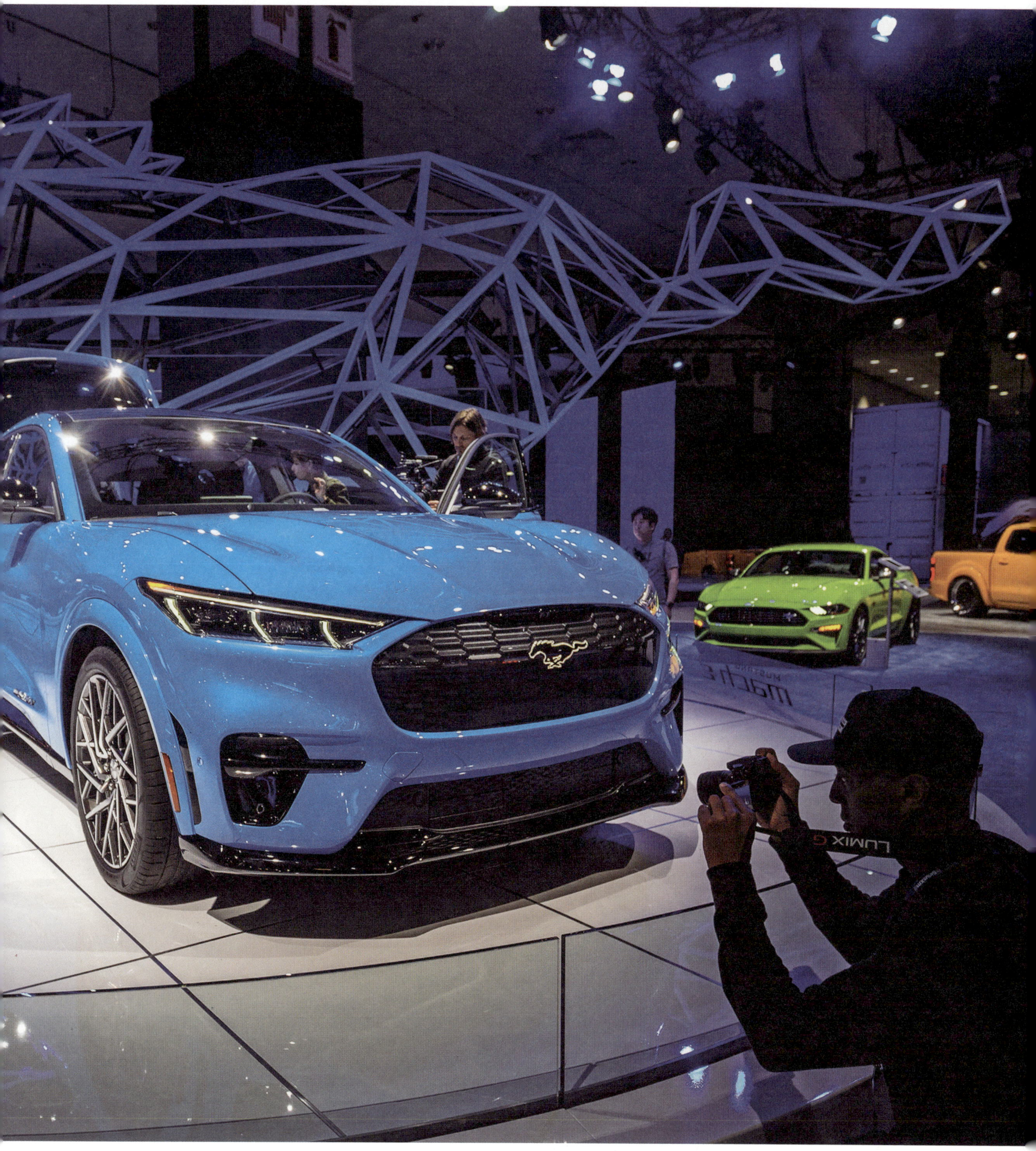
LUMIX G

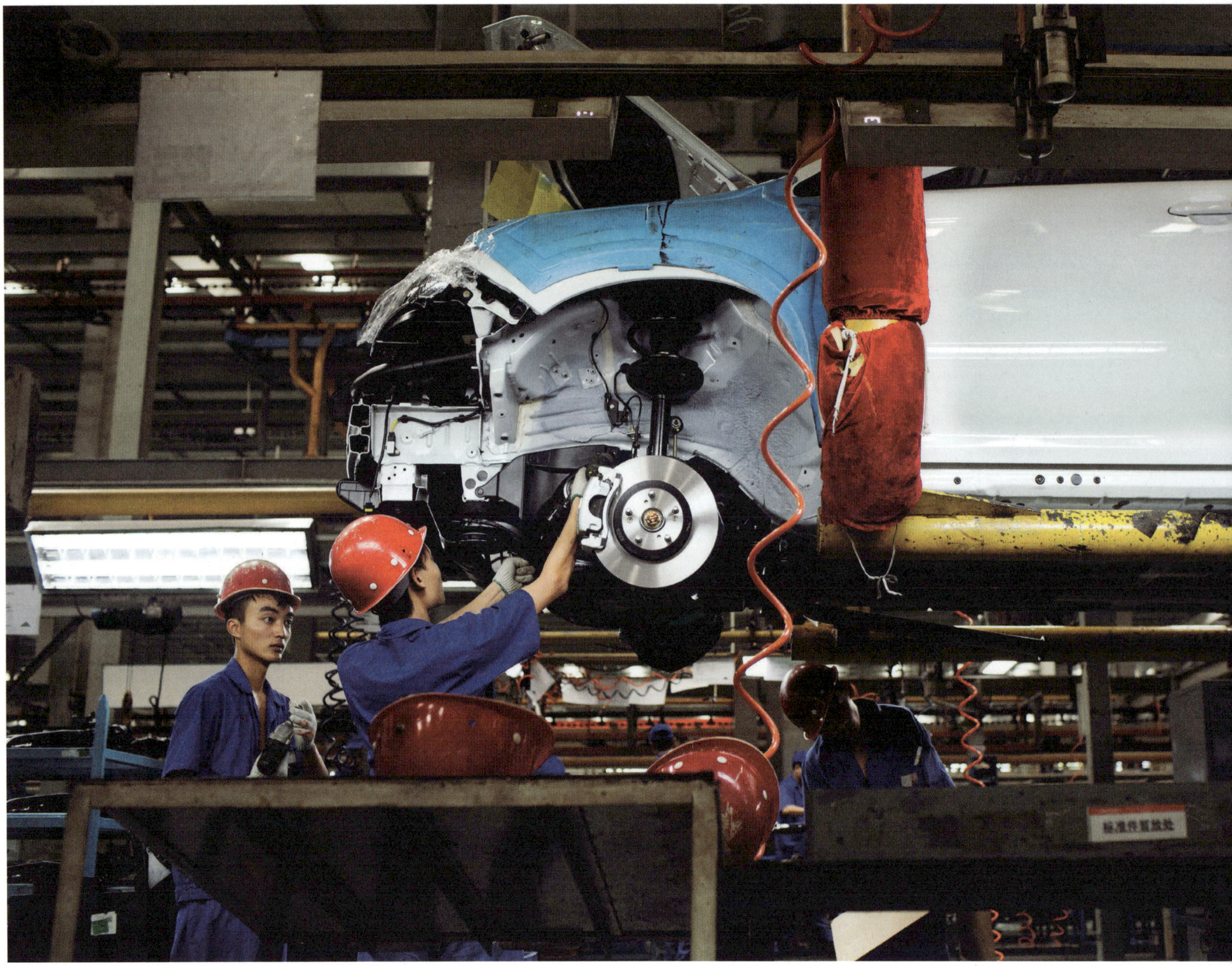

BRENT LEWIN/BLOOMBERG VIA GETTY IMAGES

on the need for a single, coordinated set of national clean air and fuel economy standards. This put an end to years of bitter and inconclusive litigation and contributed directly to the recovery of the auto industry after the great recession of 2008–2009.

NRDC's input and the California model were then essential to the automotive greenhouse gas and fuel economy standards introduced by President Obama in 2012, which mandated that new cars average 54.5 miles per gallon by 2025. Within five years of being fully phased in, the reduction in U.S. oil consumption would be equivalent to taking 85 million cars off the road. The standard was, at the time, the single-biggest action this country had ever taken to reduce carbon pollution and oil dependency.

The electric vehicle economy supports nearly 84,000 jobs across the Midwest. Currently, 13 states across the country, representing 105 million Americans, are committed to lowering tailpipe pollution through zero-emissions vehicle programs.

President Trump's announcement that he would not only roll back Obama's plan but end California's waiver under the Clean Air Act was more than just another giveaway to the oil industry. Luke Tonachel, director of the clean vehicles and fuels group, calls it a prime example of the Trump administration's "unstoppable ineptitude" that would pit auto manufacturers against each other and promise years of litigation that it would almost certainly lose. The administration has struggled to come up with any plausible rationale for rescinding the California waiver. In fact, its own analysis shows that rolling back the Obama fuel standards would add almost a billion tons of carbon pollution to the atmosphere.

In the end, lessening the harmful impact of gasoline-powered vehicles is just a transitional stage in the clean car revolution. Once again, California is in the vanguard, and NRDC is at the heart of the action. A 2014 law, cleverly titled Charge Ahead California, aims to put a million zero-emission electric vehicles (EV) on the state's roads by 2025. Fees from polluters pay for financing incentives, including cash rebates, to prospective EV buyers. Regulations like these

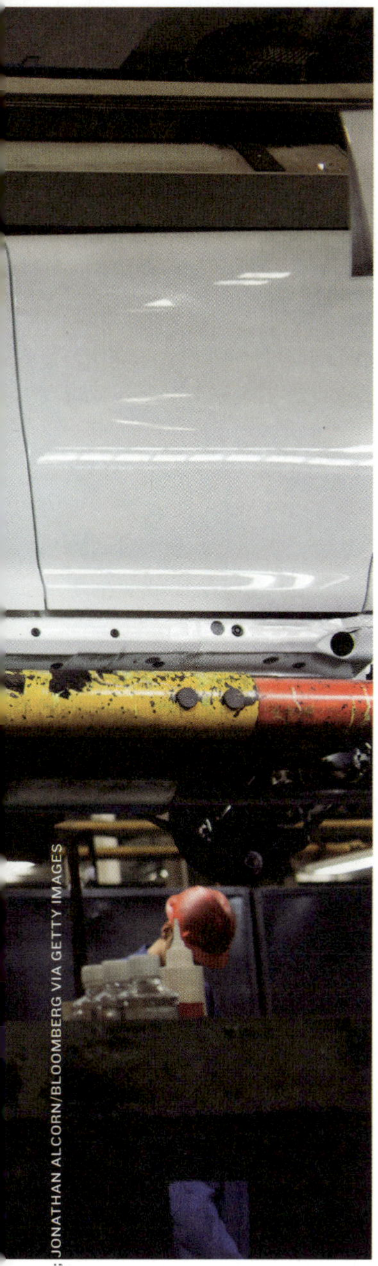

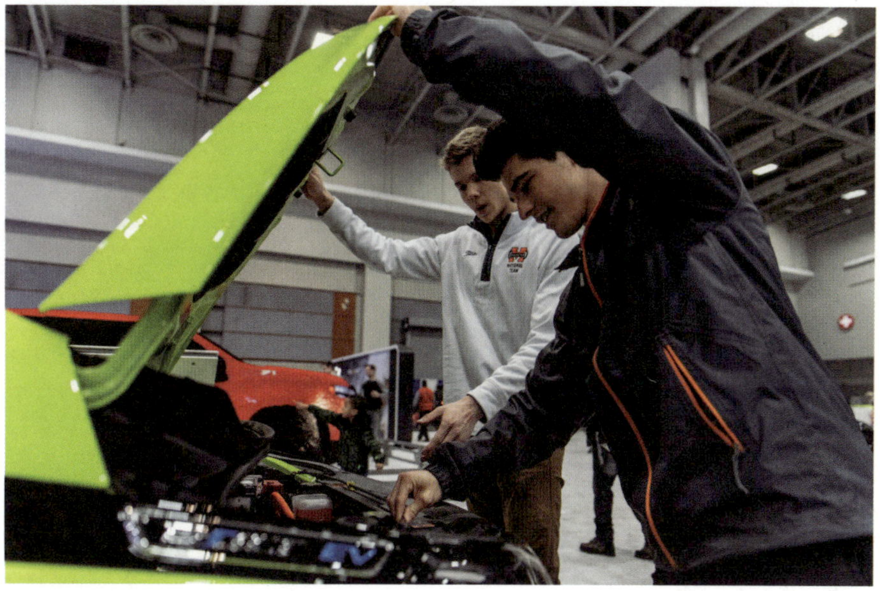

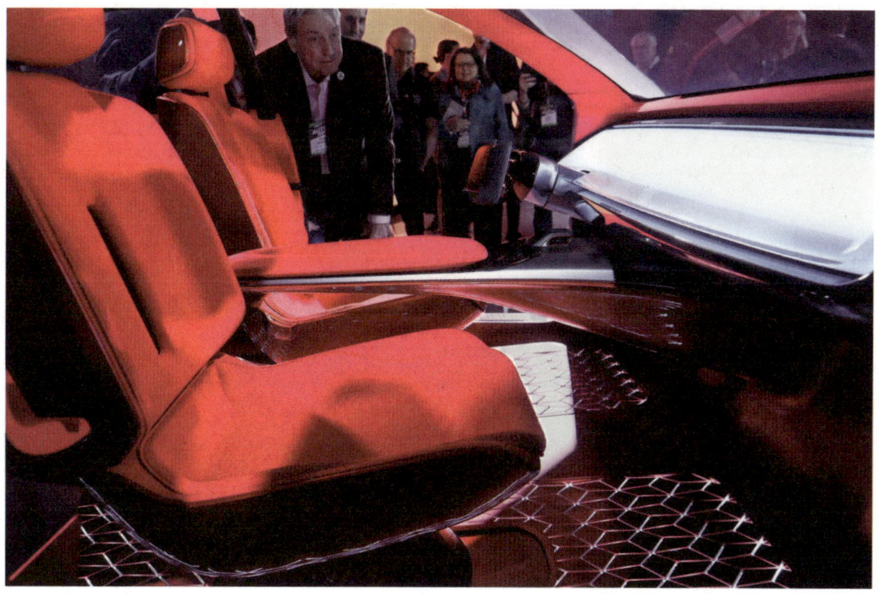

"In a quarter century spent tenaciously advocating for state clean car programs and zero-emission vehicle requirements, NRDC has fundamentally reshaped the global auto industry. Where adding more horsepower or cupholders once fell under 'innovation,' automakers now focus on efficiency and electric drivetrains. Today, America's cars are cleaner and burn less gas, and everyone has the option to drive a zero tailpipe polluting car."

—Roland Hwang, managing director of the Climate & Clean Energy Program

FROM TOP: ALEX EDELMAN/GETTY IMAGES; SHANNON STAPLETON/REUTERS; JONATHAN ALCORN/BLOOMBERG VIA GETTY IMAGES

breed innovation, and innovation in turn brings lower prices. The cost of electric car batteries has come down much faster than anyone expected. The Nissan Leaf that Roland drives is one of several models that now retail for around $30,000, and EV prices continue to fall steadily. China is now the biggest EV market in the world, and that wouldn't have happened without California's example. Meanwhile, investors, states, and utilities are realizing that there's no sense in powering clean vehicles with dirty energy. That's why updating the electric grid to handle wind and solar power is key to transforming our transportation sector.

Zero emissions by midcentury—that must be our goal. The internal combustion engine is an inherently inefficient piece of hardware, and as the clean car revolution progresses, it's destined to recede further and further in our rearview mirror—much like the tail fins of the 1950s, leaded gasoline, and, for that matter, the buggy whip.

As an expert on clean vehicle technologies, Roland Hwang has played an instrumental role in the creation and adoption of greenhouse gas and fuel efficiency standards in California and at the federal level. Here, Hwang speaks at L.A.'s Hammer Museum about the development of electric car technology and alternative fuels.

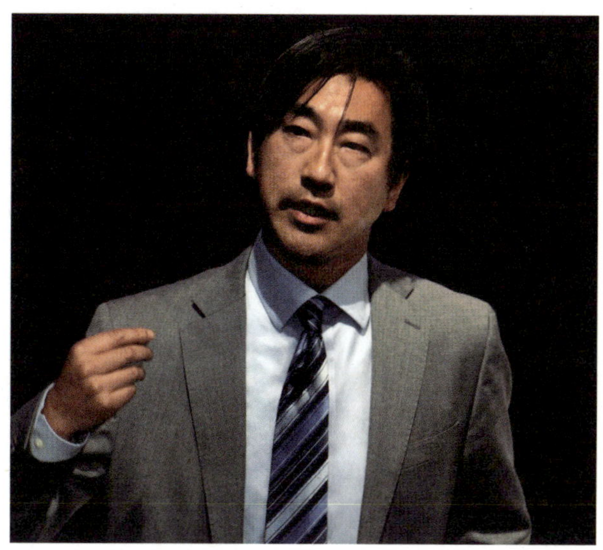

STATES OF CHANGE

IN HIS EIGHT YEARS AS CALIFORNIA'S Republican governor, Arnold Schwarzenegger used his platform as a celebrity and savvy politician to supercharge the state's position as a climate leader on the world stage. The highlight of his tenure was a pair of bills passed in 2006, Assembly Bill 32 and Senate Bill 1368. With our expert knowledge of state and federal clean air laws and decades of experience in California, NRDC was critical to the success of both pieces of legislation. Should you need further proof of our influence, Mary Nichols, who headed the clean air program in our Santa Monica office in the early 1990s, has been leading the California Air Resources Board—the lead agency in implementing both laws—since she was appointed by the governor in 2007.

Senate Bill 1368 set limits on long-term investments in dirty power plants, with the idea of starving the most polluting plants of access to utility investments. The bill, an NRDC creation from start to finish, helped launch a trend away from coal-fired power plants that continues to this day. Assembly Bill 32, dubbed the Global Warming Solutions Act, aimed to scale back greenhouse gas emissions to 1990 levels by 2020. Later extended and strengthened by Democratic governor Jerry Brown, the act was the first law in the country to take a comprehensive, long-term approach to addressing climate change and became a prototype for other states and, eventually, the federal government to follow.

We threw ourselves behind AB 32 and its architect, assemblywoman Fran Pavley, who joined us as a senior climate advisor in 2007 before returning to the legislature as a senator the following year. Nicole Lederer and Bob Epstein, the founders of Environmental Entrepreneurs (E2), magnified the power of our advocacy in Sacramento by adding the voice of the business community to stress the two bills' economic benefits. (Today, Nicole is an NRDC trustee, and Bob is the former chairman of the NRDC Action Fund.) Drawing on California's extensive regulatory authority, AB 32 capped emissions with measures that included a new market, a kind of stock exchange for carbon, usually described as a cap-and-trade arrangement. Bob also coined the term "cap-and-invest" for certain kinds of cap-and-trade schemes, such as AB 32, that auction carbon allowances and invest the proceeds in clean technologies.

As we'd hoped, California spurred other states to follow suit, especially when a federal bill, the American Clean Energy and Security Act—known as the Waxman-Markey bill—failed to make it through the Senate, after having narrowly passed the House. In 2009, 10 states in the Northeast and mid-Atlantic region came together to form the Regional Greenhouse Gas Initiative (RGGI), the first multistate market

MARIO ANZUONI/REUTERS

A worker inspects a rotor blade on top of a wind turbine in Tehachapi, California. NRDC is backing the state's efforts to reach 100 percent renewable energy by 2045.

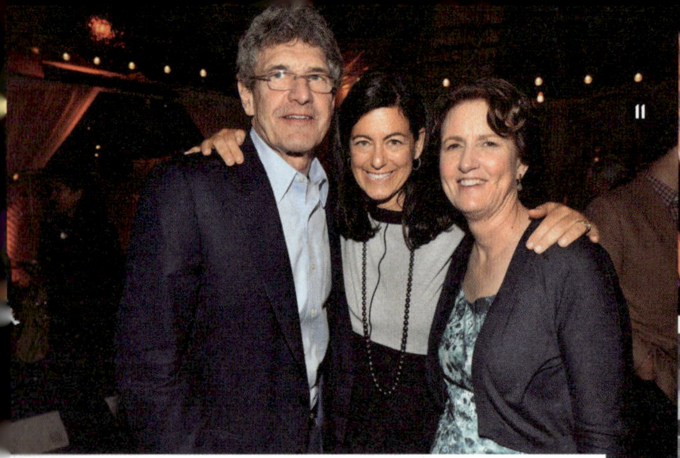

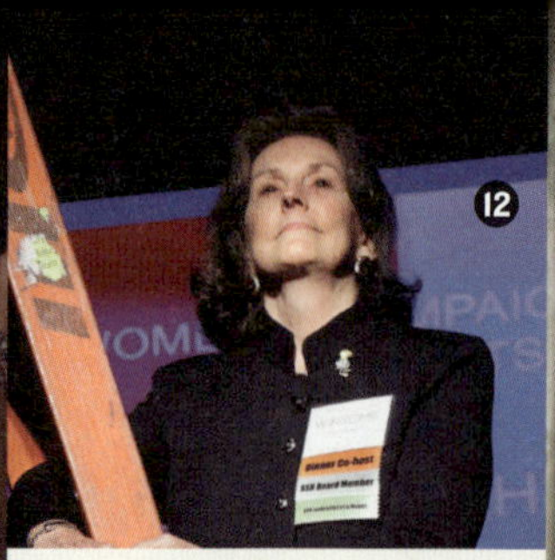

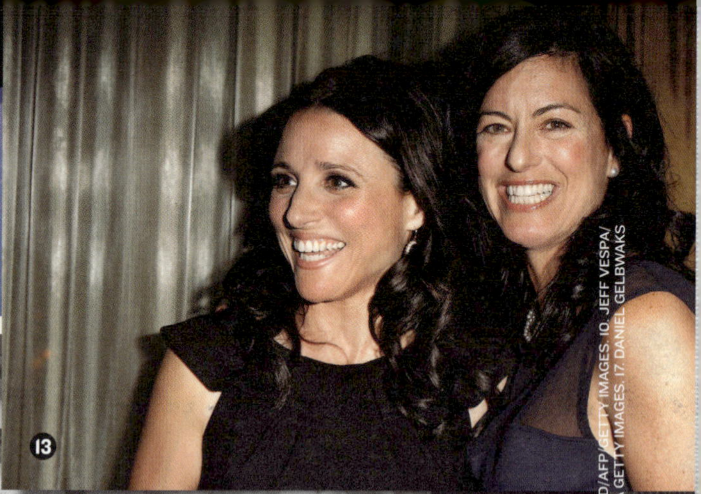

11. From left: Chair Alan Horn, trustee Laurie David, and president emerita Frances Beinecke at NDRC's Food For Thought benefit, 2014. 12. Winsome McIntosh, 2013. 13. Trustees Julia Louis-Dreyfus and Laurie David at NRDC's celebration of 20 years in Southern California, 2009. 14. Trustee Dick Ayres (third from left), former trustee Adele Auchincloss, NRDC director of climate policy David Hawkins, and former NRDC deputy director Pattie Sullivan at chair emeritus Stephen Duggan's retirement party, 1981.

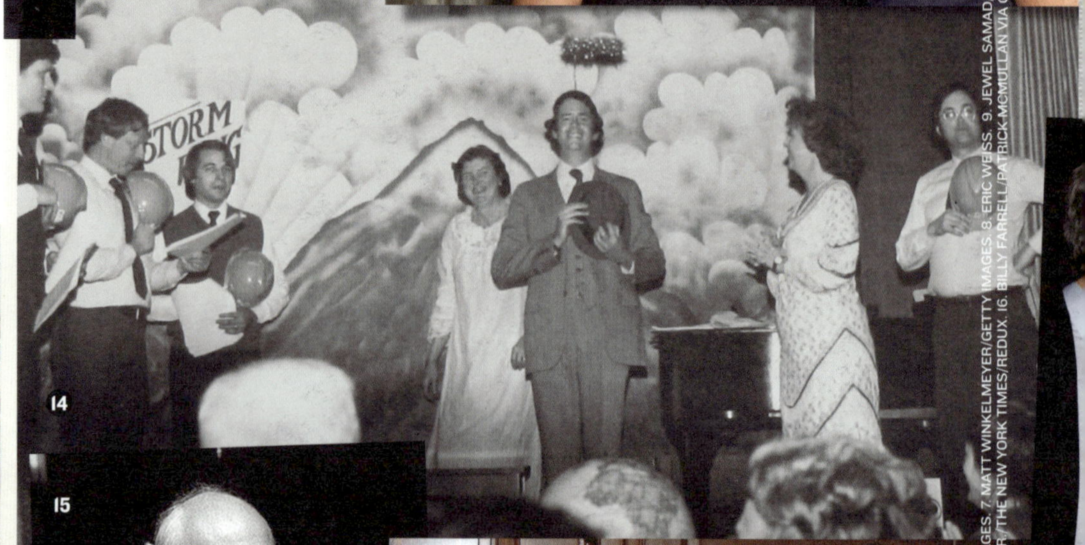

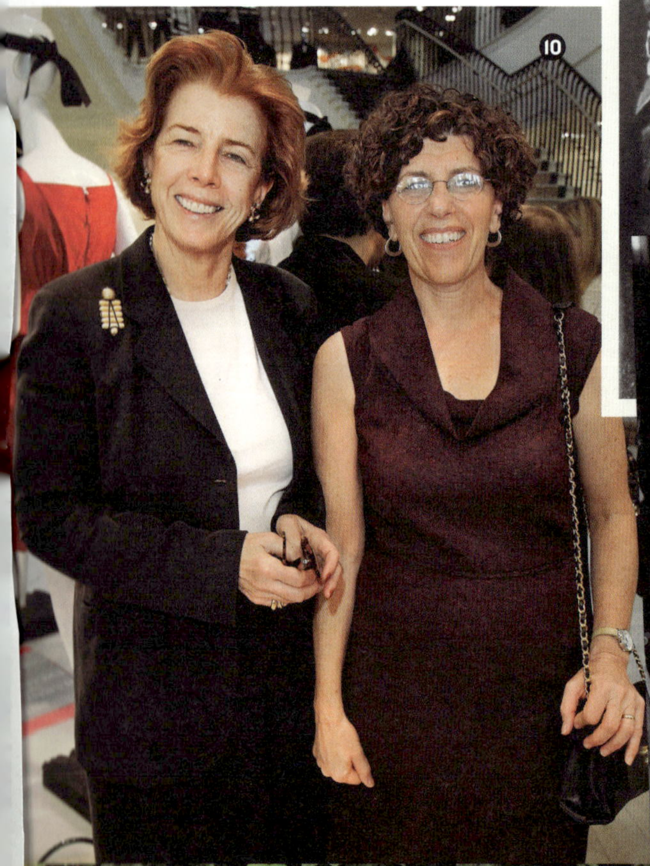

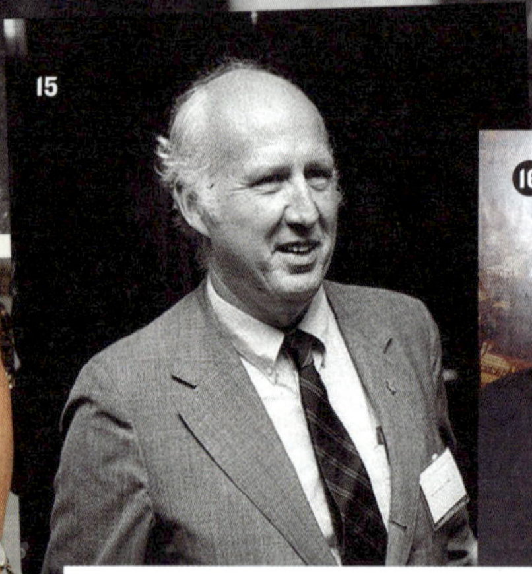

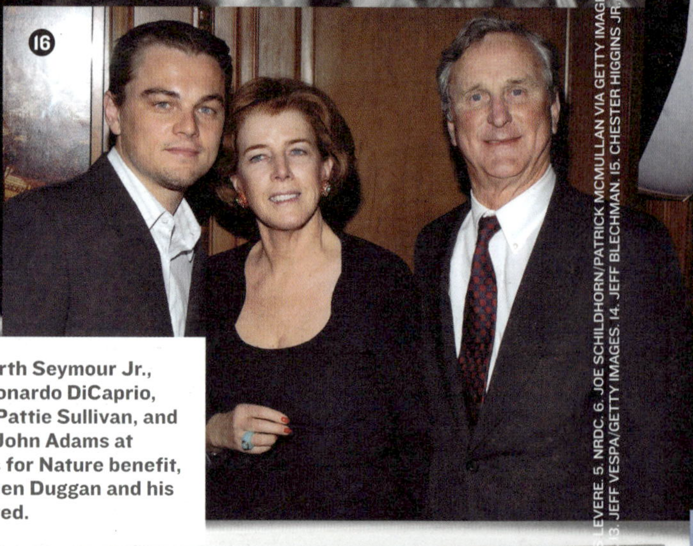

15. Former trustee Whitney North Seymour Jr., 1983. 16. From left: Trustee Leonardo DiCaprio, former NRDC deputy director Pattie Sullivan, and founding director and trustee John Adams at NRDC's seventh annual Forces for Nature benefit, 2005. 17. Chair emeritus Stephen Duggan and his wife, Beatrice "Smokey," undated.

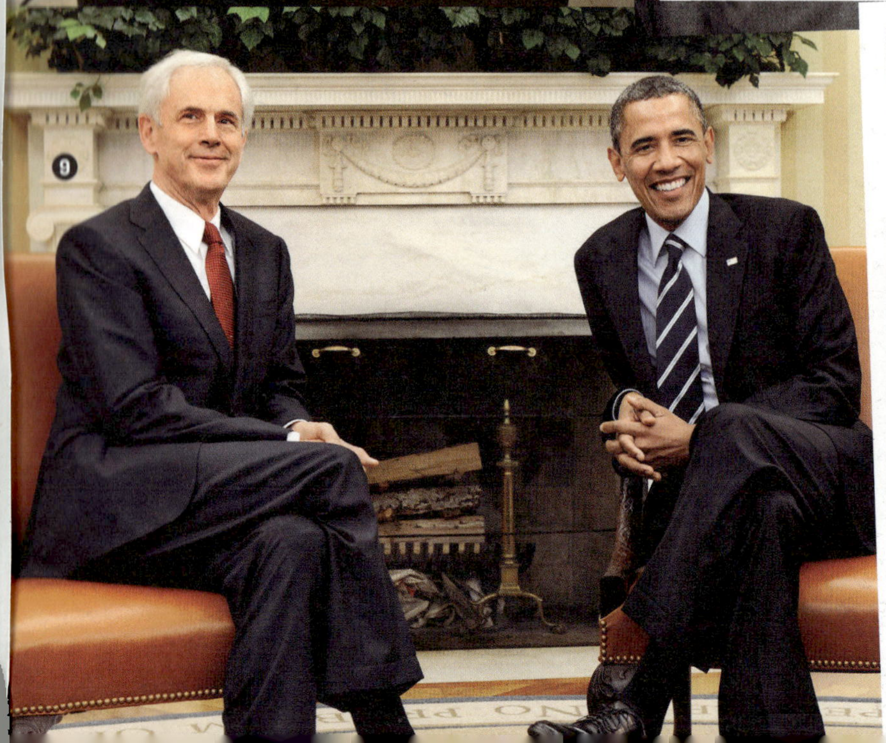

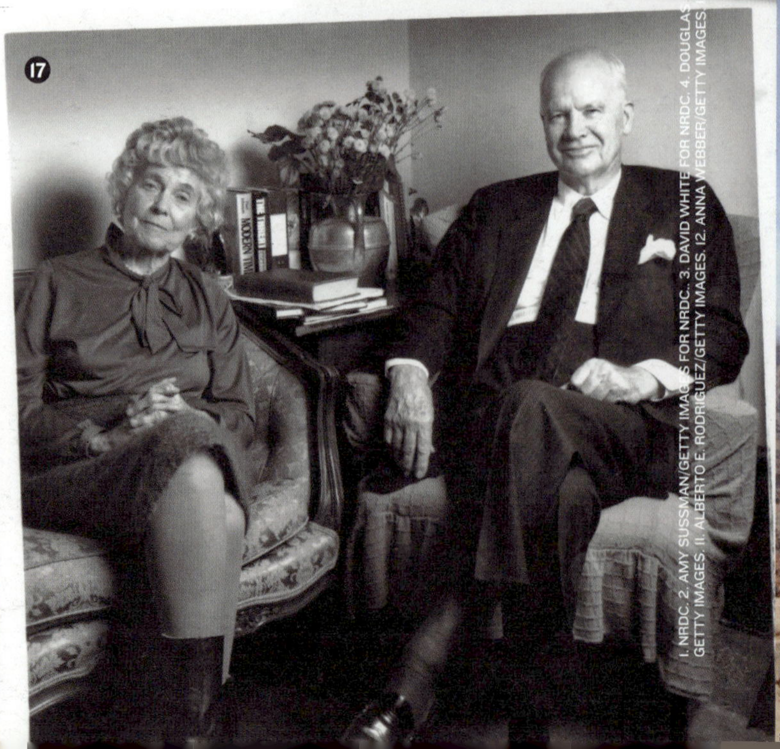

1. NRDC. 2. AMY SUSSMAN/GETTY IMAGES FOR NRDC.. 3. DAVID WHITE FOR NRDC. 4. DOUGLAS LEVERE. 5. NRDC. 6. JOE SCHILDHORN/PATRICK MCMULLAN VIA GETTY IMAGES. 7. MATT WINKELMEYER/GETTY IMAGES. 8. ERIC WEISS. 9. JEWEL SAMAD/AFP/GETTY IMAGES. 10. JEFF VESPA/GETTY IMAGES. 11. ALBERTO E. RODRIGUEZ/GETTY IMAGES. 12. ANNA WEBBER/GETTY IMAGES. 13. JEFF VESPA/GETTY IMAGES. 14. JEFF BLECHMAN. 15. CHESTER HIGGINS JR./THE NEW YORK TIMES/REDUX. 16. BILLY FARRELL/PATRICK MCMULLAN VIA GETTY IMAGES. 17. DANIEL GELBWAKS

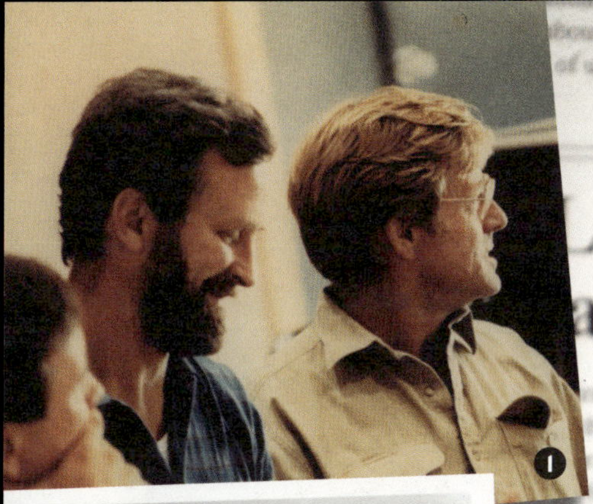

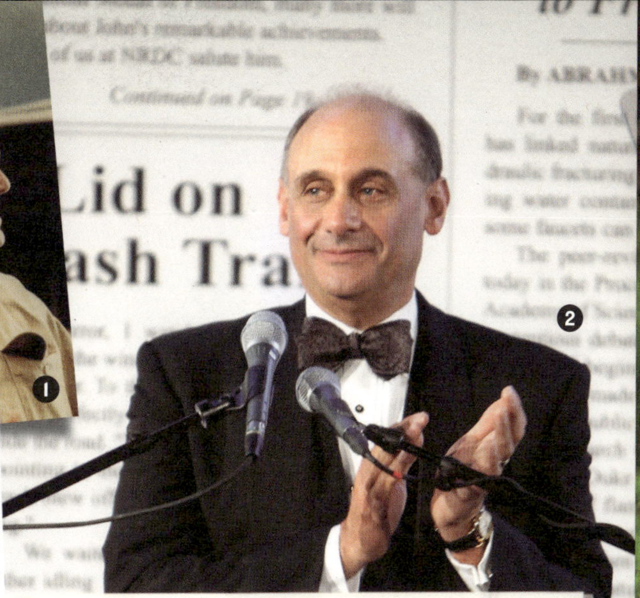

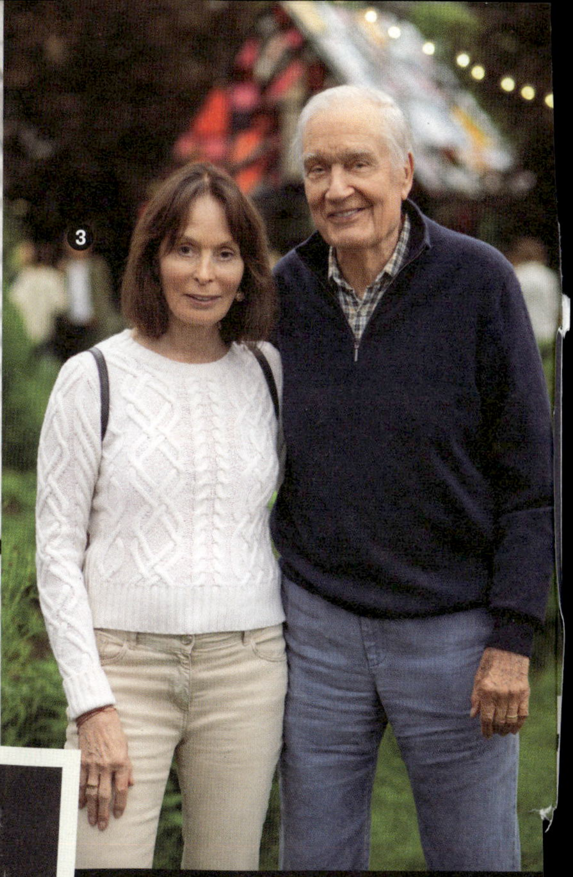

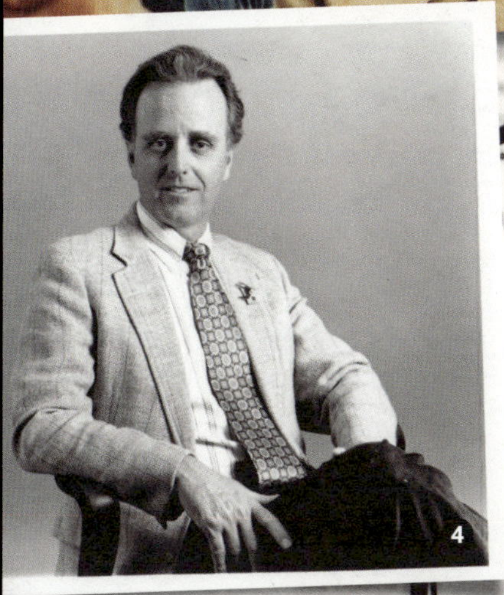

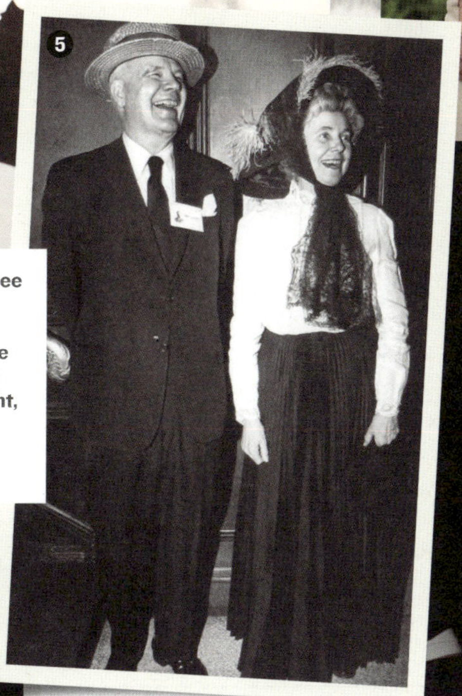

1. NRDC founding director and trustee John Adams with trustee Robert Redford at an Institute of Resource Management meeting about offshore drilling, 1982. 2. Chair emeritus Dan Tishman at NRDC's Forces For Nature benefit, 2011. 3. Trustee Frederica Perera and chair emeritus Frederick Schwarz Jr. at NRDC's farm-to-table dinner, Brooklyn, 2019. 4. Adam Albright, former vice chair of NRDC's board of directors, 1998.
5. Chair emeritus Stephen Duggan and his wife, Beatrice "Smokey," at Stephen's retirement party, 1981.

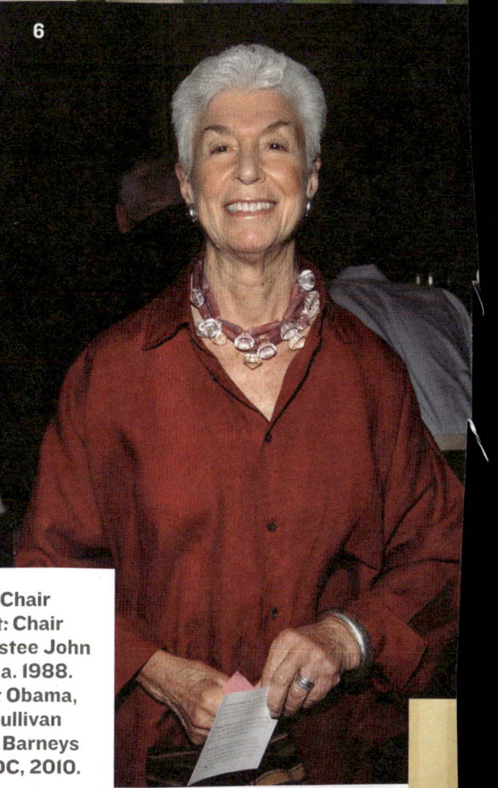

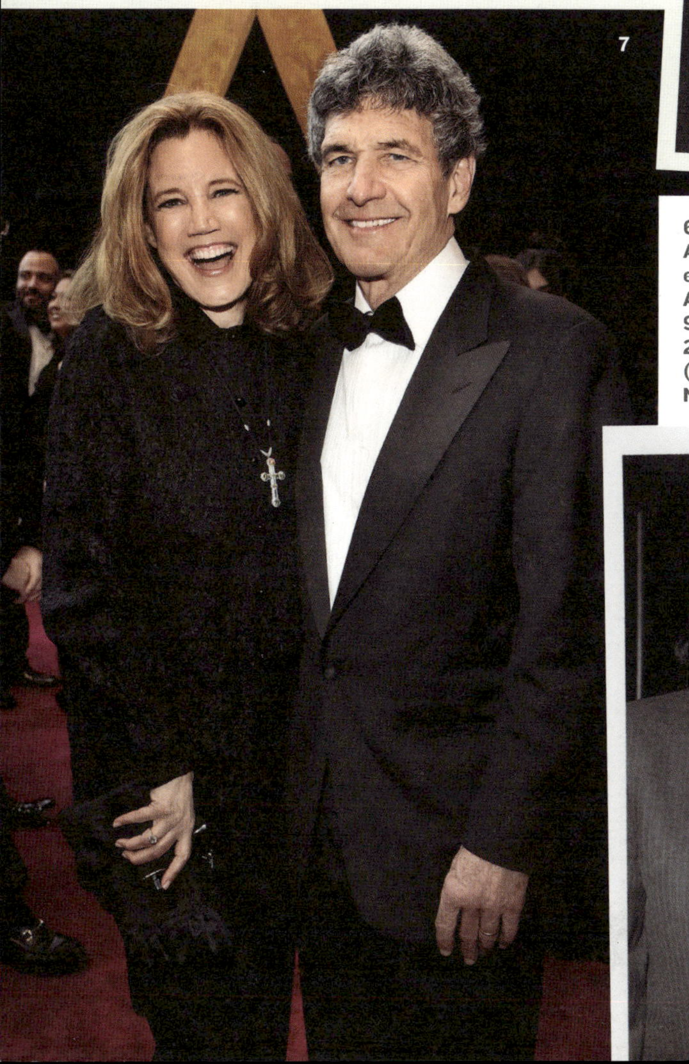

6. Honorary trustee Joan K. Davidson, 2005. 7. Chair Alan Horn and his wife, Cindy, 2018. 8. From left: Chair emeritus Bill DeWind, founding director and trustee John Adams, and former trustee Adele Auchincloss, ca. 1988.
9. NRDC cofounder John Bryson with President Obama, 2012. 10. Former NRDC deputy director Pattie Sullivan (left) and former NRDC scientist Linda Greer at Barneys New York Celebrates Nina Ricci, benefiting NRDC, 2010.

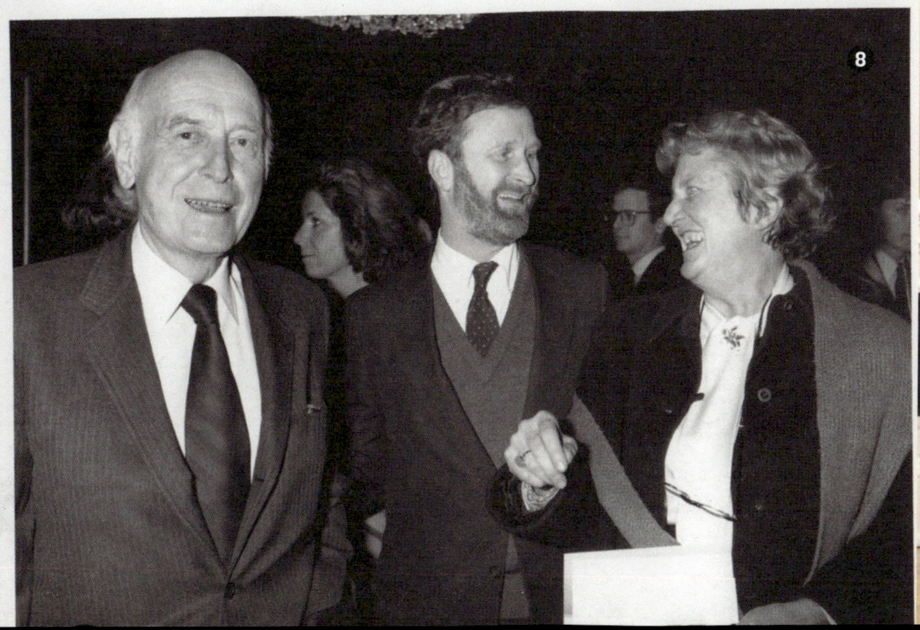

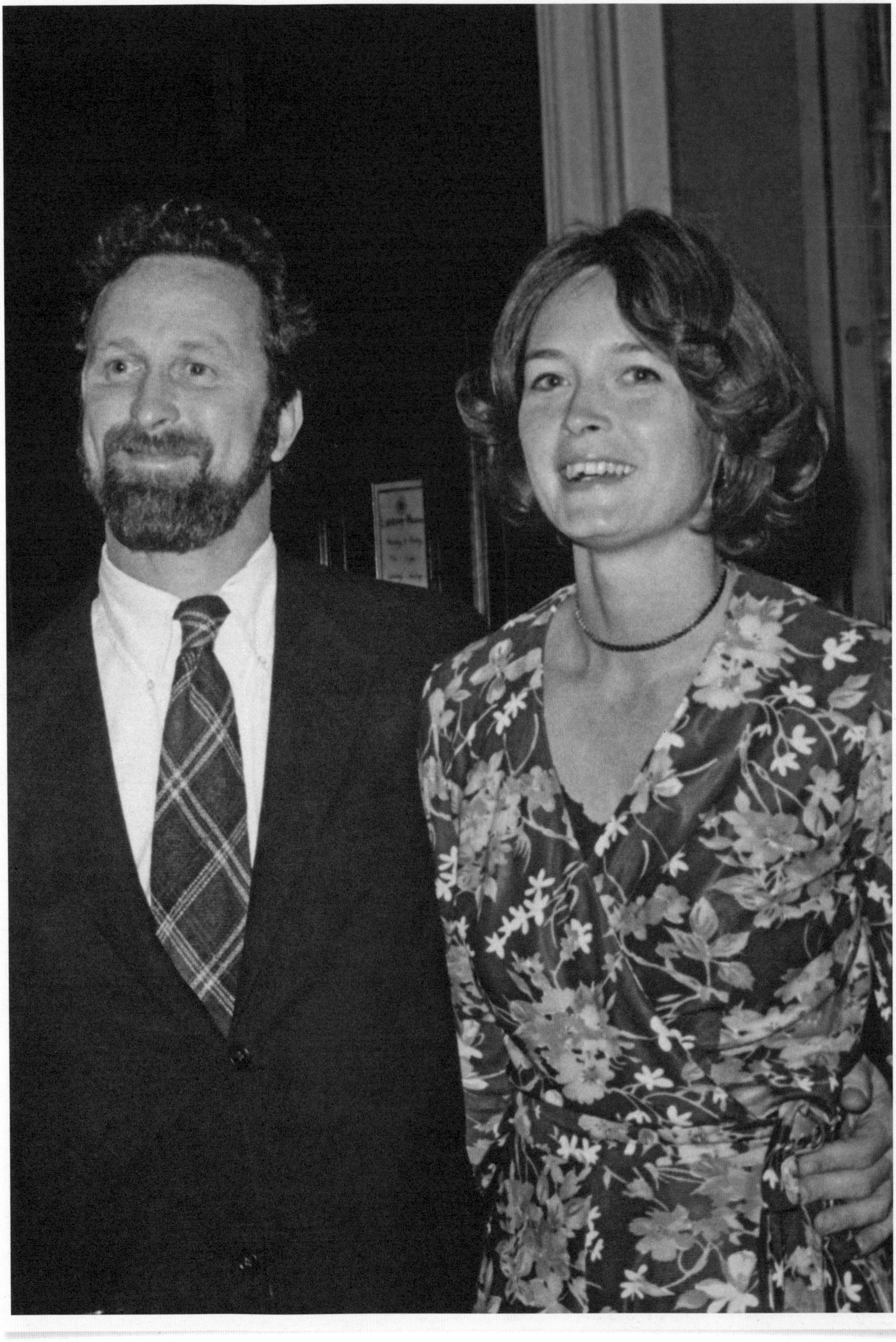

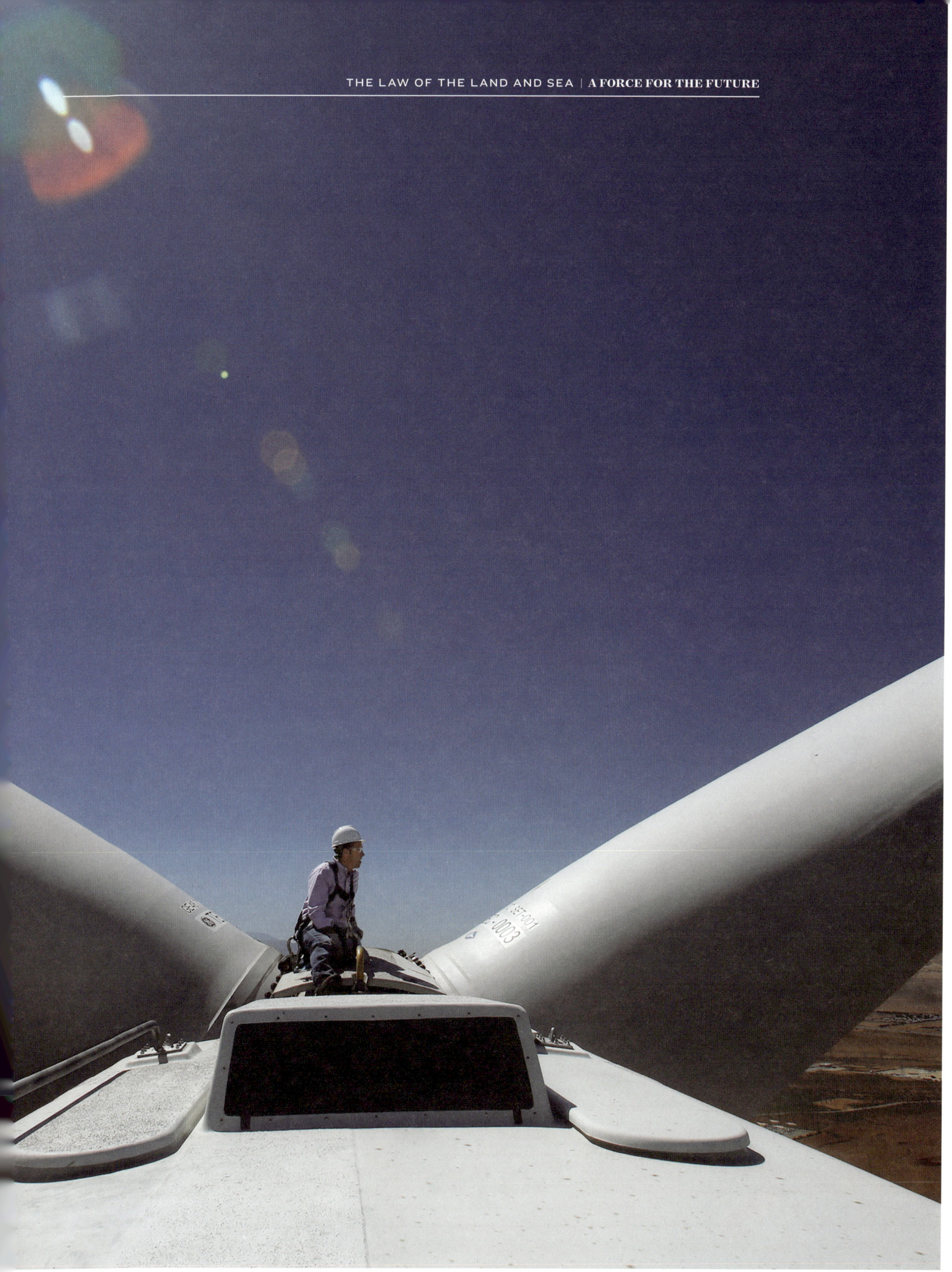

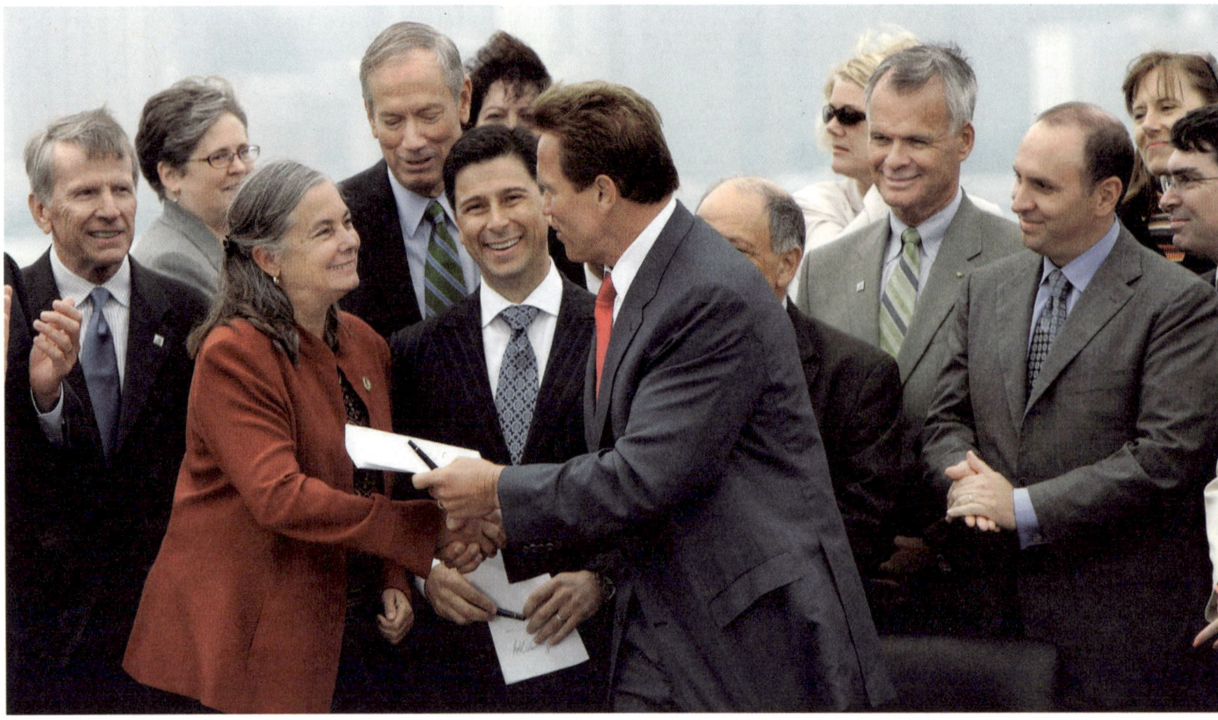

Governor Arnold Schwarzenegger hands Assembly member Fran Pavley a copy of his signed bill, AB 32, in 2006.

"When rounding up votes for AB 32, we told wavering legislators that the whole world was watching. And when the bill passed, papers from Asia to Europe to the Americas covered it—the world was indeed watching. As the fifth-largest economy on earth, what California does matters. We've become a model for other states and nations on how to decarbonize and grow an economy at the same time."

—Annie Notthoff, senior western advocacy director

of its kind and another example of cap-and-invest. No one played a bigger role in its creation than Dale Bryk, an attorney in our New York office and a formidable negotiator. Dale spent 21 years at NRDC before Governor Andrew Cuomo appointed her in 2019 to be his deputy secretary on energy and environment.

RGGI, or "Reggie" as we pronounce it, sets a regional cap on carbon emissions from power plants and sells pollution permits under this limit through regular auctions. It decreases the number of permits available each year to steadily lower the cap. States invest the auction revenues in new jobs, energy-efficiency measures, and clean renewable energy. After a decade, RGGI has outstripped expectations. In participating states, power-plant emissions have dropped by more than half and consumers have saved $1 billion on their electricity bills. The initiative has also boosted regional economic growth, created thousands of jobs, delivered billions of dollars in health benefits, and reduced air pollution and infant mortality rates. And it did so with strong bipartisan support—with both Democratic and Republican governors joining forces to launch RGGI and to consistently support and strengthen the program over time, including the consideration of the impacts on social equity and communities located near pollution sources.

The Midwest, the traditional heartland of dirty energy, has been a tougher nut to crack. Statehouses backed away from similar emissions caps due to the 2008 recession, fierce pushback from the fossil fuel lobby, and the costs of wind and solar energy still being relatively high at the time. But there's no reason to think this setback is permanent, as more and more states see the practical benefits of clean energy development.

Virginia will soon decide whether to join RGGI in 2021, and Pennsylvania recently launched a regulatory process to do so by 2022. North Carolina's new Clean Energy Plan sets similar targets. Economic models developed by NRDC have shown state leaders how cap-and-invest will not only lower bills and create jobs but also decrease reliance on costly imported energy. We're now making the same arguments to states in other regions.

The question is no longer whether we will decarbonize our energy economy. It's a matter of when and how, and even if the federal government is, for now, in thrall to the polluters, the states—with a lot of help from NRDC—are pushing the way forward and reaping the benefits.

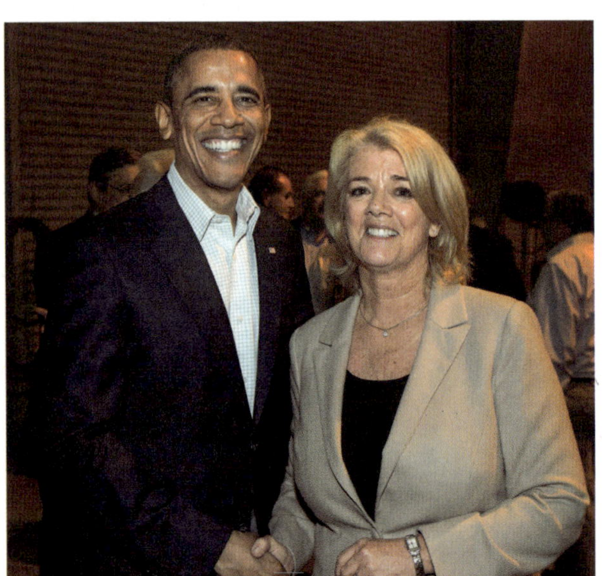

Since joining NRDC in 1982, Annie Notthoff has led efforts to encourage California to enact many of its nationally significant environmental laws. Here at the San Luis water facility in Firebaugh, California, President Obama and Notthoff shake hands after a discussion with farmers and other local stakeholders affected by the 2014 drought.

FROM TOP: DAVID PAUL MORRIS/GETTY IMAGES; PETE SOUZA/WHITE HOUSE

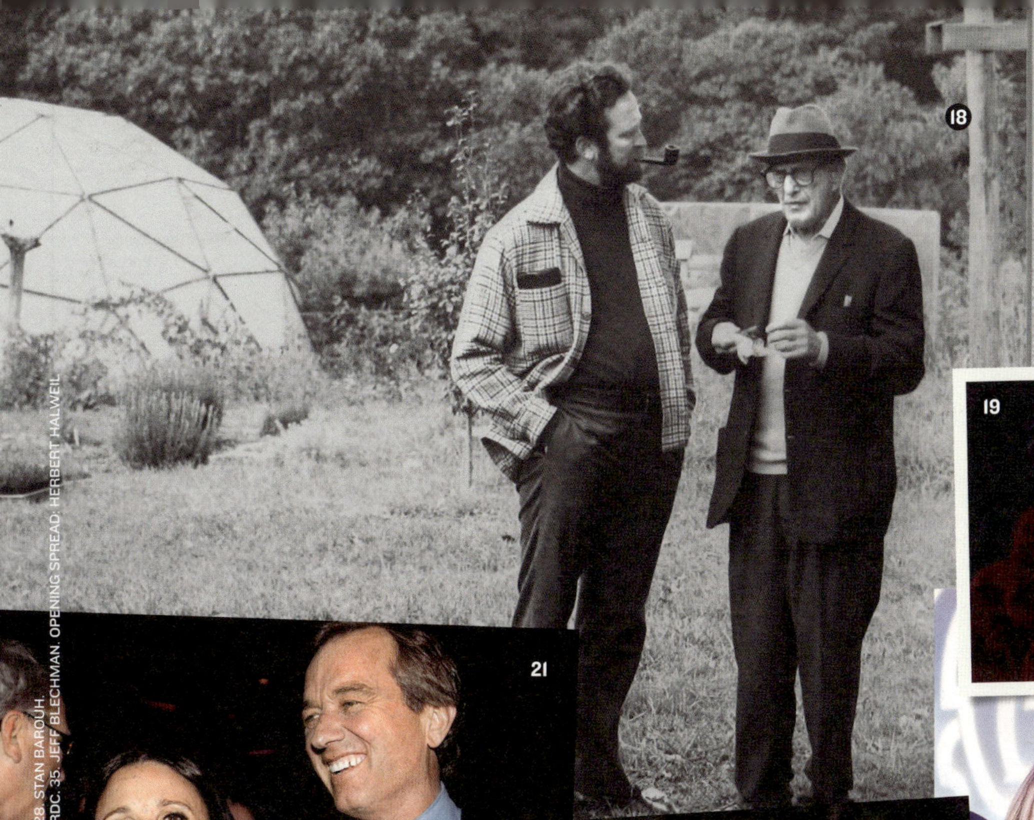
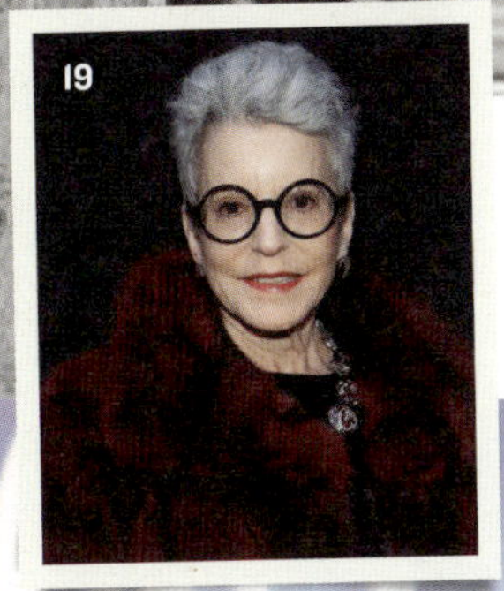
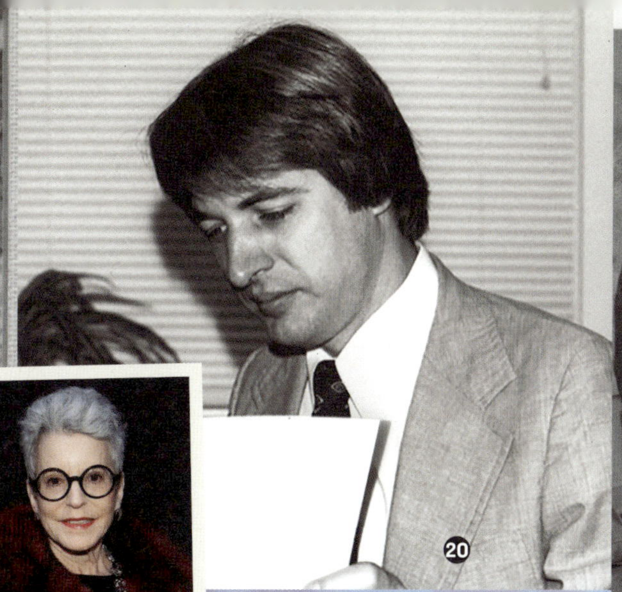
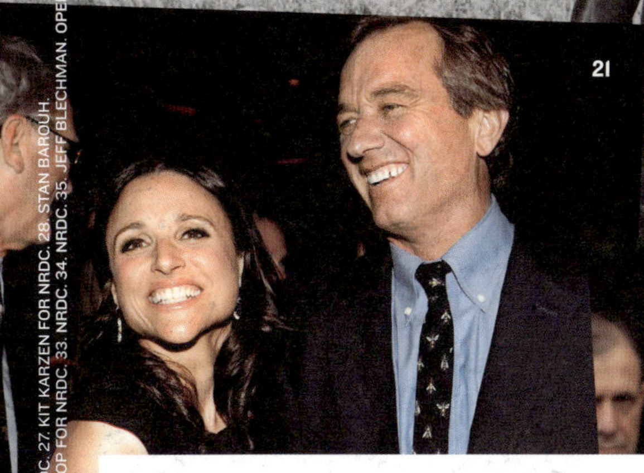
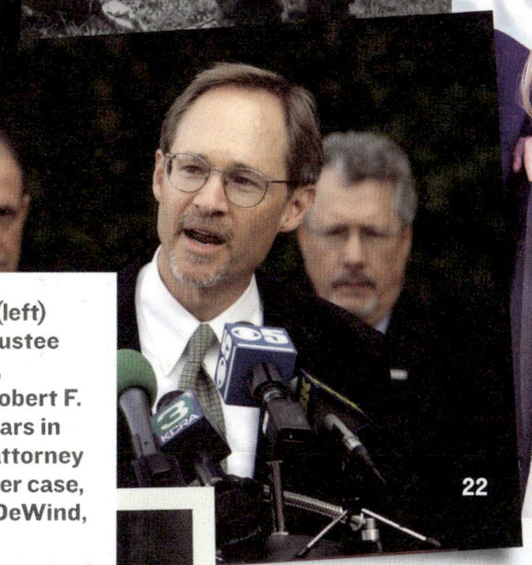
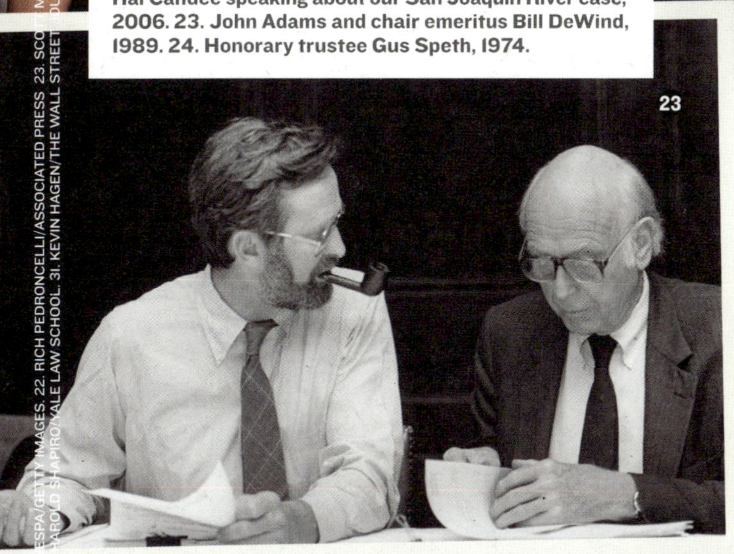
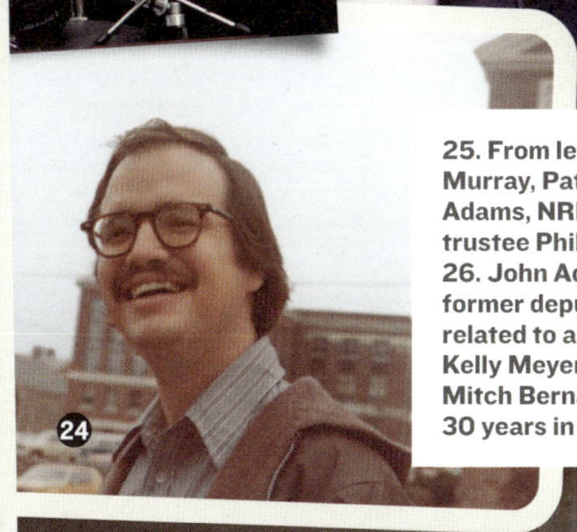

18. Founding director and trustee John Adams (left) and former trustee Jim Marshall , ca. 1970. 19. Trustee Patricia Bauman, 2015. 20. Trustee Dick Ayres, undated. 21. Trustee Julia Louis-Dreyfus and Robert F. Kennedy Jr. at the celebration of NRDC's 20 years in Southern California, 2009. 22. Former NRDC attorney Hal Candee speaking about our San Joaquin River case, 2006. 23. John Adams and chair emeritus Bill DeWind, 1989. 24. Honorary trustee Gus Speth, 1974.

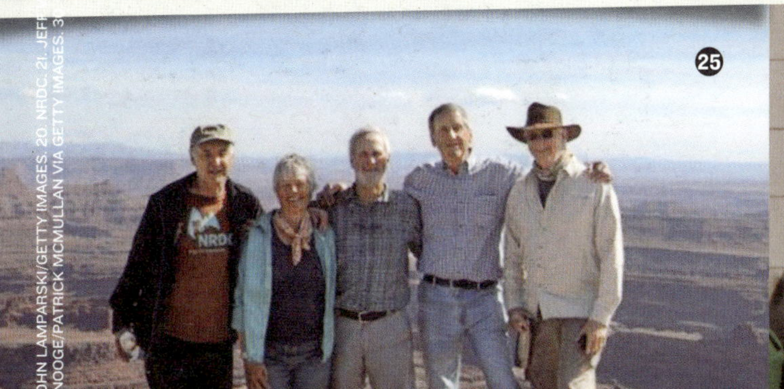
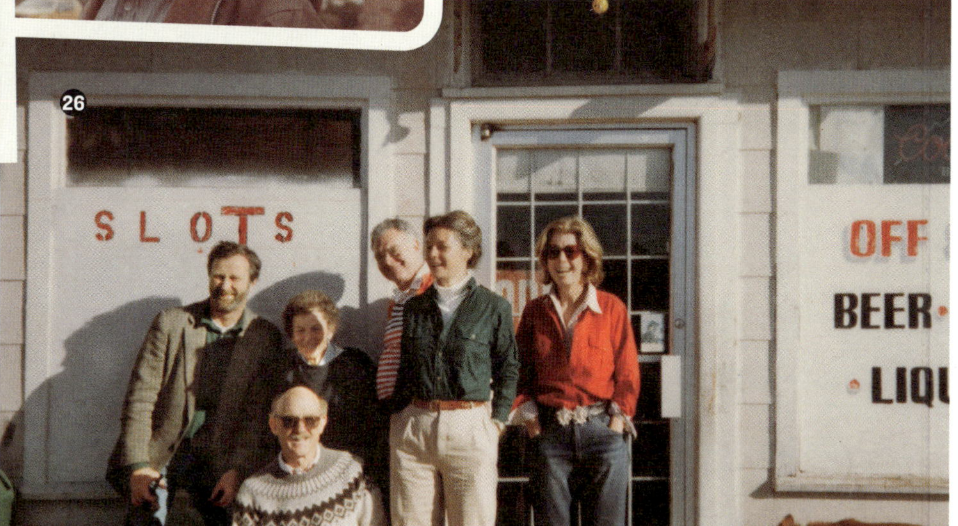

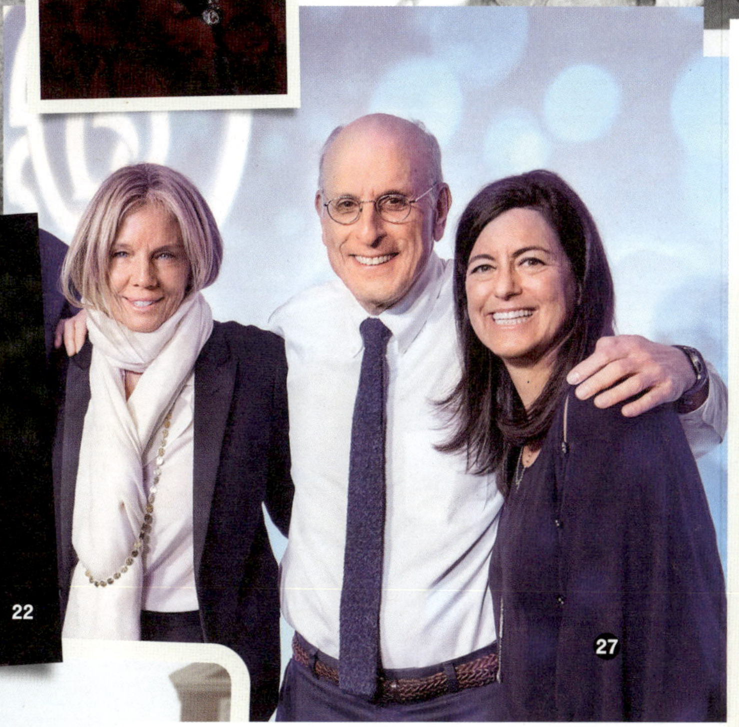

25. From left: Former NRDC director of development Jack Murray, Patricia Adams, founding director and trustee John Adams, NRDC western director Joel Reynolds, and honorary trustee Philip B. Korsant at Bears Ears National Monument. 26. John Adams (far left), Patricia Adams (green shirt), and former deputy director Pattie Sullivan (far right) on a trip related to a nuclear test in Nevada. 27. From left: Trustee Kelly Meyer, NRDC executive director and chief counsel Mitch Bernard, and trustee Laurie David celebrating NRDC's 30 years in Southern California, 2019.

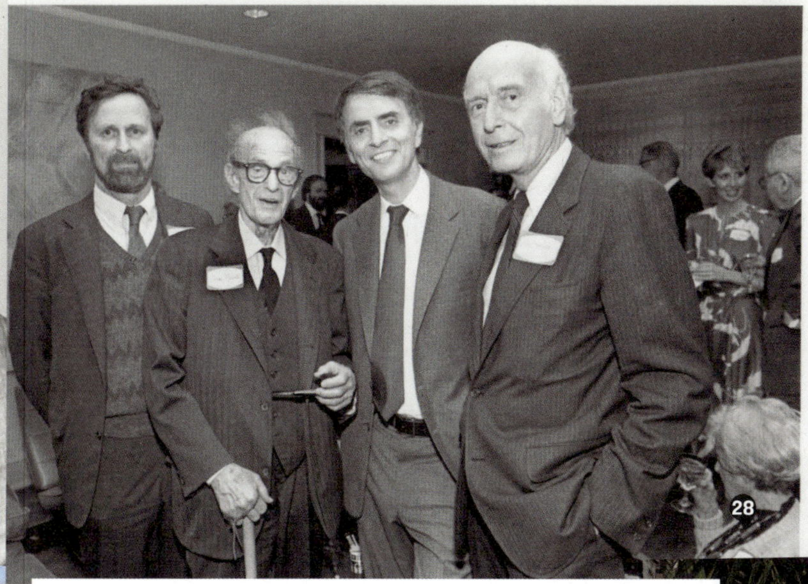
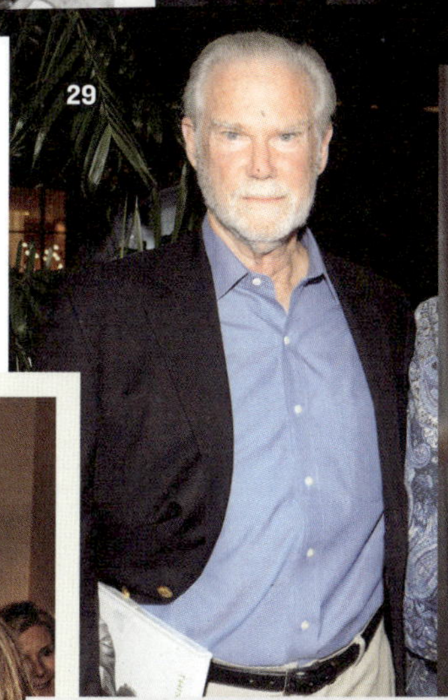
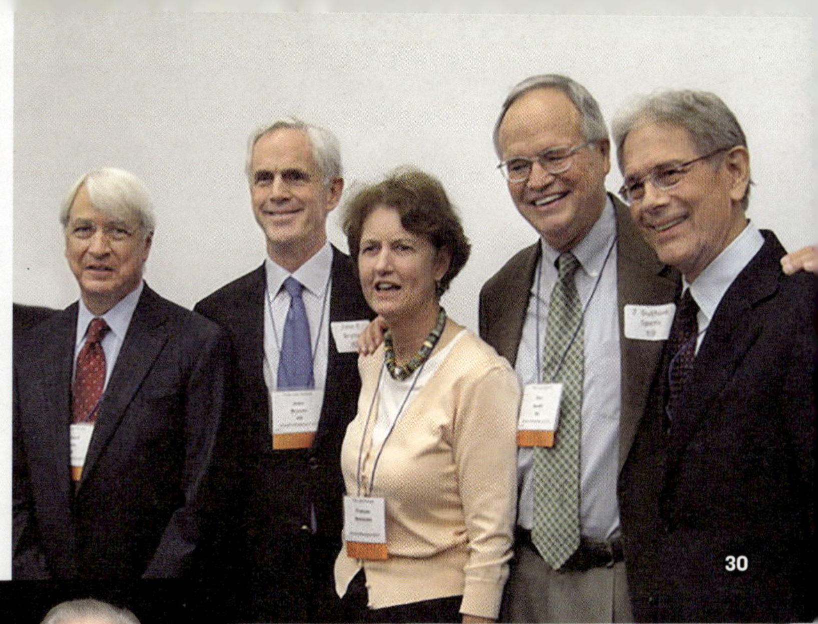
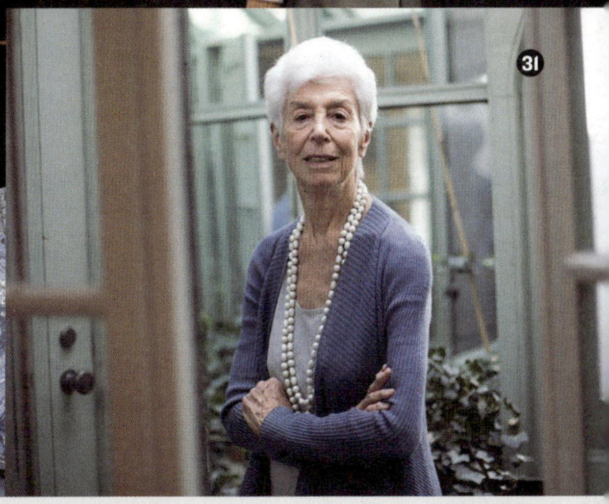
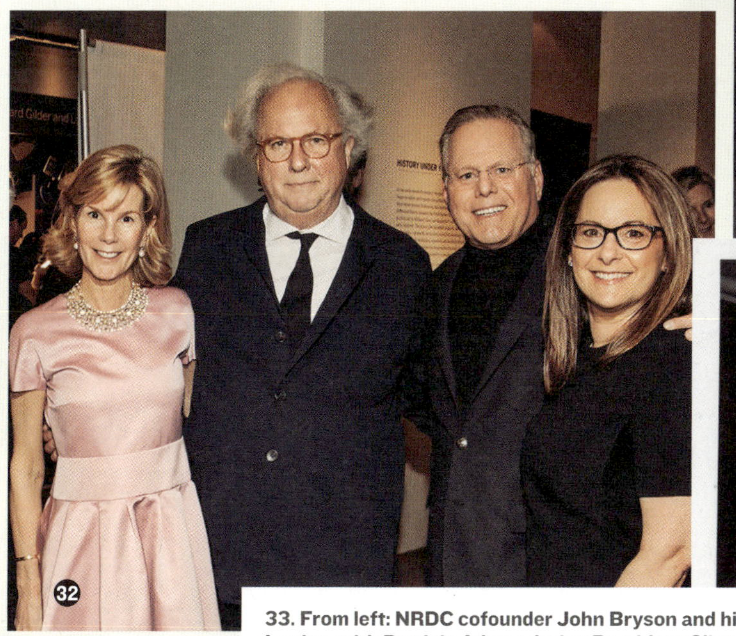

28. From left: Founding director and trustee John Adams, former trustee Jim Marshall, astrophysicist Carl Sagan, and chair emeritus Bill DeWind. 29. Honorary trustee Philip B. Korsant. 30. From left: NRDC cofounders Dick Ayres, John Bryson, Gus Speth, Ed Strohbehn receiving the Yale Law School Award of Merit, with president emerita Frances Beinecke (center), 2010. 31. Honorary trustee Joan K. Robinson. 32. From left: Trustee Anna Scott Carter and her husband, Graydon Carter, with Discovery CEO David Zaslav and his wife, Pam, at NRDC's Night of Comedy, 2019.

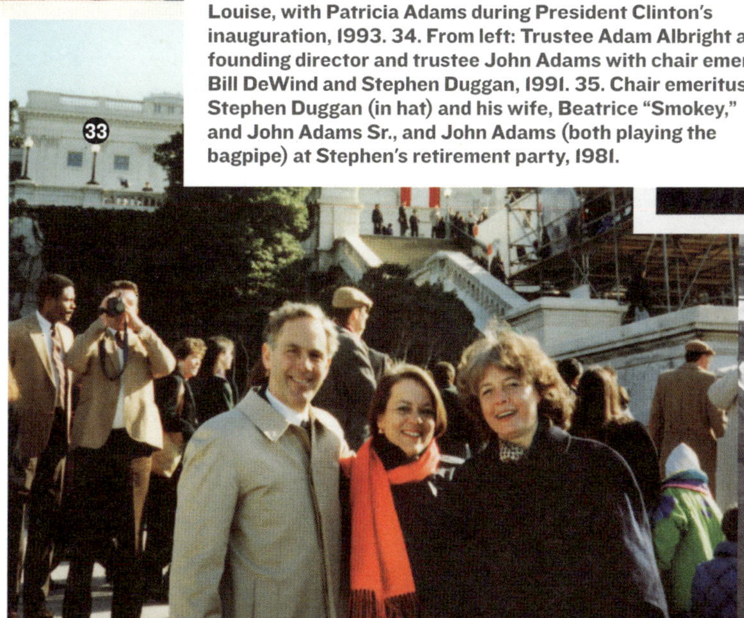
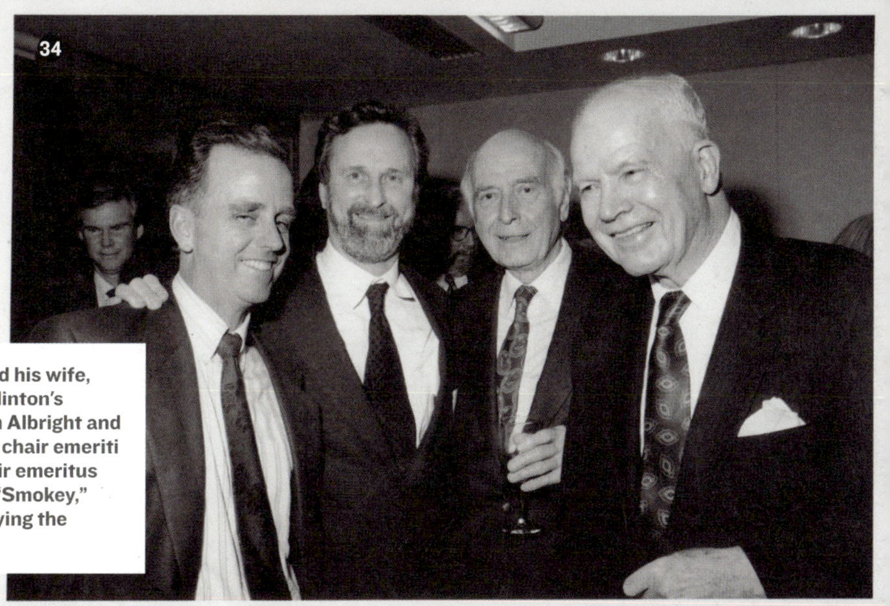
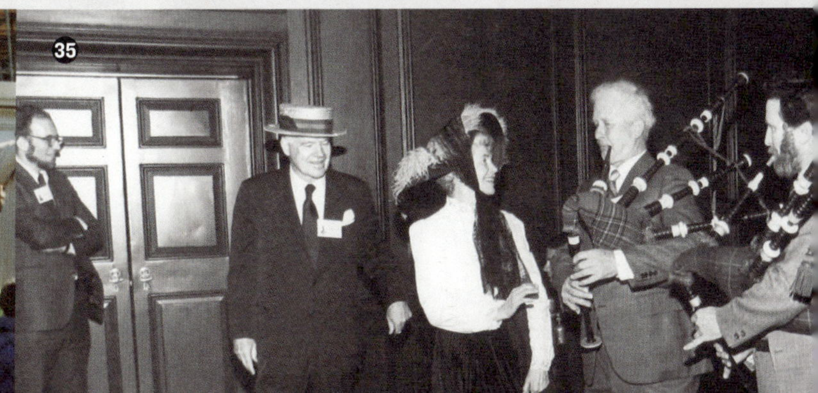

33. From left: NRDC cofounder John Bryson and his wife, Louise, with Patricia Adams during President Clinton's inauguration, 1993. 34. From left: Trustee Adam Albright and founding director and trustee John Adams with chair emeriti Bill DeWind and Stephen Duggan, 1991. 35. Chair emeritus Stephen Duggan (in hat) and his wife, Beatrice "Smokey," and John Adams Sr., and John Adams (both playing the bagpipe) at Stephen's retirement party, 1981.

JOHN LAMPARSKI/GETTY IMAGES. 20. NRDC. 21. JEFF VESPA/GETTY IMAGES. 22. RICH PEDRONCELLI/ASSOCIATED PRESS 23. SCOTT MCKIERNAN. 24–26. NRDC. 27. KIT KARZEN FOR NRDC. 28. STAN BAROUH. NOOGE/PATRICK MCMULLAN VIA GETTY IMAGES. 30. HAROLD SHAPIRO/YALE LAW SCHOOL. 31. KEVIN HAGEN/THE WALL STREET JOURNAL. 32. JUSTIN BISHOP FOR NRDC. 33. NRDC. 34. NRDC. 35. JEFF BLECHMAN. OPENING SPREAD: HERBERT HALWEIL

MOMENTS *in* GRATITUDE

LIFT HERE

Over the decades, the steadfast support and leadership of our dear friends and trustees has kept NRDC strong, focused, and prepared to protect our planet and its people far into the future.

John and Patricia Adams

Solutions Spotlight

REACHING HIGHER GROUND

With climate change already upon us, tackling this crisis and protecting Americans will now take more than cutting carbon pollution.

Looking for practical ways to help those already at risk, Rob Moore, a senior policy analyst in our Chicago office, examined the Federal Emergency Management Administration (FEMA) and its National Flood Insurance Program, which covers more than five million people in 22,000 communities. He and his team found that the maps FEMA produces to assess risk use data only from past floods, without accounting for the projected impacts of climate change.

Worse yet, in 30 states, buyers and renters don't have the right to know whether their homes have ever flooded. If you call FEMA, the agency won't tell you—until you've bought flood insurance. Catch-22. One result: The agency shells out taxpayer dollars for homeowners to rebuild again and again in the same disaster-prone places. (This is not a good strategy for an agency courting financial ruin.) And for people who want to escape flooding and move to higher ground, it typically takes more than five years for a buyout to occur with FEMA funding. Low-income households, in particular, can ill afford to wait that long, and their homes often flood again while they wait for a buyout, if one is offered at all.

As insurance rates climb and FEMA sinks ever deeper into the red, something's got to give. So in 2017, NRDC helped build broad support to pass federal legislation in the House of Representatives to help fix these problems—an increasingly rare example of common sense winning out over partisan dogma. And we continue to work with Congress in hopes of strengthening FEMA's ability to cope with the rising tide of climate-related disasters.

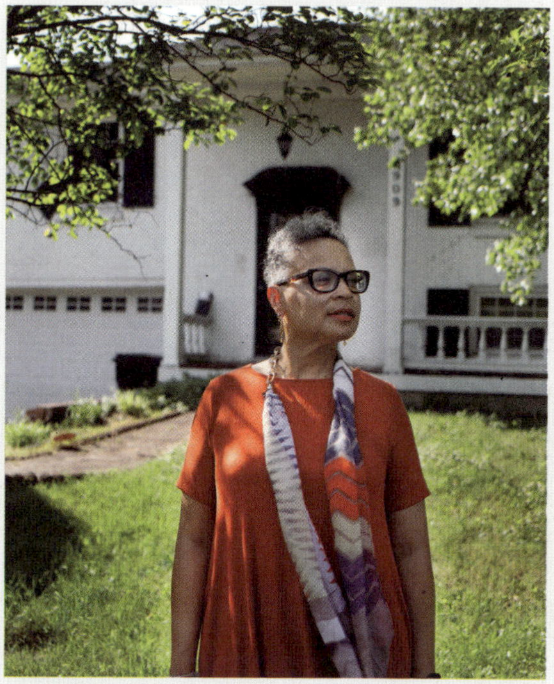

Olga McKissic stands in front of her former home in Louisville, Kentucky. The house flooded five times before She received a buyout through FEMA. Below: Floodwater from the Mississippi River inundates a house in West Alton, Missouri, in June 2019.

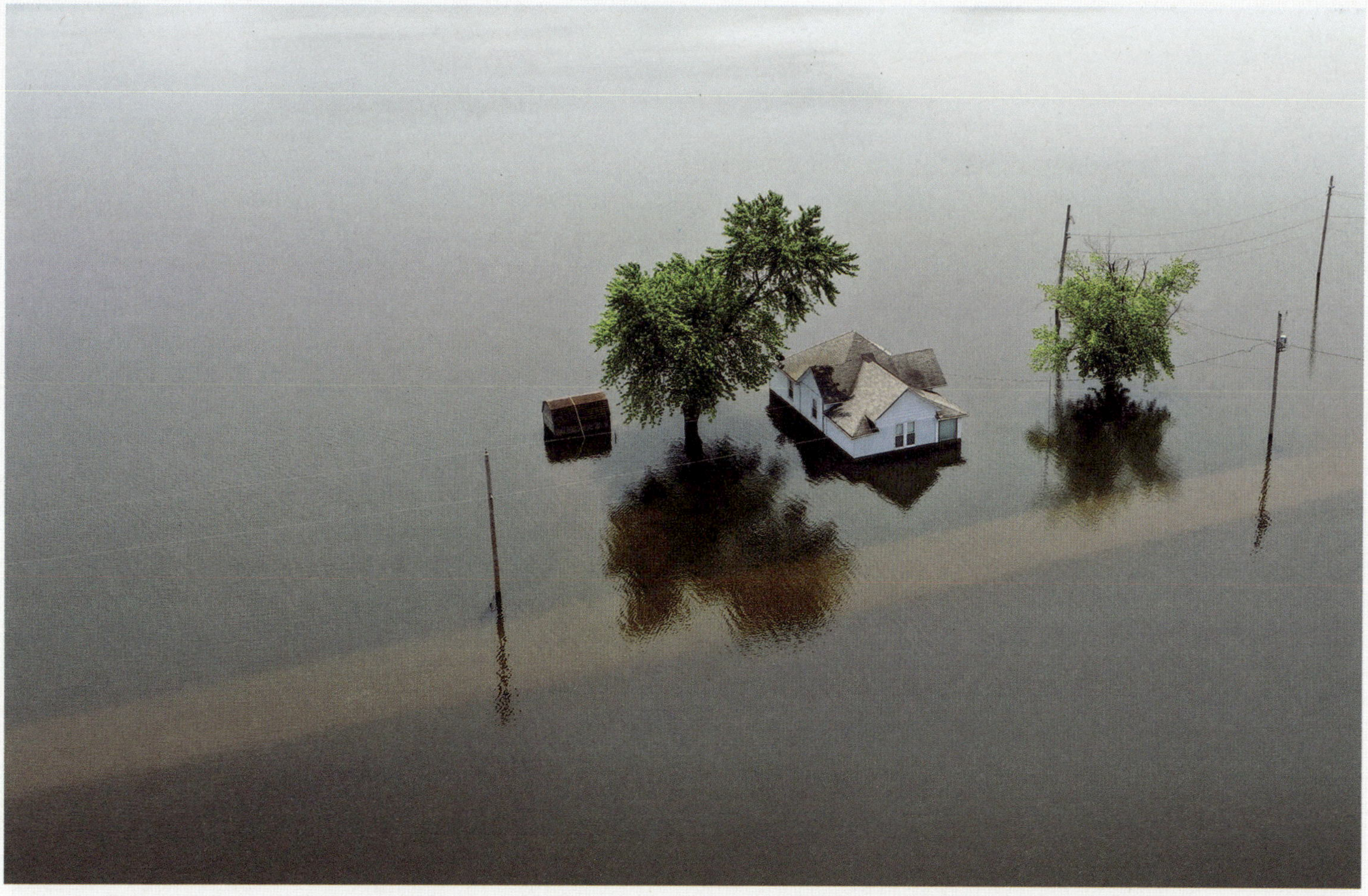

FROM TOP: LUKE SHARRETT FOR NRDC; SCOTT OLSON/GETTY IMAGES

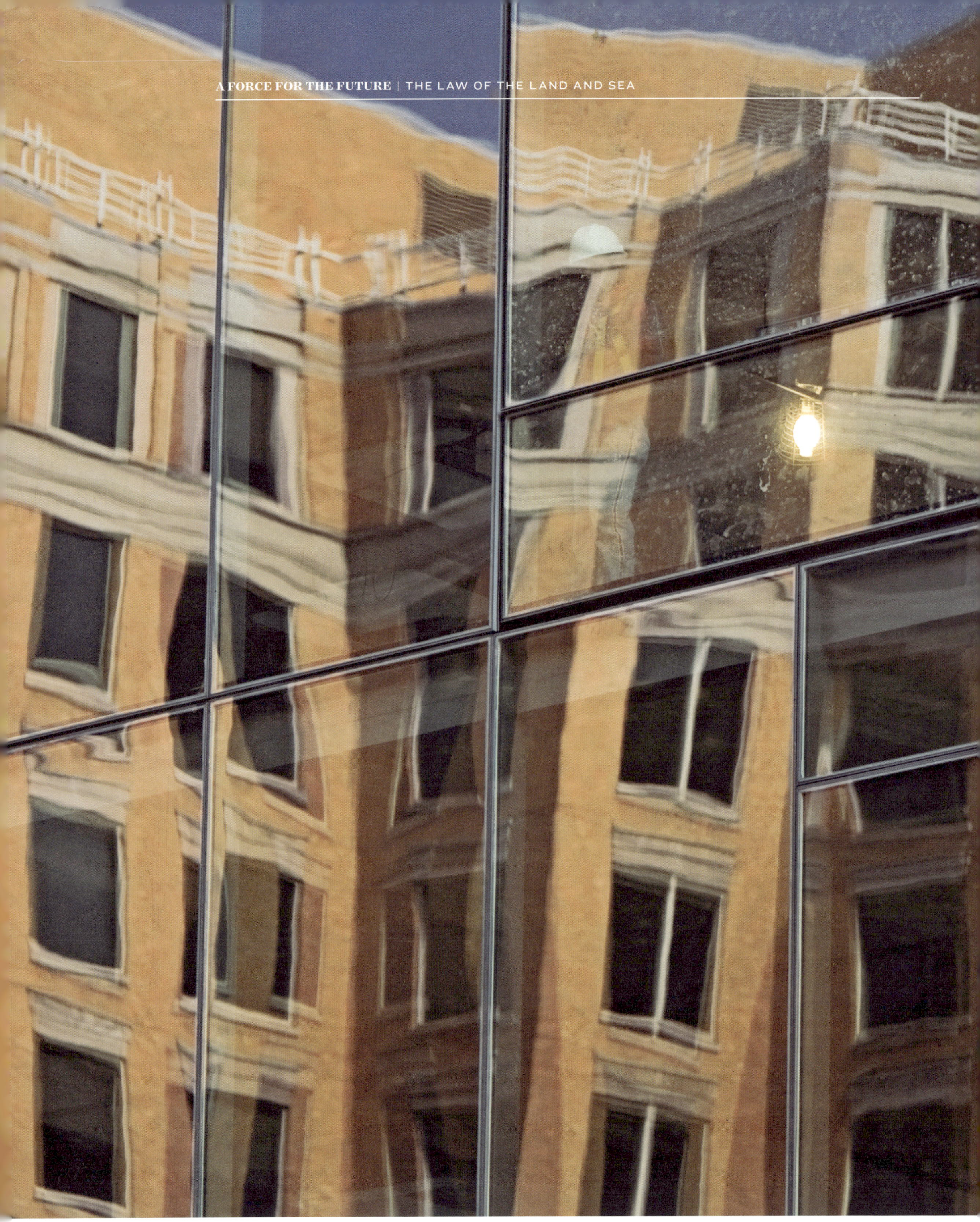

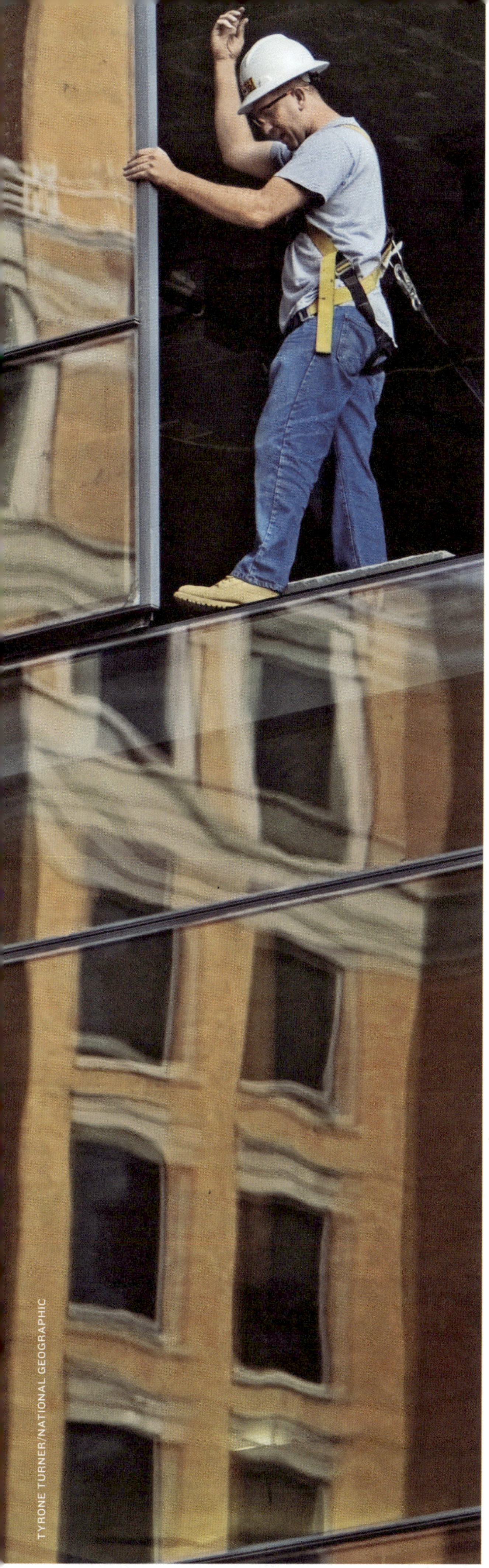
TYRONE TURNER/NATIONAL GEOGRAPHIC

ENERGY EFFICIENCY, AN UNSUNG HERO

It's easy these days to succumb to the doom and gloom surrounding the climate crisis. And with so many bad actors around, some may think that all environmentalists have to offer are sticks and no carrots, or that our main job is to haul polluters and other offenders into court. But that perspective overlooks one of NRDC's most remarkable and long-running achievements: major advances in energy efficiency.

While solar, wind, and other renewables are all vital to growing a low-carbon economy, finding more efficient ways to consume energy is the biggest contributor of all—as well as the cheapest. Energy efficiency has done more to meet the energy needs of our growing economy than oil, gas, coal, and nuclear combined. It's the main reason the country's energy consumption has increased by only about a third in the past 45 years, even as the U.S. economy has grown more than threefold. Along the way, the efficiency game has created millions of good-paying jobs and cut household utility bills by an average of $500 a year.

NRDC's fingerprints have been all over this success story ever since our first California office, headed by John Bryson (who later became the U.S. Secretary of Commerce under President Obama), led the drive for the nation's first-ever efficiency standards for refrigerators. That was in the 1970s. Since then, we've built a team of scientists, engineers, economists, policy experts, and lawyers that has cemented our reputation as national leaders on this issue. Here are just a few examples of what we've accomplished over the decades.

The codirectors of our energy program, Ralph Cavanagh and David Goldstein, are both 40-year veterans of NRDC. Ralph's singular contribution has been to transform the way energy utilities think about their business model. Traditionally, this relied on a simple equation: The more electricity and natural gas they sold, the more money they earned. NRDC showed that utilities' energy sales and financial health could be decoupled. That principle has now been embraced by utilities in 32 states and the District of Columbia.

North American utilities invested $8 billion in energy efficiency in the past year, and their belief in the value of energy efficiency grew in part from an experiment designed by NRDC in the 1980s, in collaboration with then–Pacific Power & Light and the Bonneville Power Administration, to provide professional energy audits and pay for simple measures like insulating walls and attics and installing double-pane windows. More than 90 percent of the households in Hood River County, Oregon, agreed to participate.

A new building goes up in Washington, D.C., featuring energy-efficient, triple-pane glass.

Energy efficiency has done more to meet the energy needs of our growing economy than oil, gas, coal, and nuclear combined. Along the way, the efficiency game has created millions of good-paying jobs.

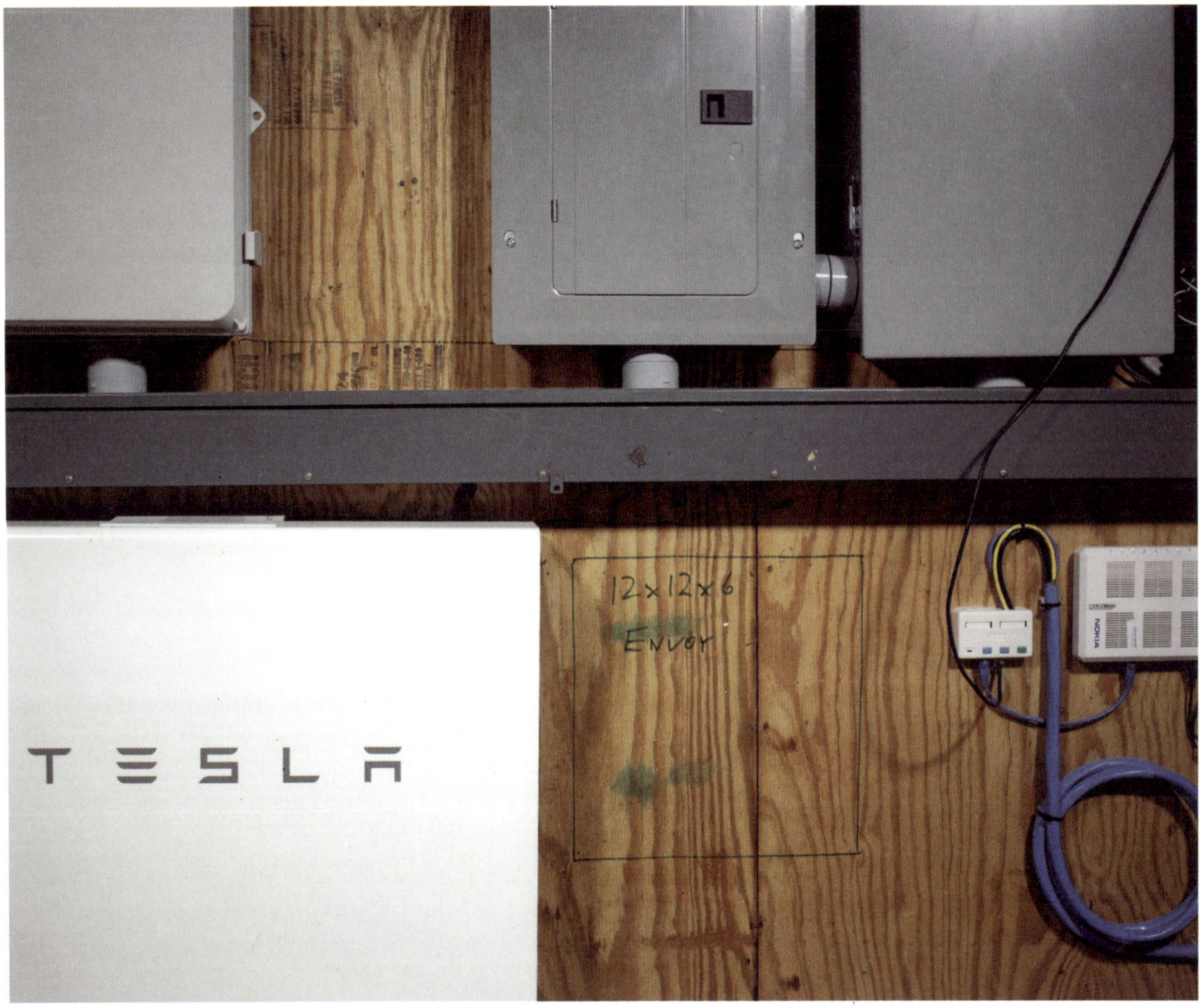

Solutions Spotlight

THE POWER PLAYING FIELD

For years, the mantra of fossil fuel lobbyists was that renewable energy would drive up our electricity bills. But those voices are notably quieter these days as the costs of wind and solar technologies plummet. Since 2009, the cost of solar has gone down by 86 percent and wind by 67 percent.

Even so, states still have a difficult time making smart decisions about their energy mix. Modeling the costs of building, financing, fueling, and operating a power plant and weighing these costs against the megawatts it could generate over its lifetime can be a complex task.

In 2019, a crack team of NRDC analysts created a user-friendly online tool that simplifies this process and allows states to make apples-to-apples comparisons between new sources of power generation. In short, the tool demonstrates the "levelized cost of electricity" for new utility-scale solar, wind, natural gas, coal, and nuclear plants. Interactive maps and tables show the most economical new energy sources for any particular state, and the evidence couldn't be clearer: Solar and wind are already the lowest-cost options in 34 states; by 2030, that number will have risen to 48, with natural gas accounting for the remaining two. As for new coal plants, says NRDC policy analyst Amanda Levin, "they're not even in the game."

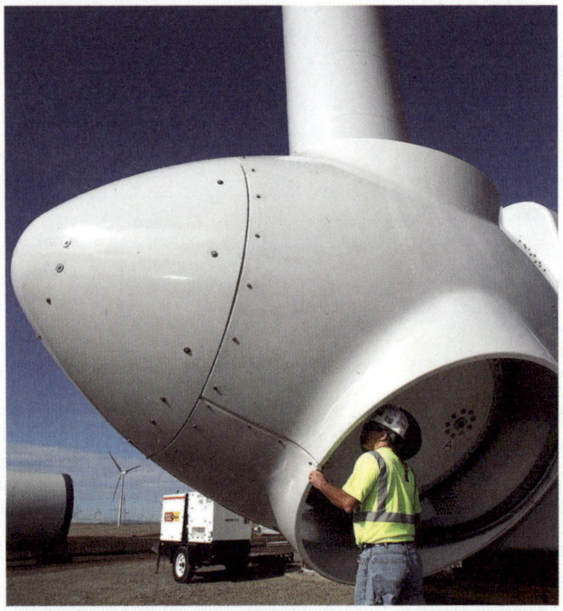

FROM TOP: LUKE SHARRETT FOR NRDC; KEN JAMES/BLOOMBERG VIA GETTY IMAGES

They saved energy—and money—and reduced the power companies' needs to build expensive new generating plants, paving the way for nationwide expansion of utility-financed energy efficiency programs.

The key to easing Americans' everyday electric demands is setting efficiency standards—some mandatory and others voluntary—and then steadily ramping them up. Building on California's early progress on refrigerators and air conditioners, David collaborated with the U.S. Department of Energy and with manufacturers to extend such standards to lighting fixtures, water heaters, clothes dryers, dishwashers, and a slew of other household appliances. Support for his work cut across party lines. David's efforts were instrumental in the Reagan administration's adoption of the 1987 National Appliance Energy Conservation Act, and it was George W. Bush who introduced the first standards for household light bulbs. Efficiency standards for appliances, equipment, and federal buildings put in place by the Obama administration (and currently being threatened by the Trump administration) promise to prevent three billion tons of carbon pollution by 2030.

Noah Horowitz, who, like Ralph and David, is based in NRDC's San Francisco office, has focused on the newest generation of home appliances. Trained as an engineer, he calculated the surprising amount of energy being consumed unnecessarily by common AC/DC adapters. That these devices converted so much of their electricity to heat, allowing much of the energy to simply escape into the air (becoming hot to the touch in the process), made no sense. When Noah came to NRDC in 1998, cellphone chargers were almost as big as the phone itself; today, thanks largely to Noah's insights, they're now not much larger than an ice cube and are dramatically more efficient. Next, we targeted what Noah calls "vampire devices"—set-top cable boxes, game consoles, computers, and monitors, which can guzzle energy from the socket even when not in use. If you think you've switched off your cable box, you may have done no more than dim the light on its digital clock. Thanks to an agreement Noah struck with the leading pay TV service providers, these boxes have cut annual energy use by 40 percent since 2012.

Over the years, NRDC has taken the lessons we've learned about efficiency to the rest of the world. We helped China and Russia formulate their first energy codes for residential and commercial buildings, and we're currently advising the Indian government on its push for more climate-friendly air conditioners as the country's consumer demand surges. But whether home or abroad, our devotion to energy efficiency is all part of our drive to sustain what Ralph calls "the irresistible momentum of the clean energy revolution."

NRDC emphasizes the importance of energy-efficient solutions—from solar panels to appliances to other home energy-saving devices—which help cut carbon pollution, create jobs, and lower electric bills.

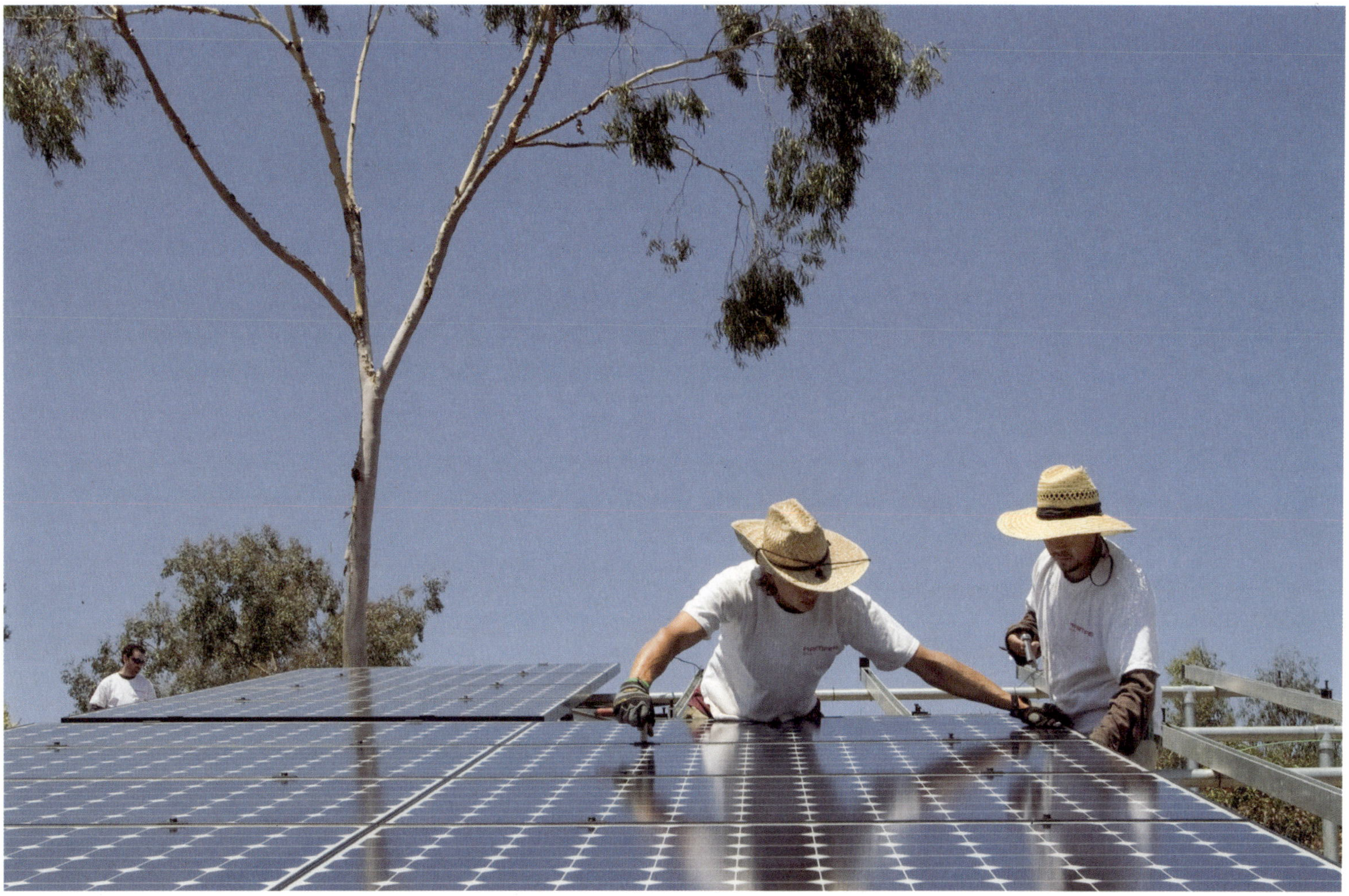

UNIVERSAL IMAGES GROUP VIA GETTY IMAGES

BATTLE FOR THE NORTH

ALASKA'S LICENSE PLATES CALL THIS land "The Last Frontier." And it's not difficult to see why. Think of the 19 million acres of untouched beauty in the Arctic National Wildlife Refuge, with its roaring rivers, towering peaks, and iconic wildlife—it's America's Serengeti. Or picture the deep greens of the majestic old-growth forests of the Tongass, one of the most important carbon sinks on the planet. But, unfortunately, the Tongass and the Arctic are also the last frontiers for extractive industries that would like nothing better than to plunder their wealth. "This region is not only the most revered place of all for the environmental movement," says Frances Beinecke. "It's where the world is changing most rapidly because of our warming climate."

NRDC has fought to protect Alaska since the 1970s, when we first responded to the timber industry's efforts to clearcut parts of the Tongass. Our work was critical to the design and adoption of the 2001 Roadless Rule, which prevented logging in 60 million acres of our national forest system, the 17-million-acre Tongass being its crown jewel. And ever since the Reagan administration first threatened to open the Arctic National Wildlife Refuge to oil drilling, we've been at the forefront of repeated successful efforts to protect it over the decades. The historic, bipartisan Arctic Cultural and Coastal Plain Protection Act, passed by the House of Representatives in August 2019, is just the latest piece of legislation we've helped to shape.

These treasured landscapes still face threats, but the widest-ranging menace to our natural heritage in Alaska comes from oil companies wanting to sink their drills deep into the floor of the Arctic Ocean and areas in the Outer Continental Shelf. For example, when President Obama announced his "all-of-the-above" energy policy in 2012, it included expanding offshore drilling on the Outer Continental Shelf—a shocking idea just two years after the Deepwater Horizon disaster. NRDC rose up to protect the Eastern Seaboard, which has not seen a drill rig in three decades. We marshaled evidence of overwhelming bipartisan opposition from governors, lawmakers, and countless communities whose well-being and economies depend on the health of their coastal waters. Under such intense pressure, the Obama administration backed down. We also hatched a plan to save the Arctic Ocean in its entirety.

The remote and frigid seas of the far north are the worst places on earth for oil drills and tankers. Even the hurricane-prone Gulf of Mexico is like a millpond in comparison to Arctic waters, which are icebound for eight months of the

Imperiled polar bears, along with gray wolves, musk oxen, caribou, and many more iconic wildlife species, roam the Arctic National Wildlife Refuge's 19 million acres.

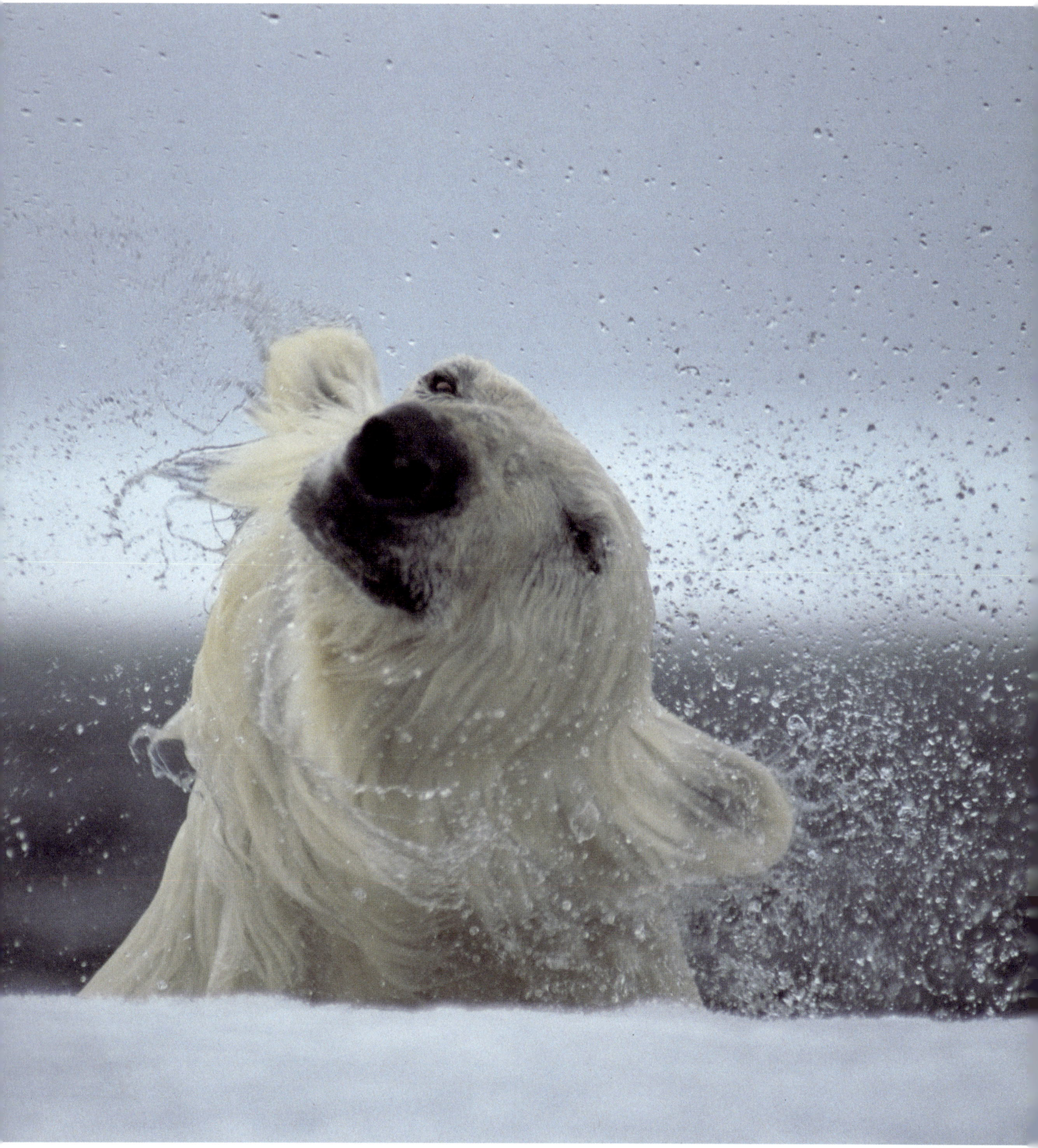

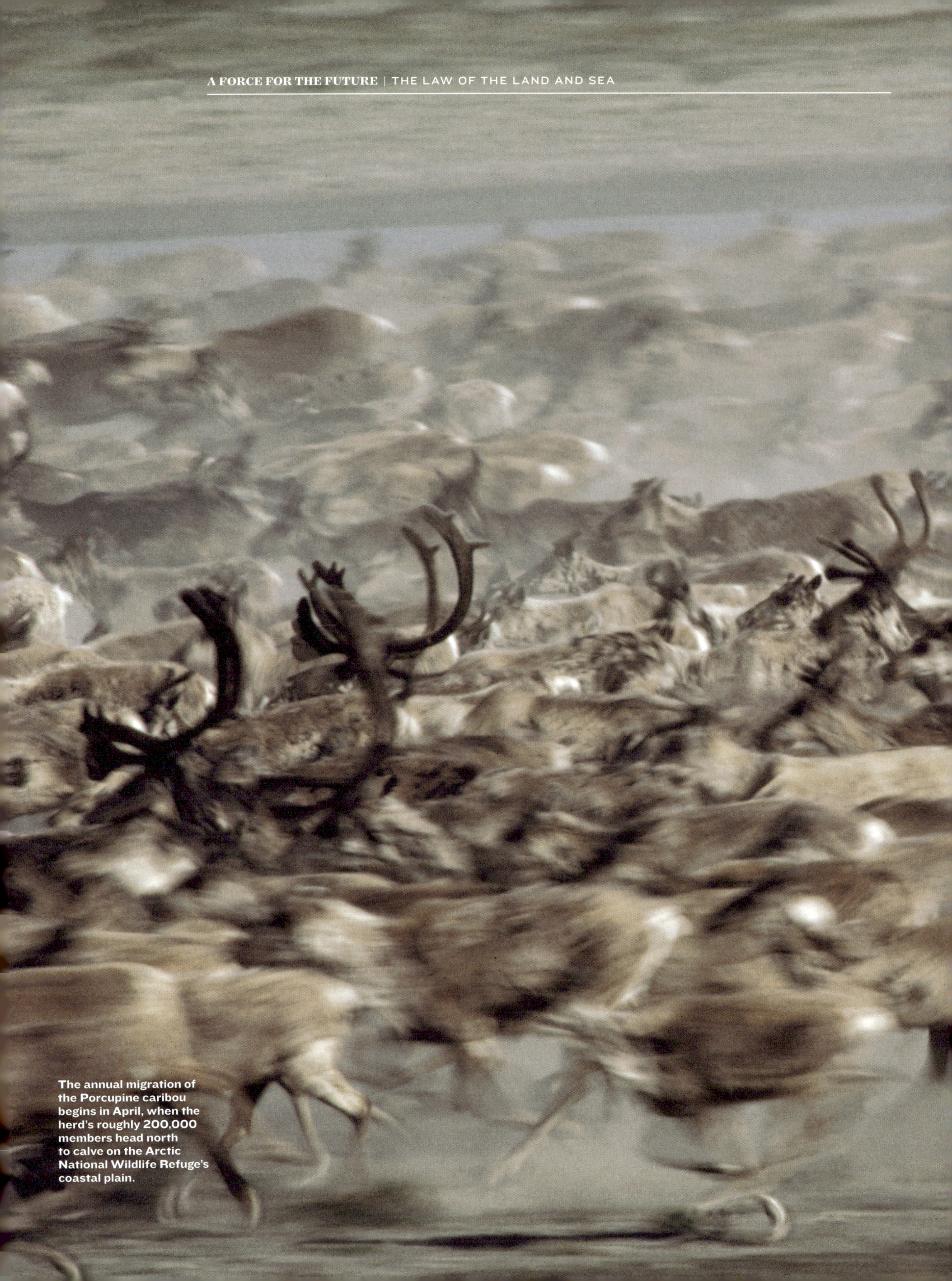

The annual migration of the Porcupine caribou begins in April, when the herd's roughly 200,000 members head north to calve on the Arctic National Wildlife Refuge's coastal plain.

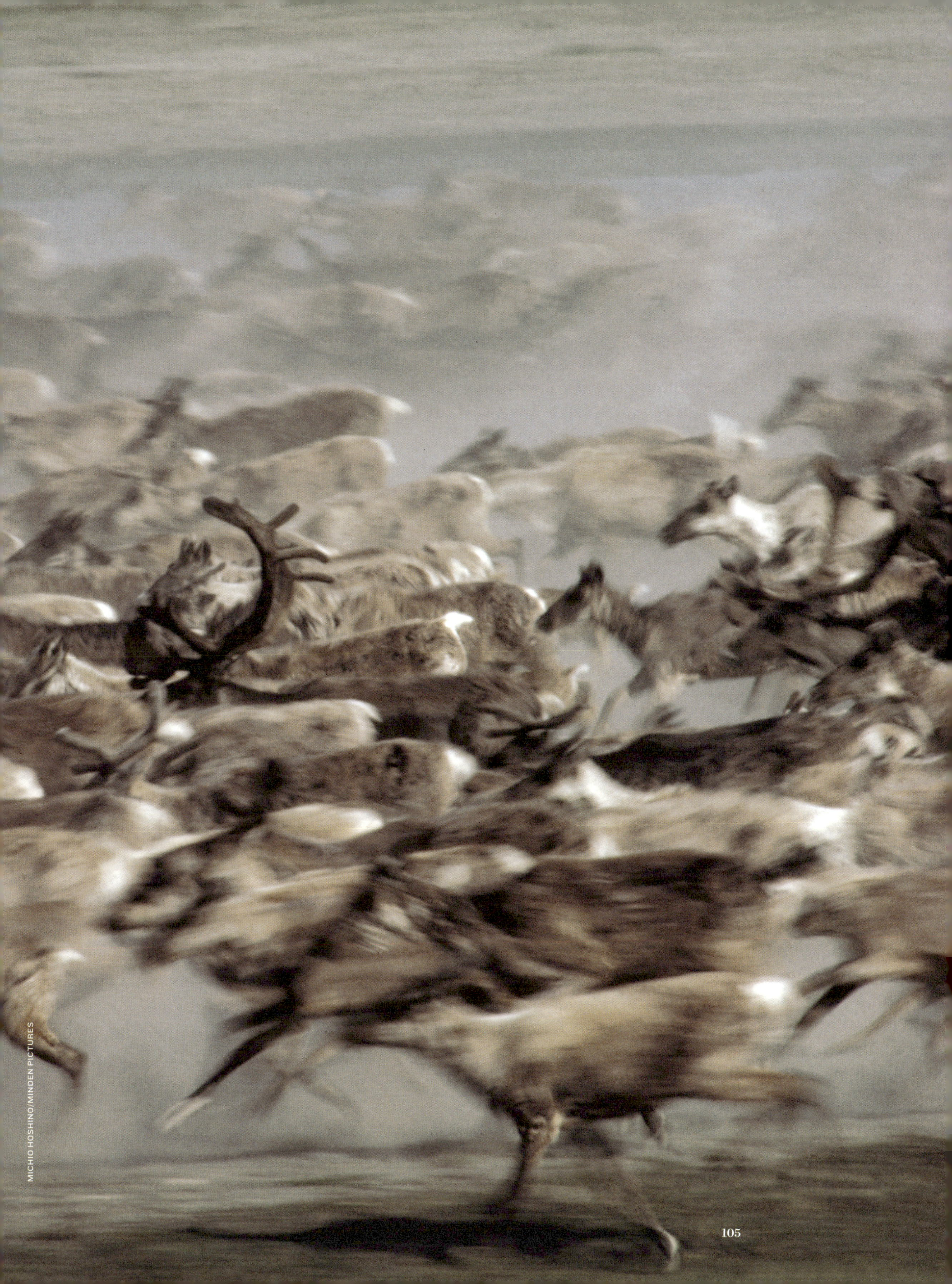

MICHIO HOSHINO/MINDEN PICTURES

FROM THE FRONTLINES

Mike Jackson

As a leader of the Tlingit tribe in southeastern Alaska, Mike Jackson has helped run summertime "culture camps" for more than 30 years. The weeklong event, held in the remote island village of Kake, is a chance to teach young people traditional ways of life, as well as to engage with them on tough issues such as suicide prevention. The campers forage, preserve seal and moose meat, smoke fish, practice totem carving, and pickle a deep-red mollusk called gumboot chiton. Mike—whose Tlingit name is Ka-oosh and who is an expert carver and former magistrate in town—credits the camp with building a stronger sense of community and improving mental health. "We reminded the youth how much they were loved and how they had a part to contribute to our tribe," Jackson says.

Both the camp and the native culture it preserves rely on the land—specifically, the Tongass National Forest. Rich in wildlife like salmon, bears, and wolves, the Tongass is one of the largest stretches of old-growth temperate rainforest in the world. Most of it is also unlogged and road-free. But its pristine state cannot be taken for granted. Threats from the logging and mining industries loom large, particularly for communities like Kake. "If you look at a satellite photo, you can tell that a lot of the logging has been around small native villages—not around cities like Juneau. It's environmental discrimination," Mike says. "Meanwhile, we're still living with the waste of historic mining from way back when there was a gold rush in Alaska."

The Organized Village of Kake, the formal designation for this primarily Tlingit community, has taken to the courts to beat back these threats. In 2001, it joined NRDC and other environmental groups in supporting the Roadless Rule, a federal law that conserved 58 million acres of wild national forests across 37 states. President Bill Clinton signed the rule into law in 2001, but it wasn't long before the George W. Bush administration began trying to roll it back. First up was an attempt to exempt the Tongass from the Roadless Rule altogether.

With the Kake tribe as lead plaintiff, NRDC and our partners at Earthjustice sued and got that exemption ruled illegal, defended our win on appeal, and persuaded the Supreme Court to leave it in place. The Bush administration could not ignore established facts showing the importance of preserving the wild Tongass, the courts said. The Roadless Rule would stand in Alaska—as would the ancient forest and the communities that it supports there. Today, despite renewed attacks on the Tongass by the Trump administration, Mike's culture camp is readying itself for its 33rd year. "We're continuing to defend our area," he says, "and thanks to our partnership with NRDC, I know we're going to put up a good fight."

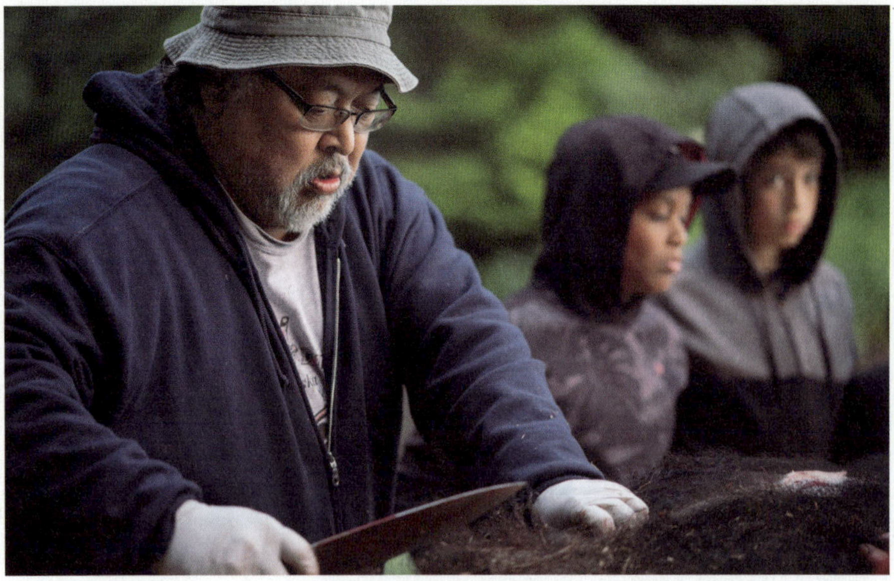

Mike Jackson at the Kake Culture Camp, 2018.

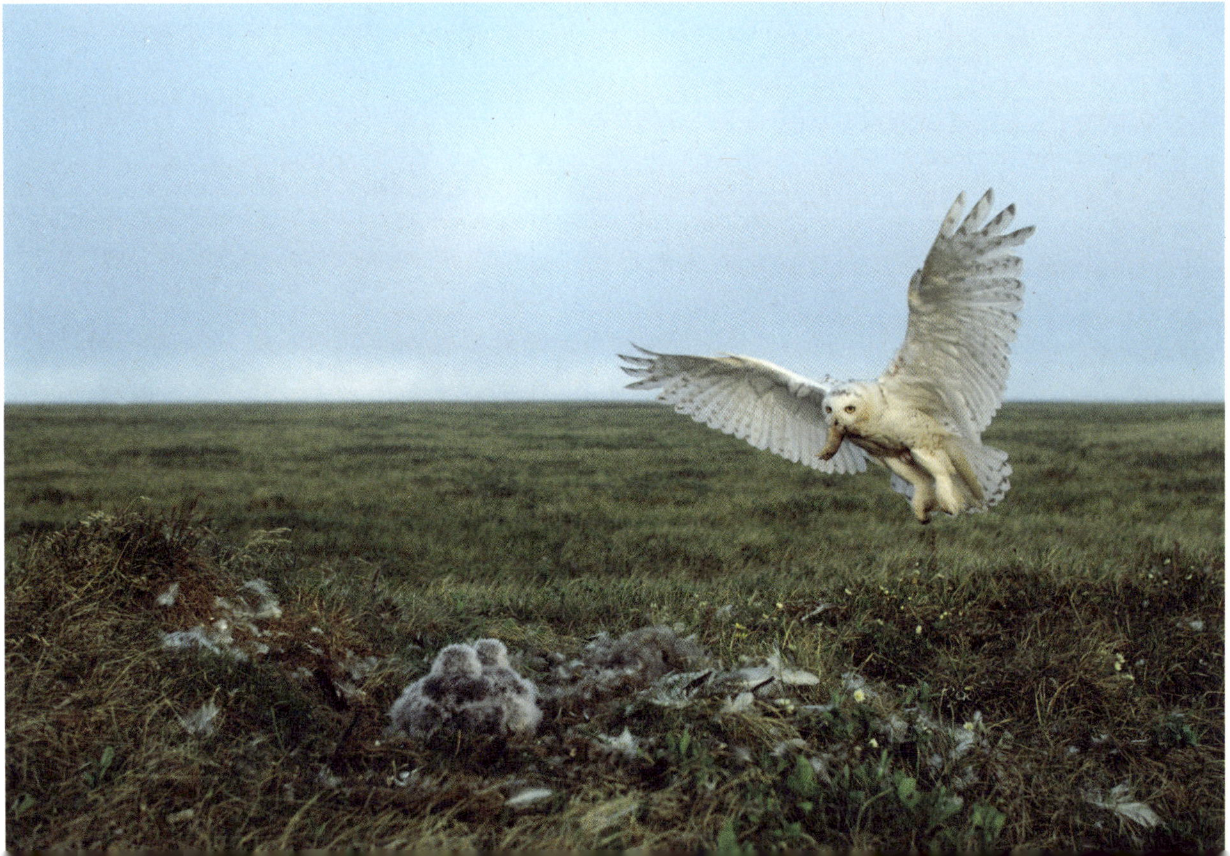

A snowy owl brings a mouse to its owlets nesting in the tundra of the Arctic National Wildlife Refuge.

FROM TOP: BETHANY GOODRICH/SUSTAINABLE SOUTHEAST PARTNERSHIP; MICHIO HOSHINO/MINDEN PICTURES

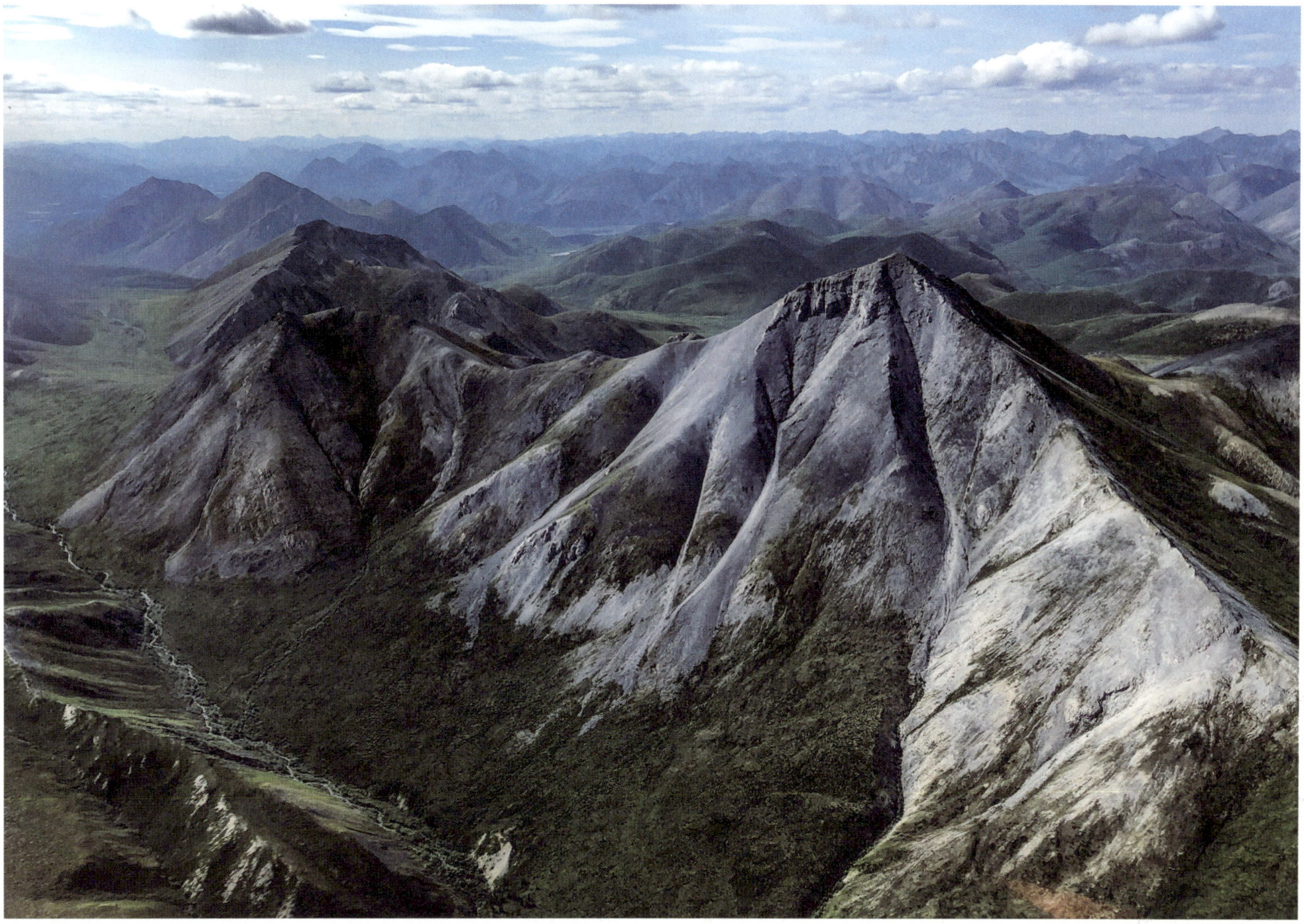

year, often shrouded in fog or darkness, and whipped by gale-force winds. Should disaster strike, help would be far away, and cleaning up an oil spill wouldn't work at all here. Even by the oil industry's own terms, the endeavor to drill the Arctic is all risk and no reward. The most recent exploration, by Shell, was an expensive fiasco. By the time the company pulled out in 2015, it had spent $7 billion for zero return. In any case, bringing that oil to market would have taken more than 20 years—by which time we will have either switched to the clean energy economy we desperately need or watched the planet's climate pass the point of no return.

NRDC built a broad-based campaign, backed by hard science, to get the Obama administration to end Arctic Ocean drilling forever. We used state-of-the-art software to model the paths of potential major spills from the sites where Shell held leases. The results were horrifying. A spill in the Chukchi Sea would travel 700 miles through the Bering Strait. A blowout in the Beaufort Sea had at least a 90 percent chance of reaching the Alaskan coast. Either scenario would put vast reaches of ocean waters, marine life, and the Arctic Refuge itself at risk.

In November 2016, Obama placed 128 million acres of the Outer Continental Shelf permanently off-limits to future drilling, including 98 percent of federal Arctic waters—a landmark victory for which NRDC can claim both authorship and leadership. Obama's legal authority rested on a provision of the 1953 Outer Continental Shelf Lands Act, which says that a president may, "from time to time, withdraw from disposition any unleased areas" offshore. There's not a word in the law about revoking such withdrawals, but soon after coming into office, President Trump tried to do precisely that. We immediately filed suit with Earthjustice, our frequent litigation partner, on behalf of a coalition of a dozen environmental and Indigenous groups.

Like all of NRDC's best litigators, Niel Lawrence, director of our Alaska project, believes in getting to the bottom of what our laws mean and how they should be enforced. Our suit walked the court through the intent, purpose, and history of the law, and showed how Trump's action flouted both the statute and the Constitution. A federal judge in Alaska agreed with us and put up a large red stop sign to our would-be ocean polluters. As we've learned, however, stop signs don't mean much to the Trump administration, and we now look forward to a rematch before the Court of Appeals for the Ninth Circuit. With the last frontier at stake, we can do nothing less.

An aerial view of mountains in the Arctic National Wildlife Refuge.

DANIELLE BRIGIDA/USFWS

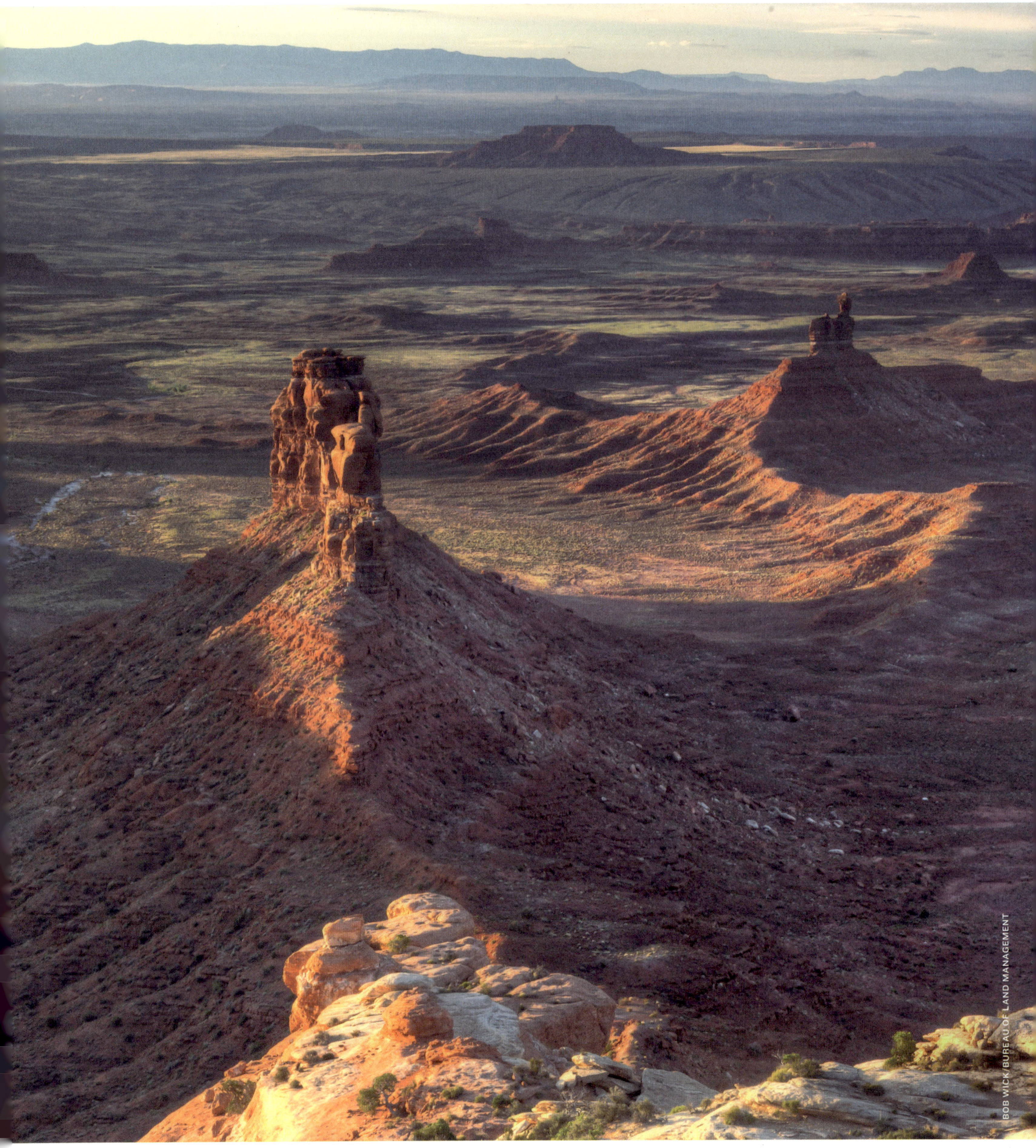

BOB WICK/BUREAU OF LAND MANAGEMENT

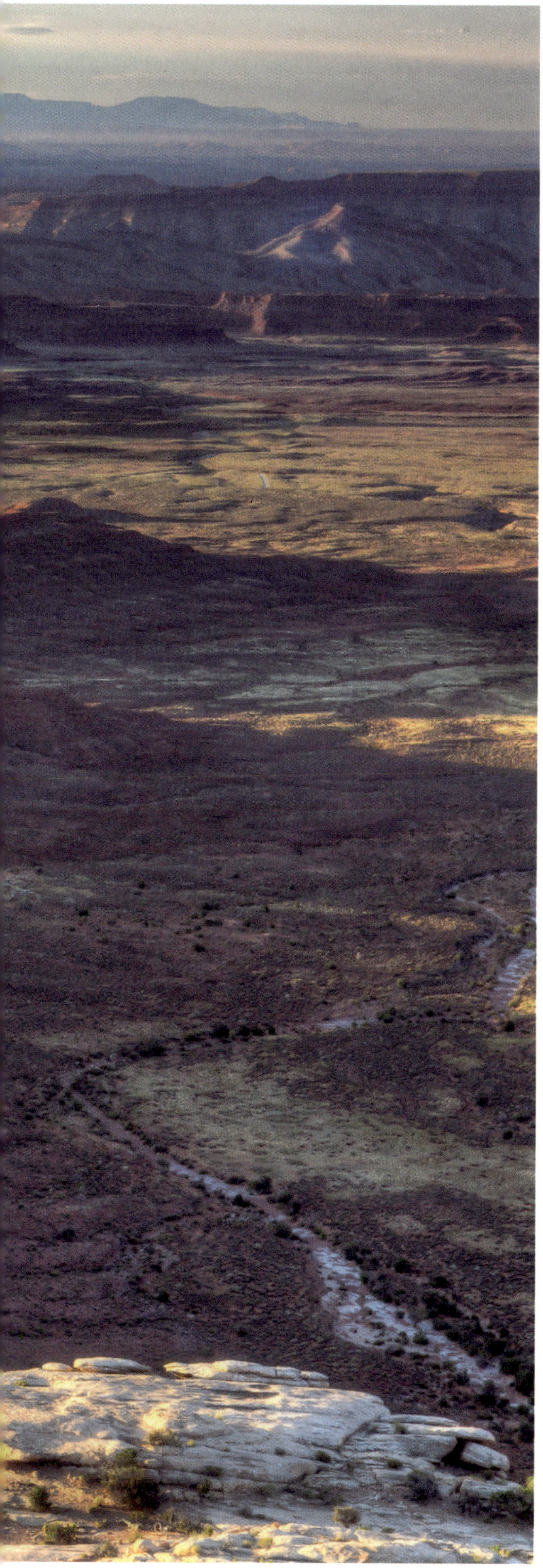

"THE LAND MANAGES US"

THE BREATHTAKING WILD LANDS OF THE West are one of America's true glories. These great, wide-open spaces contain so much of our collective history and have helped sculpt our national identity. Shielding these lands from damaging development by special interests has been a core part of NRDC's mission from the beginning. Yet huge stretches of the West are at risk from extractive industries—nowhere more so than in Utah, where more than 11 million acres of wilderness are publicly owned yet have been ineffectively managed and political opposition to federal control has often been virulent. NRDC has worked in the state for more than 30 years, in close partnership with one of the finest environmental groups in the nation, the Southern Utah Wilderness Alliance (SUWA).

During President Obama's second term, NRDC, SUWA, and others thought hard about identifying a major conservation project that could burnish his administration's legacy as a defender of public lands. In the end, the idea that fired our imaginations came not from any environmental group but from a coalition of five sovereign nations—the Navajo Nation, the Hopi Tribe, the Pueblo of Zuni, the Ute Mountain Ute Tribe, and the Ute Indian Tribe. The area they chose was a wondrous expanse of red-rock formations, labyrinthine canyons, desert mesas, and green hanging gardens. The landscape also features twin buttes that resemble the ears of a bear and gave the place its name.

The leaders of the Bears Ears campaign are the tribes themselves; our job has been to honor their vision and use our influence to support their struggle to protect their sacred lands and heritage. An environmentalist's first instinct may be to focus on the threat to Bears Ears from the oil and gas and hard-rock mining industries that covet its hidden wealth. But the intertribal coalition showed us that the land's significance runs much deeper. Bears Ears is a vast, dynamic landscape housing more than 100,000 cultural sites that are intimately woven into the creation narratives, history, and religious practices of the five tribes.

The fight for Bears Ears was radical and innovative in several ways: It was an opportunity to protect a priceless landscape on an epic scale, it united tribes who had been historic adversaries, and it outlined a novel scheme of "co-management" by federal agencies and a commission of the five tribes. And who else could be better equipped for the job? asks Kabir Green, a senior advocate at NRDC who has worked extensively on Bears Ears. Kabir likes to quote one

The ancestral homelands of several Native American tribes lie within Bears Ears National Monument. These lands are culturally, religiously, and historically important and deserve protection.

tribal member: "We don't manage land; the land manages us."

Just before leaving office, Obama signed an eloquent proclamation setting aside 1.35 million acres of Bears Ears for permanent protection as a national monument. As many presidents have done before him, Obama created the monument through the legal authority of the Antiquities Act of 1906, part of the great conservation legacy of President Theodore Roosevelt. But his successor, Donald Trump, made clear his intention to tear up Obama's proclamation. Within a few months of taking office, Trump ordered his first secretary of the Interior Department, Ryan Zinke, to "review" the status of 27 of our more than 150 national monuments, Bears Ears and the nearby Grand Staircase-Escalante obviously being his prime targets. Years of scientific study and extensive public input had preceded Obama's decision. During Trump's review, some 2.7 million Americans, including countless NRDC members, filed comments on Bears Ears, 98 percent of them in favor of its protection. But Trump ignored them, and with a single stroke of his Sharpie, he slashed the monument's acreage by 85 percent. It should come as no surprise that detailed maps produced by SUWA showed that the areas removed from protection were precisely those that fossil fuel and mining interests had set their sights on.

We lost no time in responding. Within days of Trump's decision, NRDC, SUWA, and nine other conservation groups filed a lawsuit against the administration in federal district court in Washington, D.C., which has consolidated our case with separate suits by the five tribes and by a third group of plaintiffs. Our argument is straightforward: The Antiquities Act gives presidents the right to create national monuments; it says nothing about removing them.

So far so good. In September 2019, the court denied the Trump administration's request to dismiss the case, but the fight continues in the courts. I'm confident that we'll prevail and that we'll celebrate the day when another president restores this inspirational national monument, helping to protect a unique part of this country's rich cultural fabric.

"In fighting for Bears Ears alongside five Indian nations, NRDC stood up for equity and inclusion as well as conservation. It's time we used invaluable Indigenous knowledge in making wise decisions about the lands that belong to each and every American."

—Sharon Buccino, senior director of NRDC's Lands Division

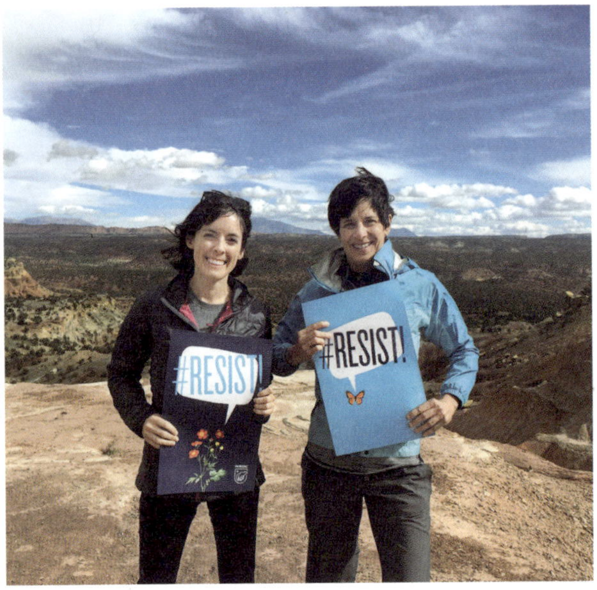

Sharon Buccino and her team supported the Bears Ears Inter-Tribal Coalition as it petitioned President Obama to create the Bears Ears National Monument in 2016 and has since been working to defend the monument in court. Here, Buccino (right) and NRDC senior attorney and managing litigator Kate Desormeau stand with protest signs near Bears Ears.

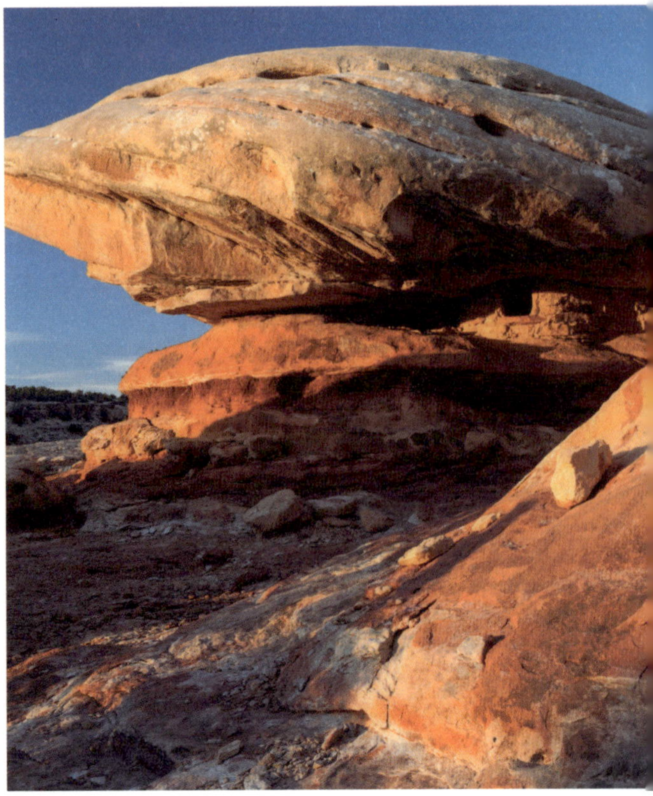

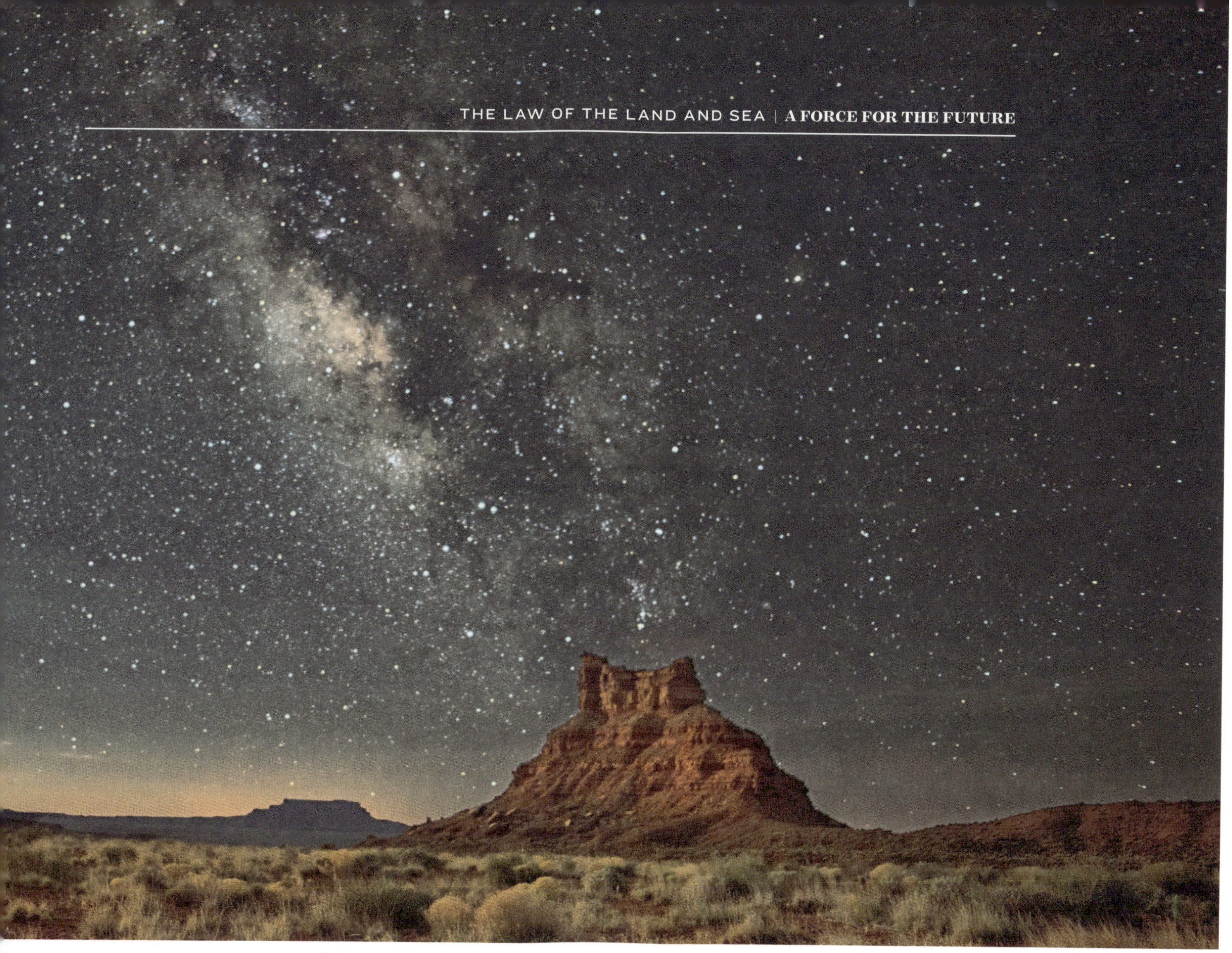

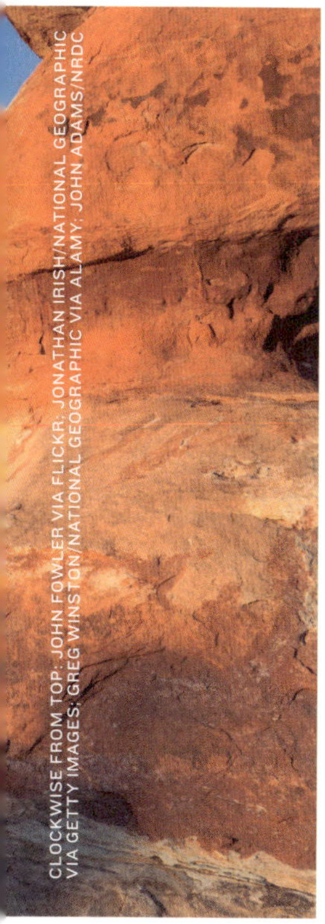

CLOCKWISE FROM TOP: JOHN FOWLER VIA FLICKR; JONATHAN IRISH/NATIONAL GEOGRAPHIC VIA GETTY IMAGES; GREG WINSTON/NATIONAL GEOGRAPHIC VIA ALAMY; JOHN ADAMS/NRDC

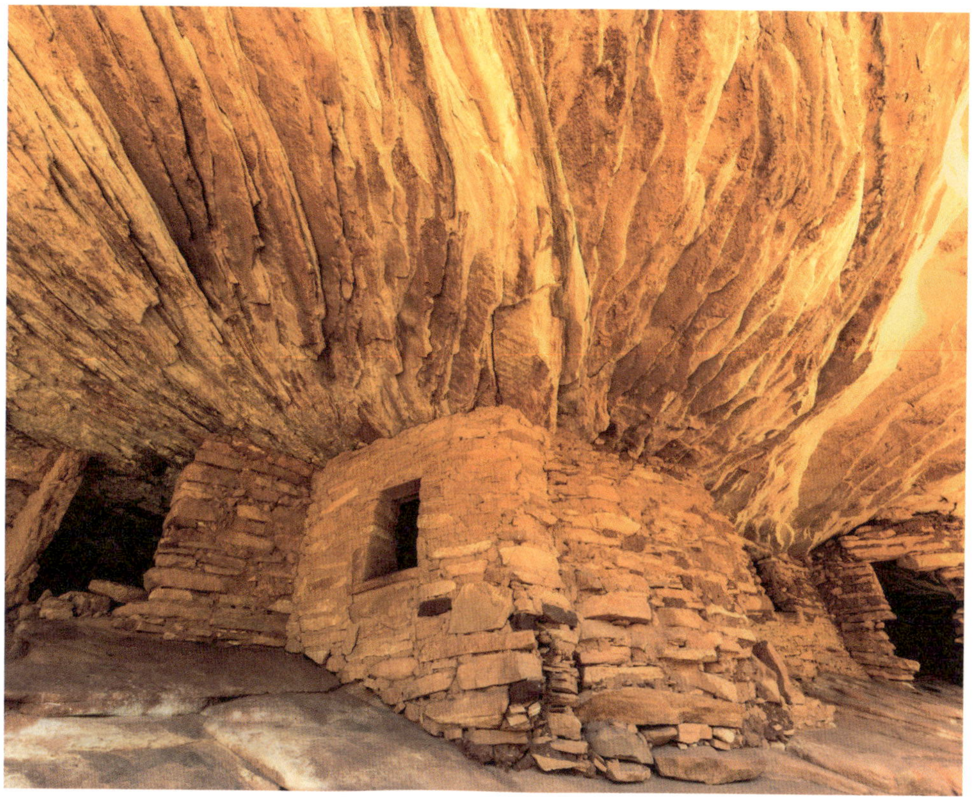

Along with its ancient dwellings, kivas, granaries, and rock art, Bears Ears also represents one of the most pristine, road-free areas in the contiguous United States, featuring a rugged labyrinth of sandstone canyons, cliffs and rock arches, meadows, and desert mesas.

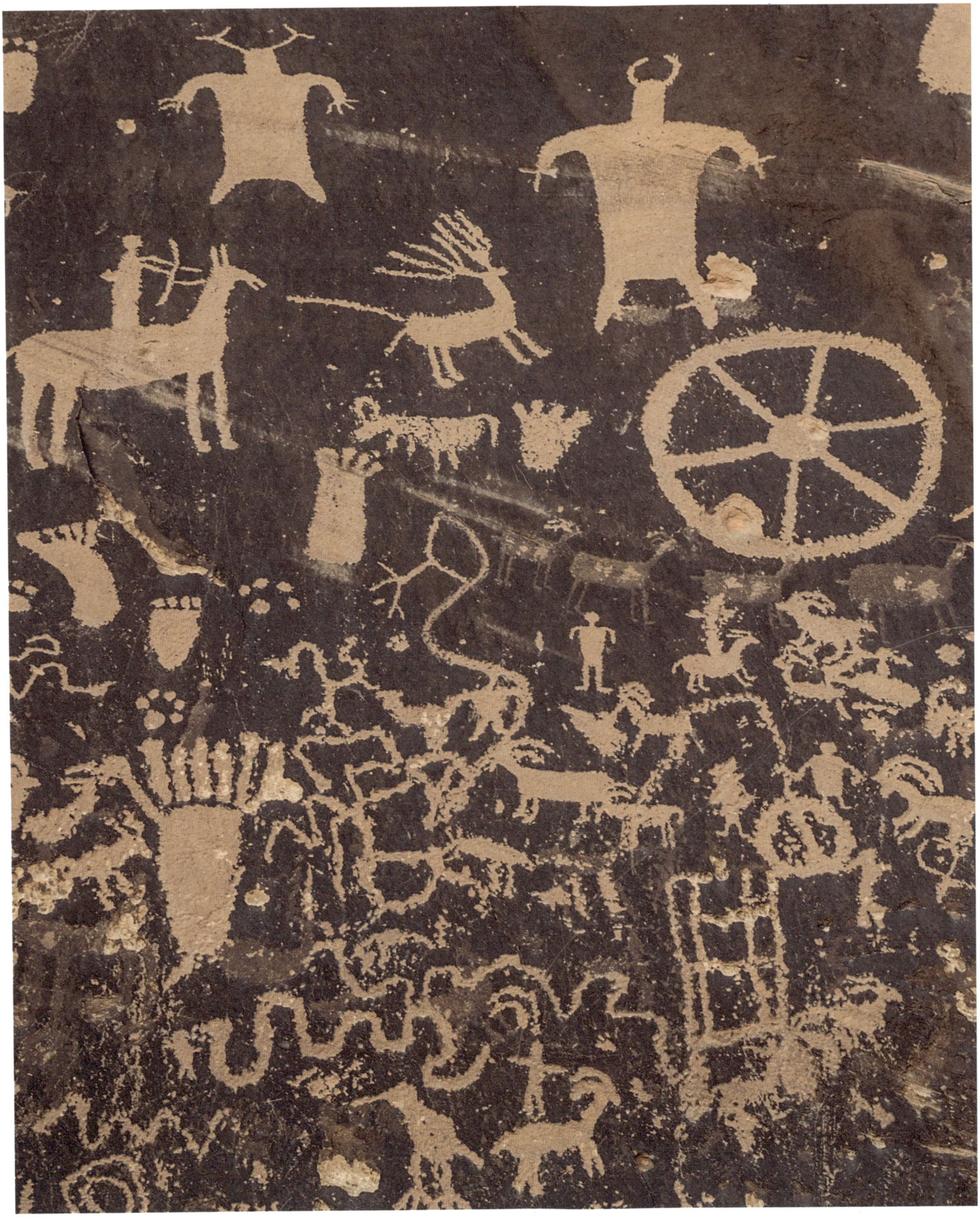

AARON HUEY/NATIONAL GEOGRAPHIC (2)

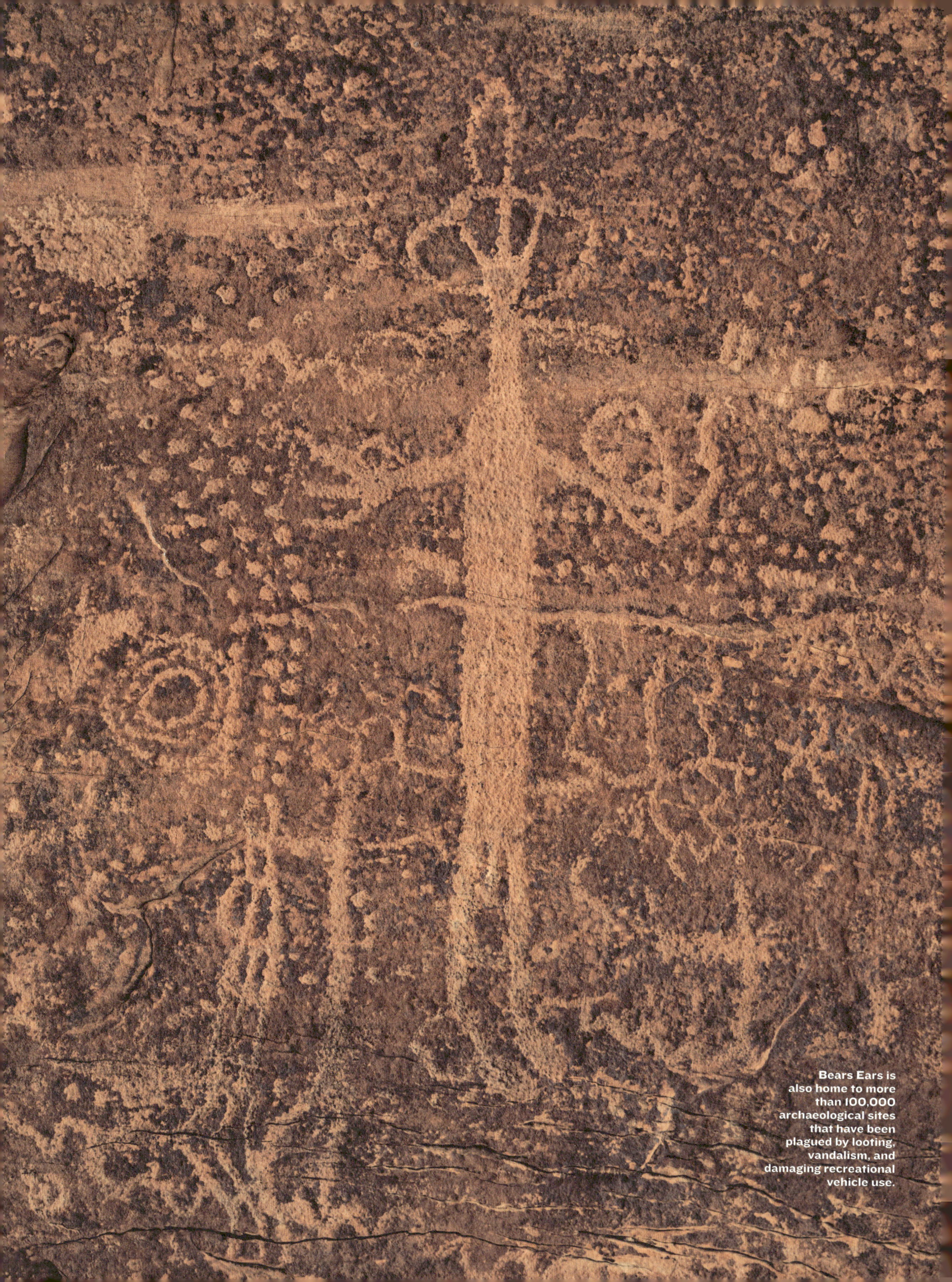

Bears Ears is also home to more than 100,000 archaeological sites that have been plagued by looting, vandalism, and damaging recreational vehicle use.

VICTORIES THAT RUN DEEP

NRDC WAS A MAJOR FORCE BEHIND A moratorium on offshore oil and gas drilling that covered the entire Outer Continental Shelf off the eastern and western coasts, the eastern Gulf of Mexico, and Alaska's Bristol Bay and lasted for more than 25 years in most of those areas. So, by the time a group of us attended the landmark Earth Summit in Rio de Janeiro in 1992, NRDC had already gained a reputation as a fierce protector of our oceans.

One hot topic in Rio was the growing threat of overfishing. The depletion of the world's coastal waters had been driving fishing fleets farther out onto the high seas, beyond the territorial jurisdiction of any single country. Soon after we returned, I asked the leaders of our oceans team, Sarah Chasis and Lisa Speer, to think of creative ways for NRDC to address the problem. What Sarah, a lawyer, and Lisa, a marine policy expert, have accomplished with their team since Rio is nothing short of extraordinary.

For starters, I don't think the United States would have supported a legally binding global fisheries treaty—the U.N. Fish Stocks Agreement that the Senate ratified in 1996—without pressure from NRDC. The agreement set strong conservation standards for managing fish that migrate over great distances, like tuna, as well as those that move back and forth between the high seas and the waters of one or more countries, such as cod. Later, in 2002, Lisa helped lead an NGO coalition through four years of tough negotiations on a U.N. moratorium to stop the abuses of bottom trawling. One of the most ruinous of all fishing techniques, bottom trawling involves dragging 200-foot-long weighted nets across the seafloor, devastating everything in their path. The U.N. moratorium, adopted in 2006, bans unregulated bottom trawling in more than 52 million square miles of the high seas. Today, supported by dedicated NRDC trustees like Claire Bernard, president of the Mariposa Foundation, and Kelly Meyer, who is passionate about ocean protections (especially in California's coastal waters), our team is immersed in negotiations for the most ambitious agreement of all: a comprehensive, legally binding global treaty to protect the ecosystems of the high seas.

We've also taken great strides toward making U.S. fisheries more sustainable. In 2005 and 2006, Sarah and the team worked to strengthen the U.S. ocean fisheries law, the Magnuson-Stevens Act, through the required setting of science-based annual catch limits. That law, which has significantly reduced overfishing in U.S. waters, is now viewed worldwide as a model for responsible fisheries management. In fact, we have recently been working to export some of these successful legal and management strategies to China, the world's largest fishing nation. Finally, we've

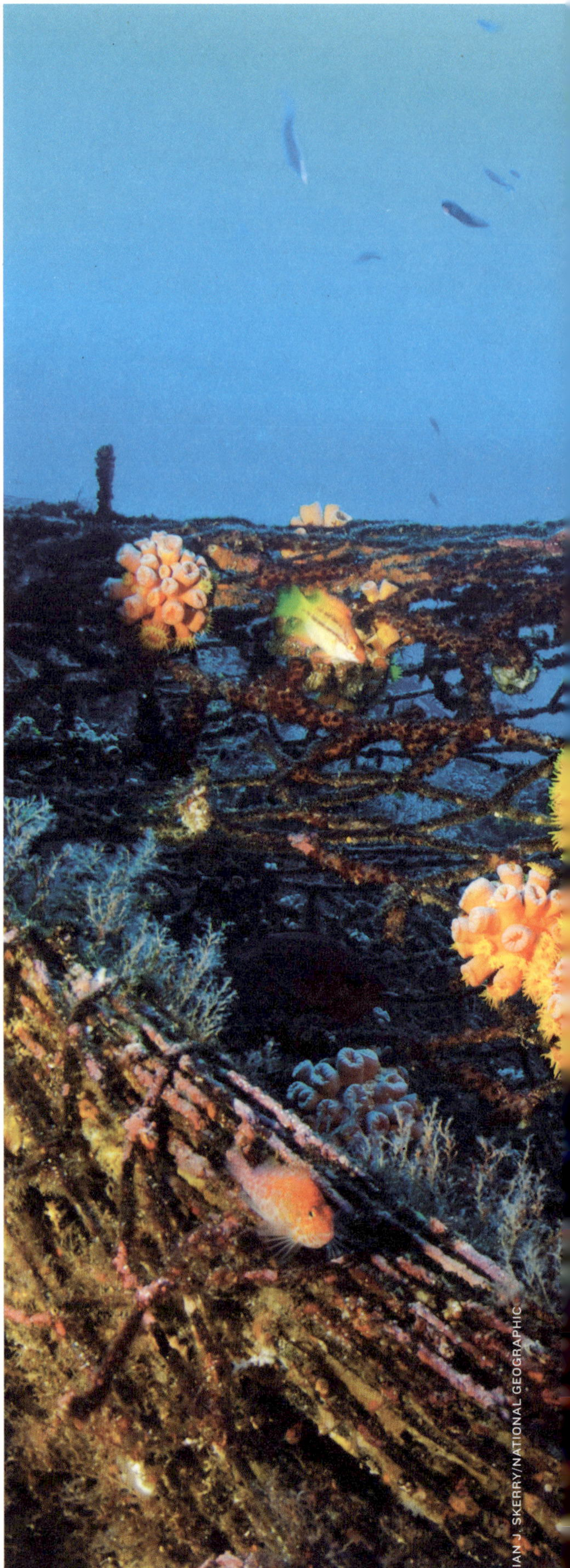

An abandoned trawl net drapes over El Bajo seamount in Mexico.

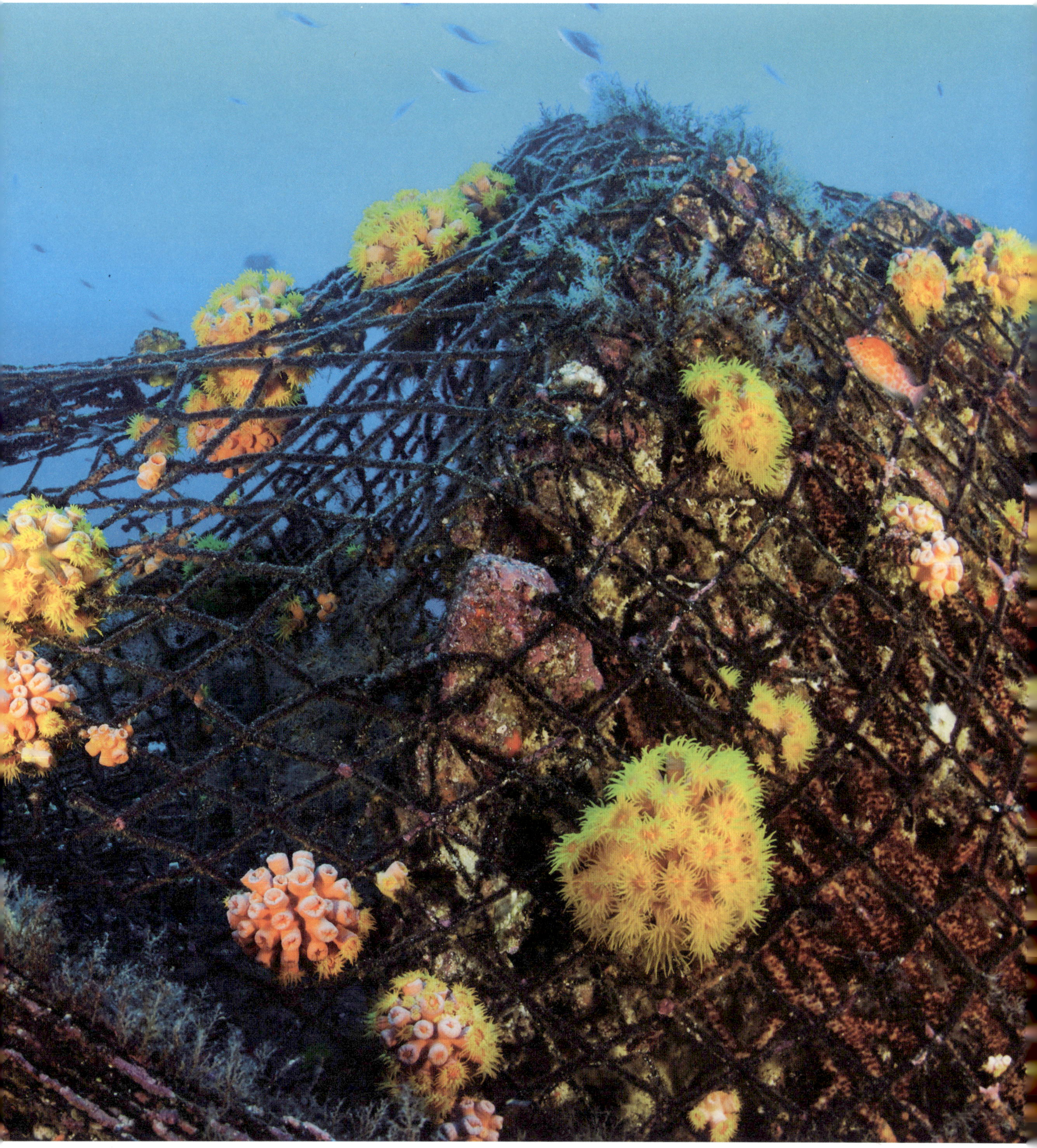

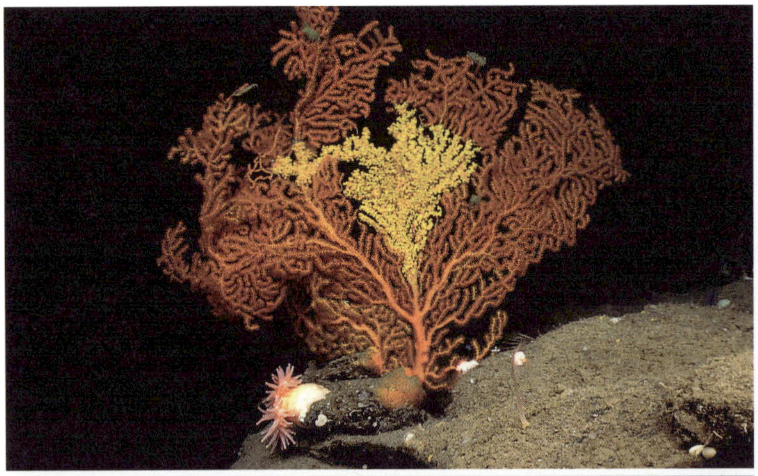

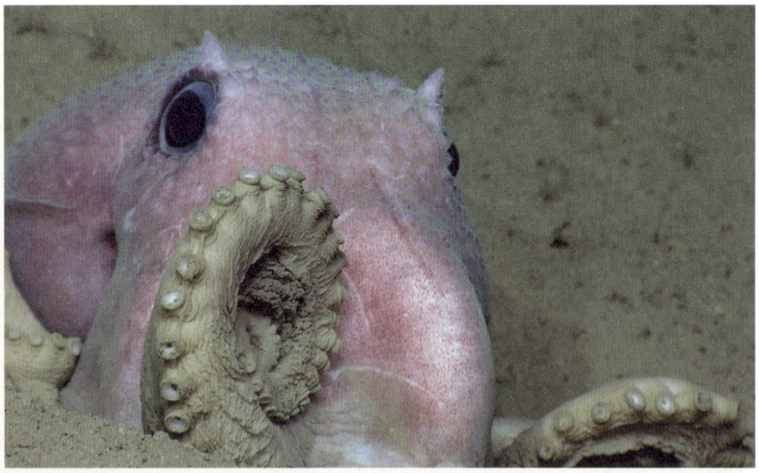

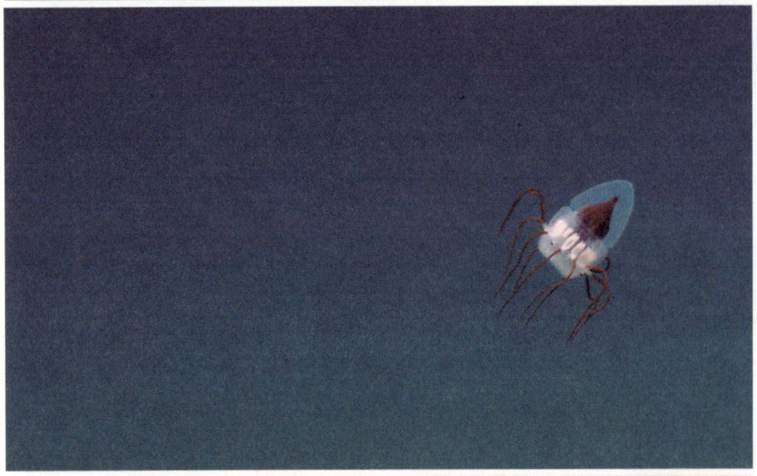

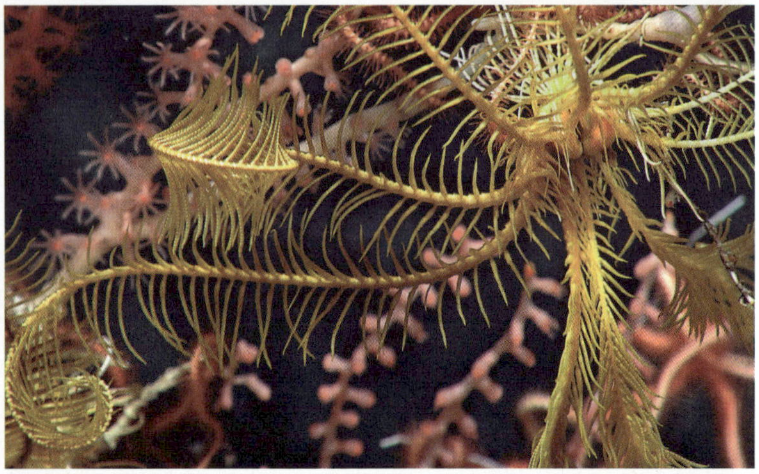

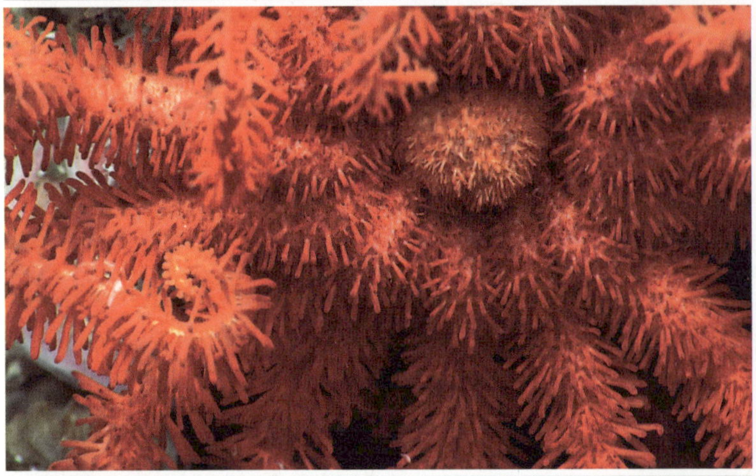

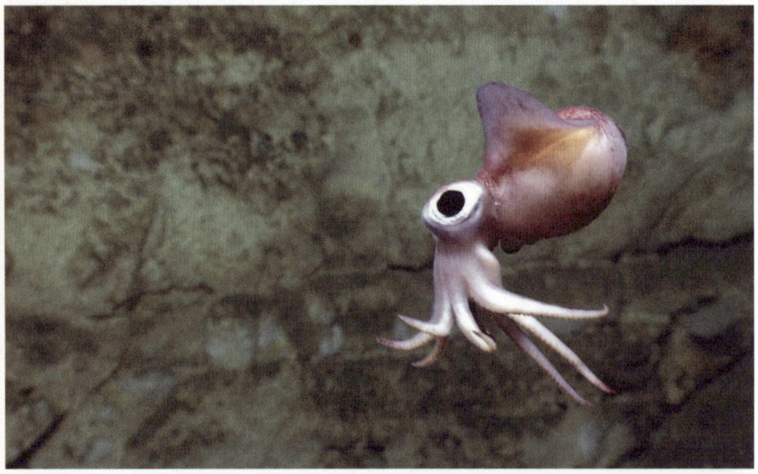

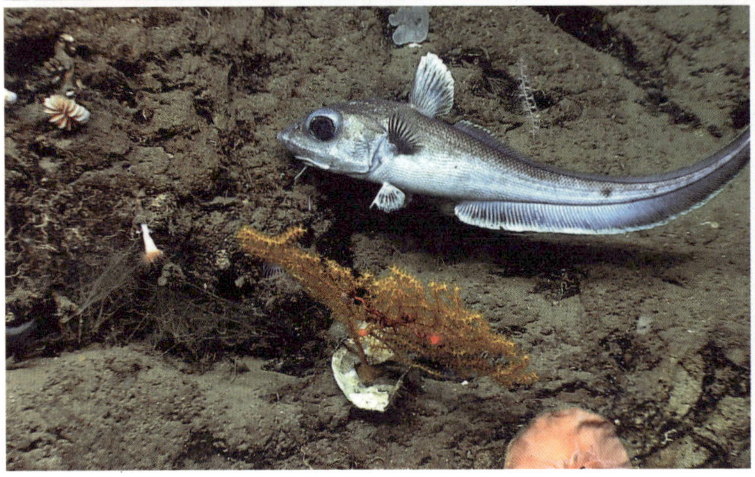

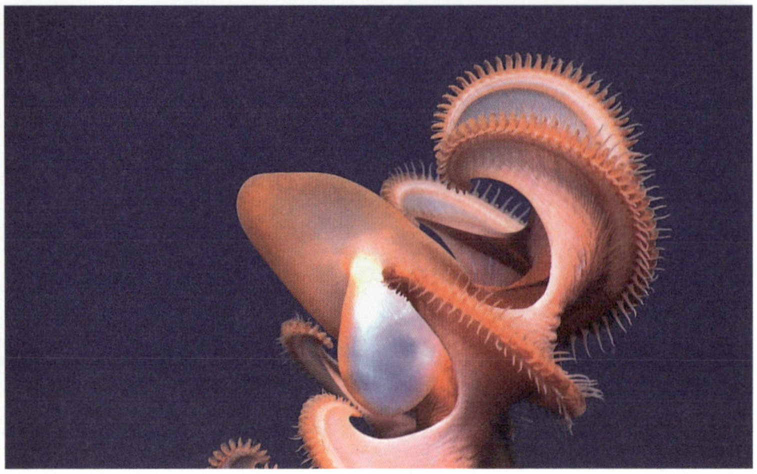

1ST ROW: NOAA OKEANOS EXPLORER PROGRAM; NOAA OFFICE OF OCEAN EXPLORATION AND RESEARCH. 2ND ROW: NOAA OFFICE OF OCEAN EXPLORATION AND RESEARCH; NOAA OKEANOS EXPLORER PROGRAM. 3RD ROW: NOAA OKEANOS EXPLORER PROGRAM; NOAA OFFICE OF OCEAN EXPLORATION AND RESEARCH. 4TH ROW: NOAA OKEANOS EXPLORER PROGRAM (2)

backed up this legal work with highly effective consumer campaigns that have led to the remarkable comeback of swordfish populations and an import ban on beluga caviar, the production of which has imperiled the dwindling population of sturgeon in the Caspian Sea.

Protecting the ocean depends on not only ending overfishing but also creating networks of protected areas. California's marine protected areas were an early example of how this can be done. Thanks to a 1999 state law that NRDC took the lead in crafting and working to implement, such areas now cover about 16 percent of California's coastal waters.

Victories like these reflect the growing scientific understanding of the importance of protecting marine ecosystems. In 2013, a remotely controlled submersible named *Deep Discoverer* gave scientists a glimpse into a previously unseen world off the coast of New England. The dramatic images from the mission showed clefts as deep as the Grand Canyon and seamounts taller than any peak east of the Rockies, all teeming with life—ancient deep-sea corals, giant fish, whales, dolphins, and hitherto unknown species. But it was also an undersea world acutely vulnerable to commercial fishing, seabed mining, and oil and gas exploration.

Within a year of *Deep Discoverer*'s journey, we launched a campaign with others to protect this wonderland in perpetuity. In 2016, President Obama responded by designating nearly 5,000 square miles—an area almost as large as Connecticut—as the Northeast Canyons and Seamounts National Marine Monument. He used the 1906 Antiquities Act, just as President George W. Bush had done in naming four marine monuments in the Pacific Ocean. Now the Atlantic Ocean has its first.

We knew the new monument would face opposition and were prepared. When industry groups challenged the monument in the spring of 2017—as well as the very authority of presidents to designate marine monuments at all—NRDC immediately moved to intervene. In 2018, the federal district court ruled in favor of the monument's designation and the use of the Antiquities Act to protect special ocean areas for future generations. In December 2019, that decision was upheld by the U.S. Court of Appeals for the D.C. Circuit. Think of these marine monuments as "blue parks," says Brad Sewell, senior director of our oceans team, who led NRDC's effort. Just as Yellowstone was the first building block in our national parks system, the canyons and seamounts of the Atlantic can do the same for our undersea treasures. That's the kind of visionary thinking we need if we're to save the oceans, along with the depths of life they contain.

The Northeast Canyons and Seamounts Marine National Monument in the Atlantic is a biodiversity hot spot, teeming with ancient corals, giant fish, and many species unknown to science. It is also an important nursery area for whales and dolphins.

FROM THE FRONTLINES

John McMurray

John McMurray remembers a time in the late 1990s when you couldn't catch a summer flounder bigger than 14 inches off the coast of Long Island. New York's waterways had become so overfished that full-grown catches were few and far between. "My whole business is driven by abundance," says John, who has been a captain of the One More Cast recreational fishing charter since 2001. "If there aren't any bluefin tuna out in the water, I don't have people signing up to fish on my boats offshore."

John grew up a "fish junkie" on the rivers of Virginia. But later, as a U.S. Coast Guard enforcement officer stationed in New York City, John witnessed the overexploitation of our seas firsthand. "There was a fleet of guys that would commercially fish for stripers," he remembers. "Back then, stripers were one of the very few management success stories at the state level. These fish were just coming back after a moratorium in the '80s and here these guys would be—catching 400 a day in the off-season out of Sheepshead Bay. It pissed me off. It pissed everyone off."

With his charter business getting off the ground, John began speaking out within the recreational fishing community about marine conservation. He became a well-known outdoors writer, publishing dozens of articles on everything from saltwater licensing to shark finning in the Bahamas. In 2008, John joined the Mid-Atlantic Fishery Management Council, the federally organized group tasked with the Magnuson-Stevens Act. The federal fisheries law that was strengthened in 2006, thanks in significant part to the efforts of NRDC, to require science-based catch limits for fish populations in the region and around the country. At about the same time, he began teaming up with conservation groups like NRDC to fight attempted attacks on the act and on how its conservation mandates were being carried out, and to spread the word in the press.

More recently, John led a group of charter captains and recreational fishermen in supporting the 2016 designation of the Northeast Canyons and Seamounts Marine National Monument. "I wrote a number of blogs and spoke to a bunch of clubs," he says, "and that made me a whole bunch of enemies." But John knew the science was on his side. He knew that the designation was necessary to protect the region's remaining biodiversity and help sustain fish populations.

"NRDC encourages the recreational fishing community to engage early and often in the political process," says John. "Some folks used to see NRDC as the bad guy—thought they wanted to take recreational fishermen off the water, but that relationship has evolved to be one of a cooperative partner with many of us."

Together over the years, our wins have added up. And so have the fish. "They really did work. We've all seen it on the water," John says. "Pretty much everything that's federally managed is way more abundant than it was 20 years ago." Populations of bluefin and yellowfin tuna, mahi-mahi, and white marlin have all rebounded in the Northeast. And the summer flounder John now catches? Big and plentiful.

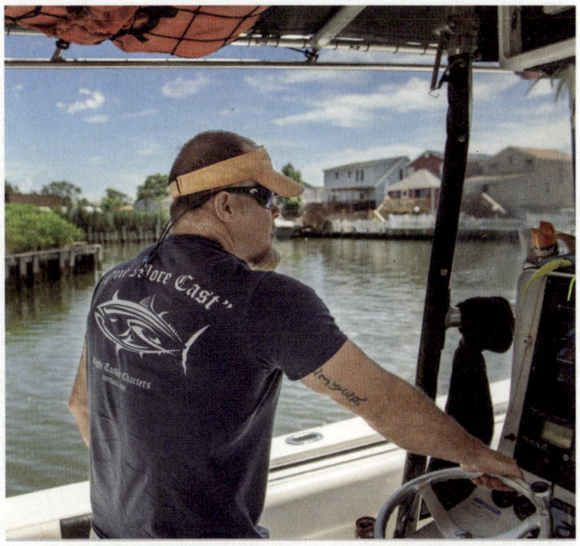

John McMurray takes his boat to the his fishing spot in Oceanside, New York.

HILARY SWIFT

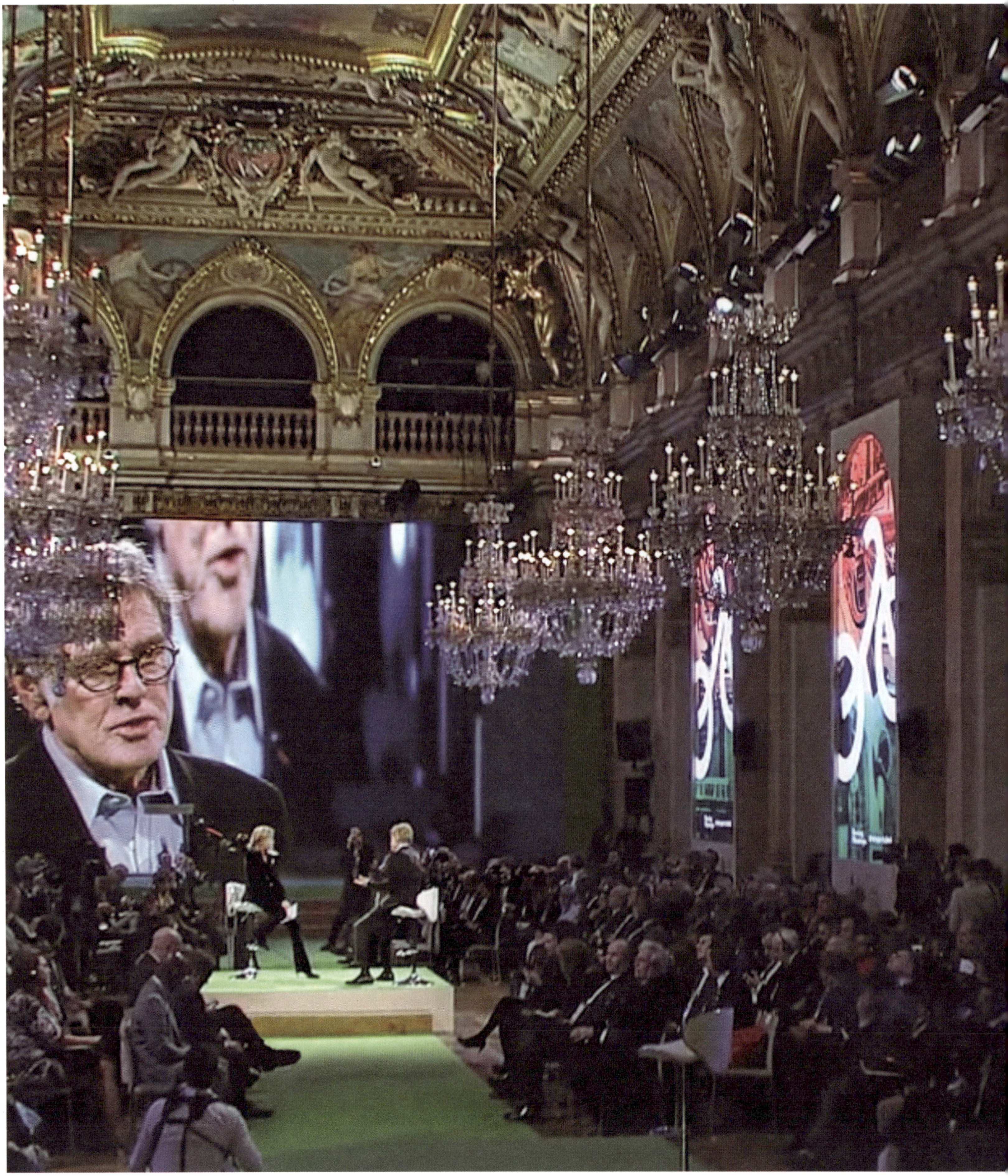

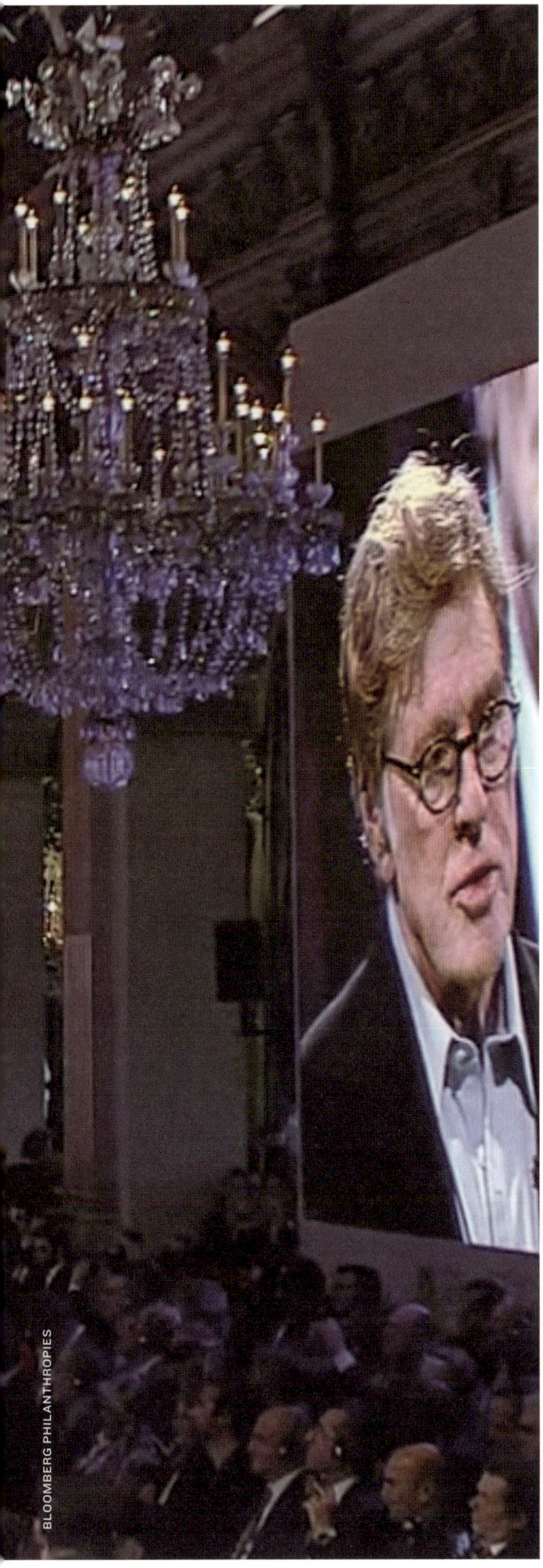

ALL EYES ON PARIS

A *FORCE FOR NATURE*, THE BOOK THAT details the history of the first 40 years of NRDC, closed with images from the landmark climate conference in Copenhagen in December 2009. While the Copenhagen conference was a bitter disappointment for many environmentalists, we glimpsed a silver lining in President Obama's 11th-hour personal intervention. He was able to solidify pledges from China and India to substantially reduce their carbon emissions. The United States would do the same.

Those last-minute developments in Copenhagen suggested the roadmap for NRDC's international climate work for the next decade and beyond. We worked tirelessly to ensure the United States set the most ambitious targets possible to hold down rising global temperatures and thereby encourage China and India to do likewise. All 195 nations of the world were asked to come up with a plan to cut their carbon pollution, but without the full participation of these three giants—the world's top emitters of greenhouse gases—any climate accord reached would've had only the dimmest hope of success.

And the voluntary targets would need to be incorporated into a formal legal framework with clear rules and accountability. The date set for a conference to reach a final agreement was 2015; the location would be Paris.

The next step was to have countries announce their targets in advance of the Paris conference, and I honestly don't believe this would have happened without NRDC's leadership. We aggressively pressed the Obama administration to come up with numbers that pushed the envelope yet were credible and achievable. We understood that the United States had to step out in front if we were to inspire China and others. This led to a formal agreement between the United States and China in 2014. The example set by the world's two biggest carbon emitters working in concert turned up the heat on other countries to come to the table in Paris with firm public commitments.

What made NRDC's role unique, in the words of Jake Schmidt, the managing director of our International Program, was that we were the only environmental group with major "boots on the ground" in both the United States

NRDC trustee Robert Redford speaks at Bloomberg Philanthropies' Climate Summit for Local Leaders event as part of the U.N. Climate Change Conference in Paris on December 2015.

What made NRDC's role unique in working on the Paris Agreement was that we were the only environmental group with major "boots on the ground" in both the United States and China.

and China. For this kind of complex negotiation, personal relationships and trust are all-important. Our Beijing office had spent years building that trust at senior levels of the Chinese government and worked closely with Chinese officials to figure out how their country could also set ambitious yet realistic targets. China's first-ever plan to cap its coal consumption (announced in 2013 and discussed earlier in this book) also reflected these goals.

In November 2015, an NRDC delegation of more than 50 staff, trustees, and donors traveled to Paris, feeling that we'd helped China and the United States reach a common understanding. What the world needed now was a system that would enshrine national targets and closely monitor the progress each country was making toward its goals. As Ronald Reagan used to say of the Soviet Union, "trust but verify." It was all well and good to set targets for 2025 or 2030, but the evidence was mounting that climate change was advancing more rapidly than we'd feared. Without constantly tracking and strengthening these targets, we couldn't be sure that we'd hold global temperatures below a catastrophic level—meaning a rise of no more than 2 degrees Celsius above preindustrial levels by the end of the century, and ideally closer to 1.5 degrees. Here, too, NRDC was pivotal, commissioning a series of technical reports that detailed how such a tracking system would work.

The next big player was India. As in Beijing, we'd built strong working relationships with officials in New Delhi, meeting regularly with the minister heading the Indian delegation. As a country committed to raising hundreds of millions of its people out of poverty, India was cautious about how deeply it could commit to slashing its carbon pollution. At the same time, it didn't want to be seen as an obstacle to an agreement the rest of the world was signing on to. Jake and Anjali Jaiswal, the senior director of our India Program, sat down with the minister to walk through the possible sticking points. It worked. One of the most rewarding symbols of our success in Paris was watching the minister exchange high fives with Jake after the gavel went down on the conference.

The Paris Agreement ultimately gathered 195 signatories, an extraordinary display of global consensus and commitment. The international climate accord entered into force on November 4, 2016, with one especially striking provision: No country could formally drop out for four years. So, even though President Donald Trump has begun the process of removing the United States from the pact, that withdrawal won't be official until the day after the 2020 U.S. presidential election. Potentially, a new administration could rejoin the agreement as soon as 30 days after taking office. Yet, regardless of that election's outcome, American states, cities, and businesses have seen the writing on the wall and are continuing to cut their planet-warming emissions, dedicate themselves to Paris' goals, and push the renewable energy revolution forward.

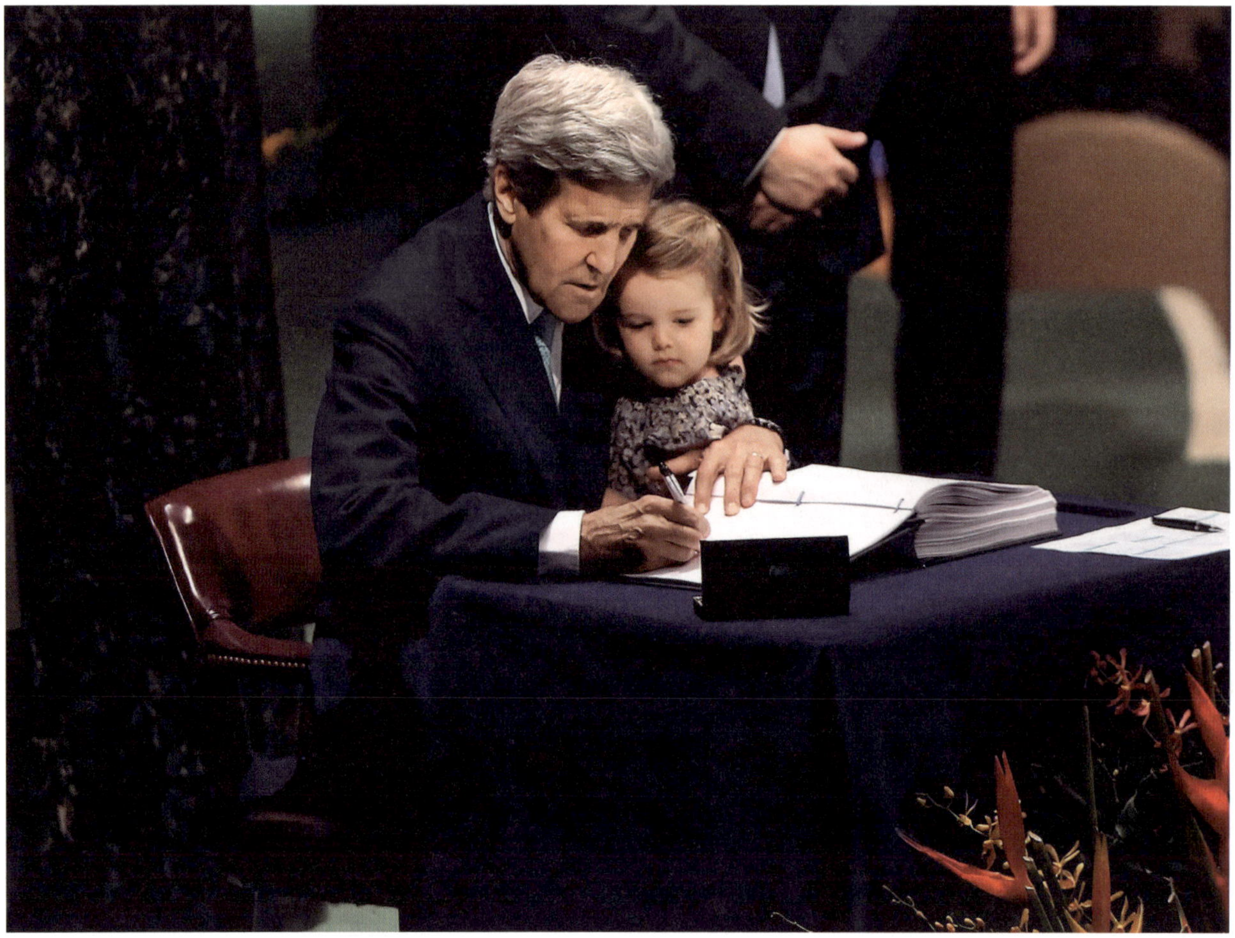

U.S. Secretary of State John Kerry holds his granddaughter as he signs the Paris Agreement on December 4, 2016. Opposite, far right: NRDC trustee Leonardo DiCaprio speaks at Bloomberg Philanthropies' Climate Summit for Local Leaders event in Paris on December 2015. Opposite, bottom: NRDC staff listen to speakers at a Storytelling for Global Action event during the U.N. Climate Change Conference in Paris on December 2015.

CLOCKWISE FROM LEFT: SPENCER PLATT/GETTY IMAGES; PETER DEJONG/ASSOCIATED PRESS; PATRICK KOVARIK/AFP VIA GETTY IMAGES; JULIA HEKIMIAN/GETTY FOR NRDC

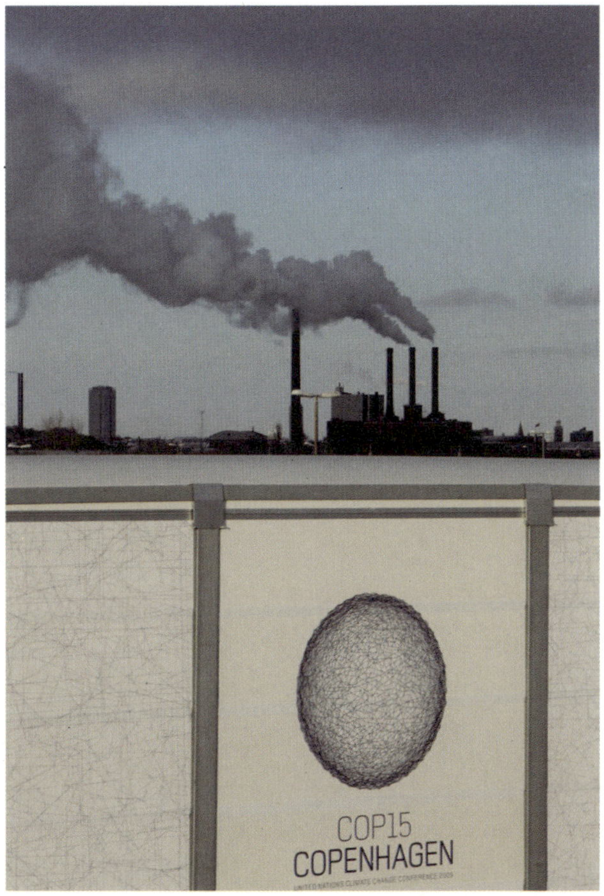
COP15
COPENHAGEN

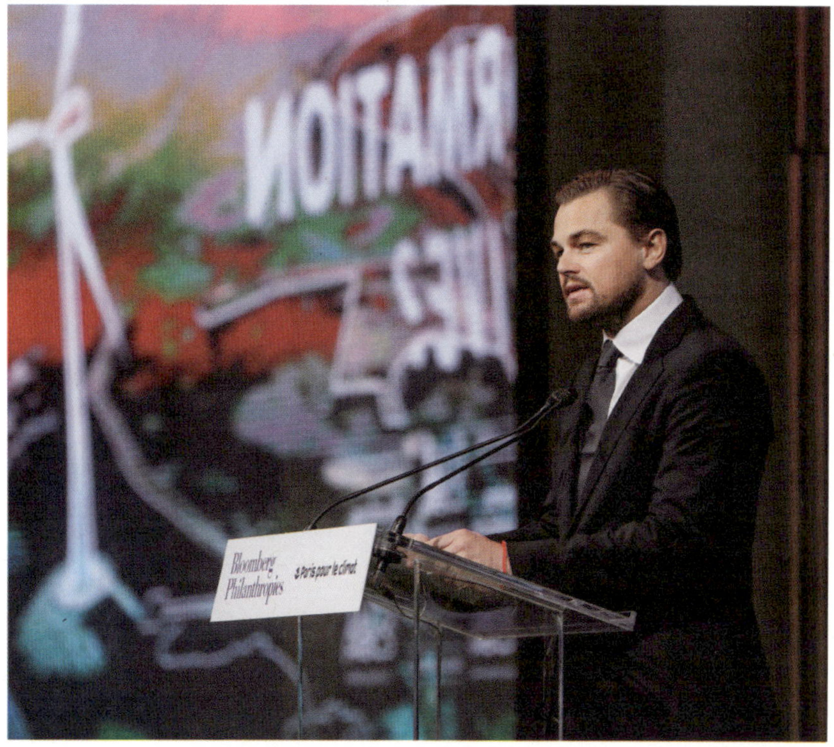
Bloomberg Philanthropies
Paris pour le climat

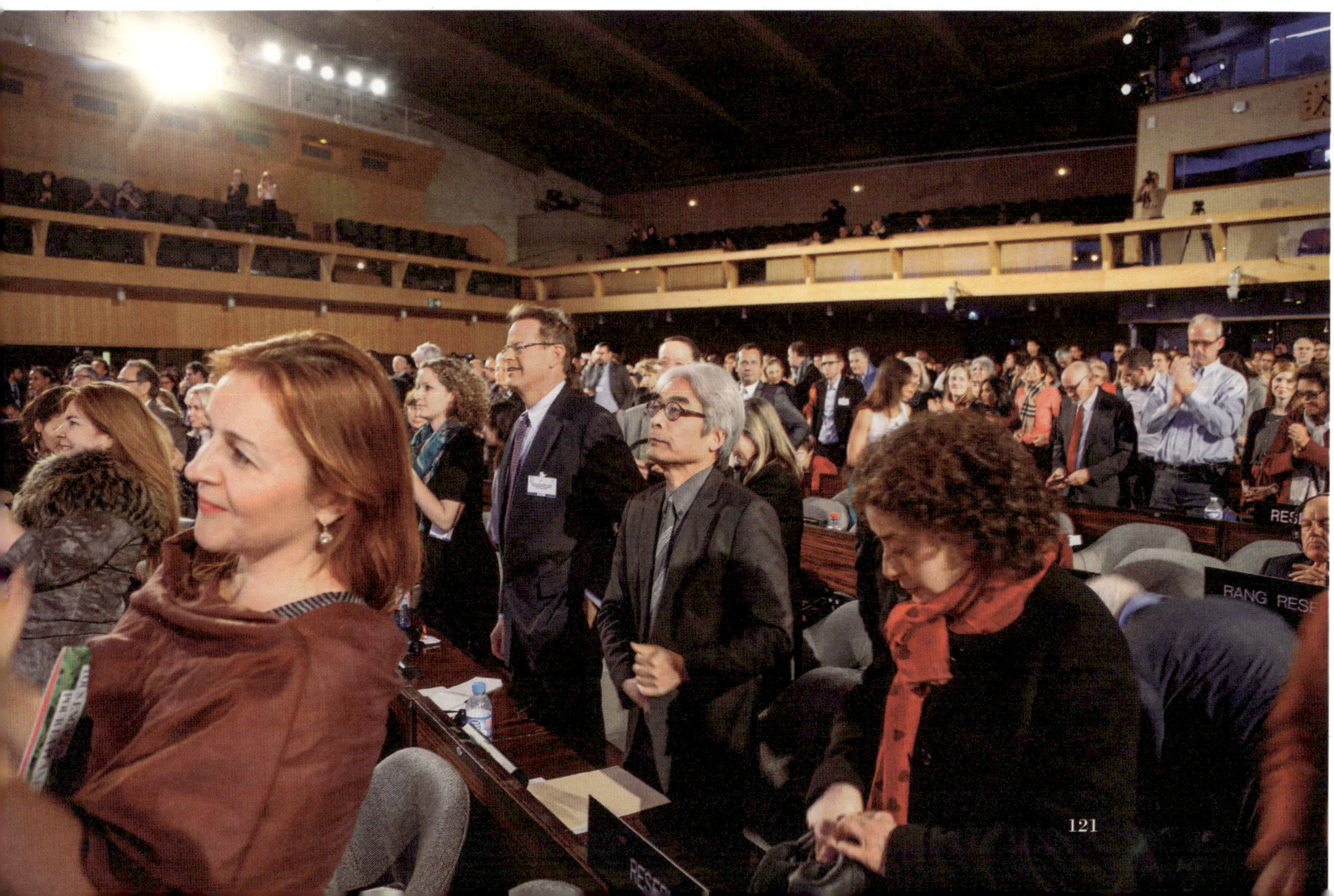
RANG RESE

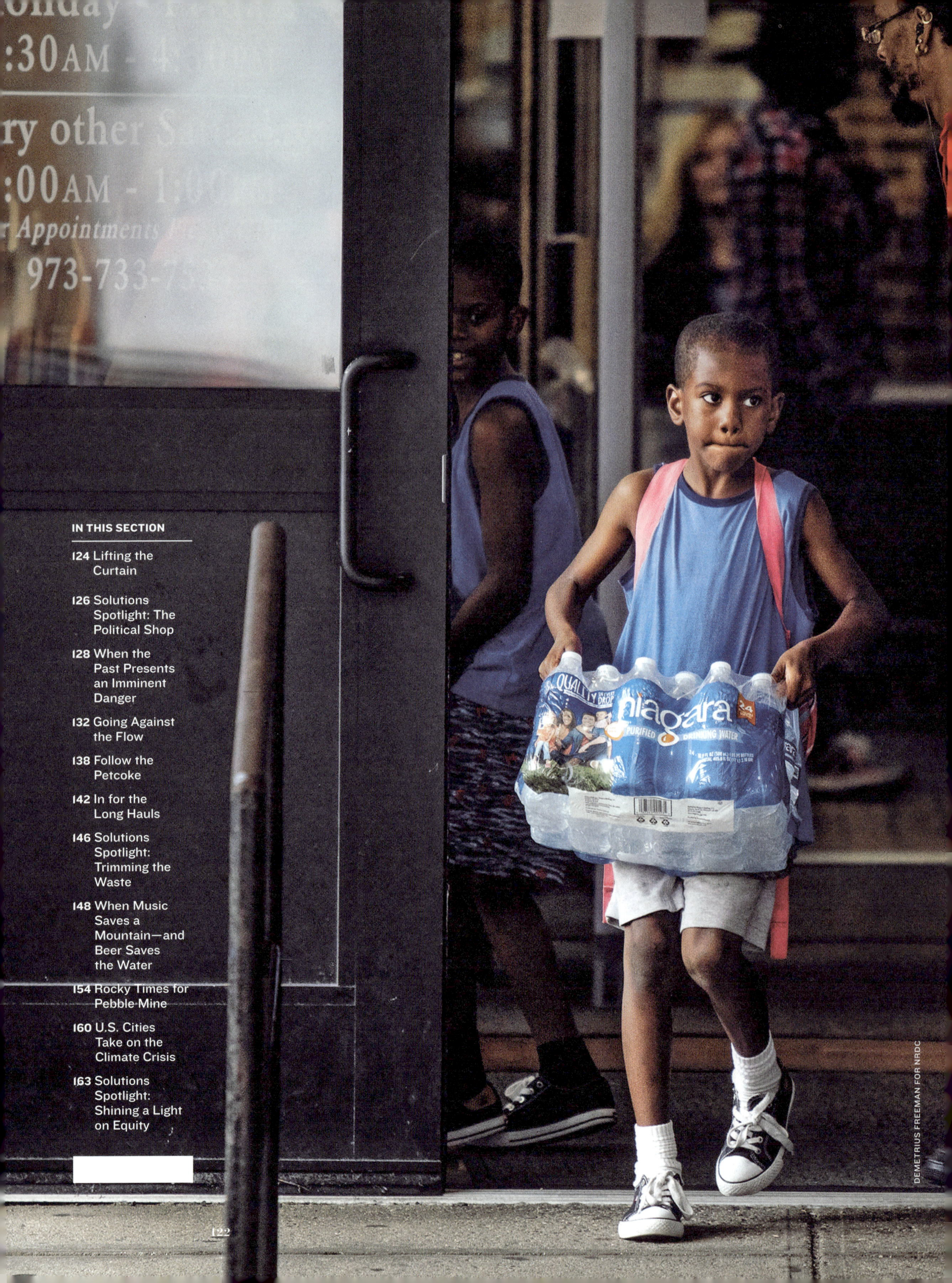

IN THIS SECTION

DEMETRIUS FREEMAN FOR NRDC

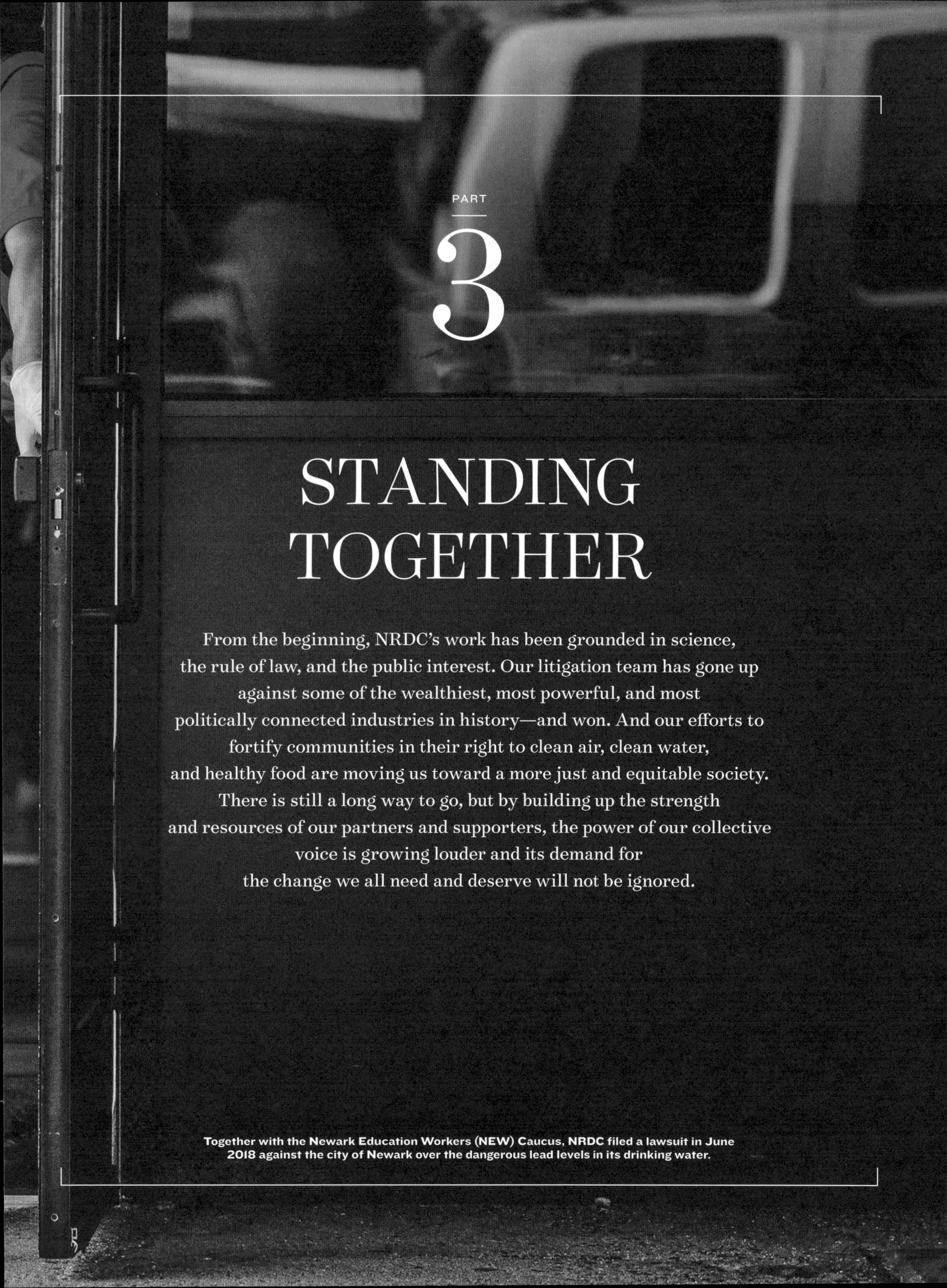

PART

3

STANDING TOGETHER

From the beginning, NRDC's work has been grounded in science, the rule of law, and the public interest. Our litigation team has gone up against some of the wealthiest, most powerful, and most politically connected industries in history—and won. And our efforts to fortify communities in their right to clean air, clean water, and healthy food are moving us toward a more just and equitable society. There is still a long way to go, but by building up the strength and resources of our partners and supporters, the power of our collective voice is growing louder and its demand for the change we all need and deserve will not be ignored.

Together with the Newark Education Workers (NEW) Caucus, NRDC filed a lawsuit in June 2018 against the city of Newark over the dangerous lead levels in its drinking water.

LIFTING THE CURTAIN

AMERICANS HAVE A RIGHT TO KNOW how the laws and policies of their country are determined and whether those policies are made with the public's interest in mind. A transparent process of public debate and commenting is essential to accomplish this, and when the government acts in secret, or has corrupt intentions, NRDC looks to the famous dictum of Supreme Court Justice Louis Brandeis: "Sunlight is the best disinfectant." One of the tools we've used to apply that principle is the Freedom of Information Act (FOIA).

As soon as George W. Bush took office in January 2001, he commissioned a task force called the National Energy Policy Development Group, headed by then vice president Dick Cheney, who was fresh off of a five-year stint as the head of Halliburton, one of the world's largest providers of services to the oil industry. When this secretive policy body unveiled its plan that May, it included more than $34 billion in subsidies for the oil and gas, coal, and nuclear industries and other polluters. The plan "read like a wish list for energy companies," said Sharon Buccino, senior director of NRDC's Land Division. Sharon is an expert on energy law, and she led our FOIA campaign, which we launched almost immediately.

We demanded the release of all relevant documents from the U.S. Department of Energy, as well as other agencies involved in Cheney's energy task force. The U.S. District Court for the District of Columbia declared that "the material which [NRDC] seeks is of extraordinary public interest," and eventually we received a trove of 13,500 pages of previously classified documents. These showed that for every meeting with an environmental or public interest group, the task force had met 25 times with industry representatives and lobbyists. The most frequent consultations were with groups like the American Petroleum Institute and the National Mining Association and companies like BP, Exelon, Chevron, and Enron. Not surprisingly, the task force's plan tracked the recommendations of the fossil fuel industry almost word for word. Having cracked the government's wall of secrecy, NRDC created a searchable online database of the documents, all downloadable, as a lasting public record of how powerful

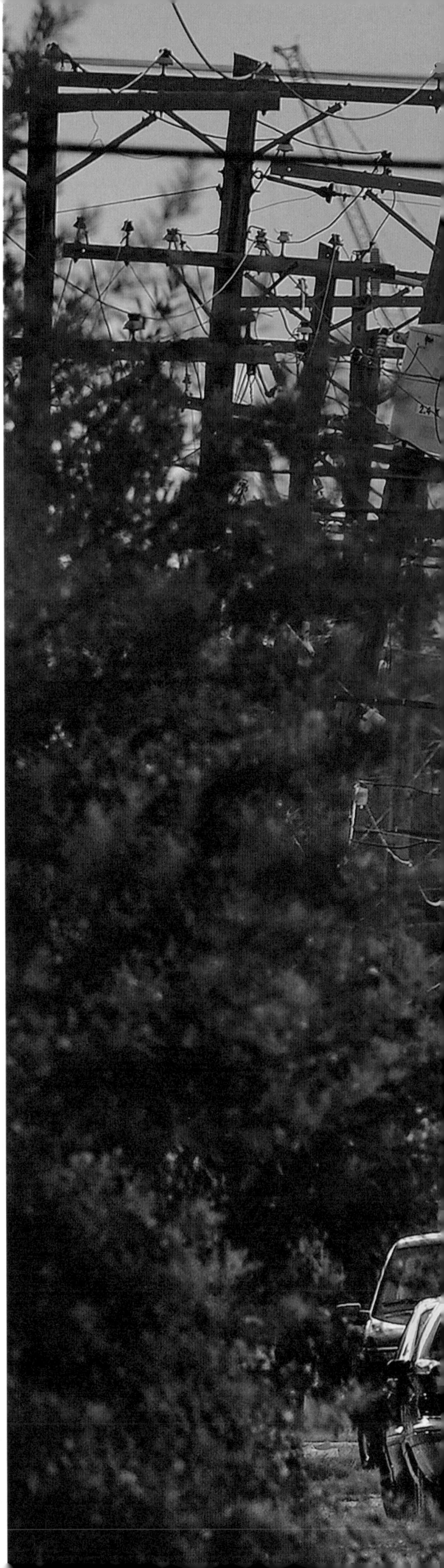

Children playing in Port Arthur, Texas, where oil refineries, and their emissions, loom over residential areas.

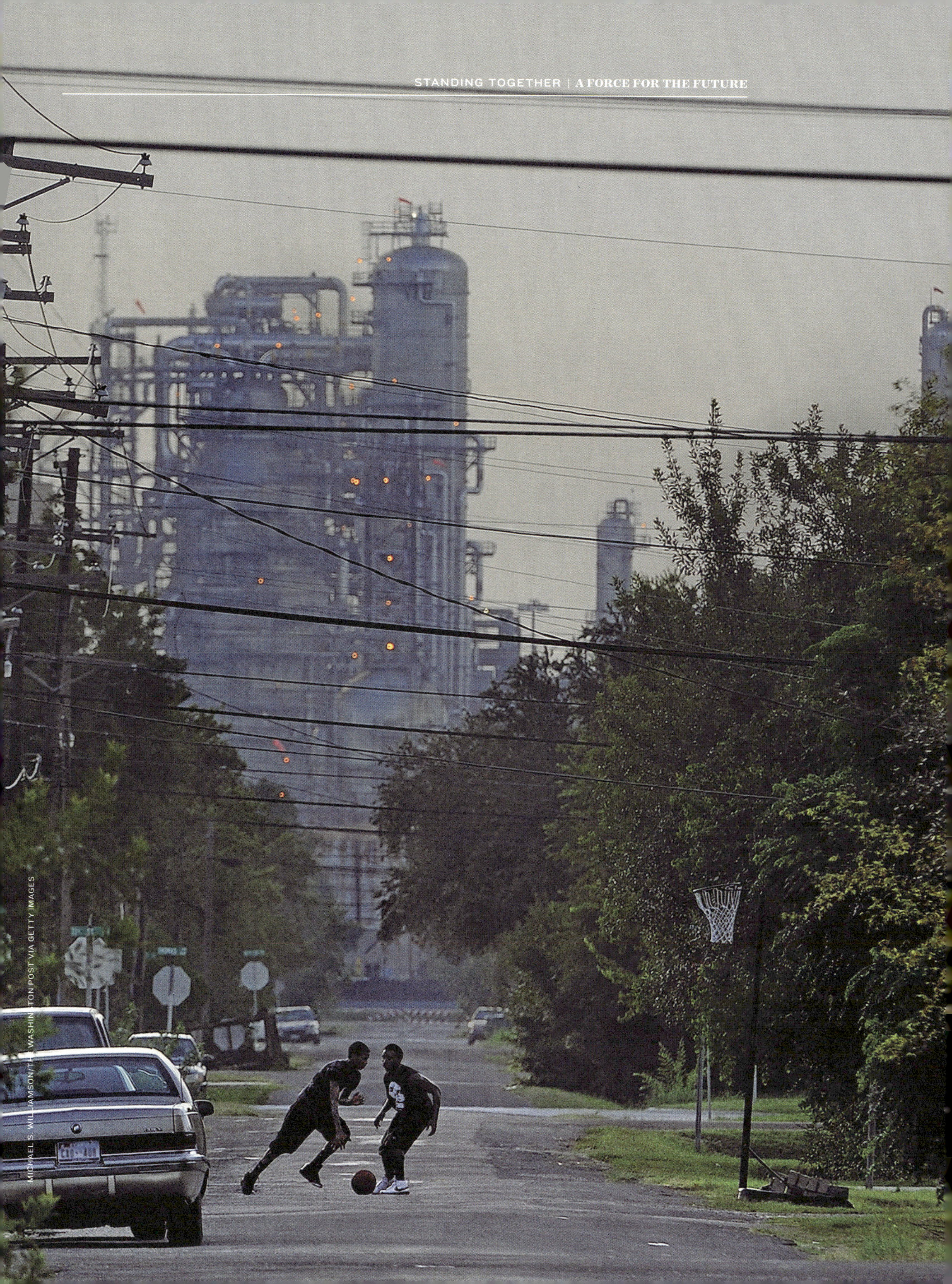

MICHAEL S. WILLIAMSON/THE WASHINGTON POST VIA GETTY IMAGES

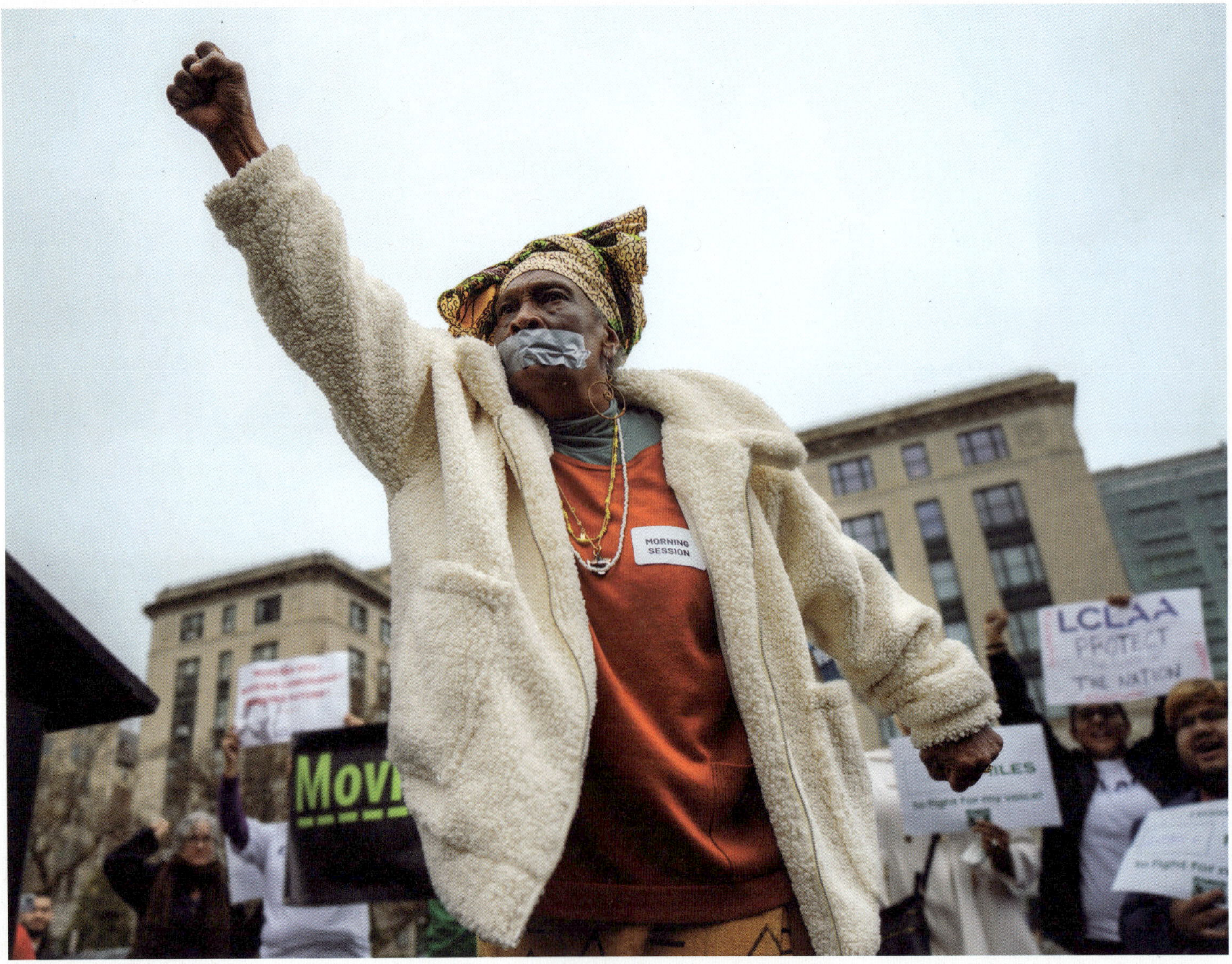

Solutions Spotlight

THE POLITICAL SHOP

For 40 years, NRDC won over politicians of goodwill—Democrats and Republicans alike—on the strength of our legal and scientific skills, our command of facts, and the power of our analysis. But in 2010, the landscape for our advocacy changed dramatically. The Supreme Court's Citizens United decision unleashed a flood of money into politics from powerful special interests, and that year congressional Democrats suffered what President Obama called a "shellacking" in the midterms. Suddenly, politicians weren't just asking if we had good ideas; they wanted to know if our ideas would win them votes.

Our response was to create the Center for Policy Advocacy (CPA) in 2012, which would arm our policy experts with new tools and strategies for persuading politicians to act on behalf of the environment and public health. Since then, the CPA has grown to include a government affairs team that lobbies federal and state policymakers, a campaigns team that mobilizes the public to encourage lawmakers to do more, and an external affairs team that builds partnerships with other politically influential voices, such as labor unions and organizations representing communities of color and young people. Meanwhile, our Environmental Entrepreneurs (E2) affiliate, founded by Bob Epstein and Nicole Lederer, works to disabuse politicians of the idea that they must choose between the environment and the economy, and the NRDC Action Fund, our sister organization, supports pro-environment politicians while holding all our elected officials accountable.

"This center is our de facto political shop," says Ed Yoon, director of CPA. "It's all about expanding our power and voice."

Dr. Mildred McClain, co-founder and executive director of Harambee House and Citizens for Environmental Justice at a protest against efforts by the Trump administration to weaken the National Environmental Policy Act, February 2020.

private interests operate behind closed doors to undermine our basic environmental and public health protections.

President Trump came into office with his own brand of secrecy. His administration actively suppresses established but inconvenient facts, shrouding them in a cynical misuse of language that seems inspired by Humpty Dumpty's declaration to Alice that "when I use a word, it means just what I choose it to mean." Words, for example, like *transparency*.

In May 2018, EPA Administrator Scott Pruitt proposed a plan he called "Strengthening Transparency in Regulatory Science," which would severely restrict the scientific research the agency could use in its rulemaking. Henceforth, the EPA could only use studies that made public their raw underlying data "for independent validation and analysis." Notably, the agency could no longer consider research that used the confidential medical records of those who had agreed to participate in its policy decisions. This would leave out numerous important peer-reviewed studies that could not make all their data publicly accessible for ethical, confidentiality reasons. Yet while the rule was proposed in the name of transparency, industry-funded research would be exempt from this restriction. After all, Pruitt argued, nothing was more sacrosanct than "confidential business information."

Pruitt was soon ousted, brought low by his personal corruption and incompetence. But the revisions to his "Secret Science rule" (or what we call the "censored science rule"), proposed in November 2019 by his successor, former coal lobbyist Andrew Wheeler, were even worse. Wheeler's version would make the rule retroactive, potentially invalidating landmark epidemiological studies like Harvard's two-decade-long Six Cities study, which documented the links between air pollution and heart disease, lung cancer, asthma, bronchitis, and premature death. With 22,000 participants, the study is considered one of the most influential ever conducted, and it shaped the public health protections of the Clean Air Act for a quarter century since its publication in 1993. Now, Wheeler would have us discount it.

NRDC responded with detailed expert comments—127 single-spaced pages of them—that tore apart the legal justifications the EPA had purported to find for its rule under eight federal environmental laws. "We forced them to make a sharp pivot to an even more farcical claim of legal authority," says John Walke, the clean air director of NRDC's Climate & Clean Energy Program. Without the authority of those eight environmental laws, Wheeler's EPA was forced to ransack the federal statute book to look for some other rationale for stripping sound science out of the rulemaking process. With the agency now on the defensive, we'll continue to press our advantage until this shameless attack on genuine science and transparency is finally scrapped.

The air quality forecast for metropolitan Los Angeles was "unhealthy for sensitive groups" on November 5, 2019—the day the Trump administration officially began withdrawing from the Paris climate agreement.

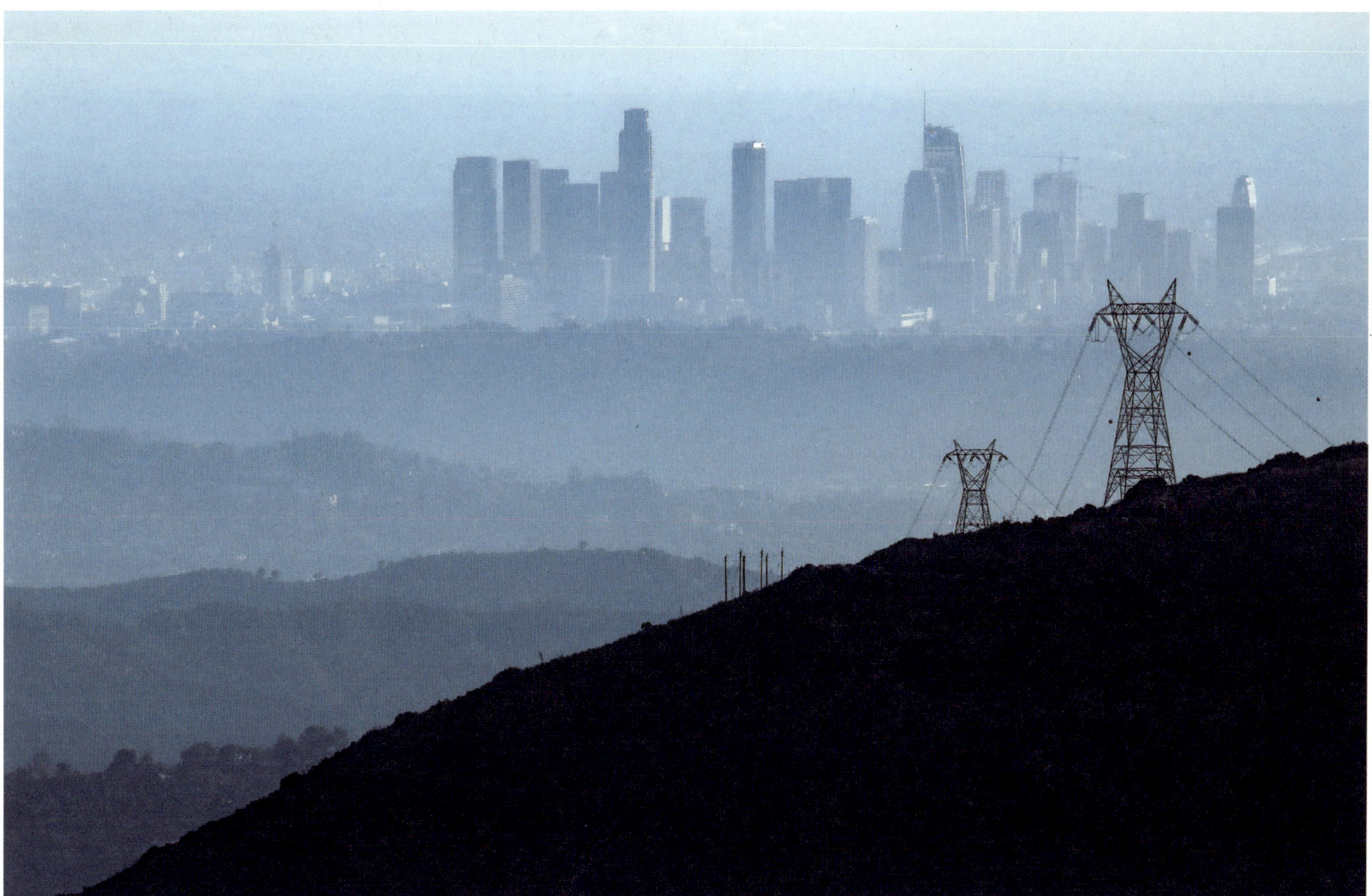

MARIO TAMA/GETTY IMAGES. OPPOSITE: TING SHEN FOR NRDC

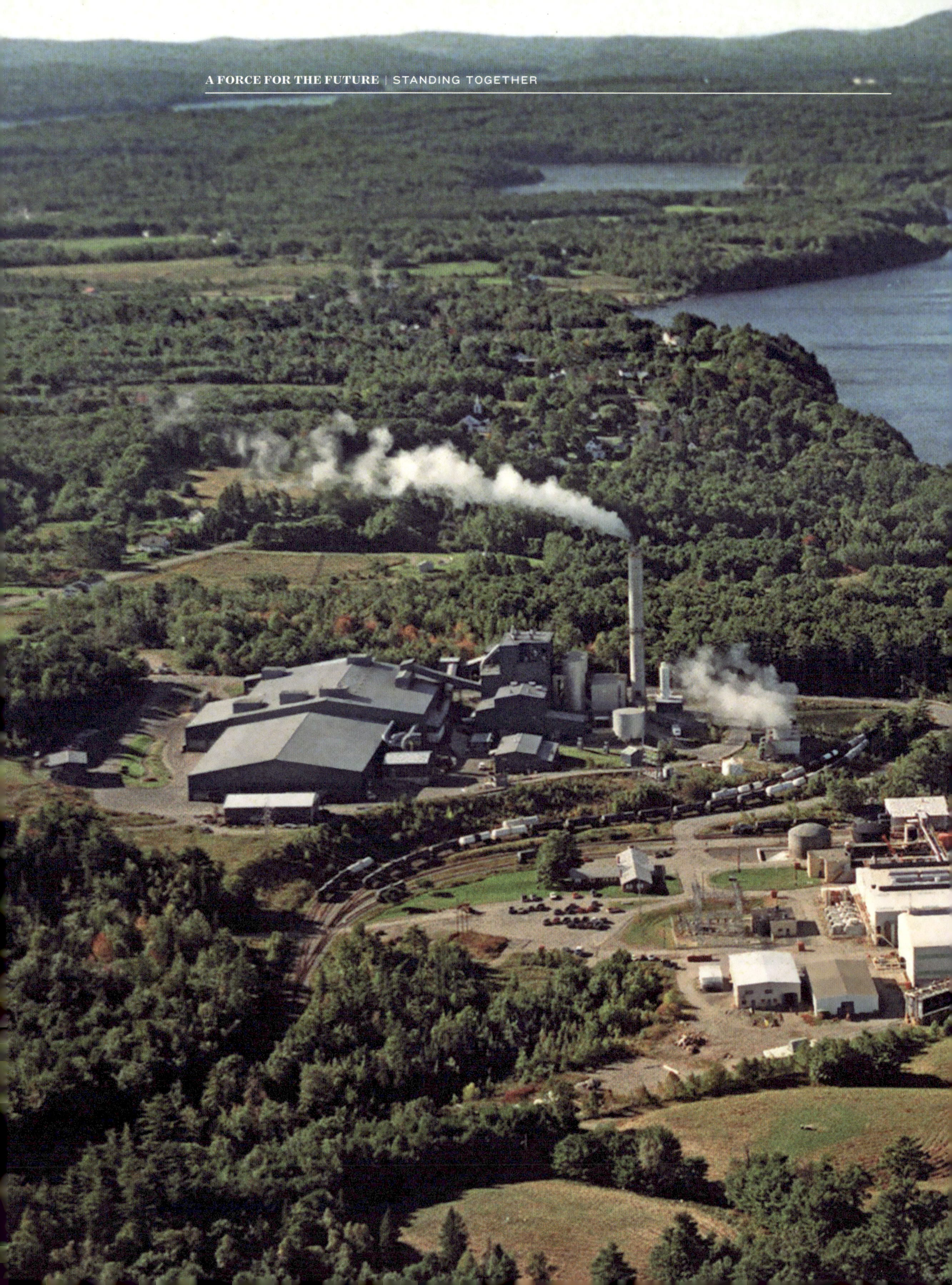

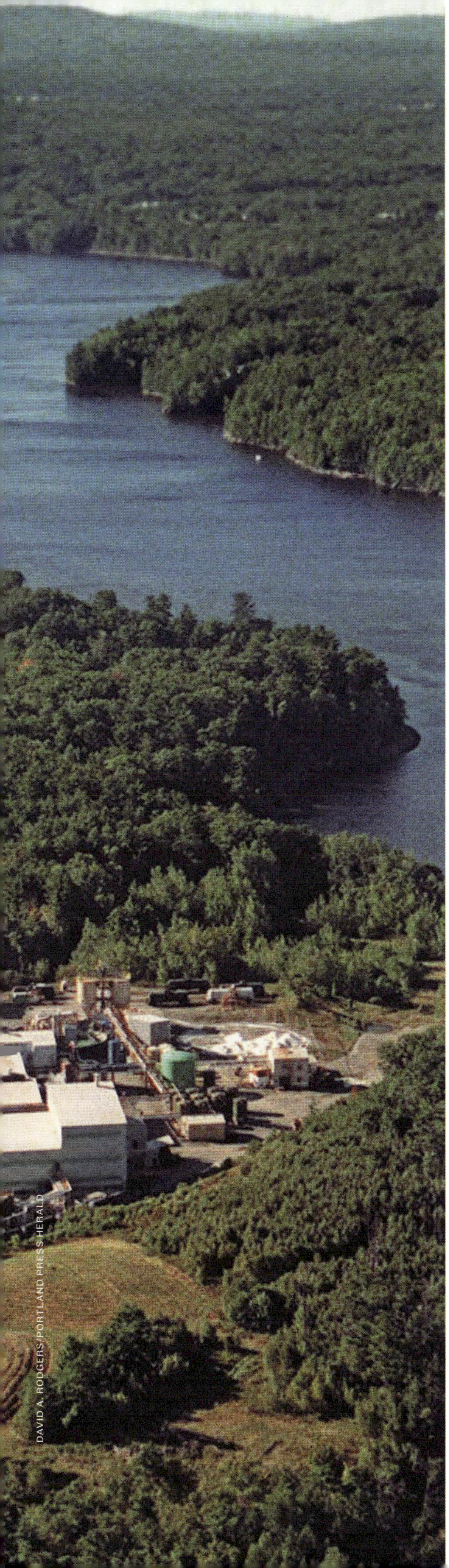

DAVID A. RODGERS/PORTLAND PRESS HERALD

WHEN THE PAST PRESENTS AN IMMINENT DANGER

IN THE NEVER-ENDING DOCKET OF LAWSUITS NRDC has taken on over the past 50 years, there are certain cases that embody what might be called our organizational DNA: fierce litigation, sound science, and a determination to stick with a case for the long haul. Take our 20-year fight against the chemical company Mallinckrodt.

Back in 1999, Frank Hatch, a longtime NRDC trustee, alerted us to press reports of mercury pollution in the Penobscot River in his beloved home state of Maine. Frank's family had a farm on the iconic waterway, which had been paddled by Henry David Thoreau and historically blessed with the biggest Atlantic salmon run in the United States—until dams, paper mills, and other industrial polluters disfigured the river in the 20th century. The contamination had the members of communities along the river worried about the impacts to local fishing jobs, wildlife, and recreation, as well as the meals they had fed their children from the Penobscot.

Mallinckrodt's chemical plant at Orrington, near the mouth of the Penobscot, used mercury as a catalyst in its production of chlorine bleach for Maine's paper mills. In 1967, at a time when the country still had no meaningful environmental laws, the plant began to spew mercury-laden sludge into the river from its sewer drains. Over the next 15 years, as much as 12 tons of the potent neurotoxin wound up on the riverbed, a dagger in the heart of the state's lobster-fishing industry downstream. If there's one thing more iconic to Mainers than the Penobscot, it's lobster.

Mallinckrodt, formerly Holtra-Chem Manufacturing, opened its Orrington chemical plant in Maine in 1967.

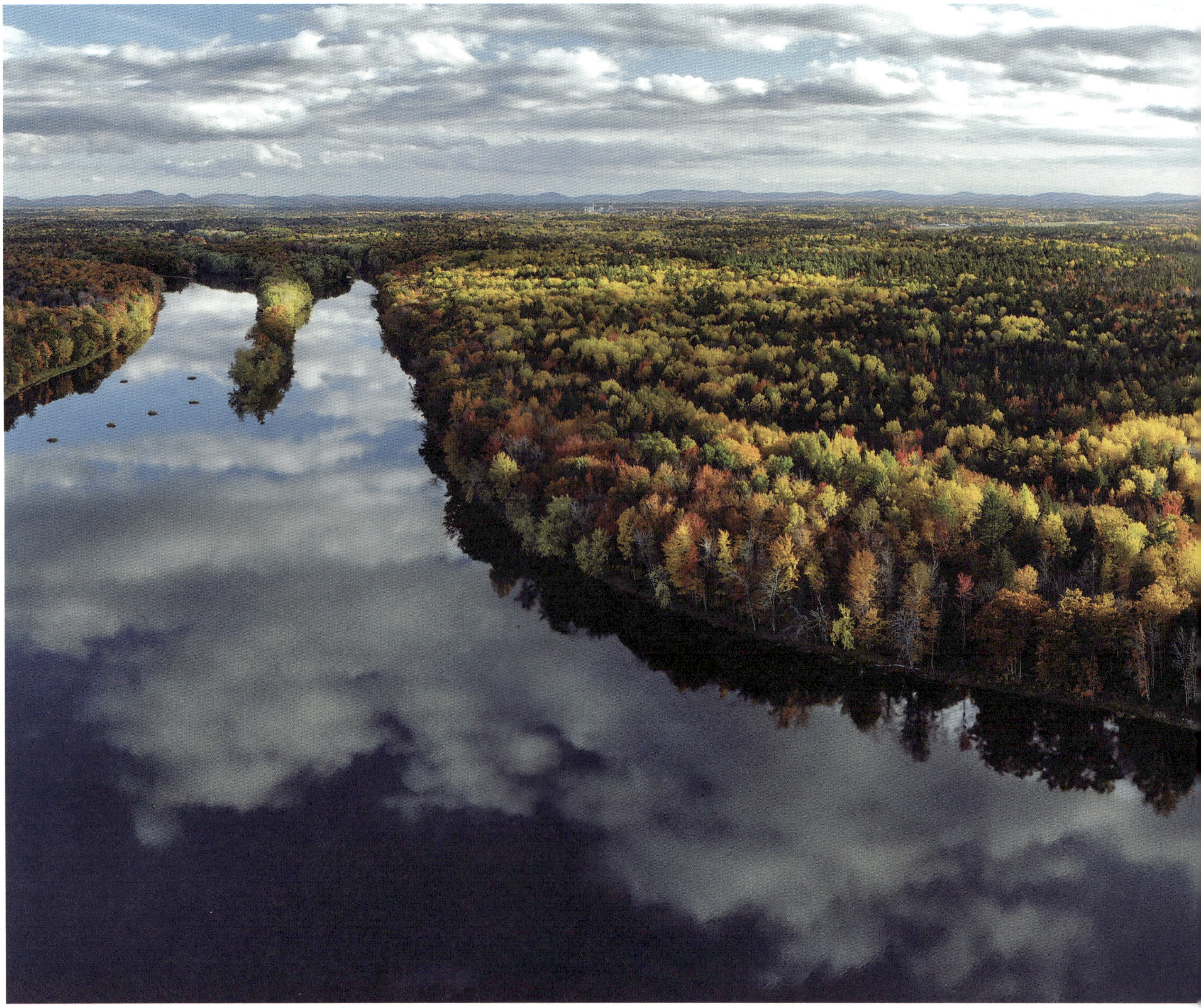

As the mercury settled into the Penobscot's sediment, microorganisms transformed it into methylmercury, which is much more toxic and steadily concentrates in animal tissues as it works its way up the food chain into fish, lobsters, and eventually the humans who eat them. The process is known as biomagnification.

We weren't optimistic about the case at first. Federal and state authorities were asleep at the wheel; local groups didn't think they stood a chance against Mallinckrodt, a powerhouse in the chemical industry; and because the pollution had occurred many years earlier, the case didn't fall within the scope of the Clean Water Act. We turned instead to another federal law—the Resource Conservation and Recovery Act (RCRA), which governs the disposal of solid waste over its entire time span, from "the cradle to the grave." Together with our local partner, the Maine People's Alliance, NRDC set out to convince a judge that the past dumping of mercury in the Penobscot presented what RCRA calls "imminent and substantial endangerment to human health or the environment."

In 2002, two of our senior attorneys, Mitch Bernard and Nancy Marks, went up in court against a phalanx of high-priced lawyers from Mallinckrodt—and won. The judge held the company responsible for the contamination and ordered it to pay for an independent scientific study to assess the extent of the problem. When Mallinckrodt balked, an appeals court upheld the ruling four years later. By accepting our interpretation of that critical phrase in RCRA—"imminent and

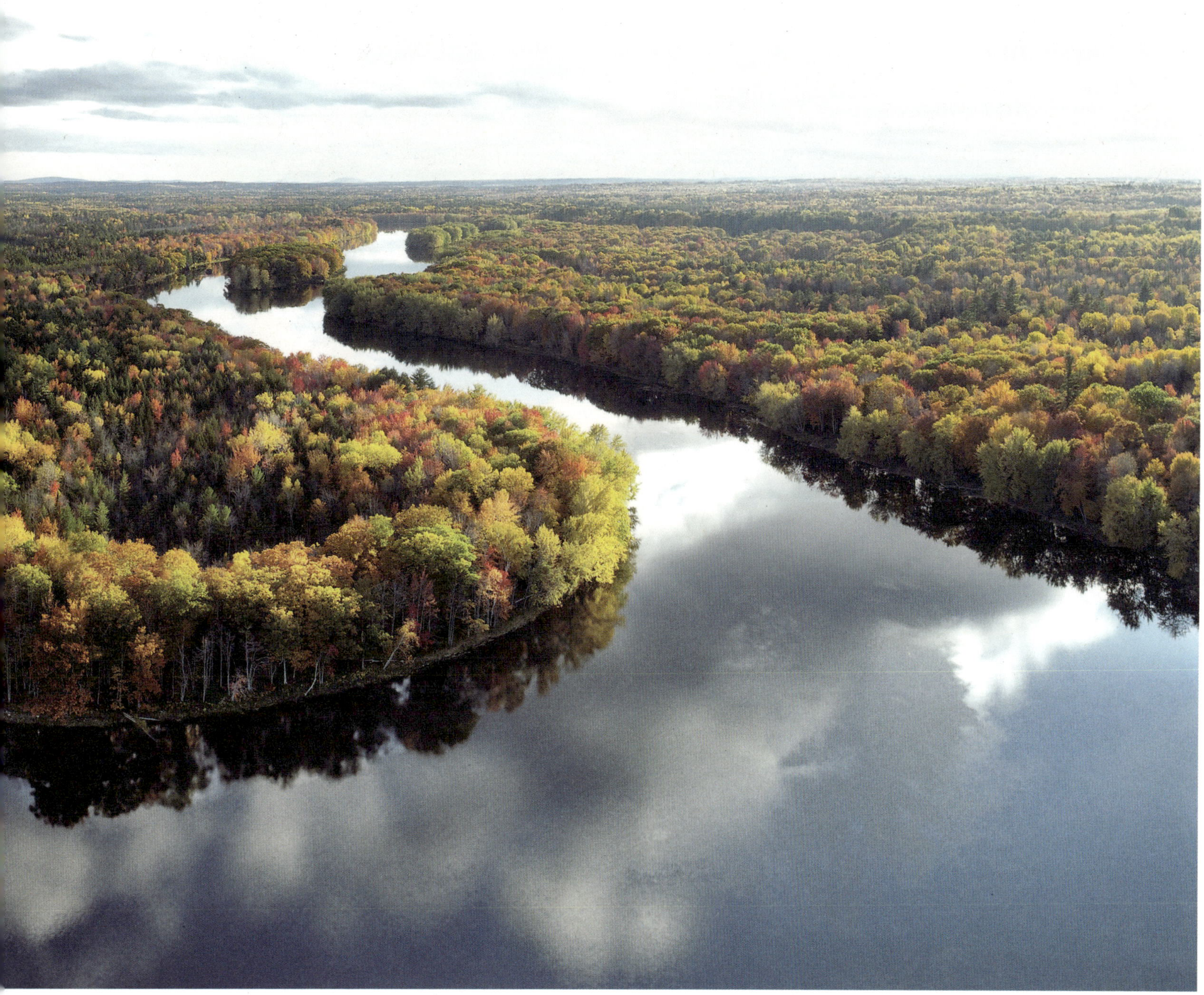

substantial endangerment"—the courts made the Mallinckrodt case a landmark in environmental law.

The panel of scientific experts duly found unsafe levels of mercury in lobsters, eels, black ducks, and marsh songbirds. The state responded by issuing an advisory, warning the public against consuming any waterfowl along the lower Penobscot—a favorite duck-hunting spot—and subsequently closed more than 12 square miles of prime lobster- and crab-fishing grounds.

The federal district court then ordered Mallinckrodt to fund another study, this time an evaluation by engineers of what it would take to clean up 20 miles of tidal river bottom downstream from Orrington, an enormously complex task. In their final report, issued in 2018, the engineers recommended dredging a million cubic yards of sediment and capping more than 200 acres of contaminated salt marshes with clean soil. Now the court must consider the cleanup plan proposed by the engineers. The estimated cost: as much as $333 million, with Mallinckrodt to foot the bill if the court approves the plan.

The case is a reminder of NRDC's first principles, Mitch says. "Polluters, no matter how powerful and no matter how well they've managed to escape government enforcement in the past, have to comply with the law. They must clean up the messes they make."

After two decades, the Mallinckrodt case isn't over, and no one can predict how long it will continue. But we're going to see it through to the very end, because that's what it takes. Winning an argument is a 100-yard dash; winning justice, as often as not, is a marathon.

SAM HESS

Orson Island sits within the Penobscot River.

GOING AGAINST THE FLOW

As the new century began, it became clear that no matter how much we accomplished in Washington, D.C., New York, and California, we needed to cover more ground in order to forestall climate change and take on the threats to clean air and water across America. We also needed concerted action at the state and regional levels, especially in our country's center. And so, in 2007, NRDC opened its Midwest office in downtown Chicago.

But you can't just parachute into a new area expecting to be welcomed with open arms. The office needed a special kind of leader, someone with deep local roots and connections. We found that person in Henry Henderson, who had served for six years as the first commissioner of the Chicago Department of Environment. Endlessly curious and gregarious, Henry seemed to know everyone in the city.

NRDC had to prove itself by adding value to the work others were already doing and by identifying an issue that we were uniquely placed to tackle. Henry quickly realized the answer was right there on the doorstep of the new office: the Chicago River.

If Lake Michigan was the pride of Chicago, the river was its shame. Raw sewage and meatpacking waste so polluted the Chicago River that the city had declared a public health emergency in 1900 and reversed the river's flow in order to send all that filth into the Mississippi watershed instead of the lake. Yet a century later, the river was still a foul-smelling eyesore.

Cleaning up the river meant taking on the Metropolitan Water Reclamation District (MWRD). Unlike almost every other U.S. city at the time, Chicago didn't disinfect its sewage, and the MWRD paid little heed to inconveniences like the Clean Water Act. MWRD's sewage effluent also contained high and uncontrolled levels of phosphorus, which fuels algae growth and creates dead zones where aquatic wildlife can't survive. Far downstream in the Gulf of Mexico, there's a dead zone roughly the size of Connecticut, and phosphorus pollution from the Chicago area was its largest single contributor. "They made a wonderful villain," says Karen Hobbs, a senior advisor and managing director of NRDC's Center for Policy Advocacy.

Henry was what you might call a strategic opportunist. Not only did he believe that a battle against the MWRD was winnable, but he also saw the potential domino effect of restoring the river and reimagining the role it could play in Chicago's civic culture. He was right on both counts.

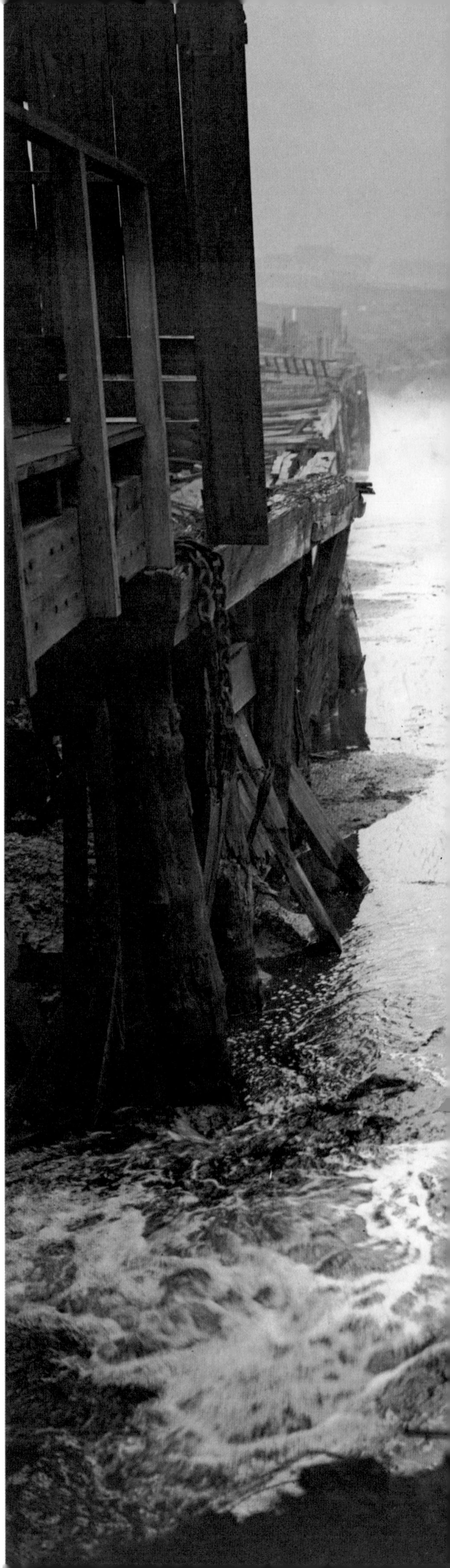

A man stands on crusted sewage in Bubbly Creek, on the South Branch of the Chicago River in April 1911.

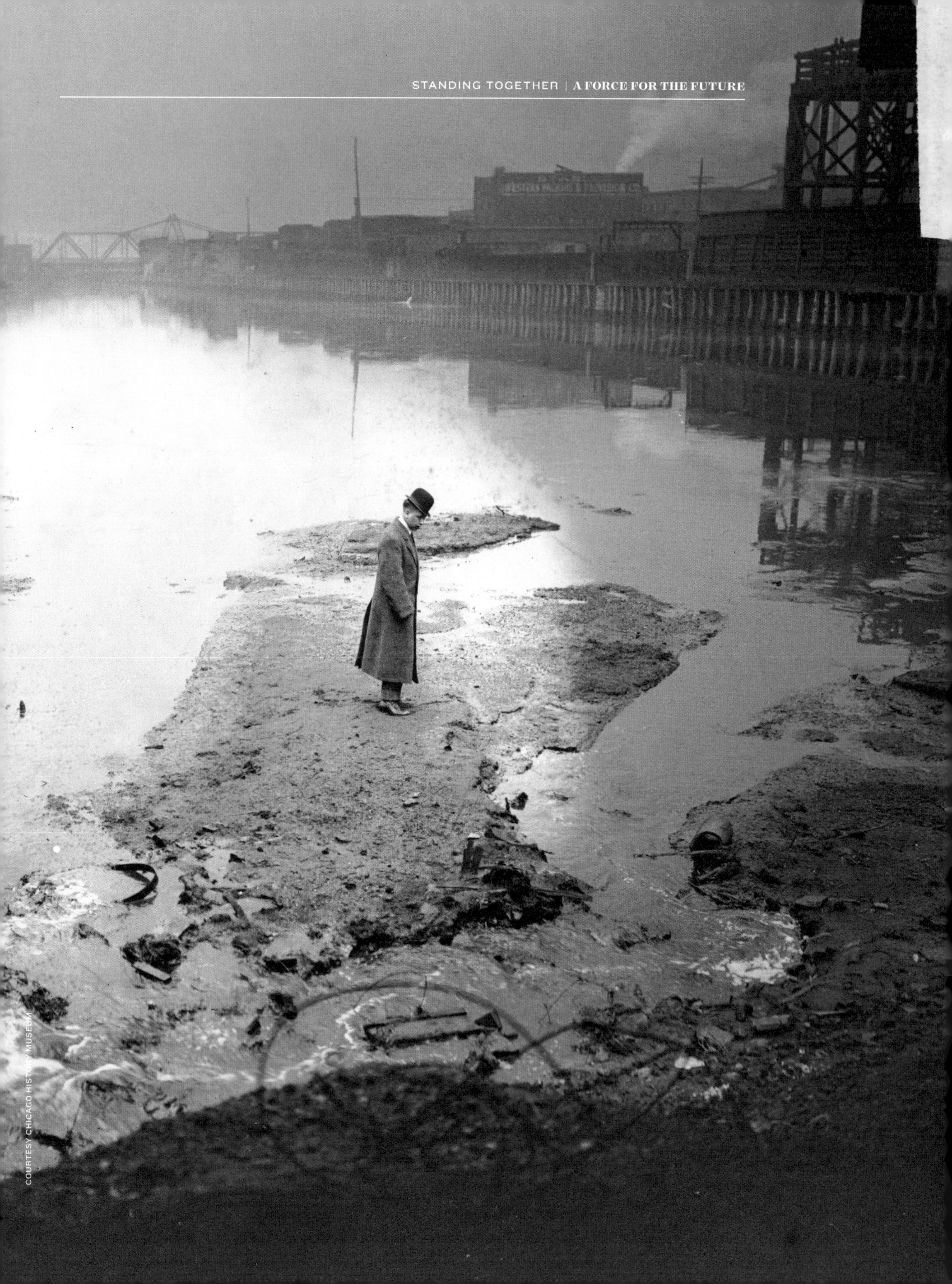

COURTESY CHICAGO HISTORY MUSEUM

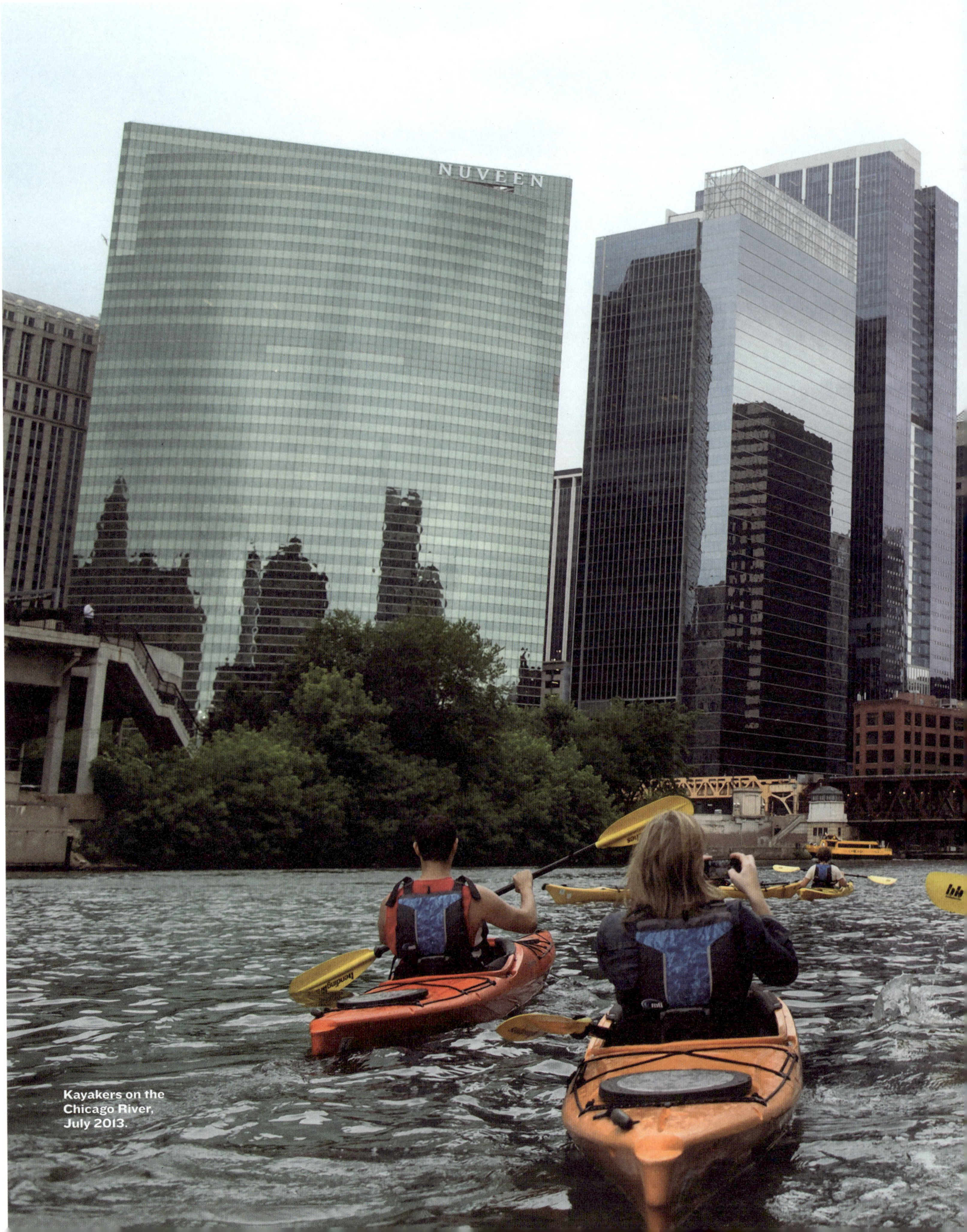

Kayakers on the Chicago River, July 2013.

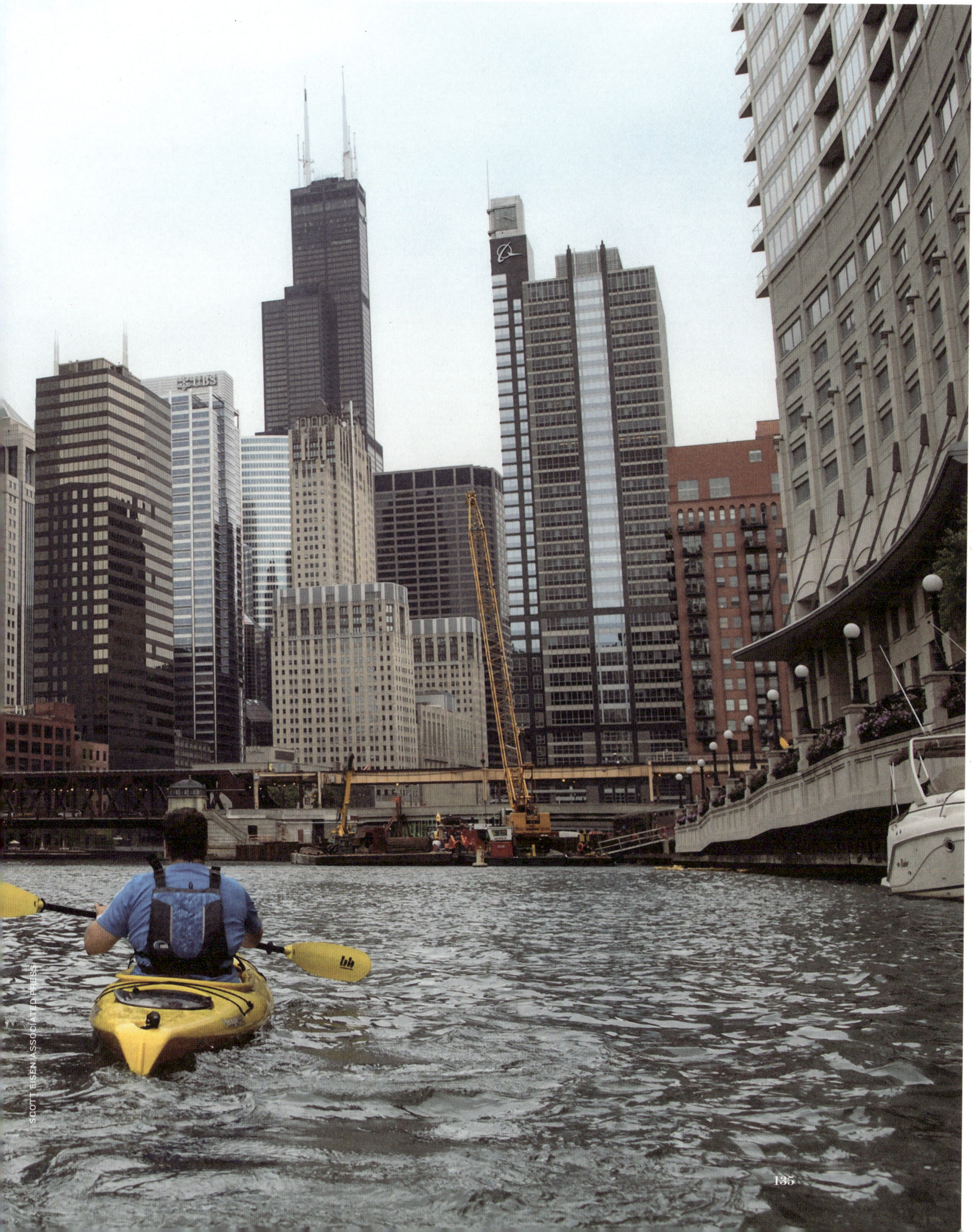

SCOTT EISEN/ASSOCIATED PRESS

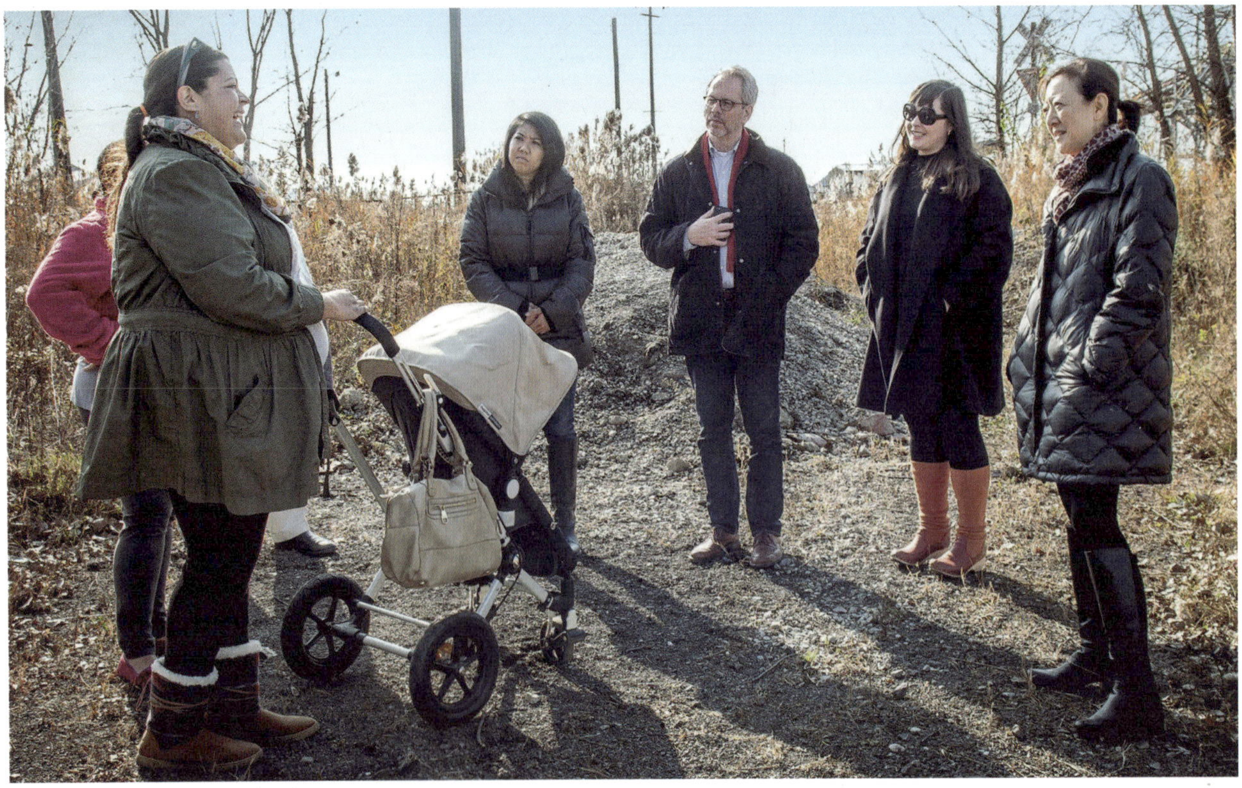

"Henry Henderson's legacy will be felt for decades to come through the economic and environmental benefits of this reimagined and cleaner river. The downtown Riverwalk is becoming one of Chicago's most popular destinations, and none of it would have been possible without Henry's optimism that the river could be more than a conveyance for sewage, or, as Henry never shied away from calling it, 'poo.' "

—Karen Hobbs, senior advisor and a managing director in the Center for Policy Advocacy

Multiple opportunities to push back at MWRD began presenting themselves, and Henry took them all. NRDC dove into Clean Water Act regulatory hearings, spearheading advocacy for disinfection and phosphorus control and filing a lawsuit against MWRD. Henry also deftly tied the water quality issues to the Asian carp that were threatening to invade the Great Lakes via the river. The Great Lakes ecosystem was already suffering the effects of several other invasive species, and the carp were voracious filter feeders capable of muscling out native fish. Viral videos of 30-pound silver carp, a type of Asian carp, leaping out of the water and hitting people in boats focused public attention on the Chicago River like nothing before.

Henry dared to posit the idea that one day an uncontaminated Chicago River might again flow in its natural direction and again nourish the lake, while helping prevent an Asian carp invasion and providing recreational and economic opportunities to the city's residents. To help visualize this possibility, he enlisted the help of an old friend, Jeanne Gang, an architect who won the MacArthur "genius award" in 2011. Gang produced renderings showing a carp barrier that would stretch across the river near the site of a defunct coal plant and a revitalized riverfront with walkways, bridges, and green infrastructure that turned an eyesore into an asset.

NRDC's advocacy in the Clean Water Act hearings culminated in a 2011 decision by the Illinois Pollution Control Board, ordering MWRD to install disinfection equipment at its three Chicago River plants. Eventually MWRD also signed a consent decree with the EPA requiring completion of its plan to control combined sewer overflows and a settlement agreement with NRDC and others to control its phosphorus discharge. Over the years, as public attention to the river grew and voters began electing more environmentally minded commissioners, MWRD slowly started to become more helpful on water quality issues. In all, the efforts benefited every community along the river and beyond.

As Henry had hoped, cleaning up the river stimulated millions of dollars in new investments, and an open sewer transformed into a tourist attraction. Henry passed away in 2018, a terrible loss to both NRDC and the city he loved. But stroll along the Chicago River on a sunny day, watching the kayakers, joggers, shoppers, and sunbathers enjoying the new riverwalk, and his legacy is right there in plain sight.

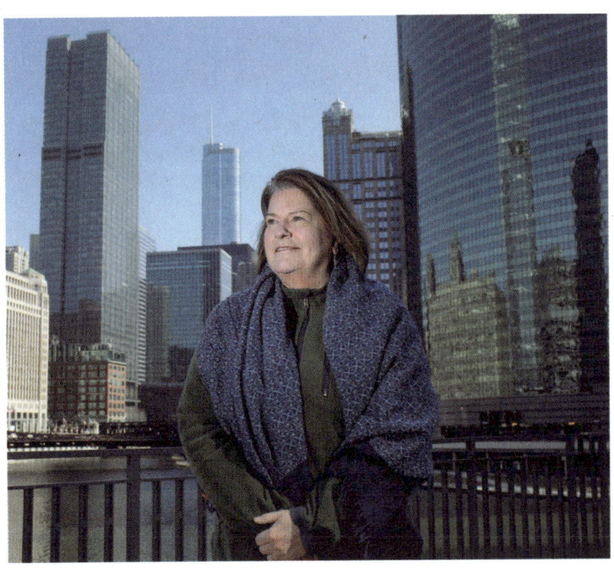

Karen Hobbs joined NRDC to work on the Chicago River and Great Lakes water policy issues and now oversees the day-to-day management of the Center for Policy Advocacy. Here, she's pictured in Chicago, with the river in the backdrop.

FROM TOP: ANGELA GUYADEEN/NRDC; JOSHUA LOTT FOR NRDC

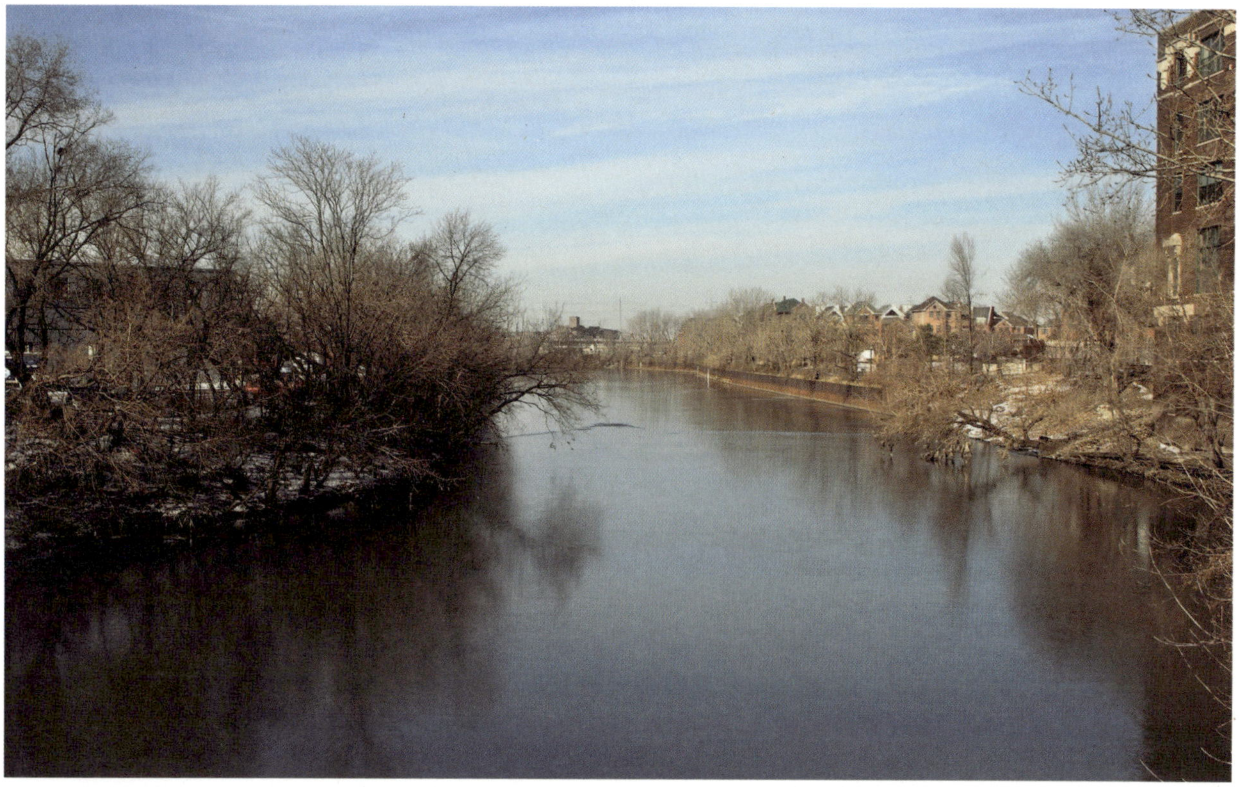

Opposite: Former NRDC Midwest director Henry Henderson (center) and former NRDC president Rhea Suh (far right) with community members of Chicago's Southeast Side. At left: The Chicago River's Bubbly Creek in 2009. Below: Chicago's new Riverwalk along the west bank of the river, 2017.

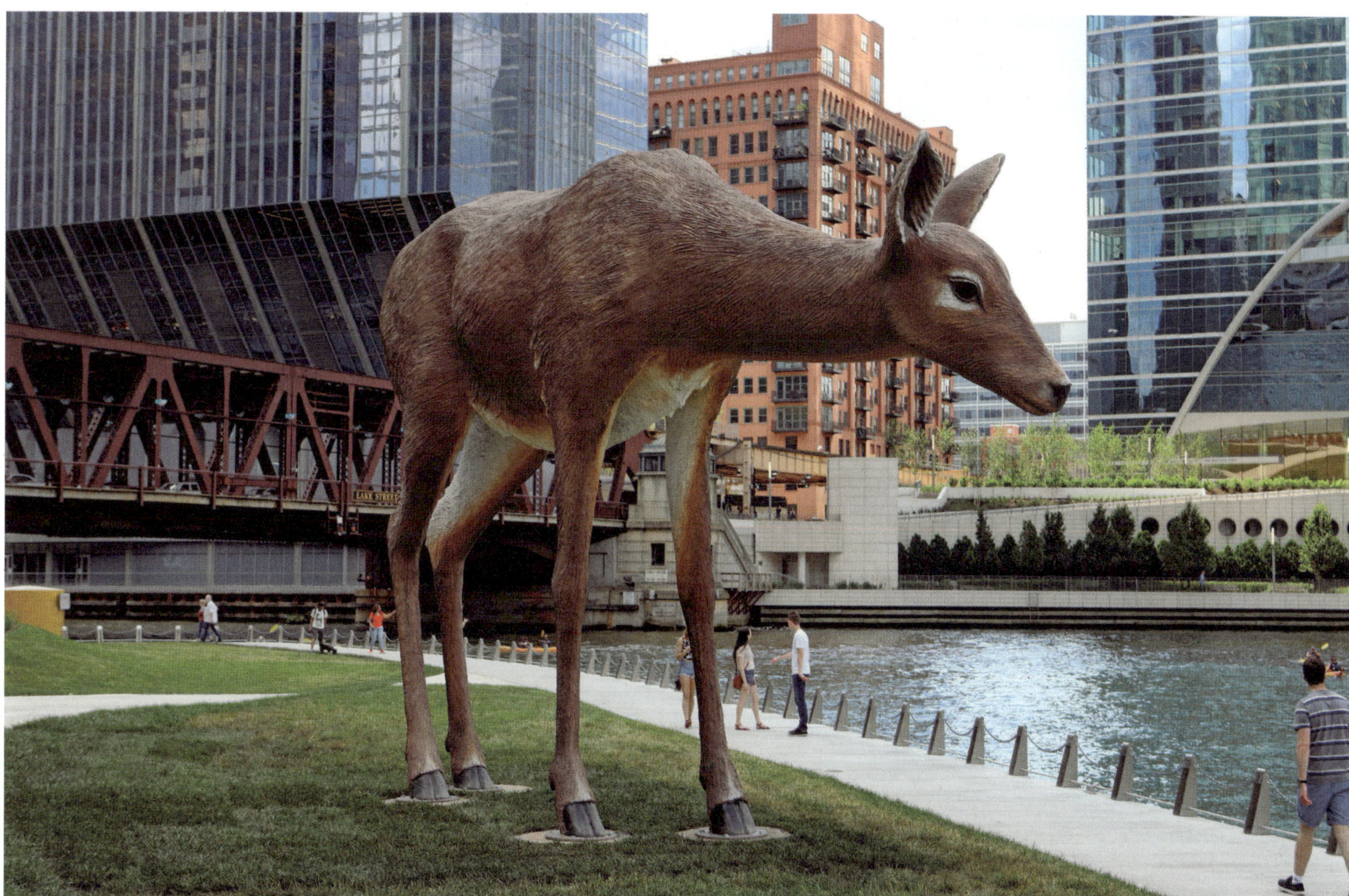

FROM TOP: FREDERICK J. NACHMAN; RAYMOND BOYD/GETTY IMAGES

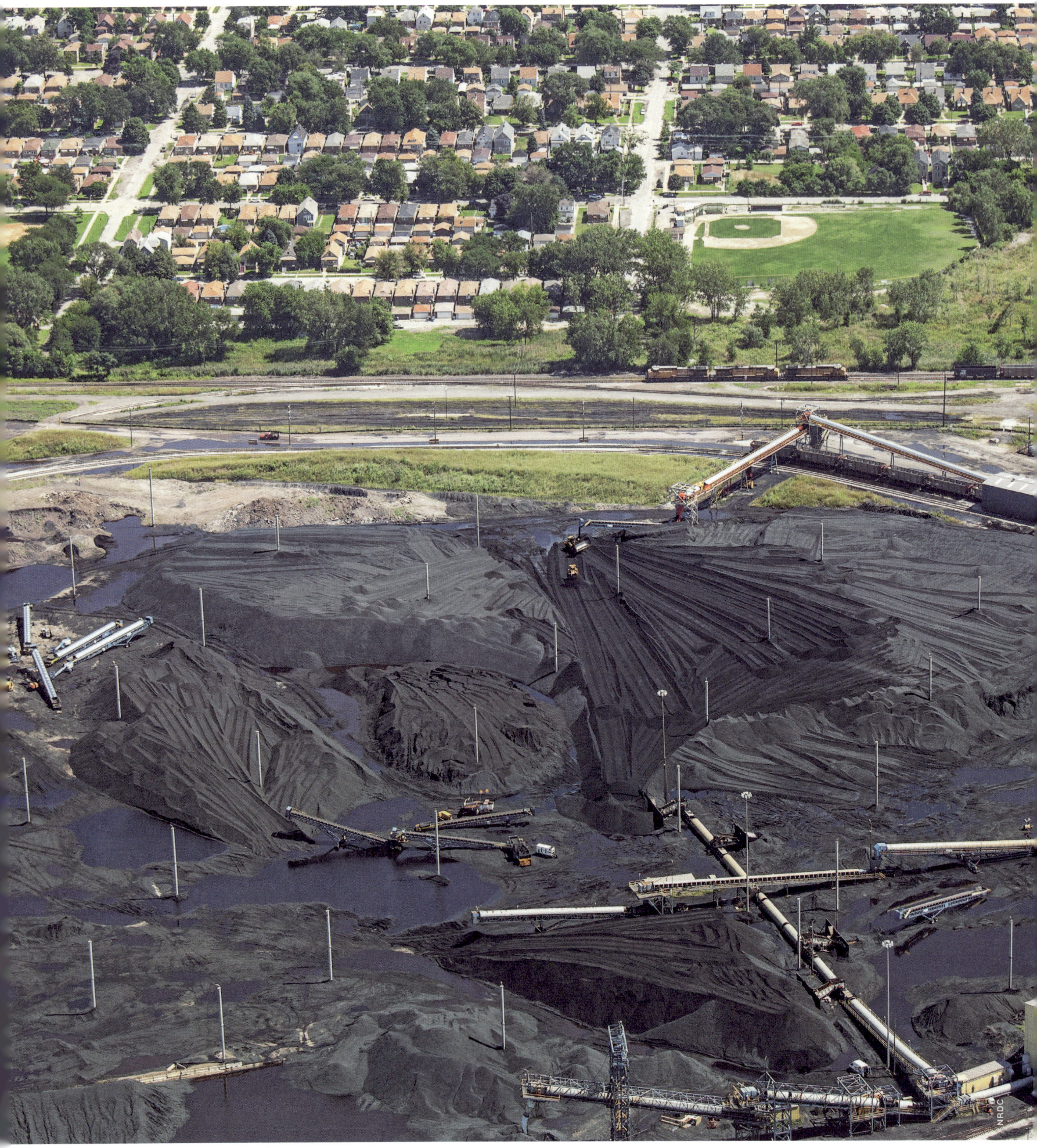
NRDC

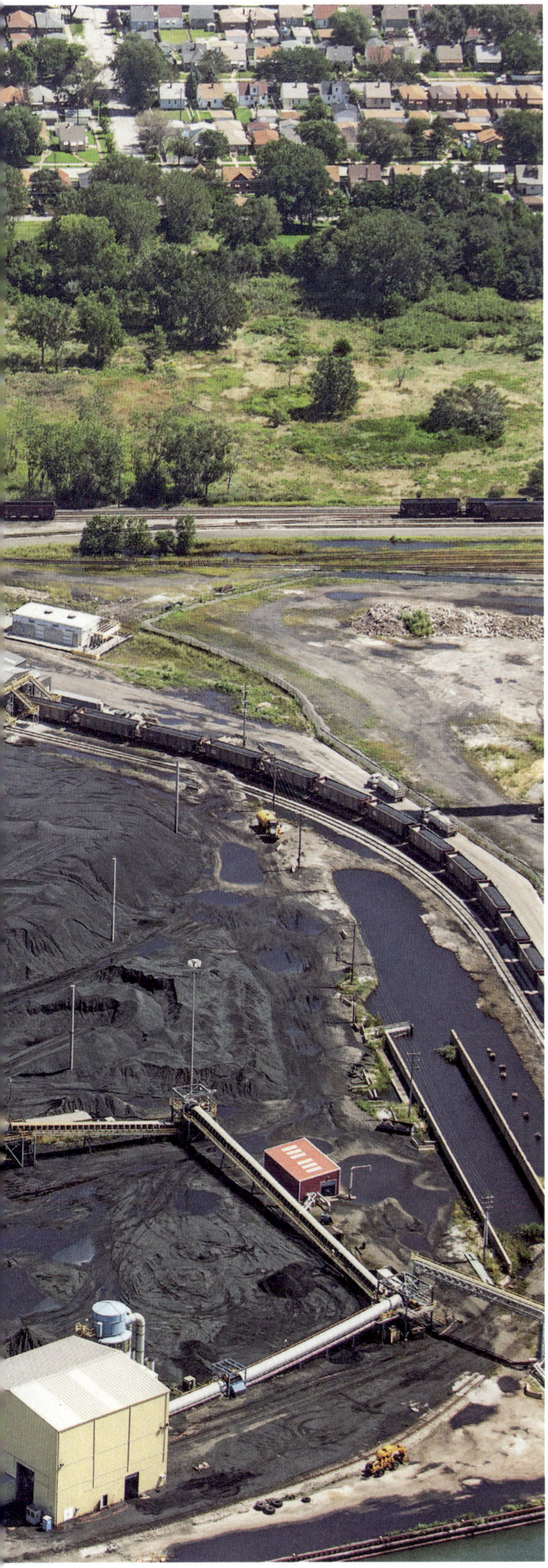

FOLLOW THE PETCOKE

SOON AFTER WE OPENED OUR CHICAGO office, we began dealing with a problem involving a substance few people had ever heard of: petcoke. This dark and gritty material is the bottom-of-the-barrel residue left over in large amounts from the refining of tar sands and other heavy oils. Petcoke, or petroleum coke, causes pollution both when burned to produce electricity and when stored next to communities en route to power plants.

Our petcoke story begins at the BP Whiting refinery, just across the state line in Indiana. BP was making money hand over fist at the time from the explosive growth of the Canadian tar sands and was looking to expand its plant. The refinery had already ignited local outrage by obtaining state permits that allowed it to increase the amount of ammonia it dumped into Lake Michigan. So when BP sought a Clean Air Act permit to avoid modern pollution controls, systematically undercounting its emissions in order to qualify, NRDC and its allies filed a challenge. In 2012, we forced a consent decree that ordered BP to install $400 million worth of pollution control equipment and established emissions standards that heavily influenced refinery regulation going forward.

It was a big win, but there is a second act to the story. Among the many other problems associated with the refinery expansion, NRDC determined that it would increase petcoke production fourfold, to an astounding two million tons a year. Petcoke is a remarkably dirty fuel. Its combustion emissions are so high that few American industries want it, so U.S. refineries ship it to China, India, Mexico, and other countries with laxer environmental standards.

While working with a local group, the Southeast Environmental Task Force, a communications specialist in our Chicago office named Josh Mogerman learned that the biggest bulk handler of the stuff was a company called KCBX Terminals—the *K* standing for Koch, as in the Koch brothers, among the biggest funders of climate-denial groups and "research." And its storage facilities were on the Southeast

Huge piles of oil refinery waste called petcoke line the banks of Chicago's Calumet River, in the city's Southeast Side neighborhood.

Side of Chicago, on the banks of the Calumet River and right next to parks and homes. Josh was shocked by what he saw: mountains of dusty, black petcoke standing six stories high and stretching for what looked like a mile along the river.

For decades, giant steel mills had dominated the Southeast Side, where residents lived by an unspoken social contract: industrial pollution might mar their neighborhood, but they'd have a guaranteed job at a good union wage in return. That deal held until the mills began to shut down in the 1980s, and the Southeast Side became a sacrifice zone. When KCBX was deciding where to store its petcoke, it went for the line of least resistance—a blighted, postindustrial community of color.

But this neighborhood also happened to be one of the cradles of the environmental justice movement, and we asked the Southeast Environmental Task Force if there was anything we could do to help, whether in court or in the media. NRDC threatened a lawsuit against KCBX—and part of me would have relished the idea of going up against the Koch brothers in court—but it never had to come to that, thanks to our media savvy.

The massive mounds of petcoke were in close proximity to the Calumet River, homes, parks, and schools, but only a handful of sprinklers mounted on poles were there to control the dust. In 2013, a windstorm blew choking clouds of black dust across a nearby ball field, and for the first time the rest of the city sat up and took notice. Josh took a *Chicago Tribune* photographer along the river, and the appalling images made the front pages. The city was embarrassed, and so was BP. The community rose up in response, and eventually Chicago adopted strict health and zoning regulations for petroleum dust, which our coalition led in crafting. As a result of our advocacy, the Illinois attorney general and the city filed lawsuits alongside the EPA. In 2015, when the city denied KCBX permission to avoid building a large enclosure for its petcoke as required by those regulations, BP agreed to stop sending petcoke to Chicago. The next day, KCBX promised to shutter one of its Southeast Side facilities and eventually remove the petcoke piles from the other, an issue we continue to monitor.

Petcoke was an object lesson in how everything connects in the world of fossil fuels, a story with a clear through line—running from the pits and tailing ponds of the Canadian boreal to the operations of the country's most powerful climate deniers and winding up in the lungs of Latino kids enjoying a baseball game on a field in Chicago.

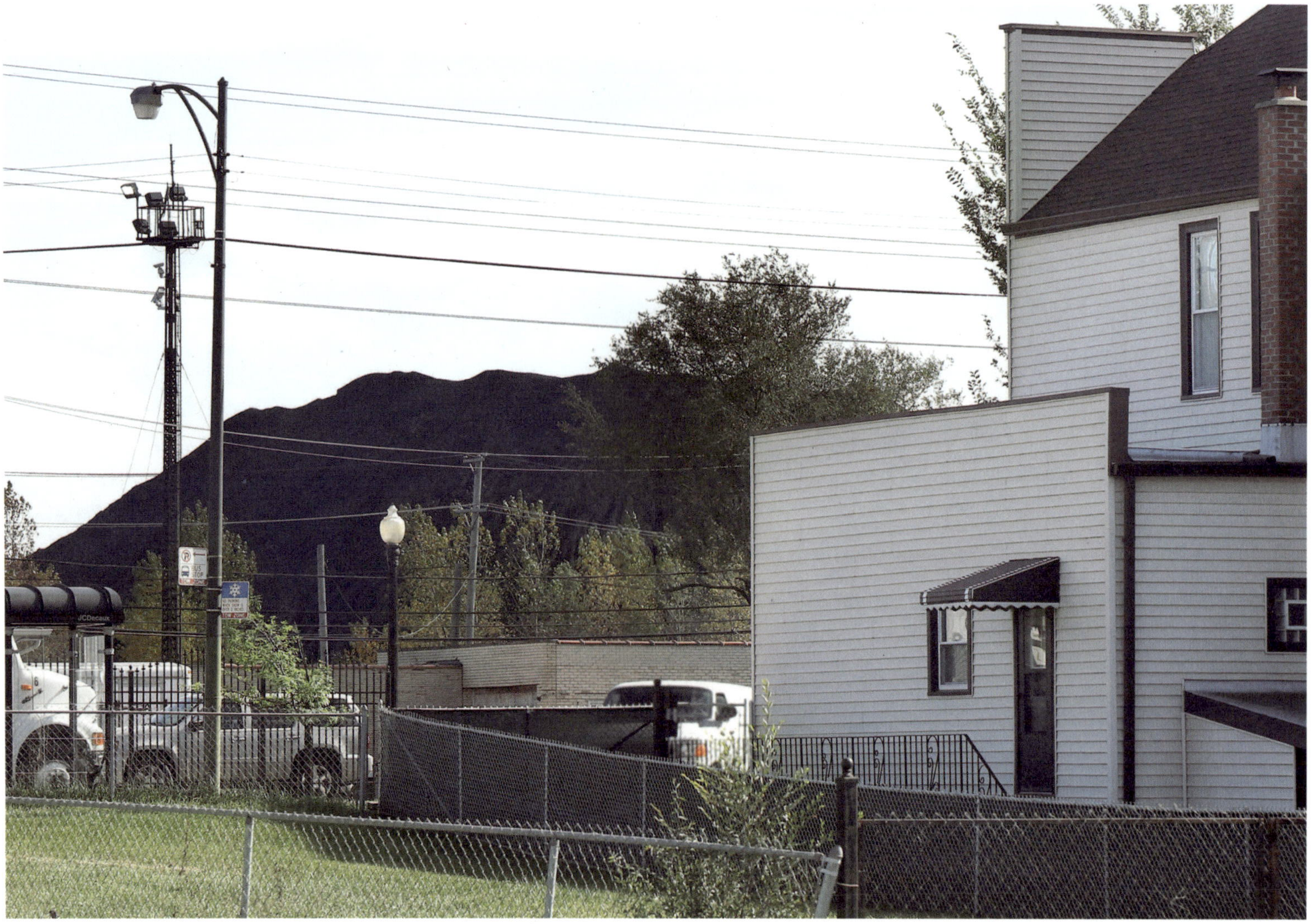

A large mound of petcoke sits near a residential neighborhood.

CHARLES REX ARBOGAST/ASSOCIATED PRESS

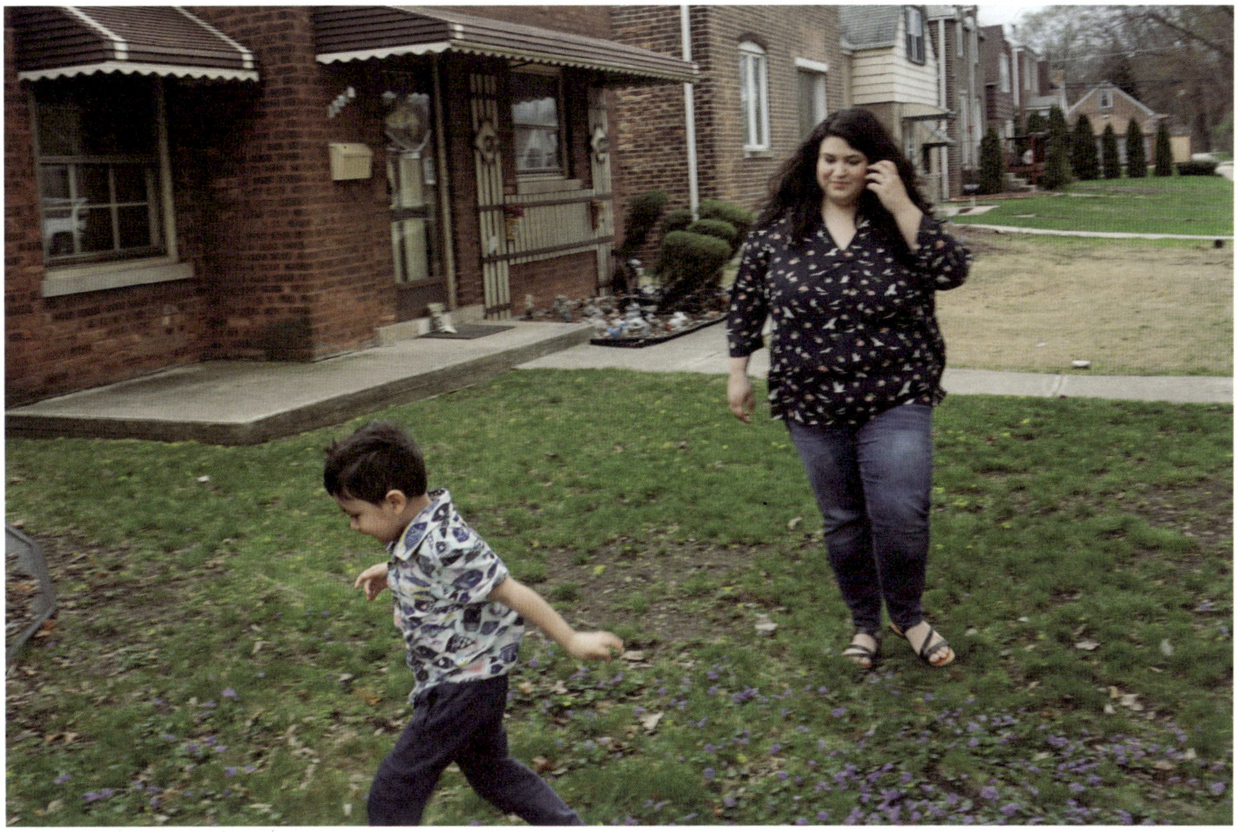

NRDC's Gina Ramirez (here with her son) has been instrumental in bringing attention to the petcoke that plagues her family and neighbors on the Southeast Side.

FROM THE FRONTLINES
Peggy Salazar

When Peggy Salazar moved into her current home on Chicago's Southeast Side 35 years ago, she immediately noticed the black dust coating the front porch of her home. Only later did she realize it was blowing in from the coal yards three blocks away. "I never guessed that stuff could travel so far," she says.

Today, as the executive director of the Southeast Environmental Task Force, Peggy is fighting the same kind of pollution—and more—as she works to transform her neighborhood into a safer, more desirable community. It hasn't been easy. "I see the changes going on in the rest of the city, and I feel like we're being ignored," she says. After the steel mills left the area in the 1990s, other dirty industries moved in. But over the past decade, Peggy and her neighbors have defeated plans to build a coal gasification plant on the Southeast Side. And with help from NRDC, they also stood up to fossil fuel giants and the city of Chicago in a successful effort to clear their neighborhood of massive, open piles of petcoke, a dusty byproduct of refining tar sands oil.

"If it weren't for NRDC's expertise and resources, we might never have had the successes we had with the petcoke situation," Peggy says. "As a small community organization, we just can't afford additional resources, and we don't have that type of talent. But they never try to run the show. They look to us, and they listen to us, and then they offer assistance. We never feel like they are stepping on our toes."

And the partnership continues. As Peggy says, "It never ends over here . . . but we have to be positive—and we don't give up."

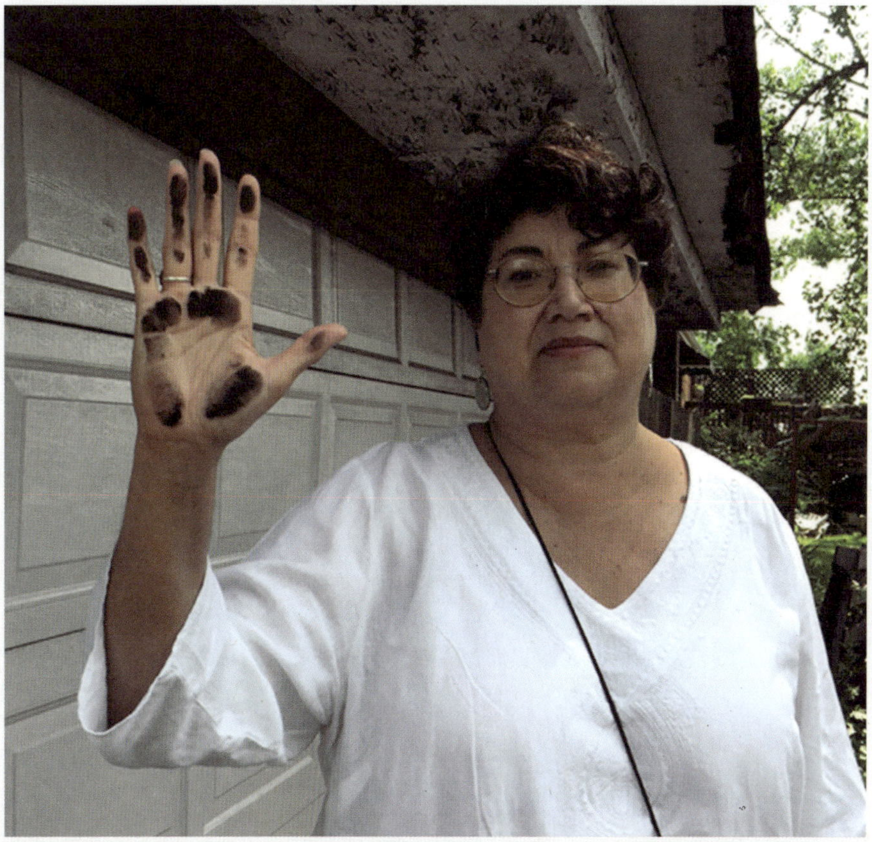

FROM TOP: REBECCA KARAMEHMEDOVIC/NRDC; ROBIN AMER/DNAINFO CHICAGO

IN FOR THE LONG HAULS

Workers at the Port of Long Beach prepare to plug in a container ship to shoreside electricity so the ship can shut down its diesel engines while at port.

TIM RUE/CORBIS VIA GETTY IMAGES

ON A TRIP TO CHINA IN 2007, FRANCES Beinecke and a group of NRDC trustees—including Dan Tishman, Tom Roush, and the late Joy Covey—visited the giant port complex at Shenzhen. Their hosts proudly showed off the port's green innovations, such as "cold ironing," where ships at berth plugged into electric power rather than running their dirty diesel engines. They explained that the changes were made because most of their container ships were bound for the Ports of Los Angeles and Long Beach, where these pollution-cutting measures were already in place. And that knowledge must have made everyone standing there proud, since the transformation of those twin California ports was largely the work of NRDC. We had acted locally and the effect went global.

In 2000, when our port saga began, the Ports of Los Angeles and Long Beach were essentially unregulated and were the main contributor to Southern California's notorious air pollution. Diesel exhaust was the main culprit, being emitted not just by the container ships but also by the 16,000 trucks per day that ran in and out of the ports, around the clock. The joke was that these ports were where old trucks went to die, spewing vast amounts of fine particulate matter (PM 2.5, which burrows deep into the lungs) along with more than 40 known carcinogens.

We'd long seen diesel as a singular threat to public health. In the 1990s, NRDC attorney Gail Feuer pinpointed one air-quality hot spot at a truck distribution center in southern Los Angeles, smack in the middle of a Latino neighborhood, and then campaigned against the four big grocery chains using it. Meanwhile in New York City, another of our attorneys, Rich Kassel, led a successful drive to get dirty buses off the streets, kicking off a worldwide revolution in the use of ultralow-sulfur diesel. Some of the worst levels of diesel emissions were coming from big bus depots, which were polluting low-income neighborhoods of color in the Bronx and other parts of the city.

On the West Coast, our involvement with the ports began when local residents asked us for help with a lawsuit against the proposed expansion of the China shipping terminal at the Port of Los Angeles. We won a $60 million settlement that created the first green shipping terminal in the world, with the cold ironing that so impressed the Chinese, dock tractors running on cleaner-burning alternative fuels,

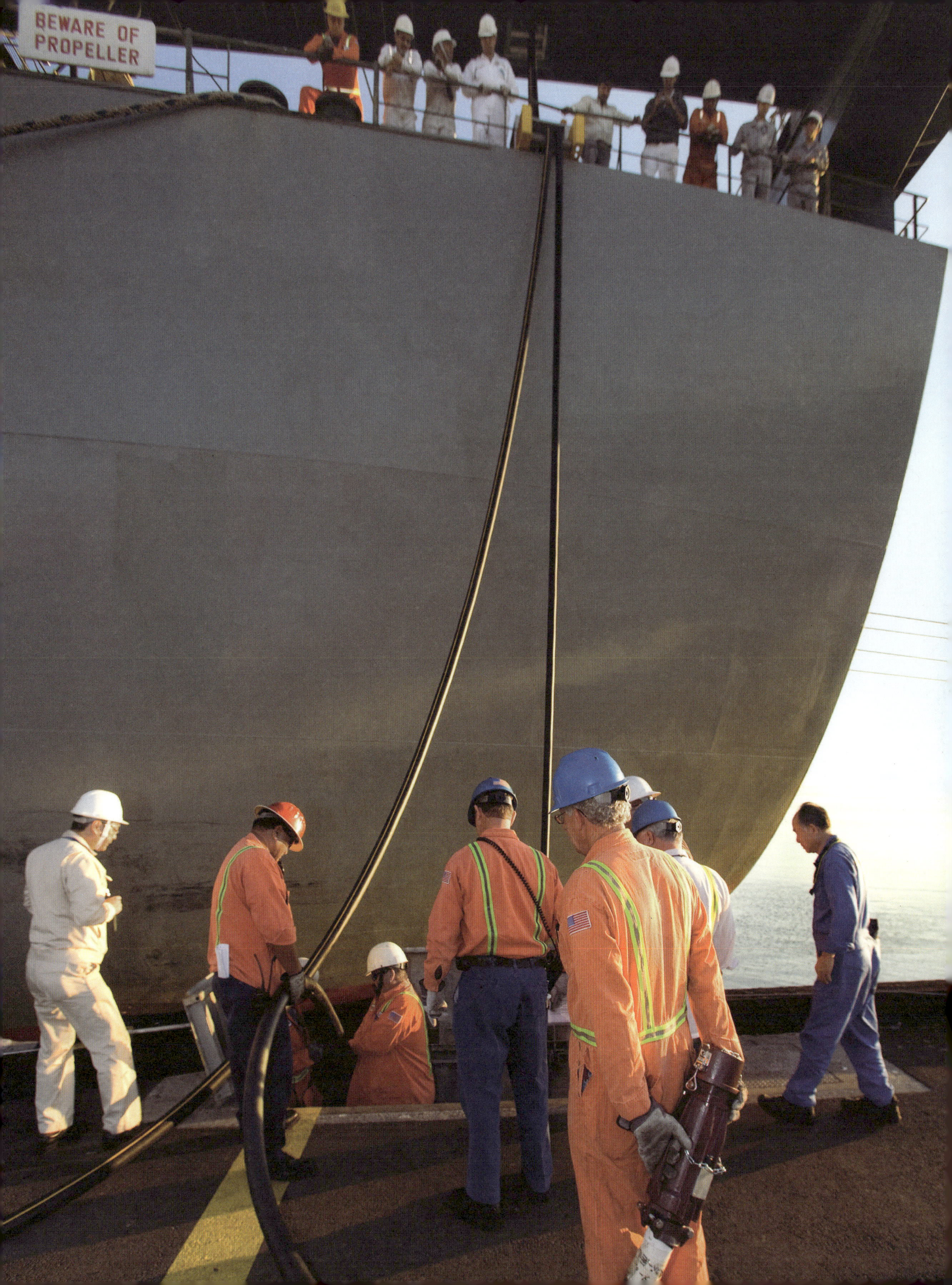
BEWARE OF
PROPELLER

"We held the ports' feet to the fire, and now every terminal project is cleaner than 20 years ago. We're changing the industry, and ports around the world are watching. And we won't stop until every community has clean air to breathe."

—Melissa Lin Perrella, senior director of NRDC's environmental justice team

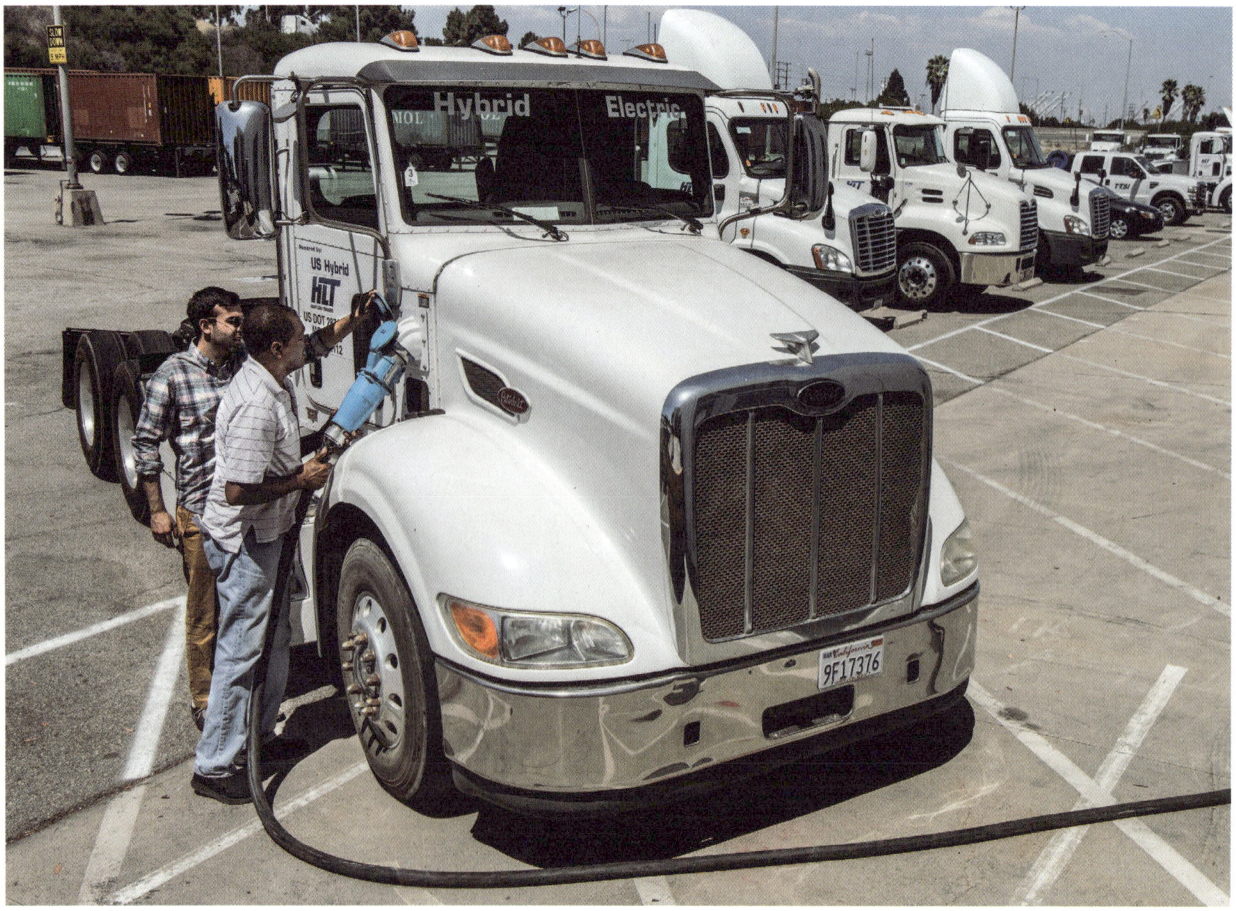

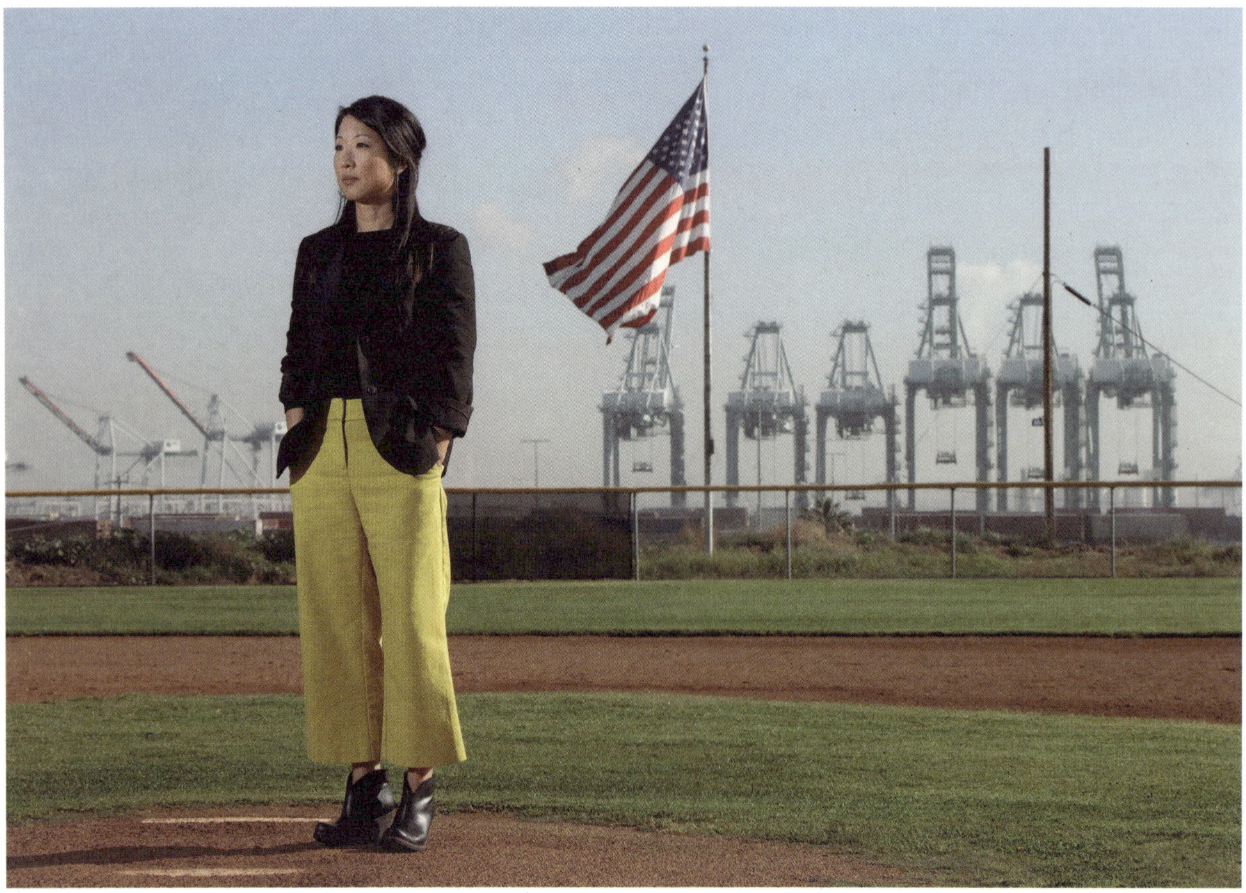

Representing communities that have been hardest hit by freight-related air pollution, Melissa Lin Perrella has led NRDC's efforts to clean up the ports of Los Angeles and Long Beach and is now expanding that work to other parts of the country. Here, she stands at the Eastview Little League baseball fields near the Port of Los Angeles.

FROM TOP: DENNIS SCHROEDER/NREL; ANN JOHANSSON FOR NRDC

grants for new private initiatives to further reduce air pollution, and a fund to mitigate the aesthetic impact of the ports on surrounding communities.

Our success in the courtroom helped forge new partnerships with environmental justice communities along the main freight corridors. Air pollution is not an equal-opportunity killer, and people living in these areas had higher-than-average risks of cancer and childhood asthma. Together, NRDC's legal expertise and the community organizing chops of groups like East Yard Communities for Environmental Justice became a force to be reckoned with. While NRDC had what Daniel Hinerfeld, one of the communication specialists in our Santa Monica office, calls "the brass knuckles of litigation" in our pocket, our larger goal was to cultivate a longer-term commitment to our new partners, founded on strong personal relationships, as they built a robust grassroots environmental justice movement.

One thing the public needed badly was hard data. For years residents had watched the big container trucks rumble past their windows, but they had no idea of how to measure the dangers the vehicles posed. For us the campaign was not just about the clean new technology for ships; the ports also had to be transparent and accountable to the community throughout their operations. In 2008, the Ports of Los Angeles and Long Beach banned old polluting trucks. And today, both ports post emissions data online, where people can check what they may be breathing in at any given moment.

Our efforts to clean up the ports have spread to their entire transportation ecosystem, including all trucks, trains, and cargo-handling equipment. The key to a future zero-emissions port is total electrification, with a transition to zero-emissions cargo-handling equipment and long-haul electric trucks being the first step. Such innovations may sound like science fiction, says David Pettit, a senior attorney who works on port issues on both sides of the Pacific. But he's confident we'll see electric trucks within the next few years, and NRDC will be there, pushing to make sure it happens as part of the broader drive for electric vehicles. "When we take on an issue like this," David says, "we don't quit."

Opposite: An electric hybrid heavy-duty truck plugs in for a charge before carrying on its duties moving freight.
Below: NRDC partners with groups like the East Yard Communities for Environmental Justice, which runs the West Long Beach Bike Toxic Tour to raise awareness of the impacts of industrial pollution on local residents.

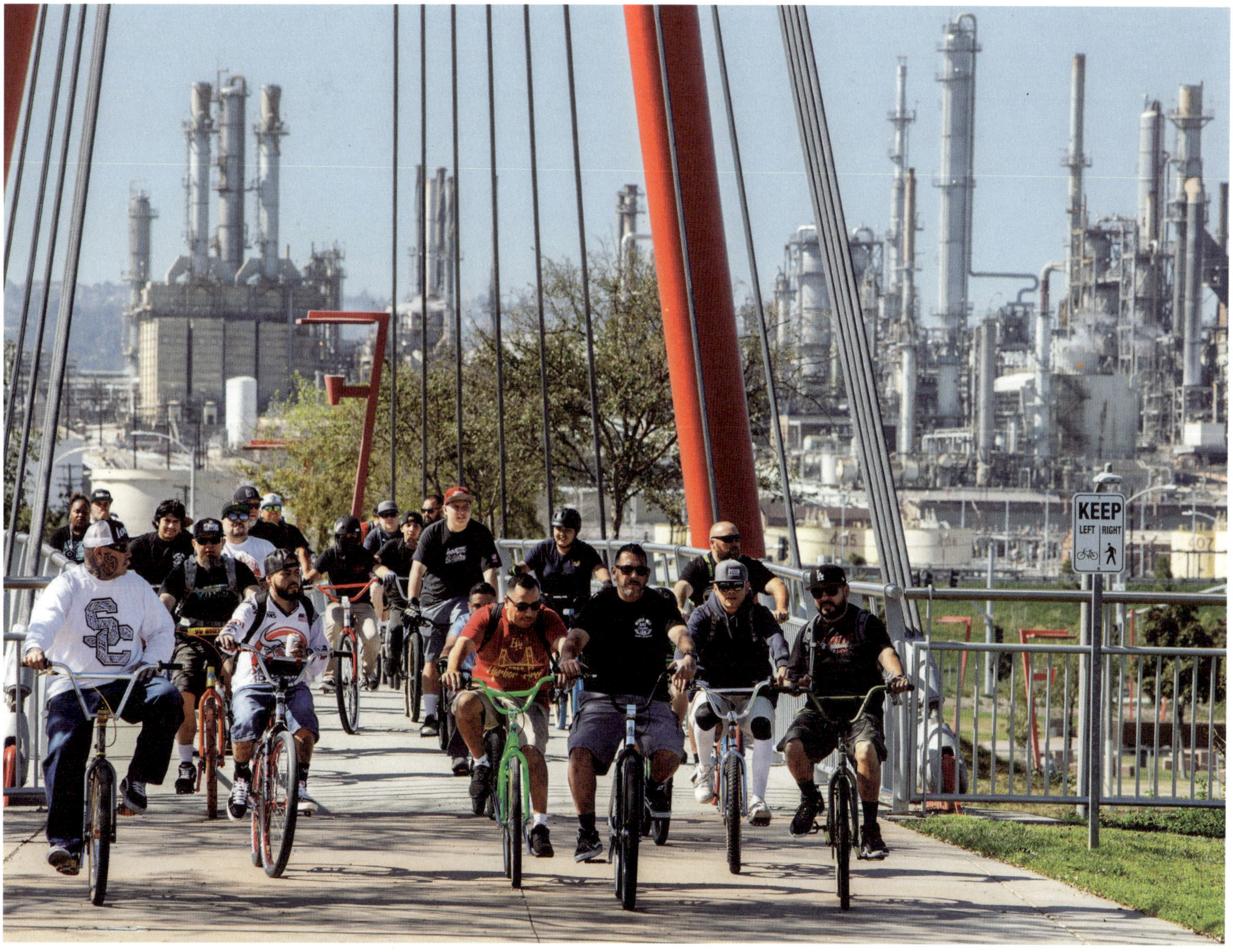

ANN JOHANSSON FOR NRDC

Solutions Spotlight

TRIMMING THE WASTE

Imagine walking out of the market with five bags of groceries and dumping two in the nearest garbage can. That's essentially what Americans do: Up to 40 percent of our food goes to waste. Restaurants serve supersize portions; food rots in our refrigerators; stores toss out perfectly edible products due to arbitrary sell-by dates and minor blemishes. By wasting so much, we squander vast amounts of energy, fertilizers, and pesticides used during food production, processing, distribution, and disposal; we also deplete water supplies and create as much carbon pollution each year as 37 million cars.

In 2012, a groundbreaking report, *Wasted,* by NRDC senior scientist Dana Gunders (now in its second edition), sparked a national debate about a problem that had been hiding in plain sight. In our Save the Food campaign, we leveraged $111 million in free publicity. But raising awareness isn't enough. Our Food Matters team has produced a tool kit of practical program and policy solutions aimed at cities, which are often in the best position to persuade local businesses to adopt better food practices while cutting their waste management costs and meeting their sustainability and climate goals. With NRDC's help, cities like Denver, Nashville, and Baltimore are already—if you'll pardon the pun—taking a big bite out of the problem.

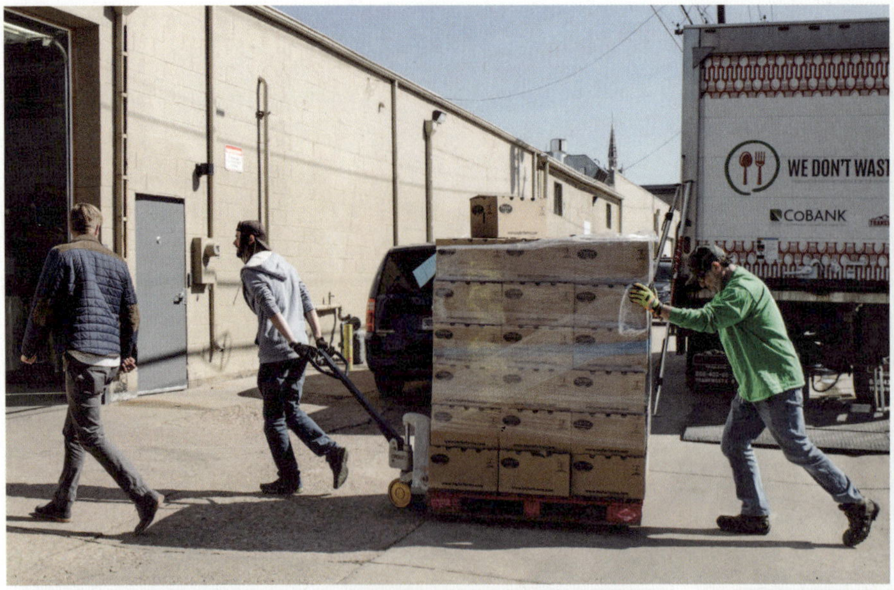

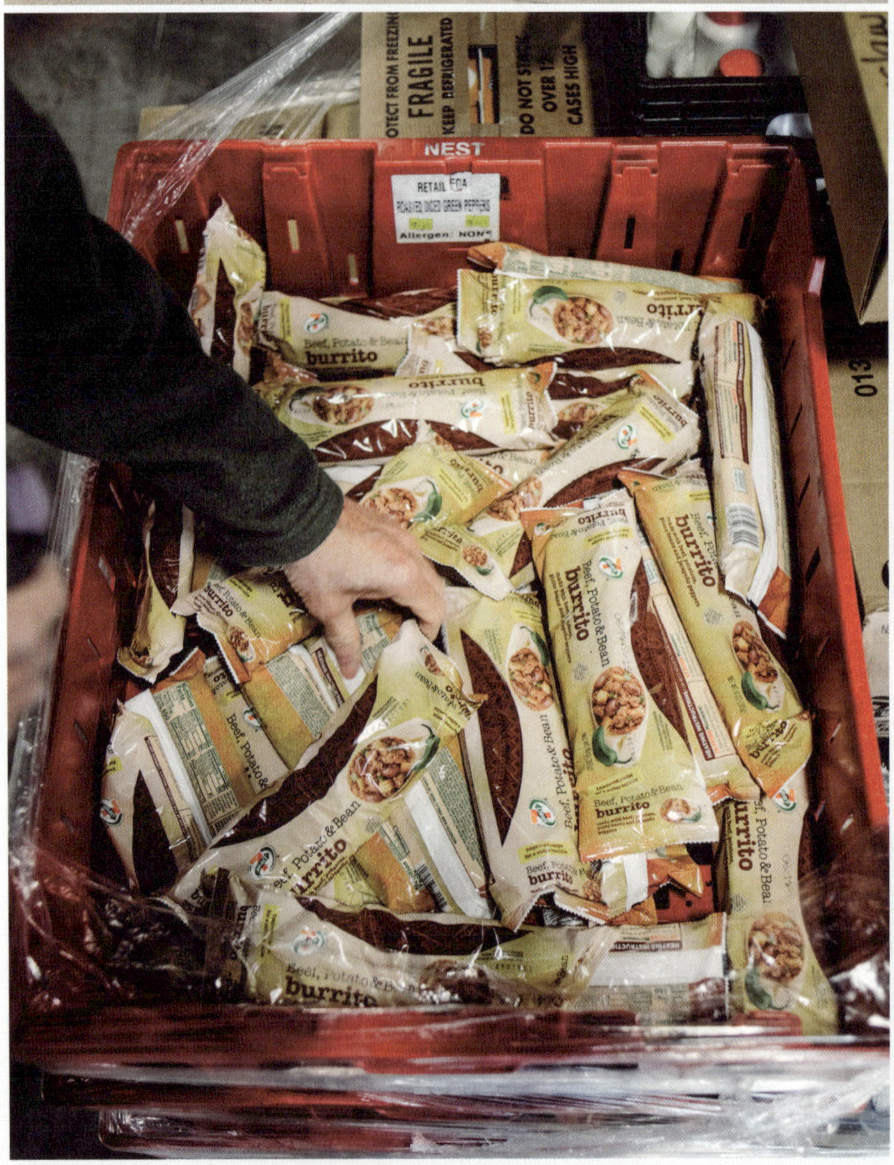

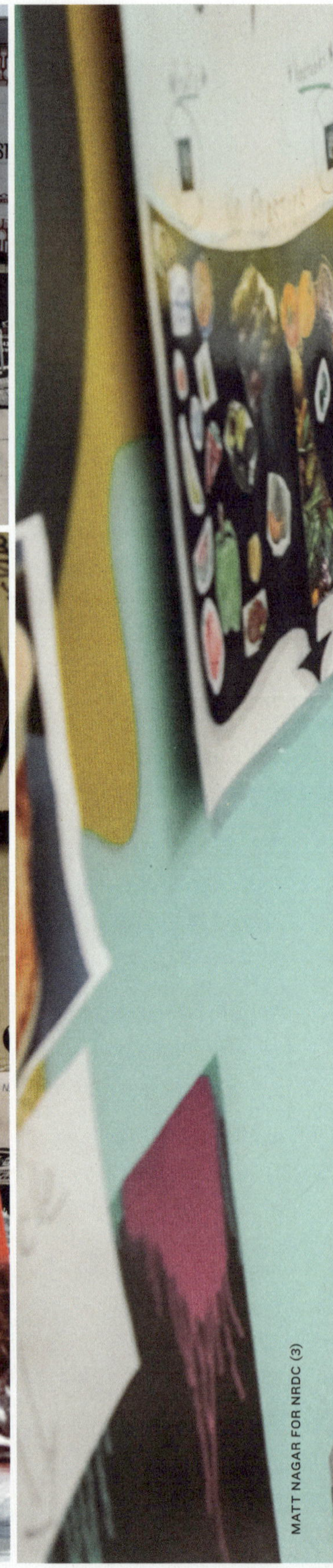

MATT NAGAR FOR NRDC (3)

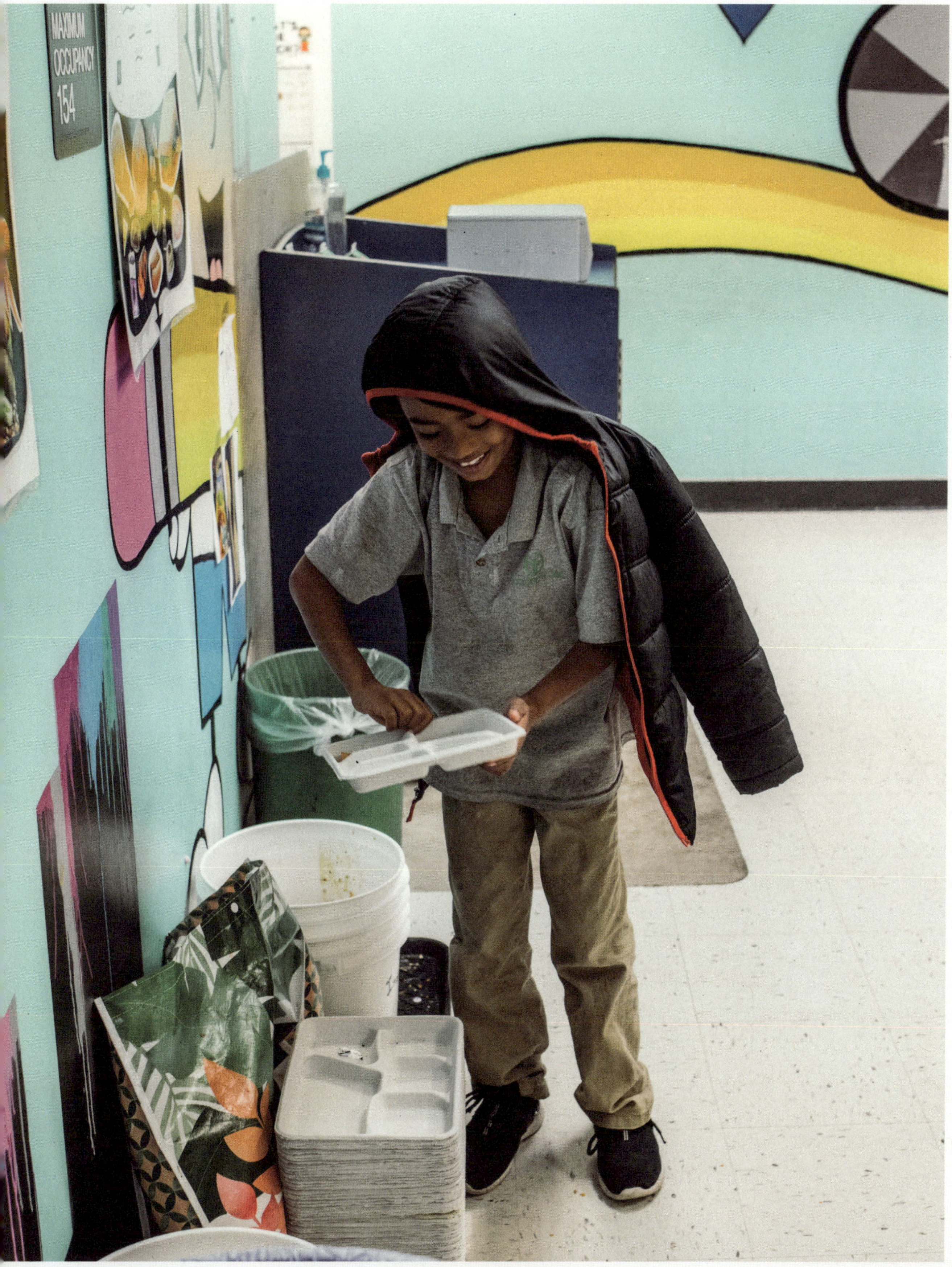

As part of the Food Matters partnership, Denver has introduced composting initiatives like this one at Academy 360. Opposite, top left: City Harvest's Jered Ratschkowsky (left) with Andrew Sanford (center) and Matt Karm of We Don't Waste during a food delivery in Denver, one of two pilot cities partnering with NRDC on the Food Matters project. Opposite, bottom: A small sample of the food items collected by We Don't Waste in one day.

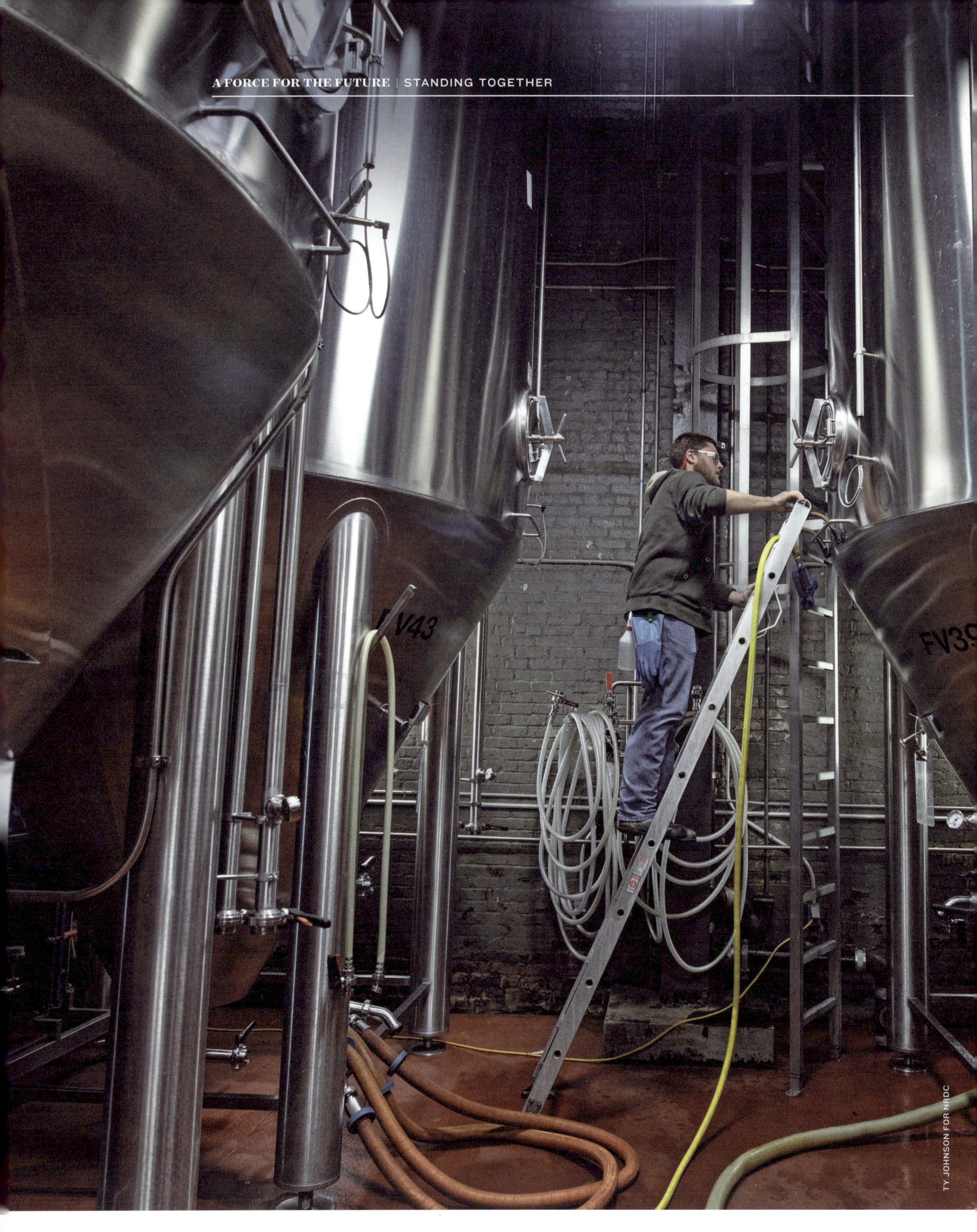

TY JOHNSON FOR NRDC

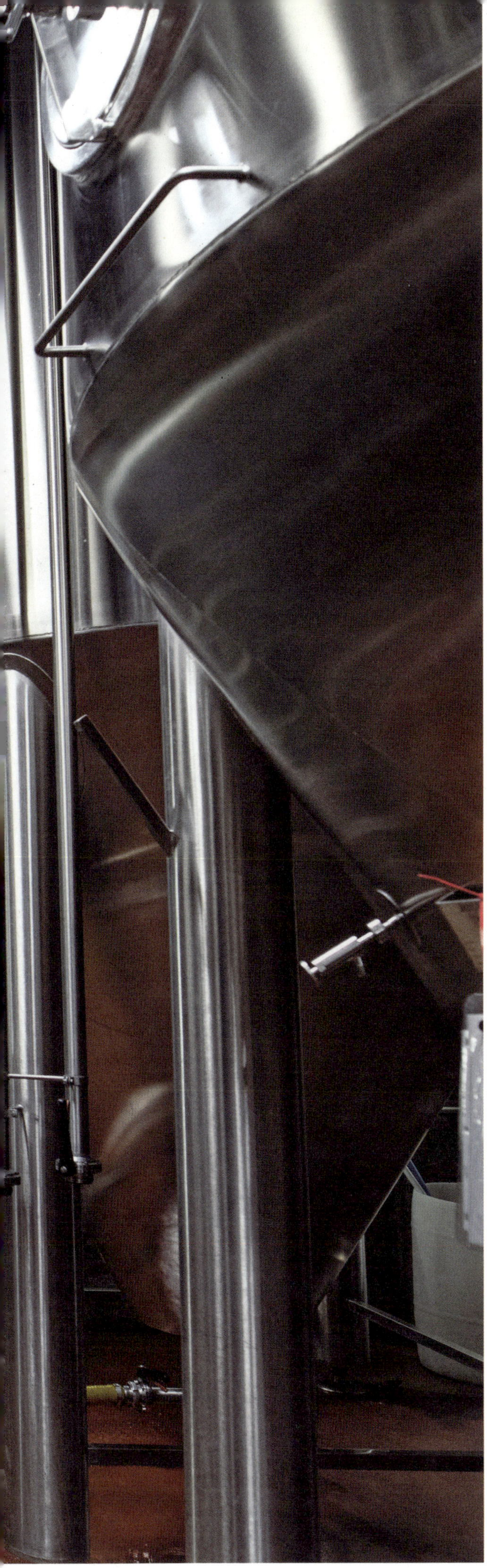

WHEN MUSIC SAVES A MOUNTAIN— AND BEER SAVES THE WATER

STRONG PARTNERSHIPS HAVE LED TO SOME of NRDC's most effective advocacy campaigns. When we bring our legal, policy, and advocacy skills to the table, we can help our partners amplify their voices. And they know we've got their backs. What we gain is their lived experience and the standing and credibility they have within their communities. Their on-the-ground efforts put a human face on our work, helping us to put down roots with new constituencies and in new places. Such partnerships connect us to the everyday concerns of countless millions of Americans and the things that enrich their quality of life—even simple pleasures like kicking back over a beer and listening to good music. Which brings us to Appalachia.

The coal industry has a political chokehold on states such as Kentucky and West Virginia, and mountaintop removal—the most destructive form of coal mining yet devised—is commonly used in the region. Companies decapitate mountain peaks with giant tractors, clearcutting and burning the forest cover and dynamiting what's left to blast open pits as deep as 1,000 feet. They then employ huge draglines to dump rock, dirt, and toxic mining waste into valleys and streams, often damaging the waterways permanently. By the early 2000s, the coal industry had obliterated more than 500 mountaintops, cleared thousands of square miles of forest, and polluted more than 2,000 miles of streams, with drastic effects on public health in downstream communities.

But while mountaintop removal is Appalachia's curse, music is its blessing. In 2009, a flash of inspiration from Rob Perks, a veteran of American Rivers and today NRDC's transportation advocacy director, brought these two forces together during a multiyear campaign to bring national attention to the issue. His idea was a resounding success. We called it Music Saves Mountains, a benefit concert that assembled some of the biggest stars in country music—Emmylou Harris, Dave Matthews, Sheryl Crow, Kathy Mattea, Naomi Judd, Alison Krauss, and many others—at the Ryman Auditorium in Nashville. If the Appalachians were the "sacred ground" of country music, Emmylou told the audience, the Ryman was its "mother church."

A worker at Brooklyn Brewery in New York City. The microbrewery is a member of NRDC's Brewers for Clean Water campaign.

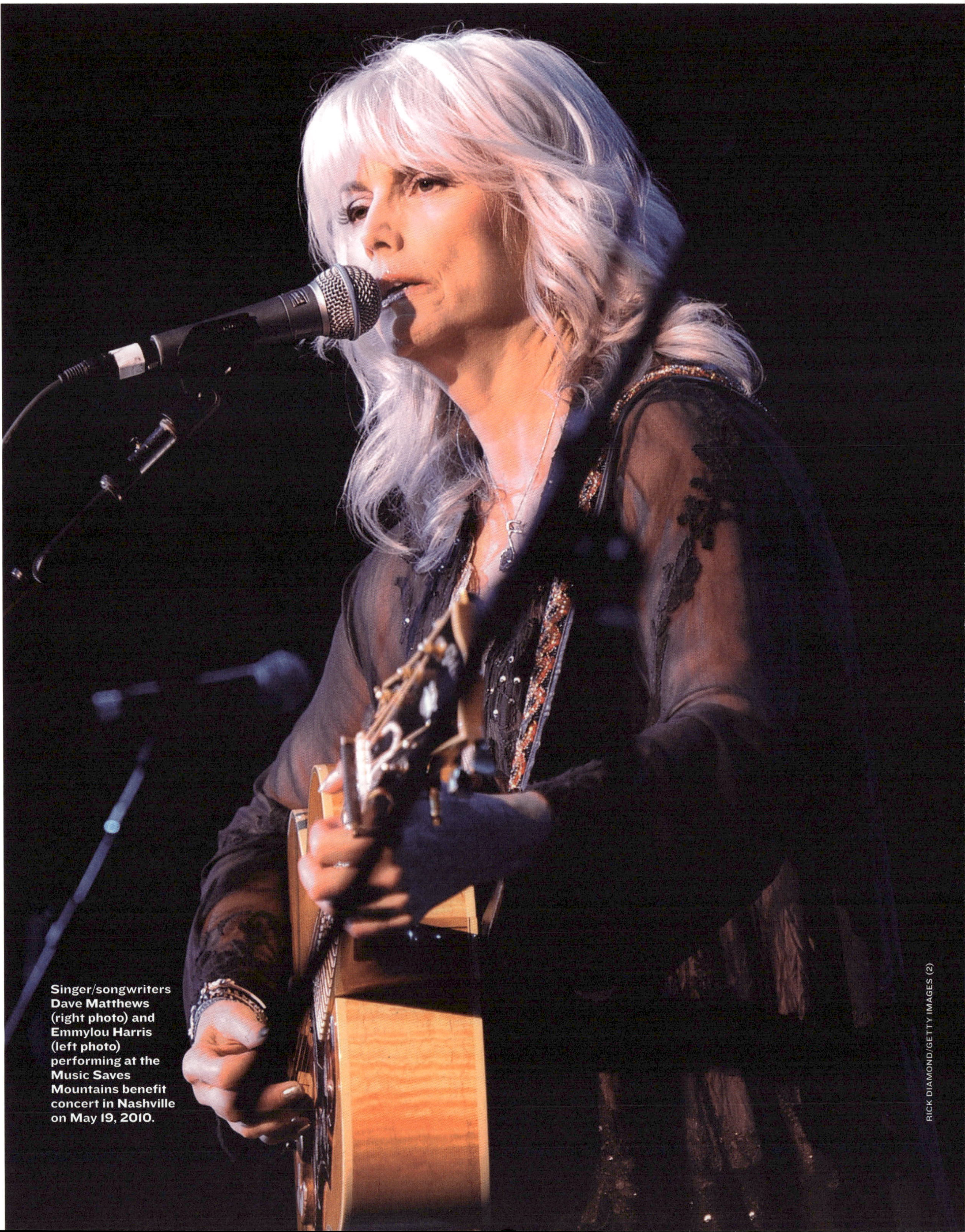

Singer/songwriters Dave Matthews (right photo) and Emmylou Harris (left photo) performing at the Music Saves Mountains benefit concert in Nashville on May 19, 2010.

RICK DIAMOND/GETTY IMAGES (2)

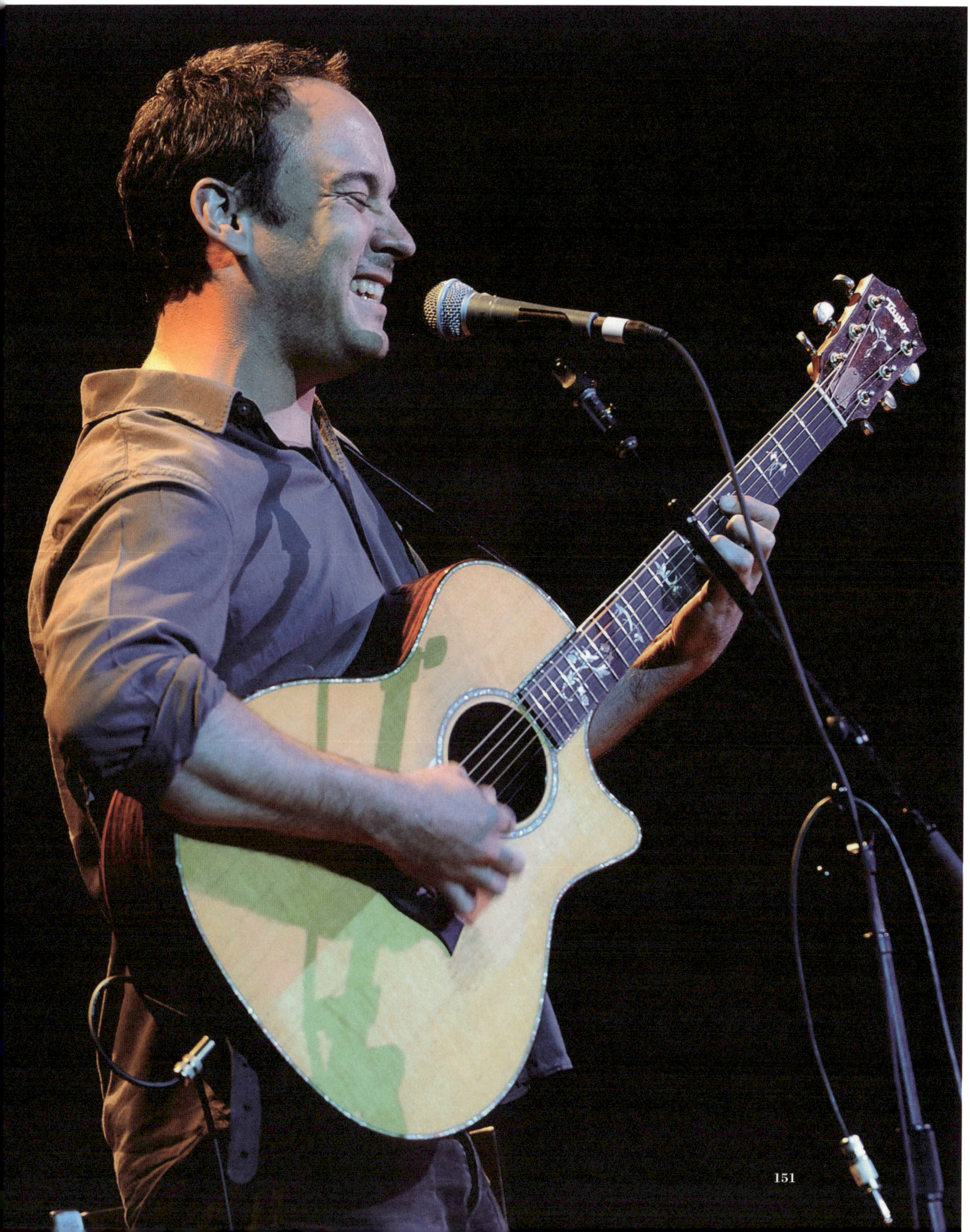
Taylor

FROM THE FRONTLINES

Chuck Nelson

Chuck Nelson considers attending the Music Saves Mountains concert 10 years ago a highlight of his life. "It was a great honor," he says. "It gave us a lot of pride in what we were doing to see these celebrities supporting us, shining a light, and letting the world see what we're going through here."

Chuck, a West Virginia native who, like the three generations before him, spent decades working underground in the state's coal mines, traveled to the 2010 benefit with his late wife, Linda, and other activists from across Appalachia. They were there to speak out against the devastating industrial operation called mountaintop removal—an environmentally brutal method of coal extraction that not only blasts the tops of mountains to rubble but also leaves many union miners jobless, pollutes water sources, and turns communities into ghost towns.

Soon Chuck joined forces with activist Larry Gibson at the Keeper of the Mountains Foundation. "It started with grassroots organizations," Chuck says. "Then NRDC got involved, and it was instrumental in pulling all different groups together. It gave us a platform where our voices could be heard in Washington and all over the country. We would not have had that opportunity if it hadn't been for groups like NRDC."

This advocacy led directly to a stricter permit process under the Obama administration that severely crippled mountaintop removal mining. But with recent regulatory rollbacks under Trump, coal companies have ramped up the practice again.

Currently, from his porch in Raleigh County, Chuck can see—and feel—a mountain being blasted away in the distance. There is still a lot of work to do, he admits. And though Chuck and his fellow grassroots activists can sometimes feel forgotten, he stays motivated by remembering what they are capable of achieving.

"There was a lot to be proud of. It's always a reminder that you can change things. It just takes people being united and sticking together and having a platform where you can get your voices heard."

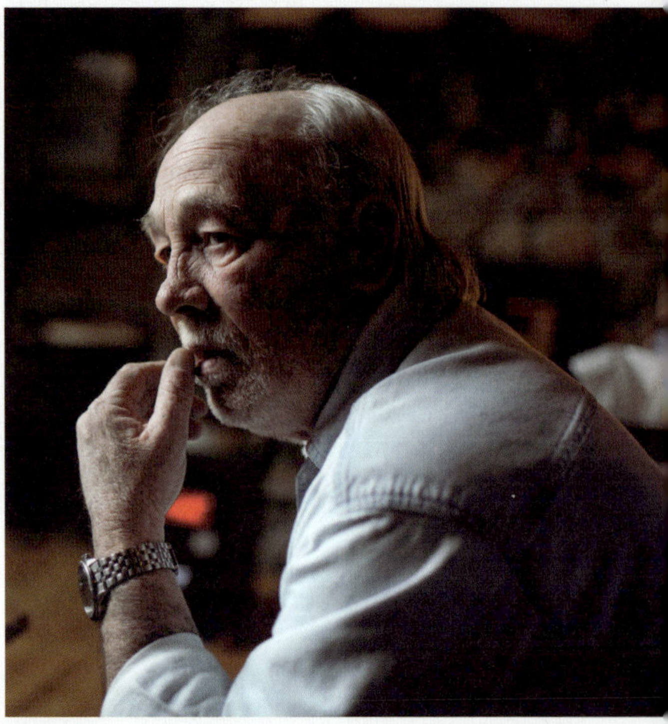

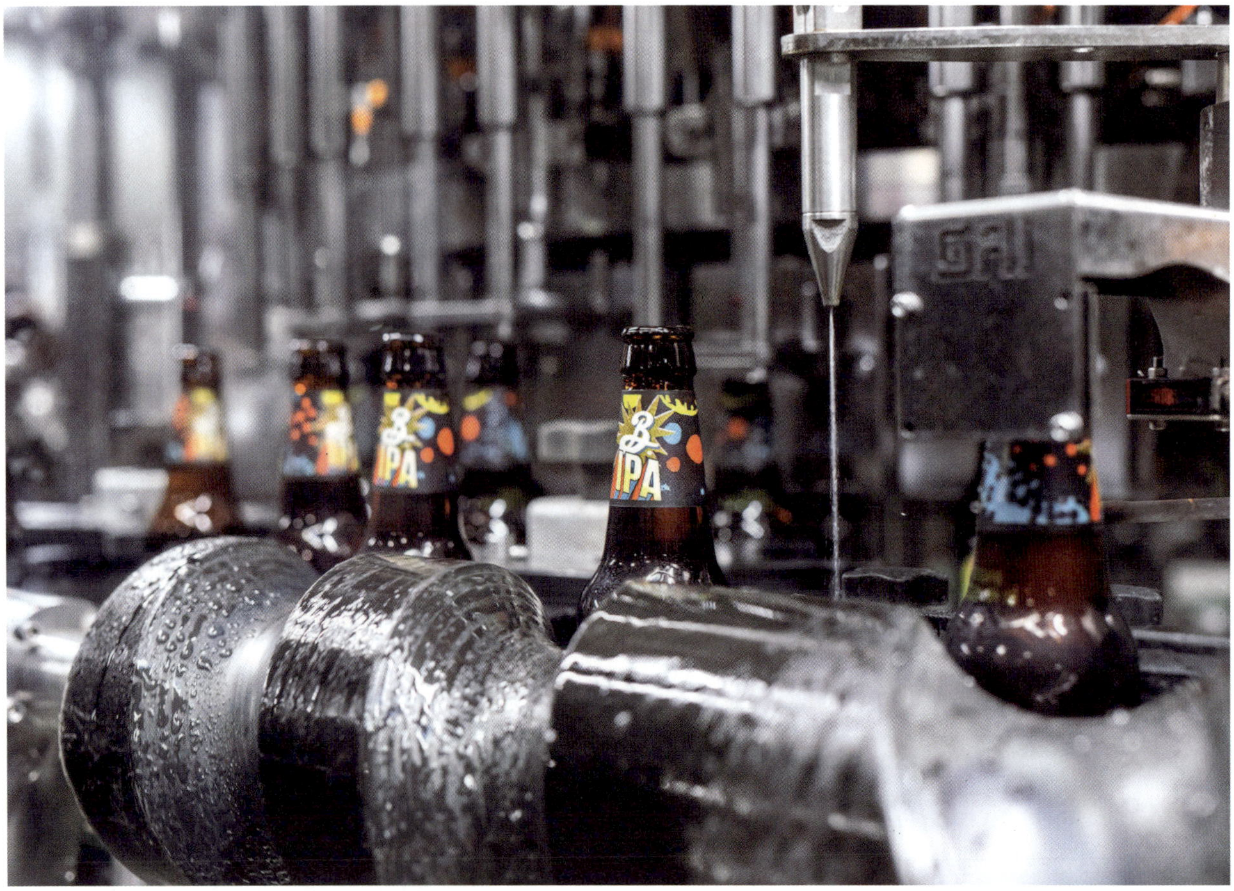

At right: Bottles of beer being processed at Brooklyn Brewery microbrewery. Opposite: An aerial view of mountaintop removal mining in West Virginia.

FROM TOP: ANDREW LICHTENSTEIN/CORBIS VIA GETTY IMAGES; TY JOHNSON FOR NRDC

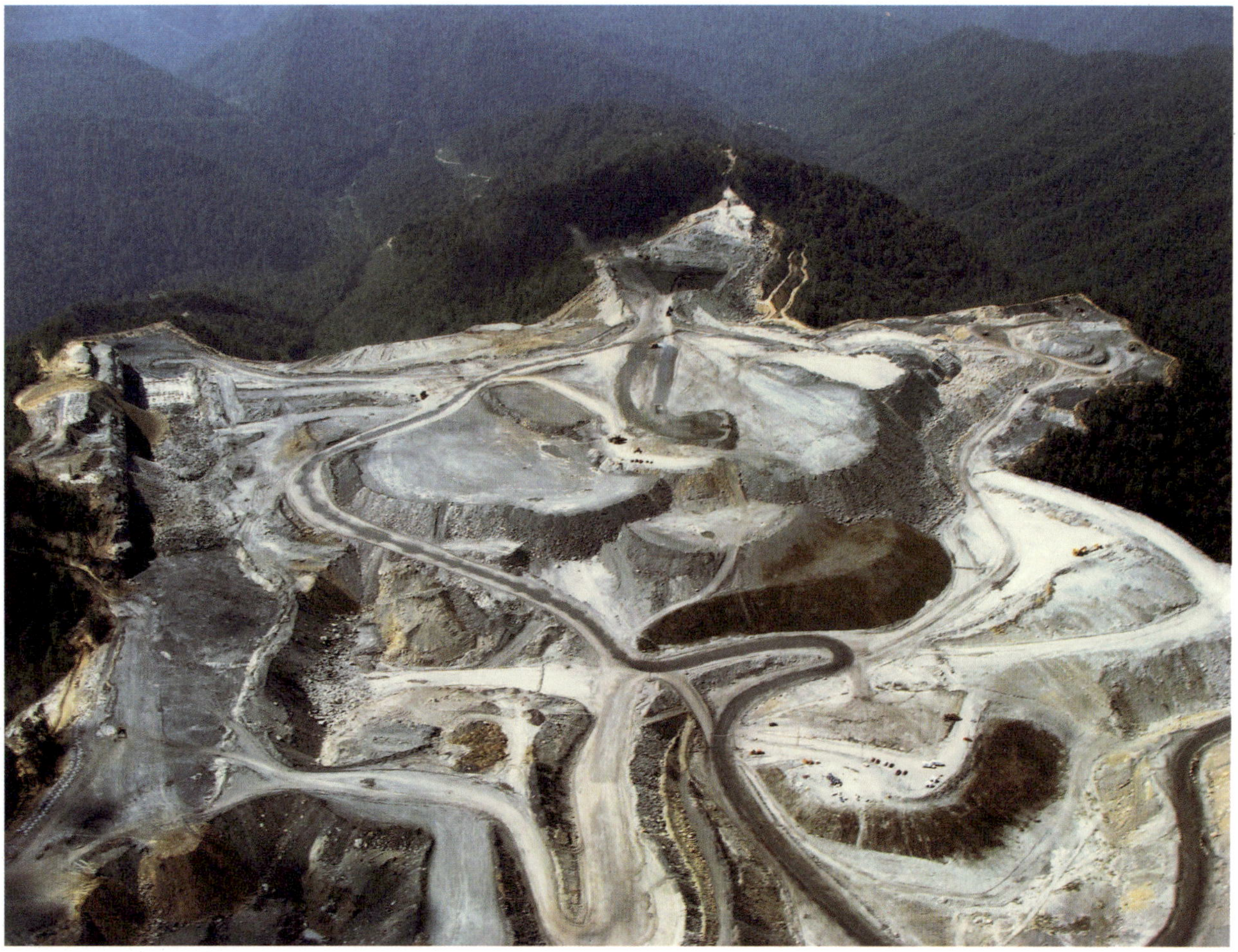

"Latino communities aren't just more likely to be affected by the climate crisis—they've also proven to contain the climate leaders who demand the systemic change we all need. We've seen that power in action as part of Voces Verdes, founded by Adrianna Quintero. This initiative built and mobilized a coalition of Latino businesses, organizations, community leaders, and public health advocates in the fight for climate action at the state and federal levels to pave the way toward a more just clean energy future."

—Linda Escalante, NRDC's Southern California legislative director

All of the concert's proceeds went to cash-starved, local grassroots groups. Five months later, in October 2010, these activists celebrated when the EPA—which earlier in the year had issued tough new restrictions on the dumping of mine waste into streams—vetoed a permit for one of the biggest mountaintop removal projects ever proposed, the Spruce No. 1 Mine in West Virginia.

You might wonder what all this has to do with beer. The connecting thread is the provision of the Clean Water Act that the EPA applied when it took action to protect the small streams that were contaminated by mountaintop removal. Pure streams and rivers also happen to be key to brewing the finest beer.

One evening in 2013, a group of NRDC staffers were gathered in a bar in Chicago, comparing notes on how the character of different beers reflects the purity and mineral content of their local water supply. The conversation prompted the idea for another innovative partnership: Why not assemble a coalition of brewers whose livelihood was directly affected by the quality of their water? And so Brewers for Clean Water was born.

BFCW began life as a group of 21 companies, ranging from small-town microbreweries to major industry players like New Belgium. At the time, the Obama administration was working to develop what eventually became the 2015 Clean Water Rule, and we targeted states with critical Senate votes, like Colorado, where New Belgium is based. The company's reputation as a leader in sustainability kicked the campaign into a higher gear, and BFCW's membership has now swelled to 114 breweries. When lawmakers have to take tough votes, local business voices are a vital influence—and the craft brewers reminded their elected officials that their industry is worth $76.2 billion a year and supports half a million jobs.

The Trump administration repealed the Clean Water Rule in September 2019, and as NRDC fights to restore its protections, the brewers are crucial allies. After all, says Russell Klisch of Lakefront Brewery in Milwaukee, the self-proclaimed beer capital of the world, "Beer can only be as good as the water it's made with."

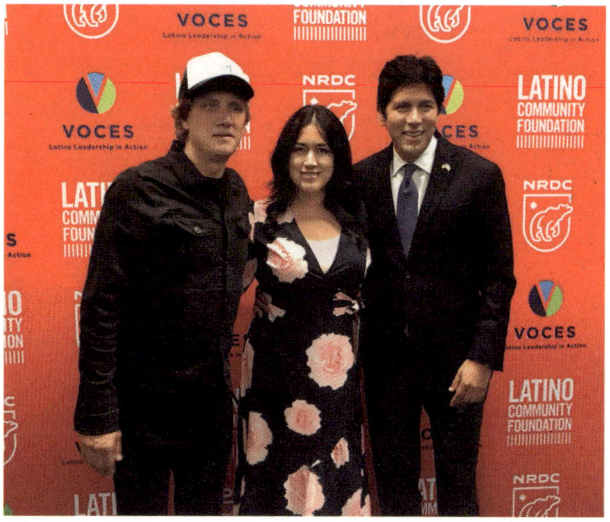

Linda Escalante works to amplify Latino voices and leadership around climate, health, and other community issues. Along with Voces Verdes, she helped create La Onda Verde, NRDC's Spanish-language communications arm. Here, she (center) attends a Latino climate leadership event at the 2018 Global Climate Action Summit.

FROM TOP: ROB PERKS/NRDC; WILSON LEE

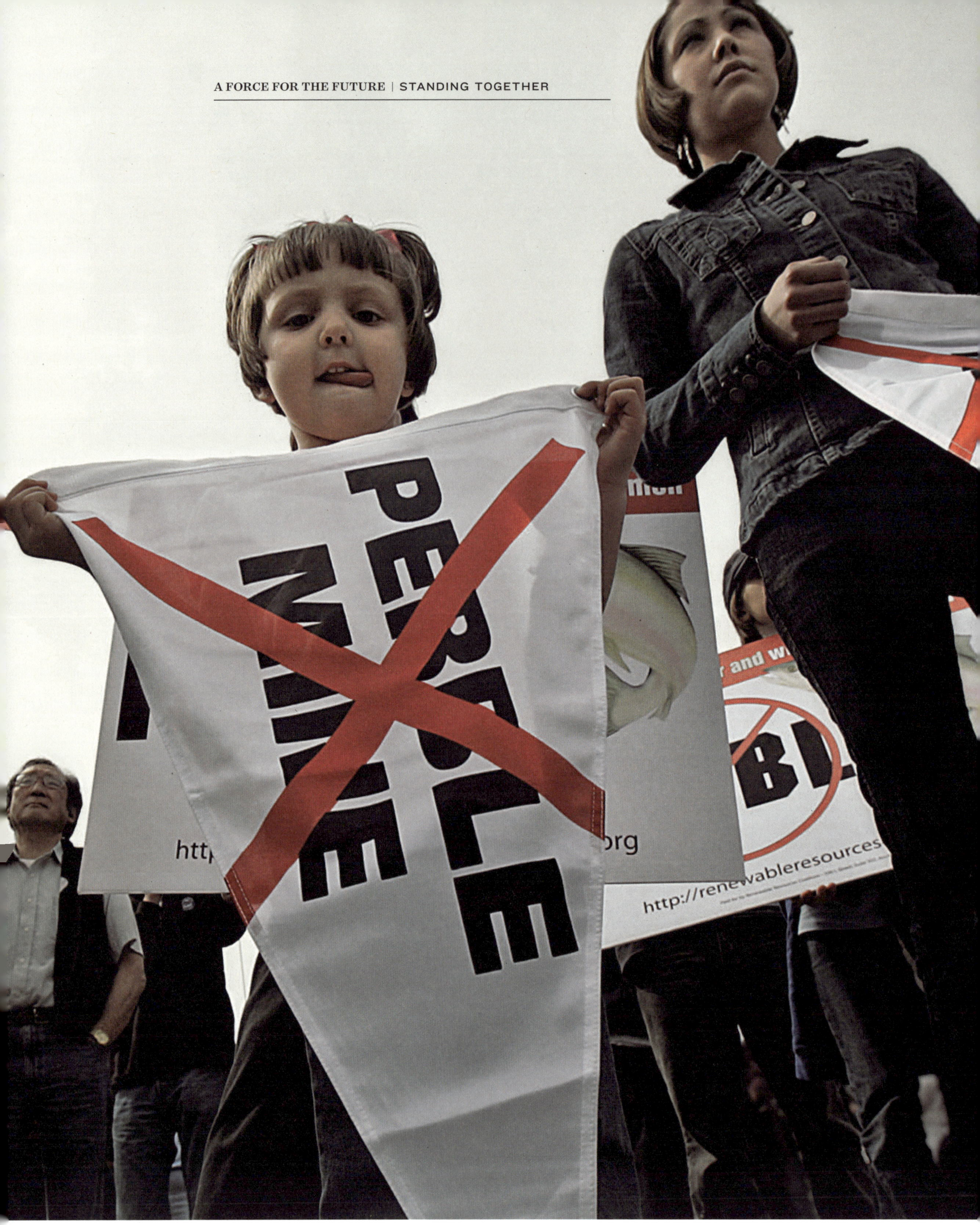
PEBBLE MINE
http://renewableresources

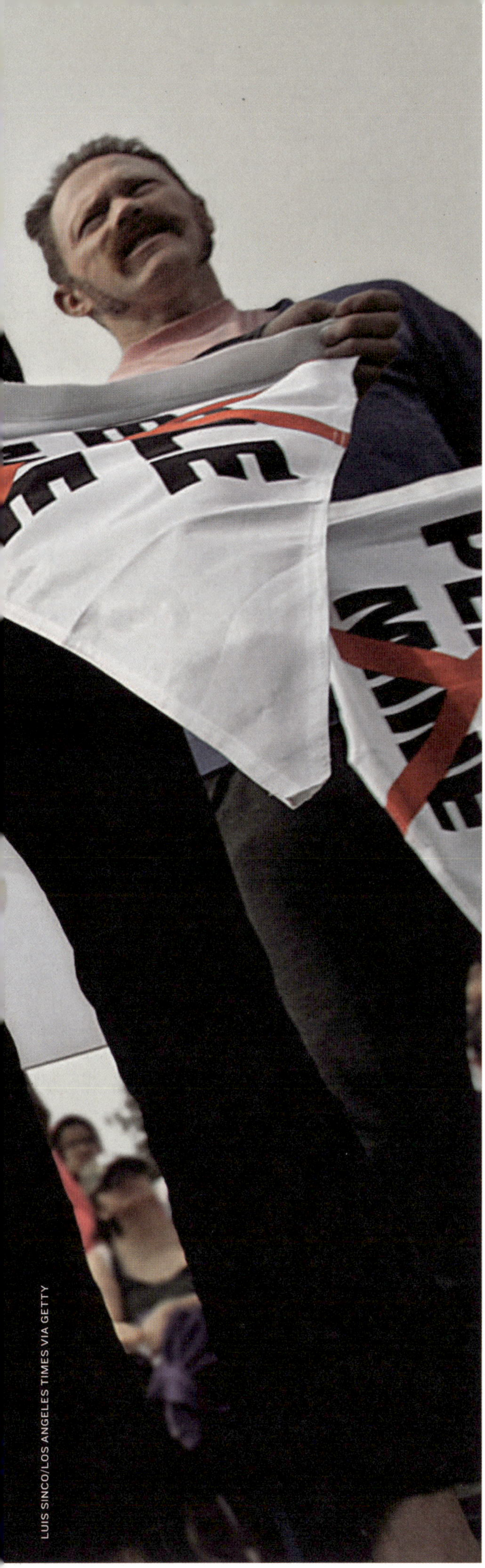

LUIS SINCO/LOS ANGELES TIMES VIA GETTY

Protestors gather in Dillingham, Alaska, at a rally against the Pebble Mine.

ROCKY TIMES FOR PEBBLE MINE

ONCE YOU'VE SEEN ALASKA, YOU NEVER forget it. My wife, Patricia, and I went there for the first time in 1977 with two of NRDC's earliest and most loyal supporters, Mike and Winsome McIntosh. We were stunned by the state's natural beauty—and horrified by the plans of extractive industries to ravage it for profit.

Thirty years later, NRDC learned that a giant gold and copper mine was threatening to do just that to Bristol Bay. With a footprint the size of Manhattan, the proposed Pebble Mine would store up to 10 billion tons of toxic waste at the pristine headwaters of one of the planet's greatest fisheries. Home to half of the world's population of wild sockeye salmon, Bristol Bay fuels a commercial fishery that brings in $1.5 billion in annual revenue and supports 14,000 jobs. The bounty of the bay—fed by a 40,000-square-mile watershed of undisturbed lakes and streams—has continuously sustained at least 31 native Alaskan tribes in the area as well as a stunning diversity of wildlife for thousands upon thousands of years.

When NRDC got involved in 2009, the Pebble Mine seemed close to a done deal. Local Alaskans had been fighting the proposal for seven years, but the state was fervently pro-mining—Sarah Palin was governor at the time—and the project's key investors were three of the most powerful mining companies in the world: Anglo American, Mitsubishi Corporation, and Rio Tinto.

Led by Joel Reynolds and Taryn Kiekow Heimer of our marine mammal team, NRDC built strong relationships with local tribes, commercial fishers, and other Alaskans and began fighting the mine on all fronts. We bought shares in the three mining companies, met with their top executives, and then raised a ruckus at their shareholder meetings.

Having already successfully confronted three industry giants, we were undeterred when a new partner showed up. We renewed our push against the company's potential financial backers.

We also paid for full-page newspaper ads featuring NRDC Trustee Robert Redford—which led to a memorable complaint by Anglo American CEO Cynthia Carroll that her mother was mad at her for pursuing something that Redford had denounced.

In Washington, D.C., we had resounding success. In 2010, President Obama pronounced Bristol Bay a "national treasure." After a rigorous three-year study, the EPA issued what's called a proposed determination under the Clean Water Act, declaring that Pebble Mine would result in "unacceptable adverse effects" including the "complete loss of fish habitat" in parts of the Bristol Bay watershed. By 2014, Rio Tinto, Mitsubishi, and Anglo American had walked away from the project.

Science had spoken, but the Trump administration made not even a pretense of listening. Instead, it threw a lifeline to the prime mover of the project, a Canadian company called Northern Dynasty Minerals. Within an hour of meeting with the company's CEO, Trump's first EPA administrator, Scott Pruitt, ordered his staff to rescind the Obama administration's determination.

Having already successfully confronted three industry giants, we were undeterred when a new partner showed up: First Quantum Minerals, another Canadian investor. We renewed our push against the company's potential financial backers, such as BlackRock, and in 2018, First Quantum became the latest major mining company to abandon the project.

Not content with ignoring the scientific evidence—and flying in the face of local opposition to the mine of more than 80 percent—the Trump administration continues to push the project forward. Pruitt's successor even allowed his agency to abrogate its authority altogether, leaving environmental oversight to the Army Corps of Engineers, which has fast-tracked its review with a permit decision expected by mid-2020. But the Army Corps' draft environmental impact statement was so slipshod that it was repudiated by the U.S. Department of the Interior, the U.S. Fish and Wildlife Service, and even the EPA's technical staff.

In addition to suing the EPA in federal court in Alaska, we have helped secure language expressing congressional concern about the Army Corps' Pebble permit review process, demanding that the agency adhere to sound science. We've followed up with more full-page ads in major newspapers—including several signed by former EPA administrators from the presidencies of Nixon, Reagan, and both Bushes, as well as President Clinton's Interior Secretary Bruce Babbitt. We've also helped unleash a publicity blitz in the Alaska media to bring pressure to bear on the state's congressional delegation. Pebble Mine is already on life support as its cash-strapped owner, Northern Dynasty, scrapes the bottom of the barrel for new partners. We're confident we'll prevail in the end. After all, if you can't save a national treasure like Bristol Bay, what can you save?

FROM THE FRONTLINES

Robin Samuelsen

Robin Samuelsen credits his two grandsons—then eight and nine years old—with encouraging him to join the fight against the Pebble Mine 15 years ago. At the time, Robin says, he was busy with his responsibilities as CEO of the Bristol Bay Economic Development Corporation. But once the lifelong Dillingham, Alaska, resident and commercial fisherman learned more about the mine—and the devastating impact it would have on Bristol Bay and its salmon fishery—he dedicated himself to stopping it from ever breaking ground.

In the years since, Robin has made numerous trips to Washington, D.C., to testify before Congress and, in 2015, to visit the White House as the guest of President Obama, whom Robin had previously taken on a tour around Bristol Bay. "He sure got an earful on Pebble," Samuelsen remembers.

More recently, Robin and other leaders from Bristol Bay joined NRDC's Joel Reynolds in Toronto at a May 2018 shareholders' meeting of First Quantum Minerals, a Pebble Mine investor. Less than two weeks later, First Quantum announced it was abandoning the project.

"It's a real honor to work with NRDC," Robin says. "Early on, we said that we couldn't take on the mining company alone and that we had to reach out to folks to help us. To have Joel [Reynolds] and his organization help us, we're very appreciative. They are making a difference along with us—this is a combined effort to save Bristol Bay and its watershed."

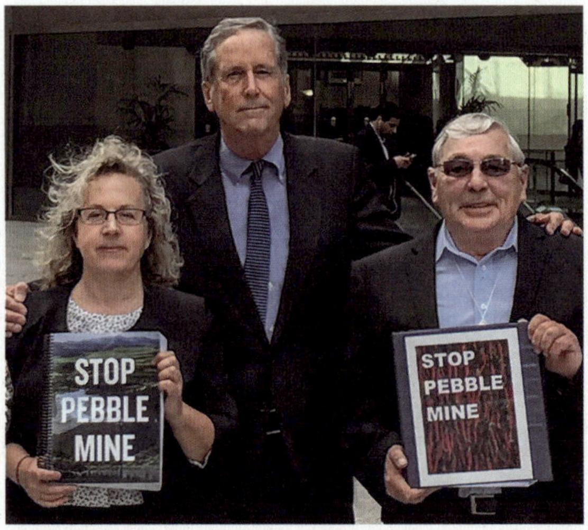

Robin Samuelson (right) with NRDC's Joel Reynolds (center).

Wood-Tikchik State Park in Bristol Bay, Alaska.

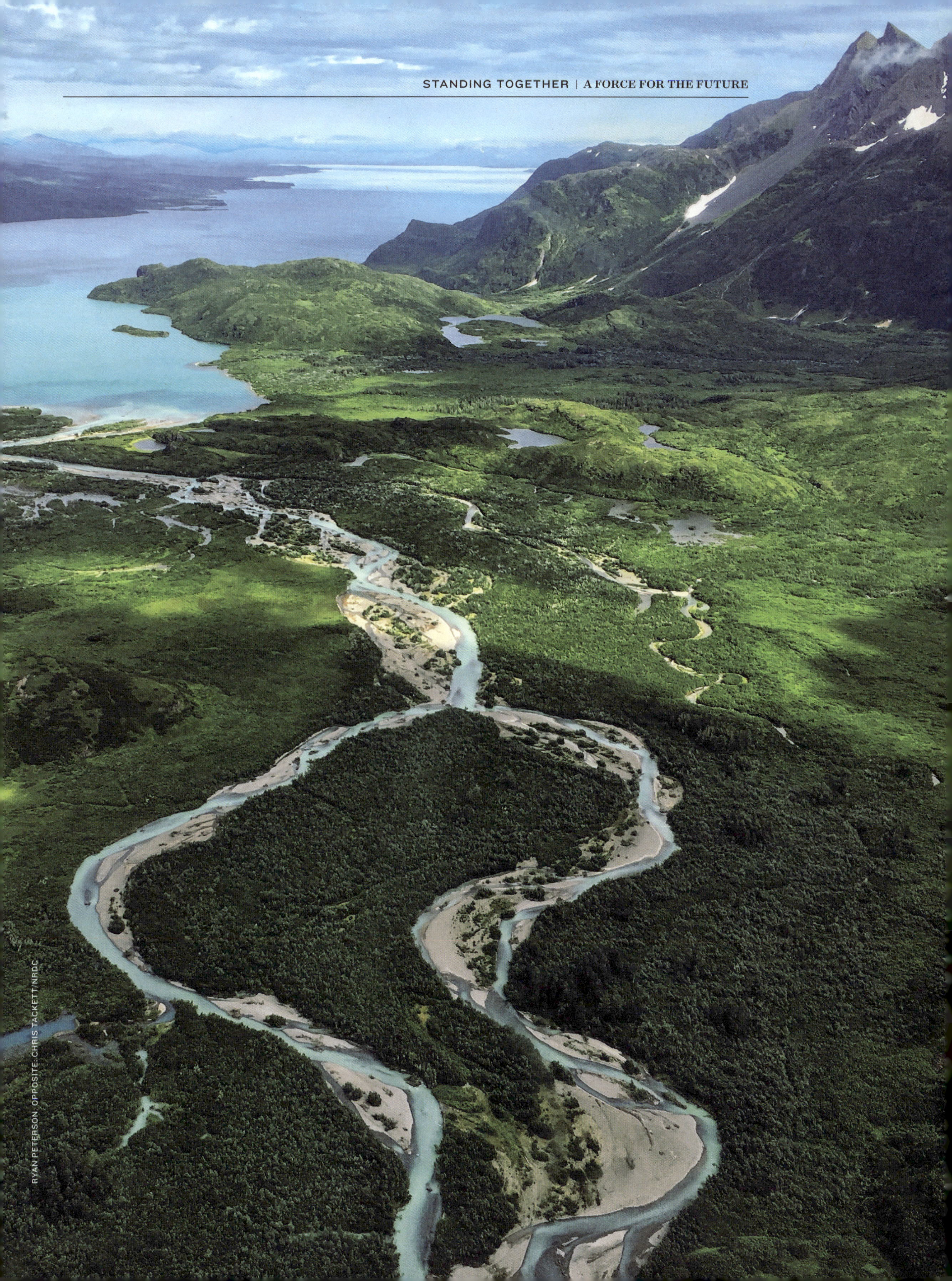

RYAN PETERSON. OPPOSITE: CHRIS TACKETT/NRDC

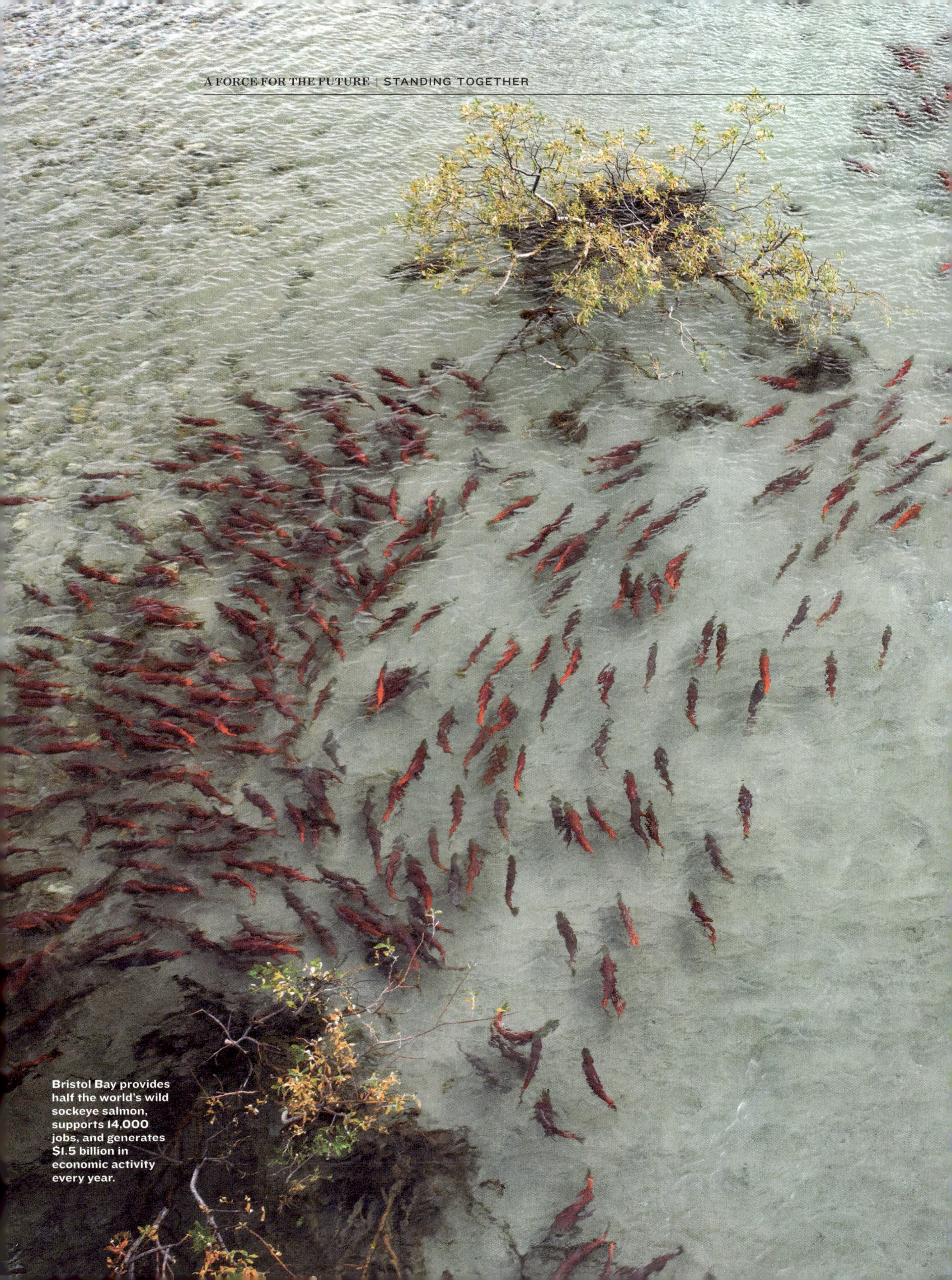

Bristol Bay provides half the world's wild sockeye salmon, supports 14,000 jobs, and generates $1.5 billion in economic activity every year.

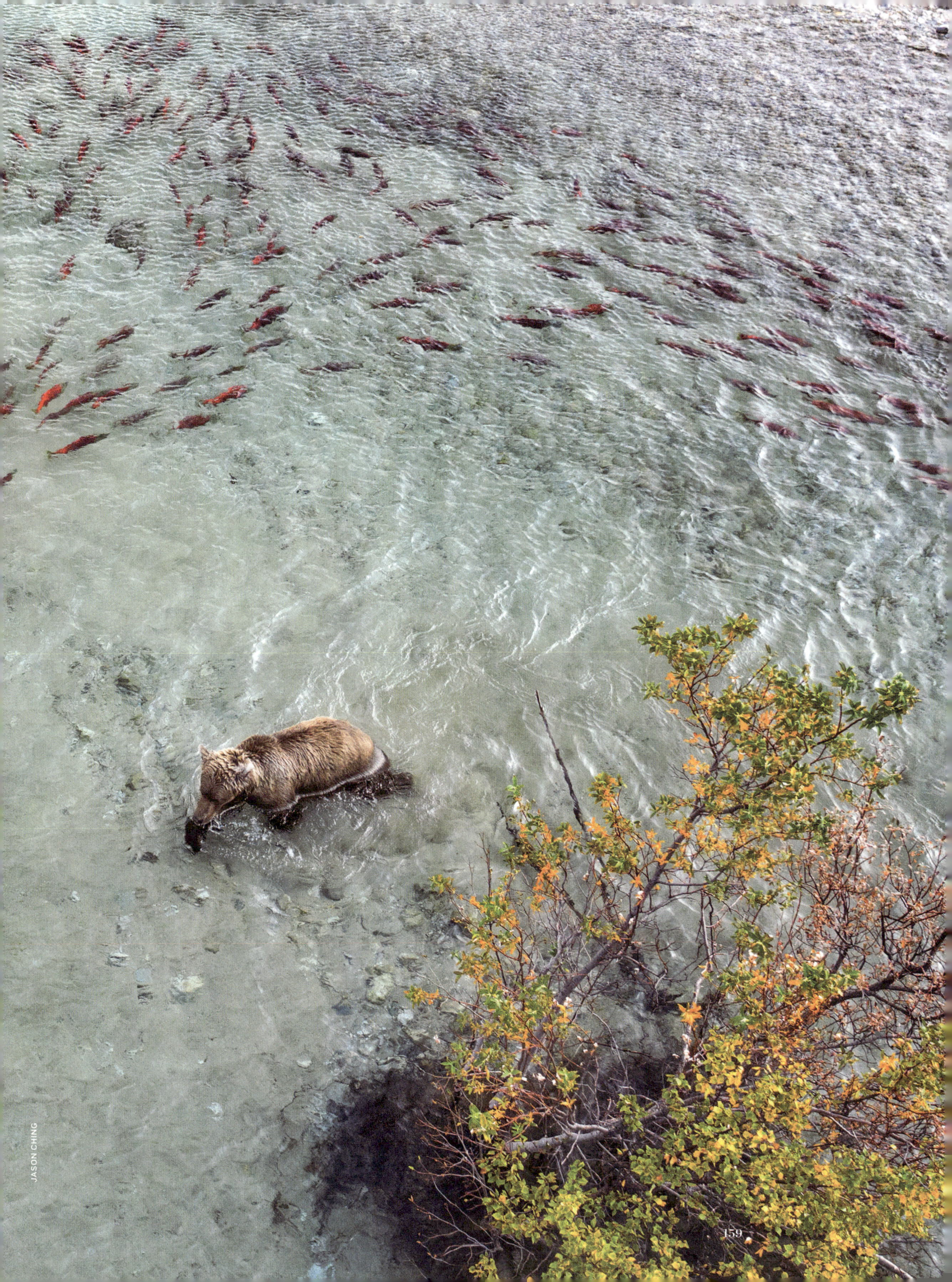

JASON CHING

U.S. CITIES TAKE ON THE CLIMATE CRISIS

In the fight against pollution and climate change, NRDC has always recognized the central importance of our cities, beginning with the first place we called home: New York City. For decades, Eric Goldstein and Mark Izeman, who spearhead our New York regional team, have worked to create a model for how to make our urban environment cleaner, healthier, and more sustainable.

In the late 1970s, we developed a blueprint that led to a complete revamping of the city's dilapidated subway system. Then we were instrumental in getting the lead out of gasoline nationwide in the 1980s and in replacing NYC's dirty diesel buses at the turn of the century with cleaner hybrid models. For decades, NRDC has worked to safeguard New York's Catskill region, which supplies clean drinking water to more than nine million downstate New Yorkers. And we have also helped to protect and clean up the Hudson River, one of the birthplaces of the modern environmental movement.

Along the way, we hired NRDC's first environmental justice director, Vernice Miller-Travis, and built robust relationships with some of the city's most dynamic community leaders. We've worked closely with groups like the New York City Environmental Justice Alliance on issues such as the placement of filthy waste transfer stations in already overburdened neighborhoods, and WE ACT for Environmental Justice, a partner with whom we have fought many battles together for clean air and children's health in the city.

With President Trump taking a wrecking ball to federal action on climate change and vowing to withdraw from

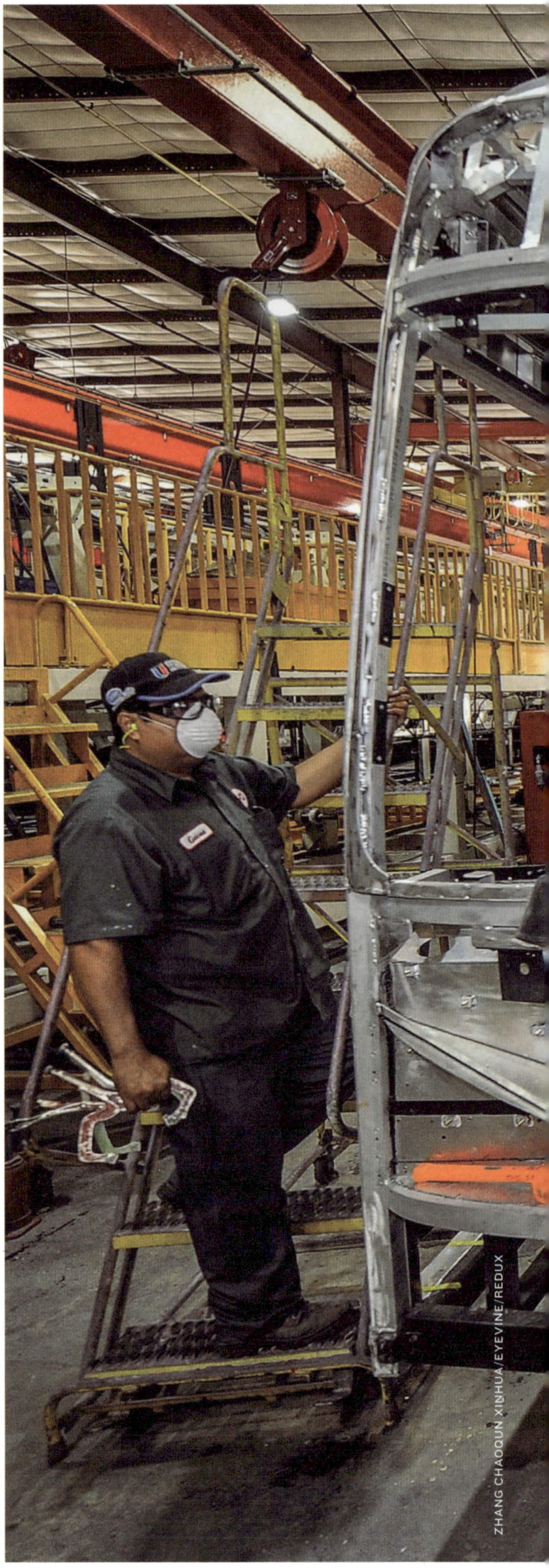

ZHANG CHAOQUN XINHUA/EYEVINE/REDUX

Workers help construct an electric city bus for Denver.

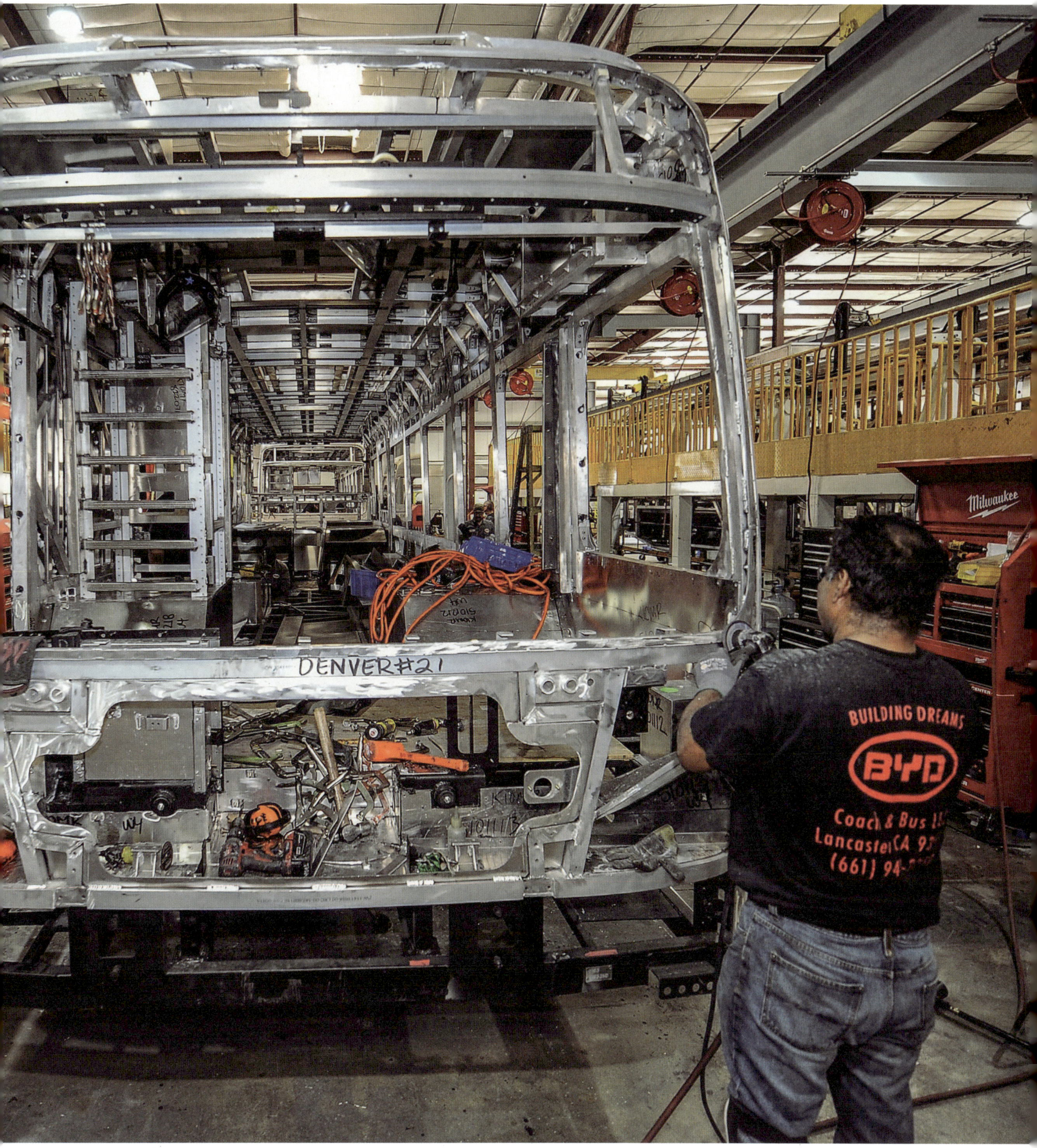
DENVER#21
Milwaukee
BUILDING DREAMS
BYD

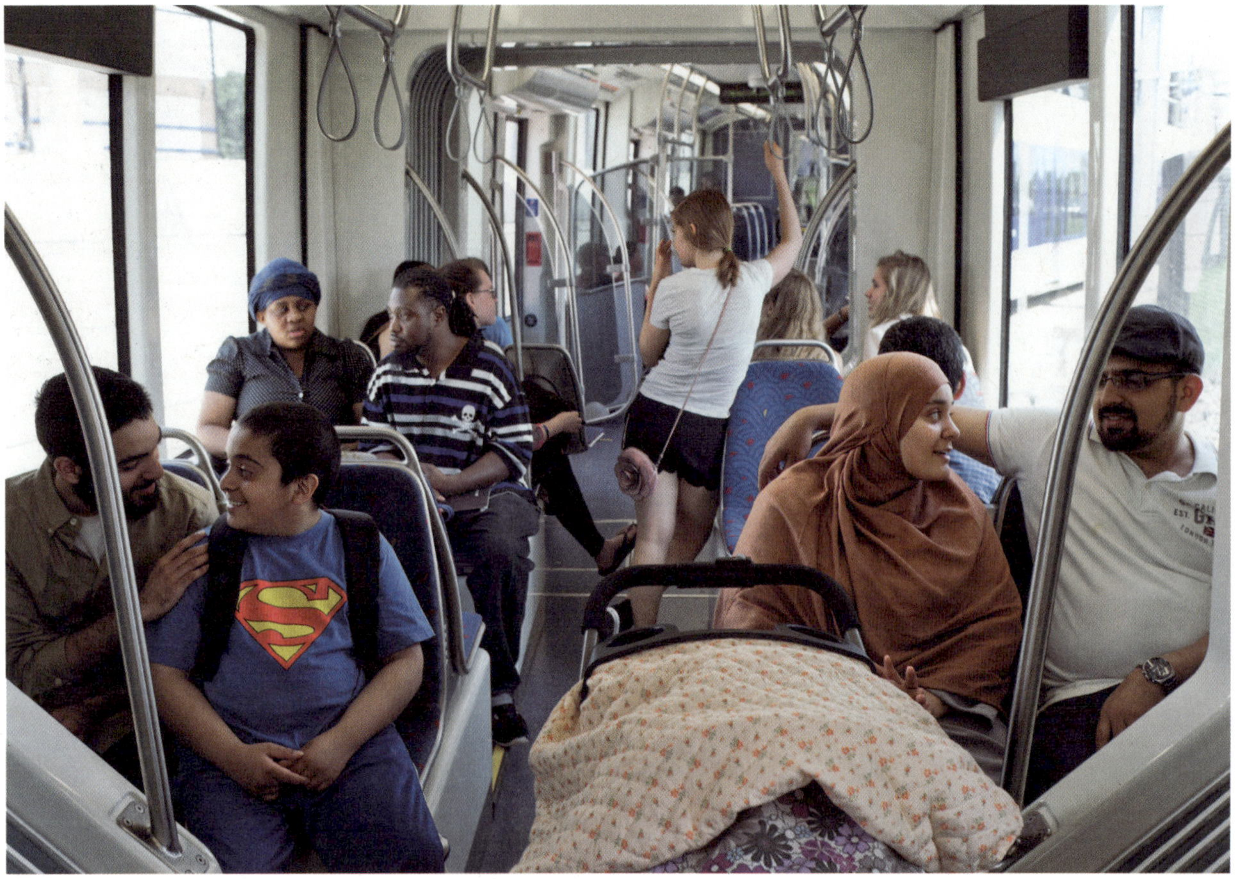

"The American Cities Climate Challenge brings NRDC's call for climate action to city halls across the country, partnering with mayors to reduce emissions while also building momentum for change at the state and federal levels."

—Chris Wheat, NRDC's director of strategy and city engagement for the American Cities Climate Challenge

the 2015 Paris Agreement, city halls around the world have been working overtime to make good on the country's climate promises. Less than a month after Trump's election, political leaders gathered in Mexico City for the annual C40 Mayors Summit, where they pledged to meet or exceed the ambitious carbon emissions targets set in Paris. The U.S. president might turn his back on the commitments made by the rest of the world, but U.S. cities would not. The following summer, hundreds of them signed a declaration with a powerful message: We Are Still In.

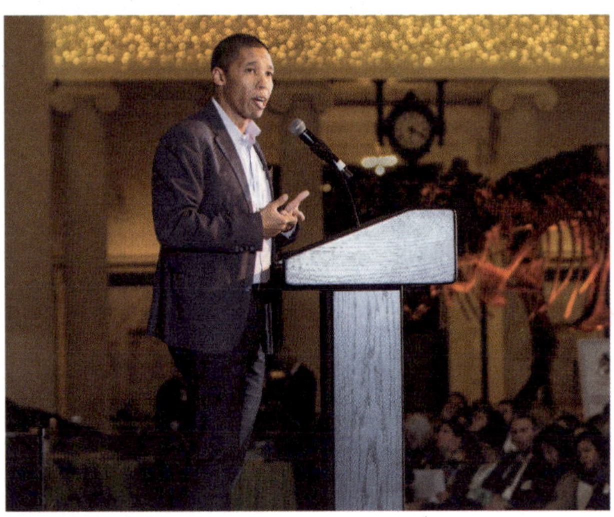

Chris Wheat oversees a team of city strategists and climate advisors and helps address any communications or political hurdles the 25 Climate Challenge cities face on their way to shrinking their carbon footprints. Here, he speaks at the 2017 Chicago Community Climate Forum at the Field Museum.

One of the most prominent signatories was former New York City mayor Michael Bloomberg. NRDC had already worked with Bloomberg's charitable foundation, Bloomberg Philanthropies, on the City Energy Project, which focused on promoting energy efficiency in buildings. Now the time had come for something more urgent and far-reaching.

Enter the American Cities Climate Challenge, a $70 million, two-year initiative announced in December 2018. Bloomberg Philanthropies chose NRDC to take the lead in designing and advocating for new policies that attack the two biggest sources of urban carbon pollution in tandem: buildings and transportation. We joined forces with Delivery Associates, a London-based consultancy that specializes in government innovation and the efficient delivery of public services, and other leading environmental and government innovation partners..

Highly competitive by design, the Climate Challenge pushes mayors to outdo each other in the scale of their ambition. More than 50 cities applied to take part, and 25 made the cut. In an effort led by Christina Angelides in our Santa Monica, California, office, NRDC has assembled a team of 30 experts in buildings, transportation, and policy advocacy. We've also built a network of 20 national partner organizations and another 68 at the local community level, bringing new constituencies and new leaders into the climate fight and ensuring that greater social equity is a core feature of each city's plans.

Take transportation, for instance. While any city would benefit from compact residential development that's close to

FROM TOP: TODD HEISLER/THE NEW YORK TIMES/REDUX; SPOON PHOTO & DESIGN

a transportation hub, each will interpret its needs differently. Some cities may emphasize bike lanes, while others may want to avoid possible sources of creeping gentrification and opt instead for faster bus lines that get people to and from work each day. Other cities' plans may include bikes, buses, and more.

Executing an ambitious city planning project can take a decade or more, but when it comes to cutting carbon pollution, we're in a race against time. That's why Climate Challenge cities must show concrete results in these first two years. As we track the progress closely, we're already seeing a whole slew of success stories. San Jose, California, has passed a new building code that bans the use of natural gas in all new construction, and the city is adding 20 miles of bike lanes that are safe for all ages and abilities. Meanwhile, Portland, Oregon, passed its ambitious Rose Lane Project, which will dedicate traffic lanes to buses across the city. And Cincinnati plans to build a 100-megawatt solar array, the largest such municipal array in the country.

The message is clear. The goal of the Climate Challenge is to shrink the carbon footprint of these 25 cities by at least 25 percent by 2025—the target set in Paris—and we're well on track to hitting it.

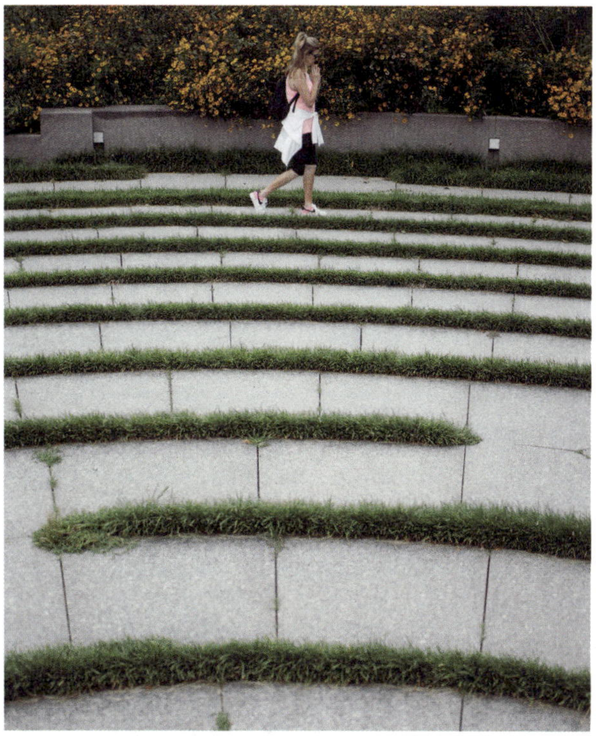

Opposite: Passengers ride a light rail line in Minneapolis. At left: Ohio River Trail park in downtown Cincinnati.

Solutions Spotlight

SHINING A LIGHT ON EQUITY

NRDC has shown for decades that the cheapest and cleanest way to curb our reliance on fossil fuels is energy efficiency. When the Obama administration proposed its Clean Power Plan in 2014, we took the opportunity to address a neglected area of this climate strategy: the unfair energy burden that falls on low-income households.

Whether living in high-rise public housing projects, subsidized private housing, or mobile homes in rural areas, these families pay a disproportionate amount of their income on heat and electricity, often literally forced to choose between keeping the lights on and paying the rent. This is why we launched Energy Efficiency for All (EEFA), an advocacy project funded by the JPB Foundation. A partnership among NRDC, the National Housing Trust, Elevate Energy, and the Energy Foundation, EEFA creates networks and builds power at the state and local levels to promote efficiency (and thereby lower power bills) through innovative financing initiatives, incentives for utilities, and holistic building retrofits, especially in multifamily dwellings.

Twelve state coalitions now participate in EEFA, up from the original nine, and so far the program has benefited more than 200,000 renters. It's a whole new way of thinking about energy efficiency—measuring success not just by the amount of carbon pollution it prevents but by the contributions it can make to greater social equity.

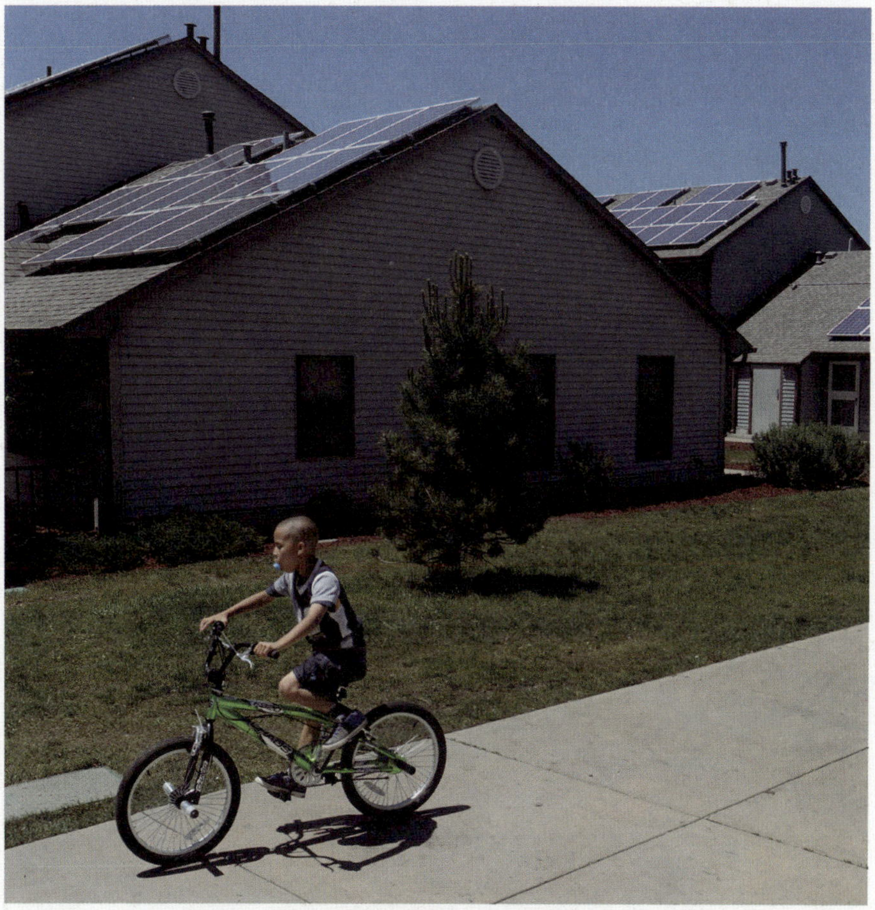

FROM TOP: LUKE SHARRETT FOR NRDC; CYRUS MCCRIMMON/THE DENVER POST VIA GETTY IMAGES

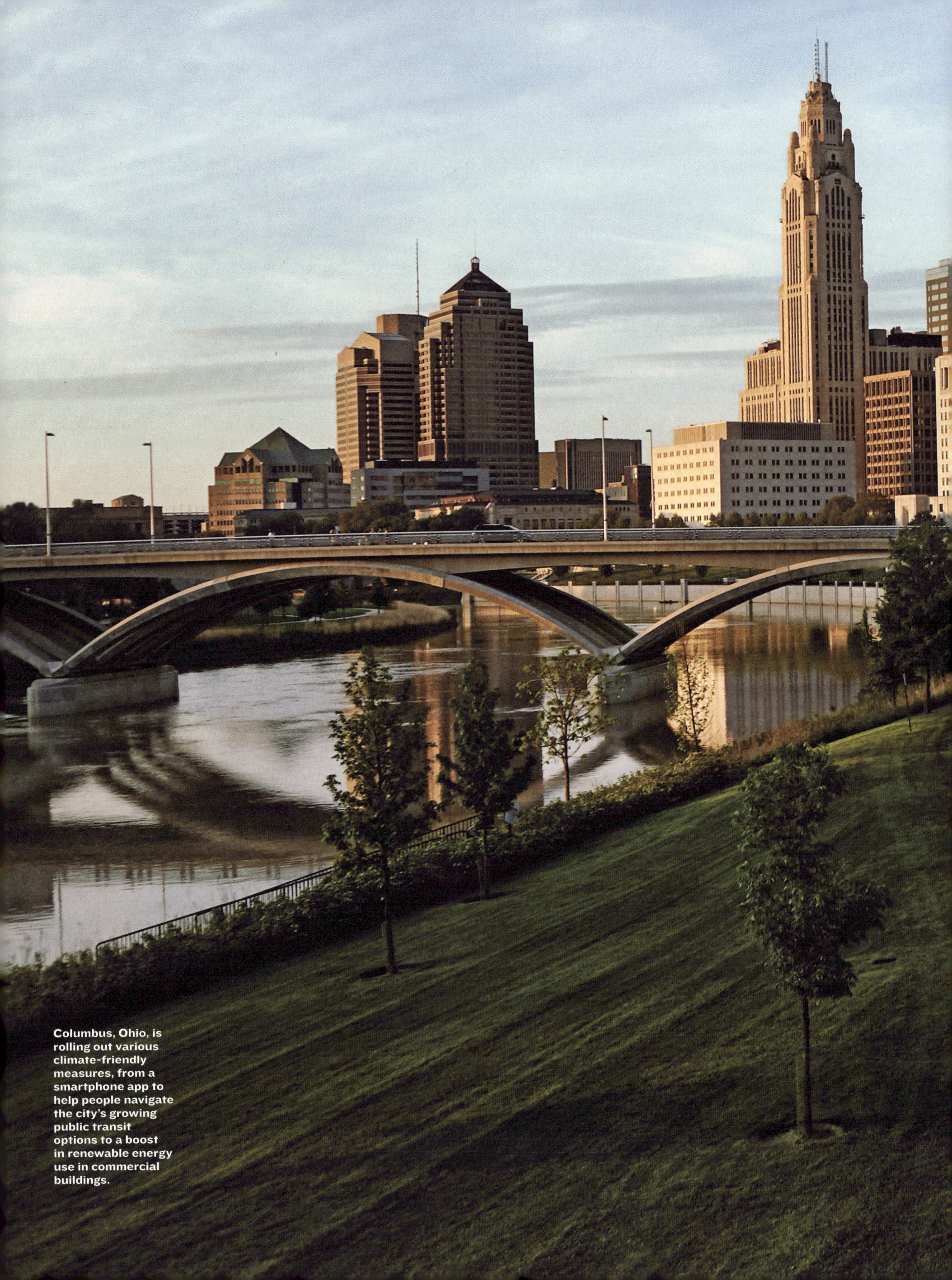

Columbus, Ohio, is rolling out various climate-friendly measures, from a smartphone app to help people navigate the city's growing public transit options to a boost in renewable energy use in commercial buildings.

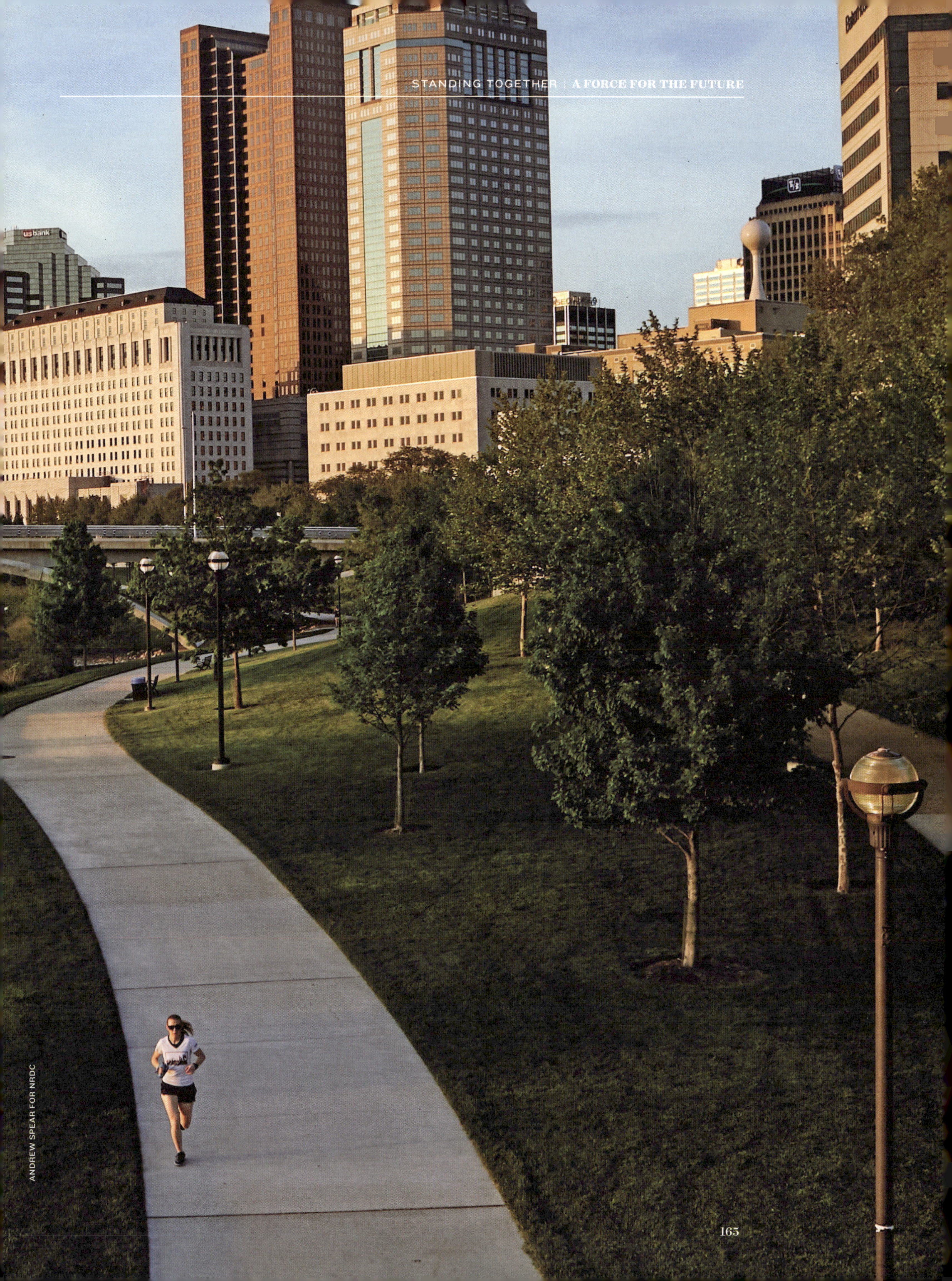

ANDREW SPEAR FOR NRDC

EPILOGUE

Gina McCarthy

NRDC PRESIDENT AND CHIEF EXECUTIVE OFFICER

"WHAT KEEPS YOU UP AT NIGHT?" I GET ASKED THAT A LOT. It's not just the current, and seemingly endless, efforts to gut environmental rules and standards, to expand the exploitation of public lands, or to sideline government scientists—it's the sense of uncertainty and hopelessness that has gripped our country. According to a 2018 poll by the Yale Program on Climate Change Communication, the majority of Americans are both worried about climate change and convinced that we will fail to address it.

That has got to change. There are so many reasons to be hopeful. Now is not the time to throw in the towel—it's time to go all in.

I am often reminded of something 16-year-old climate activist Lana Perice told the *Los Angeles Times* in 2019: "I feel proud knowing that my generation isn't going down without a fight." I couldn't agree more. Throughout history, younger generations have pushed progress forward by making noise—in the streets, in the classrooms, in the halls of government, and in the courtroom. In fact, it's how NRDC got its start. Today, that tradition carries on.

I am so inspired by the young people who are standing up and demanding climate action, and my generation has to fight right alongside them. We all have to stand up if we want the people we love to have a better, healthier, more prosperous tomorrow. As a mother, a grandmother, and someone who has dedicated her entire career to this cause, I refuse to let my family and these young heroes down.

In my twenties, I started out as a local health agent in my hometown of Canton, Massachusetts. I had to deal with hazardous waste sites, contaminated drinking water, and other challenges that hit close to home for a lot of people, including myself. Working with these issues during the early days of environmental regulations was never easy. I would sit down at kitchen tables with neighbors who were worried about whether pollution was harming the health of their families, and these conversations were often difficult because the science needed to answer their questions wasn't yet available, the environmental laws to address them were just being drafted, and the technology that could offer solutions was decades away. All too often, the best I could do was let people know that someone was on their side.

But those early experiences taught me how to listen, how to really talk with people honestly about what I knew and didn't know, and how to work through the problems and deal with the uncertainties together—as a team. Since then, the country has made so much progress. We have

Everything we do—every lawsuit, every report, every policy brief, every petition, every tweet—is a tool for communities suffering from the negligence of our political leaders in the fight against the climate crisis.

come a long way in our understanding of the science behind environmental issues and in our development of the technical solutions needed to clean up our messes, to protect public health, and to defend our precious natural resources.

Over the past three decades, those families, successes, and challenges led me to NRDC, and they still motivate me today. They remind me how important it is for us to show up, stay focused, be honest, work hard, and have each other's backs. These values are at the core of NRDC's remarkable history and why I am beyond proud to lead NRDC's team—now more than 700 strong. And I promise you we will work every day to make sure that the communities on the frontlines of environmental degradation know that every single one of us is working for them. We have their backs!

After all, NRDC has been fighting—and winning—"impossible" battles for the past 50 years. And we're not going to let up. There is also no group of people better equipped to overcome climate change, our biggest crisis yet.

NRDC has just the right mixture of scientific rigor, policy expertise, innovation, legal strength, and people power—the very same recipe that John Adams used when he founded this organization 50 years ago. And boy, has it paid off for all of us.

- **Scientific rigor:** Our marine scientists developed a system to determine safe catch limits for at-risk fish populations, providing science-based policy solutions that governments have used to bring populations back from the brink, including more than two dozen species here in the United States.
- **Policy expertise:** Today, our experts are at work around the globe, teaming up with China to take on smog and helping India roll out its ambitious renewable energy plan.
- **Innovation:** NRDC problem-solvers recently devised a brilliant plan to help California's already stressed grid deliver power to a new generation of electric vehicles.
- **Legal strength:** NRDC litigators just keep beating polluters in courts across the country and holding government agencies accountable when they fail to follow the law or ignore science.
- **People power:** When the Mitsubishi Corporation tried to build a salt factory where gray whales breed, NRDC brought massive public pressure to bear, which led to the protection of the last whale lagoon, an essential nursery for newborn calves, along the Baja California coast.

NRDC is going to continue to lead the charge to break our dependence on fossil fuels and speed the transition to a renewable energy economy. We are going to keep defending clean air and children's health. And we will continue to work for communities where families who are struggling economically must, all too often, also confront high levels of pollution and the disastrous onslaught of climate change.

At NRDC, we see everything we do—every lawsuit, every report, every policy brief, every petition—as an opportunity to build hope for a healthier and safer today and a brighter tomorrow.

From the saving of Storm King Mountain in the 1970s to the defense of the ozone layer in the '80s to the blocking of offshore drilling near our coastlines in the '90s and beyond, young people have always driven NRDC forward. The next generation of NRDC lawyers, scientists, advocates, and specialists are building on that legacy and are an unbelievably formidable force. Meanwhile, our youngest activists are fighting for safe drinking water, blocking fossil fuel infrastructure, confronting environmental racism, and much more.

Progress is about having a plan, having the right people to implement it, and getting the public behind it. The fighters of NRDC across the generations are living reminders of what we can achieve with passion, commitment, and unflinching resolve.

Fear is paralyzing, and the world needs to move. So when feeling overwhelmed, look to those fighting for change and join them. The fighters of NRDC are living reminders of what we can achieve with passion and commitment. Together, we are an unstoppable force for a better future.

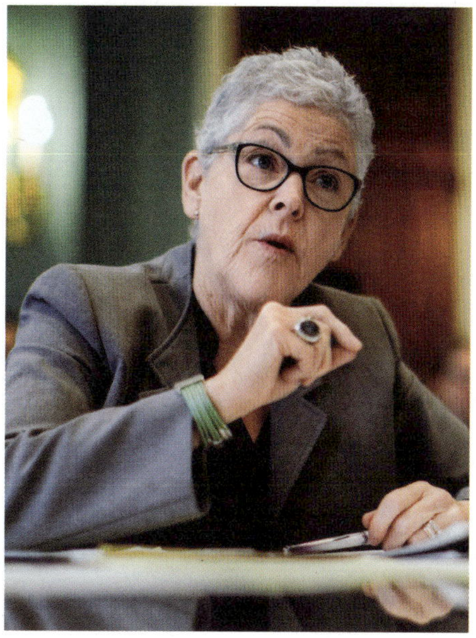

TING SHEN FOR NRDC

Gina McCarthy testifies during a House Select Committee on the Climate Crisis hearing in February 2020.

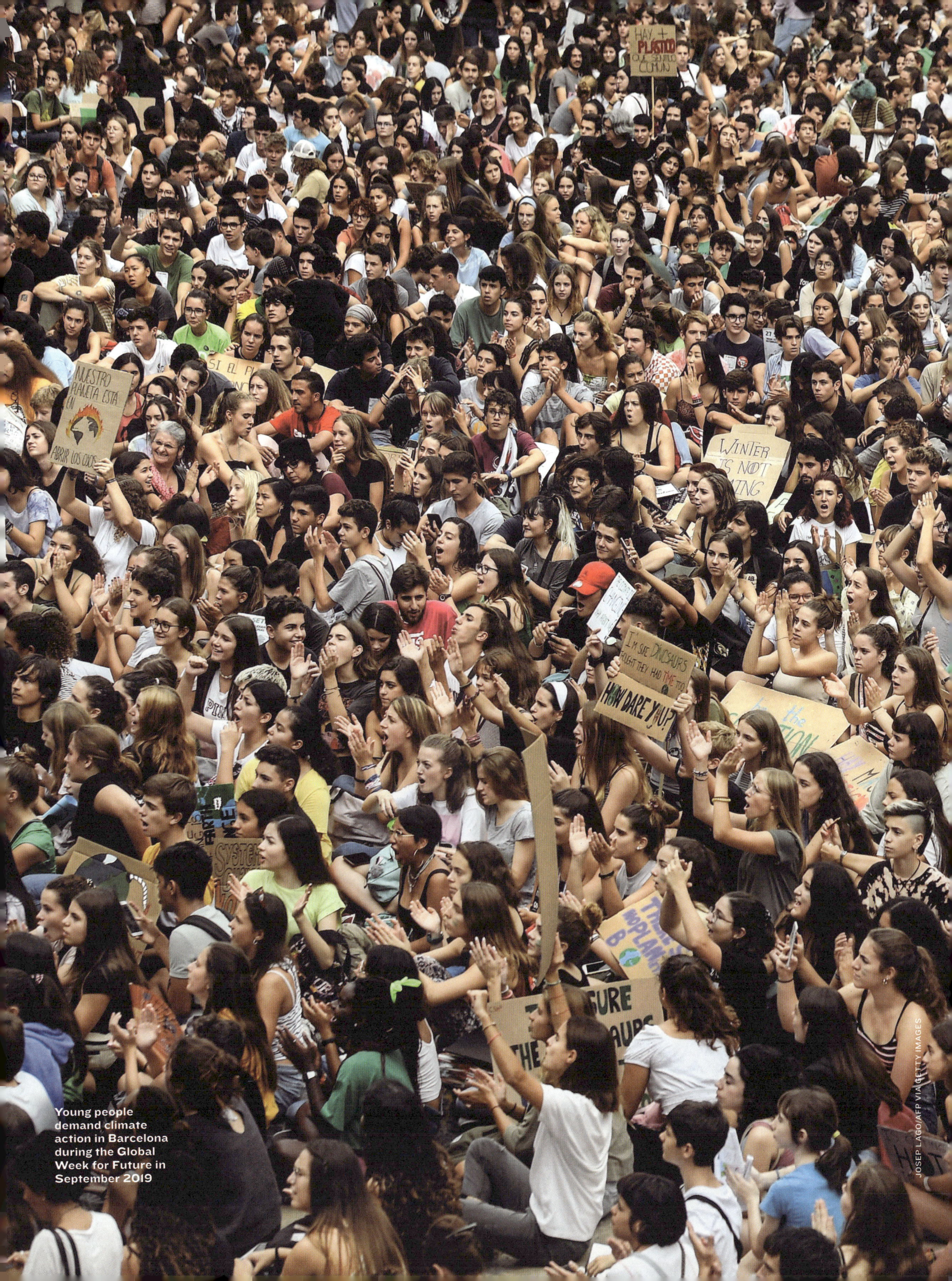

Young people demand climate action in Barcelona during the Global Week for Future in September 2019

JOSEP LAGO/AFP VIA GETTY IMAGES

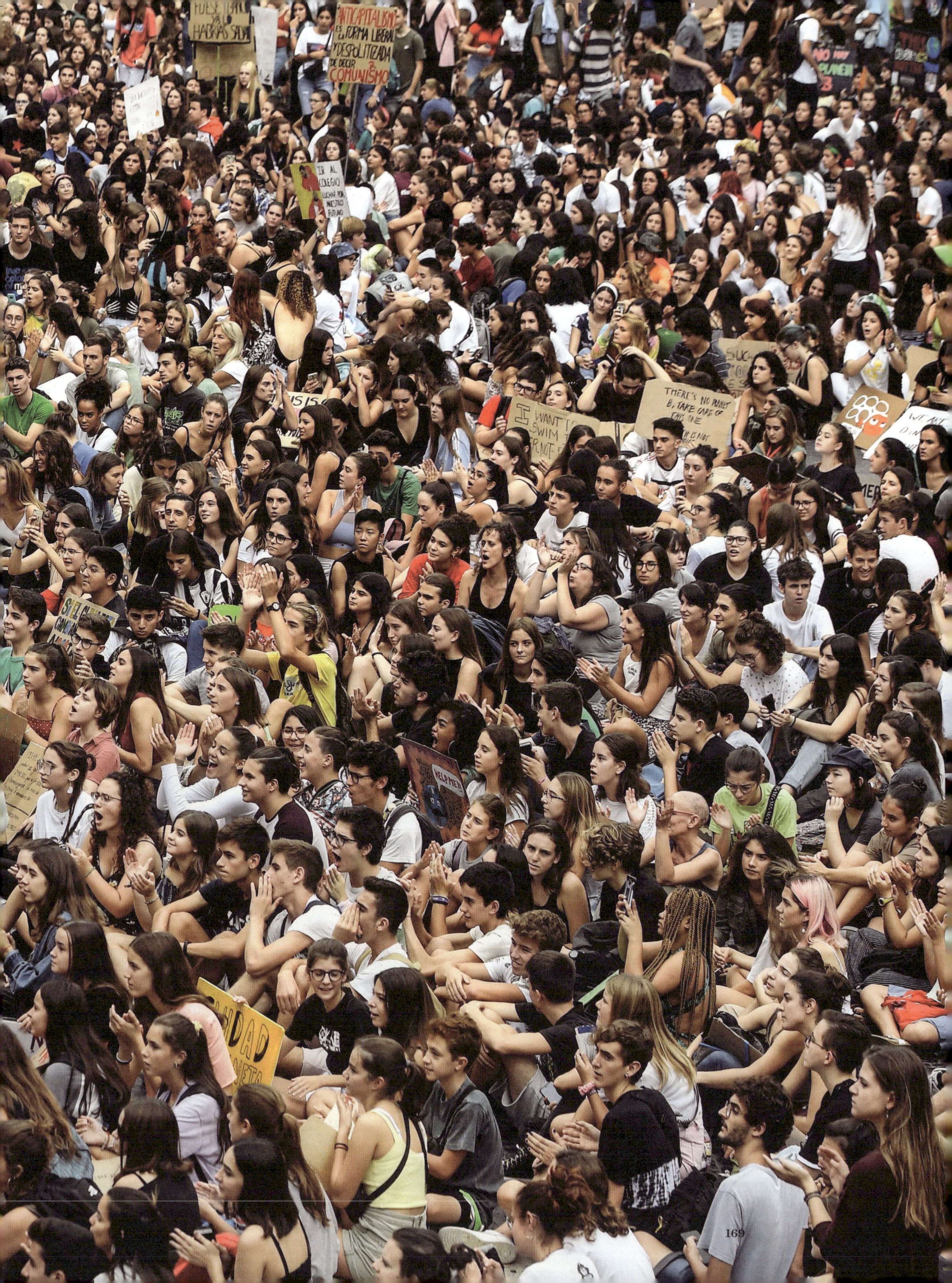
THERE'S NO PLANET B, TAKE CARE OF THIS ONE

NRDC TRUSTEES 1970 TO PRESENT

"Environmental issues often demand that NRDC think and act creatively as it cultivates new allies and learns to use new levers of power. When working alongside Indigenous populations, that has meant learning from those who have lived with the land for millennia and finding ways to empower them."

—Adam Albright was a vice chair of NRDC's board of directors from 1985 to 2015. Adam and his wife, Rachel, started the philanthropic ARIA Foundation, which awards grants to progressive advocacy groups such as NRDC.

"Over the decades, as habits and media preferences changed, NRDC evolved, too, with an increased investment in building a robust online membership program. We are deeply grateful for our members. Whether they connect with us digitally or through traditional mailings, our members' loyalty is unmatched."

—Honorary Trustee Philip B. Korsant, an investor and a former president of Ziff Communications Company, was a member of NRDC's board of trustees for more than two decades and played a foundational role in reenvisioning NRDC's membership fundraising campaigns.

† Deceased

INDEX

A FORCE *for the* FUTURE

INSIDE NRDC'S FIGHT TO SAVE THE PLANET AND ITS PEOPLE

John H. Adams

Printed and bound in the United States of America.

First edition

ISBN 978-0-7892-1372-3

10 9 8 7 6 5 4 3 2 1

Library of Congress Cataloging-in-Publication Data available upon request

—

End sheets: Jens Mortensen. Photographs within the end sheets by Daniel Gelbwaks, Douglas Levere, Scott McKiernan, Joshua Horowitz, Alex Berliner, Stan Barouh, Chase Roe.

—

For bulk and premium sales and for text adoption procedures, write to Customer Service Manager, Abbeville Press, 655 Third Avenue, New York, NY 10017, or call 1-800-ARTBOOK.

Visit Abbeville Press online at www.abbeville.com.

ABBEVILLE PRESS

Printed on 100% Recycled Paper

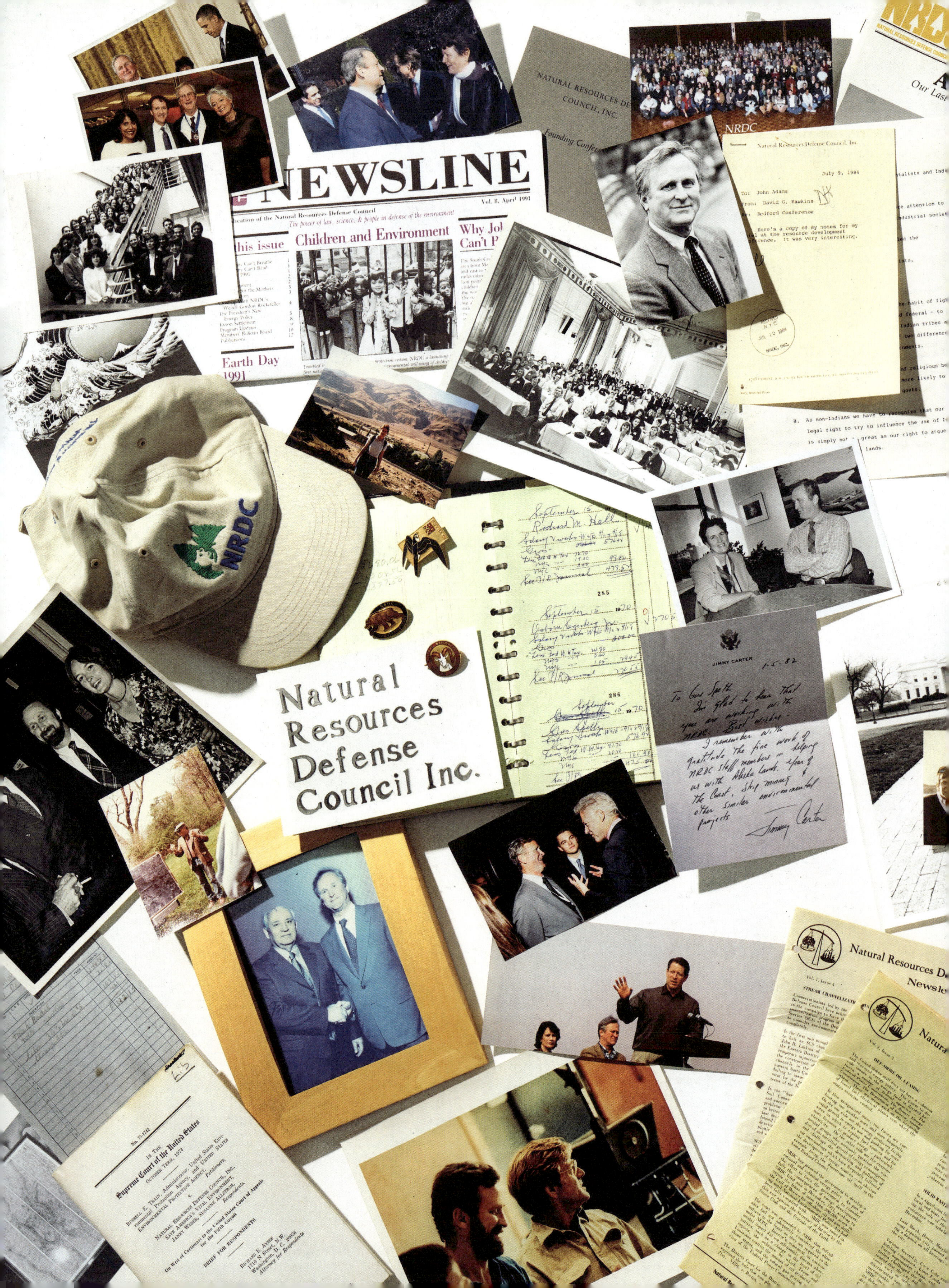
NEWSLINE
Children and Environment
Earth Day 1991
Natural Resources Defense Council Inc.
NRDC
JIMMY CARTER
NATURAL RESOURCES DEFENSE COUNCIL, INC.
Natural Resources Defense Council Newsletter